CW01662780

Cultures of Intoxication

Edited by Phil Withington and Angela McShane

OXFORD
UNIVERSITY PRESS

OXFORD
UNIVERSITY PRESS

1 Great Clarendon Street, Oxford OX2 6DP

Oxford University Press is a department of the University of Oxford.
It furthers the University's objective of excellence in research, scholarship,
and education by publishing worldwide in

Oxford New York

Athens Auckland Bangkok Bogotá Buenos Aires Cape Town
Chennai Dar es Salaam Delhi Florence Hong Kong Istanbul Karachi
Kolkata Kuala Lumpur Madrid Melbourne Mexico City Mumbai Nairobi
Paris São Paulo Shanghai Singapore Taipei Tokyo Toronto Warsaw

with associated companies in Berlin Ibadan

Oxford is a registered trade mark of Oxford University Press
in the UK and in certain other countries

Published in the United Kingdom
by Oxford University Press Inc., New York

© The Past and Present Society, 2014

The moral rights of the author have been asserted
Database right Oxford University Press (maker)

First published 2014

All rights reserved. No part of this publication may be reproduced,
stored in a retrieval system, or transmitted, in any form or by any means,
without the prior permission in writing of Oxford University Press,
or as expressly permitted by law, or under terms agreed with the appropriate
reprographics rights organization. Enquiries concerning reproduction
outside the scope of the above should be sent to the Rights Department,
Oxford University Press, at the address above

You must not circulate this book in any other binding or cover
and you must impose this same condition on any acquirer

A catalogue for this book is available from the British Library

Library of Congress Cataloging in Publication
Data (data available)

ISBN 0-19-871562-7
ISBN 978-0-19-871562-7

Subscription information for Past & Present is available
from:jnls.cust.serv@oup.com

Typeset by Cenveo Publisher Services, Bangalore, India
Printed by Bell and Bain Ltd, Glasgow, UK

Past and Present Supplements

Supplement 9, 2014

Cultures of Intoxication

Edited by Phil Withington and Angela McShane

President of the Past and Present Society
J. H. Elliott

Vice-President
Keith Thomas

Editorial Board
Chris Wickham (Chair)
All Souls College, Oxford
David Cannadine (Vice-Chair)
Princeton University
Gadi Algazi
Tel Aviv University
C. A. Bayly
St Catharine's College, Cambridge
Anna Bayman
Paul Betts
St Antony's College, Oxford
David Blackbourn
Vanderbilt University
Michael Braddick
University of Sheffield
Sebastian Conrad
Freie Universität Berlin
Peter Coss
Cardiff University
Marwa Elshakry
Columbia University
Eric Foner
Columbia University
Roy Foster
Hertford College, Oxford
Ruth Harris
New College, Oxford
Matthew Hilton
University of Birmingham
Joanna Innes
Somerville College, Oxford
Colin Jones
Queen Mary University of London
Alan Knight
St Antony's College, Oxford
Sarah Knott
Indiana University
Mark Mazower
Columbia University
Rana Mitter
St Cross College, Oxford
Robin Osborne
King's College, Cambridge
Judith Pollmann
Instituut voor Geschiedenis, Leiden
Alice Rio
King's College London
Lyndal Roper
Oriel College, Oxford
S. A. Smith
All Souls College, Oxford
Selina Todd
St Hilda's College, Oxford
Megan Vaughan
King's College, Cambridge
Alexandra Walsham
Trinity College, Cambridge
Evelyn Welch
King's College London

Editors	**Supplement General Editor**	**Associate Editor**	**Supplement Sub-Editor**
S. A. Smith	Matthew Hilton	Anna Bayman	Catherine Macduff
Alexandra Walsham			

Submissions should be made via the online submission system: http://mc.manuscriptcentral.com/past. Intending contributors should request a copy of 'Notes for Contributors'. Other communications, editorial correspondence, etc., should be addressed to The Editors, Past and Present, 103 Walton Street, Oxford OX2 6EB, UK. Tel: +44 (0)1865 511147; E-mail: editors@pastandpresent.org.uk.

© *World Copyright: The Past and Present Society, 2014.*

Photocopying and reprint permissions: single and multiple photocopies of extracts from this Journal may be made without charge in all public and educational institutions or as part of any non-profit educational activity, providing that full acknowledgement is made of the source. Requests to reprint in any publication for public sale should be addressed to Oxford University Press. This policy may be reviewed by the Past and Present Society from time to time. More information can be obtained from Rights and New Business Development, Journals Division, Oxford University Press, Great Clarendon Street, Oxford OX2 6DP, UK. Tel: +44 (0)1865 354490 or 353695; Fax: +44 (0)1865 353485; E-mail: journals.permission@oup.com, www.oxfordjournals.org/access_ purchase/rights_permissions.html

The Past and Present Society is a company limited by a guarantee registered in England under company number 2414260 and a registered charity under number 802281. Its registered office is at 9400 Garsington Road, Oxford.

Typeset by Cenveo Publisher Services, Bangalore, India, and printed by Bell and Bain Ltd, Glasgow, UK

Cultures of Intoxication

CONTENTS

List of Illustrations

Introduction: Cultures of Intoxication

Phil Withington

Why intoxication?

Intoxication figures prominently in George Orwell's *Animal Farm*. In the very first sentence we learn that 'Mr Jones, of the Manor Farm, had locked the hen-houses for the night, but was too drunk to remember to shut the pop-holes'.[1] It is this drink-induced negligence that allows the animals to gather in the barn to hear Old Major give his prophetic diatribe against humanity. Old Major concludes his rousing speech by warning the assembled animals

> that in fighting against Man, we must not come to resemble him. Even when you have conquered him, do not adopt his vices. No animal must ever live in a house, or sleep in a bed, or wear clothes, or drink alcohol, or smoke tobacco, or touch money, or engage in trade. All the habits of Man are evil.[2]

Sometime later it was because Jones, descending into alcoholism, 'went into Willingdon and got so drunk at the Red Lion' that he forgot to feed the animals and precipitated the farmyard insurrection. When the animals stormed the farmhouse, 'Some hams hanging in the kitchen were taken out for burial, and the barrel of beer in the scullery was stove in with a kick from Boxer', the redoubtable carthorse and hero-worker of the revolution. It comes as no surprise that the fifth commandment of the now renamed 'Animal Farm' becomes 'No animal shall drink alcohol'—a maxim as portentous as 'All animals are equal'.[3]

It is, in turn, the discovery of the pleasures of intoxication by the revolutionary intelligentsia—the pigs—that marks at once the final dissipation of the revolutionary dream and the transformation of the pigs into humans. Finding a case of whisky in the cellar, the despot Napoleon and his entourage

[1] George Orwell, *Animal Farm*, introduced by Malcolm Bradbury, ed. Peter Davison (London, 2000), 1.

[2] Ibid., 7.

[3] Ibid., 13, 16, 17.

 © The Past and Present Society

experience first sweet intoxication and then the hangover from hell. Thereafter they learn to brew their own beer (growing barley on land previously put aside for retired animals) and change the fifth commandment to 'No animal shall drink alcohol *to excess*'.[4] When Boxer becomes too old to work the pigs do not put him out to pasture, as promised. Rather they surreptitiously send him to the knackers' yard and buy more whisky with the profits. When Napoleon starts walking on two legs he also takes to smoking a pipe.[5] And when the pigs finally morph into humans they are entertaining local farmers in Jones's old drawing room with drinks, toasts, speeches, and a game of cards. Watching confusedly through the windows, the other animals watch Napoleon stand and declare 'I will give you the same toast as before, but in a different form. Fill your glasses to the brim. Gentlemen, here is my toast: To the prosperity of Manor Farm!' The tragic denouement has been reached:

> There was the same hearty cheering as before, and the mugs were emptied to the dregs. But as the animals outside gazed at the scene, it seemed to them that some strange thing was happening . . . what was it that seemed to be melting and changing? . . . The creatures looked from pig to man, and from man to pig, and from pig to man again: but already it was impossible to say which was which.[6]

Orwell's beautifully told fable captures much of the premise behind this volume. First, there is the intimation, substantiated by archaeologists and anthropologists, that intoxication is a universal and essential feature of the human condition—as quintessentially human as dwelling houses, clothing, money, trade, and inequality.[7] As such, it is a subject that demands as much serious historical attention as any of the other 'habits of man'. Secondly, Orwell conveys how the connotations, rituals, and sociology of intoxication are nevertheless culturally and historically specific: he invokes, that is, a perennial feature of human existence that also invites comparative and cultural analysis. In the case of *Animal Farm*—in which animals are also metaphors

[4] Ibid., 78–9, 83.

[5] Ibid., 91, 98.

[6] Ibid., 102.

[7] Andrew Sherratt, 'Alcohol and its Alternatives: Symbol and Substance in Pre-Industrial Cultures' in Jordan Goodman, Paul E. Lovejoy, and Andrew Sherratt (eds), *Consuming Habits: Global and Historical Perspectives in How Cultures Define Drugs* (London, 2007), 11–46; E. Margaritis and M. K. Jones, 'Beyond Cereals: Crop-processing and *Vitis vinifera L.* Ethnography, Experiment and Charred Grape Remains from Hellenistic Greece', *Journal of Archaeological Science*, 33:6 (2006), 784–805; M. K. Jones, *Feast: Why Humans Share Food* (Oxford, 2007).

for the labouring classes of Europe in the early twentieth century—intoxication emerges at once as an integral feature of seigniorial and bourgeois culture and the means to critique those cultures on moral and political grounds. As depicted by Orwell, it was a source of masculine distinction that distinguished governors from the governed; that facilitated class solidarity among erstwhile political rivals; and that distracted elites from their paternalistic, social, and economic obligations. Thirdly, Orwell also nicely evokes the experiential attractions and transformative power of intoxication. For Mr Jones, drunkenness was not so much a symptom of his social and personal decline as its cause, his love of alcohol ensuring the transition from successful farmer to habitual 'inebriate'. For the pigs, alcohol and tobacco are not simply the mark of acquired status but also visceral pleasures that transform their bodies and personalities before the very eyes of the other animals. The first shock of whisky and the altered state it induced—the otherwise tyrannical and reclusive Napoleon singing songs he'd previously banned and then donning a bowler hat and racing around the farmyard—augured the longer transition of pigs into men.[8] The evening of healths and sociability, with the faces melting and changing, sees that transition concluded.[9]

Cultures of Intoxication accordingly provides a multi-disciplinary and comparative view of a perennial human 'habit'—a view that also privileges and in some instances reconstructs intoxication as an experience and practice in its own right. By this is not meant the raw and individual undulations of altered consciousness that, for example, the cultural theorist Walter Benjamin tried to transcribe in the late 1920s—what Benjamin styled the 'ecstasy of the trance' (*Rauschgluck*) induced by hashish.[10] The 'ecstasies' of most people remain far beyond the historical record and, by their very nature, are notoriously difficult to recollect and convey. (It is with good reason that Patty, the narrator of Jonathan Franzen's 2010 novel *Freedom*, notes that 'The autobiographer is mindful of how dull it is to read about someone else's drinking';[11] and Benjamin's own accounts of *Rauschgluck* are hardly among his most illuminating 'scientific' experiments.) Rather the volume seeks to recover the configuration of factors—social, political, cultural, material—that have combined to shape and inform such experiences and practices in the past, in the present, and over time. For some contributors this has indeed meant hazarding the feelings and perceptions induced by intoxicants

[8] Ibid., 78.

[9] Ibid., 102.

[10] Walter Benjamin, *On Hashish*, introduced by Marcus Boon, ed. Howard Eiland (Cambridge, Mass., 2006), 13, 18.

[11] Jonathan Franzen, *Freedom* (London, 2010), 61.

and the circumstances of their consumption: in the symposia of ancient Greece, for example, or the dance floors of contemporary San Francisco and Hong Kong. For others it has involved deconstructing the manner in which 'experience' and 'cognition' are themselves defined and represented, be it in the 'countercultural' theories of the 1960s, the virulent colour schemes of contemporary brain scans, the symbolism of Renaissance painting, or the conduct literature of early modern England. Three chapters focus more particularly on the materiality and tacit rules of practice, exploring the artefacts of seventeenth-century 'political drinking', the physical taste of opium during the Japanese occupation of Taiwan, and conventions of political patronage and sociability in eighteenth-century Stockholm. And three chapters narrate the remarkably ambiguous and complicated intersections between drinking, modernity, and power as witnessed in the Islamic Middle East, West and South Africa, and Spanish colonial and post-colonial America.

'Intoxication' is, of course, a word used to describe many different kinds of 'altered state'—not merely the physiological and neurological effects of plants, beverages, and chemicals but also religious ecstasy, hypnotic trance, musical reverie, intense collective joy.[12] Conversely there are plenty of other terms that invoke the experiences and practices associated with this particular kind of consumption, the most usual of which in contemporary parlance is 'drugs'.[13] Given that this volume is concerned only with intoxication derived from consumables—eight chapters focus on alcohol, four on opiates and hallucinogens—then its choice as presiding paradigm requires explanation. There are, in fact, at least four reasons why it is the term of choice. Unlike that of drugs, the vocabulary of intoxication is etymologically and semantically precise, having always depicted artificial alterations of consciousness. It is relatively neutral, certainly without the ideological connotations of drugs. It is encompassing, accounting for all substances with demonstrable physiological and neurological impact. And it depicts a cognitive and social condition (intoxication) as well as the substances that induce it (intoxicants).

A quick genealogy of the language makes these attractions clear. 'Intoxication' derives from the Greek (*toxikos*, 'pertaining to arrows or archery'), alluding to the poisons placed on their tips, and traditionally invoked notions of danger, ambiguity, and margins.[14] The vocabulary most likely became known to Europeans though the Latin *toxicare*, 'to

[12] Nicholas Humphrey, 'Introduction: Altered States', *Social Research*, 68:3 (2001), 585.

[13] Jacques Derrida, 'The Rhetoric of Drugs', repr. in Anna Alexander and Mark S. Roberts (eds), *High Culture: Reflections on Addiction and Modernity* (New York, 2003), 19–44.

[14] I would like to thank Martin Jones for discussions on this subject.

smear with poison', and was translated into national vernaculars from the sixteenth century.[15] Robert Cawdrey listed 'intoxicate' as 'poisoned' in his 1604 dictionary of 'hard words' and John Bullokar defined it as 'To betwitch, to amaze, to extremely dull one's spirit' in 1618.[16] Early metaphorical uses usually referred to bewitchment by harmful others: witches with their herbs, or Catholics with their rituals.[17] Indeed it was only from around 1650 that the vocabulary also began to mean 'drunkenness' with any regularity: in 1658 Edward Phillips took 'intoxication' to mean 'a poisoning, or envenoming'; by 1678 he had added 'also a fuddling or making drunk'.[18] A century later, Samuel Johnson effaced any sense of poisoning from the term: 'intoxicate' meant simply 'to inebriate: to make drunk' and 'intoxication' was 'the act of making drunk; the state of being drunk'.[19] But when the noun 'intoxicant' was coined in the second half of the nineteenth century, it was not limited to alcohol. On the contrary, for Romantic poets and toxicologists alike it became a generic category for all substances known to intoxicate.[20] This was in almost direct contradistinction to the Old French term 'drug', which until the end of the nineteenth century was used primarily to describe 'An ingredient used in physic; a medicinal simple' and less commonly to denote 'anything without a value'.[21] Different medicines had different qualities—including stupefaction and stimulation—but these qualities varied according to the drug and were not inherent to the word. It is only relatively recently that 'drug' has acquired its presiding connotations of illegality, addiction, danger, and harm on the one hand and subversion, counter-culture, and hedonism on the other. Indeed the contrasting semantics of 'intoxicant' and 'drug' since the 1860s would make for an interesting and important study.

[15] Cathy Shrank, 'Beastly Metamorphoses: Losing Control in Early Modern Literary Culture' in Jonathan Herring, Ciara Regan, Darin Weinberg, and Phil Withington (eds), *Intoxication and Society: Problematic Pleasures of Drugs and Alcohol* (Basingstoke, 2012), 202.

[16] Robert Cawdrey, *Table Alphabetical of Hard Usual English Words* (1604); John Bullokar, *English Expositor* (1618).

[17] Shrank, 'Beastly Metamorphoses', 203–5.

[18] Edward Phillips, *New World of Words* (1658, 1678).

[19] Samuel Johnson, *A Dictionary of the English Language: in which the Words are Deduced from their Originals, and Illustrated in their Different Significations by Examples from the Best Writers, Volume I* (London, 1775).

[20] Charles Baudelaire, *Artificial Paradises*, trans. and introduced by Stacy Diamond (New York, 1996); www.oed.com/view/Entry/98570?redirectedFrom=intoxicant#eid [accessed 24 September 2013].

[21] Johnson, *Dictionary*; Virginia Berridge, 'Altered States: Opium and Tobacco Compared', *Social Research*, 68:3 (2001), 662.

The accretion by the word 'drug' of so much rhetoric makes it extremely problematic as a term of social or historical analysis.[22] The concept of intoxication, in contrast, invites consideration of all consumptive experiences and practices involving intoxicants,from the mild stimulation of afternoon tea, to the inebriation of rounds in the pub, to Benjamin's ecstatic trances.[23] The chapters that follow accordingly demonstrate, in the first instance, the experiential importance of the social contexts and connections in which and through which these habits and rituals are enacted: the sociology of consumption, in terms of those included and excluded from the act; the objects and materials used to consume; the locations and topographies of consumption. Secondly, the chapters intimate the variety of discourses that have imbued these practices with meaning and sense, both for individual partakers and societies at large. These include grand cultural traditions, not least the complex and often contradictory values forged by the ancients and appropriated by Europeans—and subsequently the wider world—since the Renaissance. But they also include more makeshift feelings of spirituality, invigoration, comfort, or solidarity claimed by particular groups at certain moments for specific intoxicants, be it in contemporary nightclubs or seventeenth-century alehouses. Thirdly, there are constant reminders of the close relationship between intoxication and power. This is true in the conventional sense of scientific, political, and colonial authorities using knowledge, technology, and the economy to try and control the uses, semiotics, even the taste of intoxicants. But it is also true in the sense noted by Orwell, of intoxicants and their consumption constituting power and, indeed, making power work: as the lubricant of political patronage; the pledge of ideological loyalty; the rites of manhood; the embodiment of taste, civility, privilege, subordination, and exclusion.

The chapters are a reminder, finally, of the remarkable extent to which so much consumption was and remains *immanently intoxicating*. That is, because intoxicants have been traditionally used for a host of purposes other than transformations in consciousness—not least in everyday diet, physic, and sociability—the potential and inadvertent loss of cognitive and bodily control emerges as an endemic feature of social life both past and present.[24]

[22] Derrida, 'The Rhetoric of Drugs'.

[23] Mary Douglas, *Constructive Drinking: Perspectives on Drink from Anthropology* (London, 2000); Benjamin, *On Hashish*, 53.

[24] Berridge, 'Altered States', 655; Virginia Berridge, *Opium and the People: Opiate Use and Drug Control Policy in Nineteenth and Early Twentieth Century England*, 2nd edn (London, 1999); Keith Wrightson, 'Alehouses, Order, and Reformation in Rural England, 1590–1660' in Eileen Yeo and Stephen Yeo (eds), *Popular Culture And Class Conflict 1590–1914: Explorations in the History of Labour and Leisure* (Brighton, 1981), 1–6.

It haunts the civil conversation of Renaissance dinner tables, the political wrangling of Swedish parliaments, the hard toil of mining for gold in Africa, the business of Iranian or African royal governance, even Christian Communion. Contrariwise, it transpires that one of the key aspirations and sources of legitimacy for civil and colonial authority since the fifteenth century has been not the eradication of intoxication so much as the conceit of controlled consumption. In theory at least, to be able to retain demonstrable levels of self-discipline and stamina in the midst of both immanent and purposeful intoxication distinguishes (usually male) elites from the incontinent and indiscriminate masses. A key insight of this volume, therefore, is that how societies recognize and deal with this threat of latency is quite as integral to their cultures of intoxication as the deliberate pursuit of neurological and physiological transformation. And as Orwell well knew, it is both kinds of intoxication—the immanent and the purposeful—that help define societies and a person's place within them.

Drugs and civility

Cultures of Intoxication does not emerge, of course, out of the historiographical blue. On the contrary, intoxicants and their consumption is a multifaceted subject that has attracted a host of studies, both scholarly and popular, in a variety of disciplinary fields.[25] Traditional lines of research range from the economic history of particular intoxicants, such as beer, to the institutions and social milieus in which they were consumed, such as alehouses and taverns.[26] They vary from the epistemological frameworks by which the causes and effects of intoxication are understood, such as medicine, to the legal, moral, and political means by which they are debated and policed.[27]

[25] Wolfgang Schivelbusch, *Tastes of Paradise: A Social History of Spices, Stimulants, and Intoxicants* (New York, 1992); Stuart Walton, *Out of It: A Cultural History of Intoxication* (Harmondsworth, 2000).

[26] Richard W. Unger, *Beer in the Middle Ages and the Renaissance* (Philadelphia, 2004); Peter Mathias, *The Brewing Industry in England 1700–1830* (Cambridge, 1959); Judith M. Bennett, *Ale, Beer, and Brewsters in England. Women's Work in a Changing World 1300–1600* (Oxford, 1996); Peter Clark, *The English Alehouse: A Social History 1200–1830* (Harlow, 1983); Thomas Brennan, *Public Drinking and Popular Culture in Eighteenth-century Paris* (Princeton, 1988); Peter Thompson, *Rum, Punch and Revolution: Taverngoing and Public Life in Eighteenth Century Philadelphia* (Philadelphia, 1999); Roy Rosensweig, *Eight Hours For What We Will: Workers and Leisure in an Industrial City, 1870–1920* (Cambridge, 1983).

[27] B. Ann Tlusty, *Bacchus and Civic Order: The Culture of Drink in Early Modern Germany*, (Charlottesville, VA, 2001), especially ch. 3 and 5; Roy Porter, 'The Drinking Man's Disease: The Pre-History of Alcoholism in Georgian Britain', *British Journal of*

They encompass the metaphorical, aesthetic, and representational aspects of intoxication as well as the role of intoxicants in constructing social, national, and gendered identities.[28] There are overlaps with historians of food and drink, in discussions of the nutritional or social value of intoxicants.[29] Drugs (whether produced by early modern apothecaries or global pharmaceutical companies) carry obvious interest for historians of medicine.[30] Political historians are interested in alehouses, taverns, and coffeehouses as places of political discourse and sociability.[31] Historical geographers are concerned with the spatial politics of intoxication.[32] The list could go on. Yet while the historiographical interest in intoxication is clearly extensive, and reflects just how multifaceted the subject is, it also makes for a somewhat fractured and disparate field of enquiry in which the cumulative importance of intoxication, both synchronically and diachronically, is not always recognized. It is unusual, for example, for the consumption of alcohol and tobacco to be treated together, never mind caffeine and opiates; and until now it is only in biographies of particular commodities, such as Brian Cowan's study of coffee, or the place of an intoxicant in a single community, such as Ann

Addiction, 80 (1985), 385–96; Harry W. Paul, *Bacchic Medicine: Wine and Alcohol Therapies from Napoleon to the French Paradox* (New York, 2001); Herring et al., *Intoxication and Society*.

28 Schivelbusch, *Tastes of Paradise*; Piero Camporesi, *Exotic Brew: the Art of Living in the Age of Enlightenment* (Cambridge, 1998); Kathleen McCormack, *George Eliot and Intoxication* (Basingstoke, 2000); James Nicholls and Susan J. Owen (eds), *A Babel of Bottles: Drink, Drinkers and Drinking Places in Literature* (Sheffield, 2000); Tanya Pollard, *Drugs and Theatre in Early Modern England* (Oxford, 2005).

29 Craig Muldrew, *Food, Energy, and the Creation of Industriousness: Work and Material Culture in Agrarian England, 1550–1780* (Cambridge, 2007); Martin Jones, *Feast: Why Humans Share Food* (Oxford, 2007).

30 David Courtwright, *Dark Paradise: Opiate Addiction in America Before 1940* (Cambridge Mass., 1982); Berridge, *Opium and the People*; Roy Porter and Milulas Teich (eds), *Drugs and Narcotics in History* (Cambridge, 1995).

31 Phil Withington, 'Public Discourse, Corporate Citizenship, and State-Formation in Early Modern England', *American Historical Review*, 112:4 (2007), 1016–38; Mark Knights, 'John Locke and Post-Revolutionary Politics: Electoral Reform and the Franchise', *Past and Present*, 213:1 (2011), 41–86.

32 Angela McShane and James Kneale, 'Histories and Geographies of Intoxicants and Intoxication: An Introduction', *The Social History of Alcohol and Drugs*, 25:1–2 (2011), 6–14; James Kneale, 'Modernity, Pleasure, and the Metropolis', *Journal of Urban History*, 28 (2000), 647–57; David Beckingham, 'An Historical Geography of Liberty: Lancashire and the Inebriates Acts', *Journal of Historical Geography*, 36:4 (2002) 388–401.

Tlusty's study of drinking in Augsburg, that the economic, cultural, social and political converge.[33]

Andrew Sherratt, in his introduction to the 1995 volume *Consuming Habits*, has outlined by far the most coherent agenda for starting to think comparatively and historically about what he termed 'peculiar substances'.[34] This agenda centred on 'plant products whose derivatives are now classified as "drugs" and subject to legal prohibition and regulation'. Sherratt looked primarily to archaeology and anthropology in order to overcome 'the inhibitions which our recent history has imposed', arguing that the 'discourse of "drugs" is no model for the often subtle uses of psychoactive substances in the past' or, indeed, in places where 'traditional practices continued'.[35] For Sherratt, modern 'usages and definitions' were not only specific to 'capitalism and the Industrial Revolution', they were also 'misleading as a framework for approaching the great variety of ways in which organic substances have been used by human beings to alter their mental states'.[36] The way to circumvent the tyranny of modernity was fourfold. Sherratt proposed a long 'genealogy' of substances that also encompassed 'a comprehensive understanding of other cultures'. He took 'peculiar substances' to be part of the 'anthropology of consumption', whereby psychoactive substances should be considered 'alongside a variety of other meaningful consumables'. He emphasized that these substances should be 'considered not so much a category in themselves but as one aspect of a potentially wide range of activities', their meaning and significance determined by specific context, consumers, and function. And Sherratt argued that the economic significance of intoxicants should also be recognized, not merely under capitalism but also in indigenous, traditional, and pre-historical economies.[37]

This approach to intoxicants and their uses is extremely powerful. It suggests that intoxication understood as an act of consumption has potentially as many meanings as partakers, and can occur in a range of settings to serve a variety of functions. It posits that just as there are a host of intoxicants, from the mildly stimulating to the deeply narcotic, so there is a spectrum of intoxicating behaviour, from caffeine breakfasts to opiate slumbers: that there are

[33] Brian Cowan, *The Social Life of Coffee: The Emergence of the British Coffeehouse* (Newhaven, 2005); Tlusty, *Bacchus*. See also David Hancock, *Oceans of Wine: Madeira and the Emergence of American Trade and Taste* (New Haven, 2009).

[34] Andrew Sherratt, 'Introduction: Peculiar Substances' in Goodman et al., *Consuming Habits*, 2.

[35] Ibid., 5.

[36] Ibid., 1.

[37] Ibid., 6–8.

intoxications, that is, rather than intoxication. It emphasizes the peculiar importance of peculiar substances to political economies, whether makeshift, commercial, industrial, or global. It highlights the material culture of intoxication, and how identities and relationships are articulated not simply through substances but also through the objects and paraphernalia of consumption. And by turning to pre-modern and indigenous practices, it challenges the current hegemony of medical and regulatory expertise, which reduces 'drugs' to their bodily impact and legal status.

In a very real sense, therefore, *Cultures of Intoxication* carries on from where *Consuming Habits* left off. There remain, nevertheless, two aspects of the story told by *Consuming Habits* that this volume looks specifically to address. In the first instance, because Sherratt and his collaborators turned to intoxicating habits that are neither modern nor western in order to circumvent the contemporary rhetoric of drugs, they ended up reinforcing the impression that it is precisely this rhetoric that is the defining feature of intoxication in the modern era. *Consuming Habits* fails, that is, to develop or outline an historical and comparative anthropology of modernity itself, instead taking the language of drugs generated by political and scientific institutions since the late nineteenth century to be hegemonic and even normative. Secondly, in addition to conflating modernity with drugs, *Consuming Habits* also testifies to the implacability of what Norbert Elias long ago termed the 'civilizing process'. Chapters by Jordan Goodman and Woodruff D. Smith focus, for example, on the impact of colonial intoxicants—or what Goodman terms *excitantia*—on European diets and sociability during the seventeenth and eighteenth centuries. They argue that the introduction of these commodities was integral to the spread of civility, with tobacco, coffee, tea, chocolate, and sugar becoming 'commercial capitalistic substitutes for indigenous European drugs' and alcohol. These new comestibles 'embodied moderation, as opposed to excess; mildness, as opposed to harshness; sobriety and wakefulness, as opposed to drunkenness and wantonness'.[38] The inference is that while intoxicants like alcohol and indigenous herbs and plants became the stuff of traditional and, increasingly, lower class consumption, colonial 'soft drugs' served as the lubricants of modern sobriety, respectability, and industry.[39]

[38] Jordan Goodman, 'Excitantia: or, How Enlightenment Europe Took to Soft Drugs' in Goodman et al., *Consuming Habits*, 132; Woodruff D. Smith, 'From Coffeehouse to Parlour: the Consumption of Coffee, Tea, and Sugar in North-Western Europe in the Seventeenth and Eighteenth Centuries' in Goodman et al., *Consuming Habits*, 154–5.

[39] Jan De Vries, *The Industrious Revolution. Consumer Behaviour and the Household Economy, 1650 to the Present* (Cambridge, 2008).

Since the publication of *Consuming Habits* the tendency to think about modern intoxication in terms of transgressive and pathological drugs rubbing against the bounds of 'civil' and healthy normality has become, perhaps, even more entrenched. In academic circles at least, one reason for this is the burgeoning aesthetic and philosophical interest in what has been termed 'narcotic modernity'.[40] This is the sensibility, usually traced back to Romanticism, that valorizes and indeed fetishizes drugs as both a source of profound illumination and a mode of counter-cultural resistance—a tradition of modern thought usually traced from Thomas de Quincey's *Confessions of An English Opium Eater* through Charles Baudelaire's *Artificial Paradises* to Walter Benjamin's 'protocols' and the expanding vista of drug culture thereafter.[41] In the meantime, however, a bio-political historiography has fostered a much more pejorative and possibly more socially pervasive conception of drugs. The field combines interest in 'scientific and technical developments in the drugs area' with the social, political, and regulative issues and morbidities that result.[42] Approaches range from the empirical, sceptical, and policy-minded research of Virginia Berridge to the more strident medico-idealism of David Courtwright.[43] There are also obvious overlaps with the social and neurological sciences.[44] What is constant, however, is the focus on and characterization of intoxicants—drugs—as a medical, social, and political problem.

The most synoptic and ambitious history to come out of this tradition—Courtwright's *Forces of Habit*—is a case in point.[45] This argues that humanity since around 1500 has undergone a 'psychoactive revolution' in which

[40] Dave Boothroyd, *Culture on Drugs: Narco-Cultural Studies of High Modernity* (Manchester, 2006), 9, citing Avital Ronell, *Crack Wars* (Lincoln, Nebraska, 1992); Derrida, 'Rhetoric of Drugs', 27, 29; Alexander and Roberts, *High Culture*, 3.

[41] Boon, *Road to Excess*, 7; Baudelaire, *Artificial Paradises* ; Boothroyd, *Culture on Drugs*, 105–11; David Frisby, *Fragments of Modernity* (Cambridge, MIT, 1986), 1–3, 187–265.

[42] Roy Porter, 'Introduction', in Porter and Teich (eds), *Drugs and Narcotics in History*, 3.

[43] See Virginia Berridge, *Marketing Health. Smoking and the Discourse of Public Health in Britain, 1945–2000* (Oxford, 2007); Alex Mold, *Heroin: The Treatment of Addiction in Twentieth-Century Britain* (Illinois, 2008); Alex Mold and Virginia Berridge, *Voluntary Action and Illegal Drugs: Health and Society in Britain Since the 1960s* (Palgrave, 2010); James Nicholls, *The Politics of Alcohol: A History of the Drink Question in England* (Manchester, 2009); David Courtwright, 'Addiction and the Science of History' *Addiction*, 107 (2012), 486–92.

[44] Jonathan Herring et al., 'Starting the Conversation', in Herring et al., *Intoxication and Society*, 1–30.

[45] David Courtwright, *Forces of Habit: Drugs and the Making of the Modern World* (Cambridge, Mass, 2001).

'people everywhere have acquired progressively more, and more potent, means of altering their ordinary waking consciousness'.[46] Courtwright's somewhat reductive explanation for this process is that 'psychoactive trade benefited mercantile and imperial elites in ways that went beyond ordinary commercial profits'. 'Drugs'—and he uses the word deliberately and inclusively—were at once astonishingly lucrative and a remarkably effective means to 'control manual labourers and exploit indigenes'.[47] Their traffic accordingly served two ends: the vulnerable or desperate drink, inhale, or inject as an antidote to the hopelessness of their situation; and since the sixteenth century various interested parties have induced and manipulated these habits for profit and power.[48] In the meantime the respectable classes turned to the milder and more civil pleasures of colonial *excitantia*. It is only since the end of the nineteenth century, with transformations in medical knowledge and the concomitant medicalization of political power, that this long phase in global stupefaction and exploitation has begun to be called to account.

A question underpinning this volume, therefore, is what happens to this narrative and the assumptions that frame it when the polarized and deeply politicized concept of drugs is replaced with the vocabulary of intoxication. The short answer is that while drugs and all their rhetoric remain an important part of the story, that story nevertheless becomes altogether longer, more variegated, encompassing, and (in what is a key and recurring word in the chapters that follow) *ambiguous*. While each of the contributors provide detailed explications of this ambiguity, the next section outlines in more schematic terms some of the most striking aspects of the relationship between intoxication and historical change over the last half-millennium.

Intoxications past and present

Since the late fifteenth century at least, intoxicants and their consumption have been deeply implicated in—and so shaped by—processes conventionally associated with early modern and modern societies. This is not to suggest, of course, that immanent and purposeful intoxication was not also integral to social life before 1500. Nor is it to argue for a sudden and decisive discontinuity in how cultures of intoxication are structured: quite the opposite. It is to note, with Sherratt, a set of transitions and intensifications that cumulatively are distinctive. But it is also to suggest that there is more to these changes insofar as intoxication is concerned than simply drugs and civility.

[46] Ibid., 2.
[47] Ibid., 4.
[48] Ibid., 2, 59.

Most obviously, intoxicants have been integral to commercial, capitalist, and industrial developments. This is certainly true in terms of the establishment of global trading networks in 'new' commodities like tobacco, caffeine products, and subsequently opiates and cocaine. Indeed one proponent of 'deep history' has joined Courtwright in arguing that 'modernity was created' when intoxicants previously specific to particular regions 'fell together into a new [global] framework'.[49] The entrenchment of tobacco as a staple in the seventeenth century, of sugar, tea, and coffee in the eighteenth century, of opium in the nineteenth century, and of cocaine and heroin in the twentieth century is accordingly well known.[50] As economically significant was the domestic commercialization of traditional alcohols, like wines and beers, and the development of new technologies to produce distilled liquors at scale.[51] These alcohols formed the vanguard of Europe's commercializing economies, meeting the variegated needs of expanding national populations.[52] They were also lucrative exports both within Europe and beyond.[53] From a European perspective, the Dutch were crucial to these developments. In England, for example, modern Dutch beer-brewing techniques were superseding traditional ale production by the later sixteenth-century. Made with hops, beer was transportable, durable, and encouraged economies of scale. Its production in London alone rose from an estimated 51 million litres

[49] Daniel Lord Smail, *On Deep History and the Brain* (Berkeley, 2008), 186.

[50] Jordan Goodman, *Tobacco in History* (London, 1993); Sidney W. Mintz, *Sweetness and Power: The Place of Sugar in Modern History* (New York, 1985); Cowan, *Social Life of Coffee*; Berridge, *Opium and the People*; David T. Courtwright, 'The Rise and Fall and Rise of Cocaine in the United States' in Goodman et al., *Consuming Habits*, 215–38; Courtwright, *Dark Paradise*.

[51] John Chartres, 'No English Calvados? English Distillers and the Cider Industry in the Seventeenth and Eighteenth Centuries' in John Chartres and David Hey (eds), *English Rural Society, 1500–1800* (Cambridge, 1990); Unger, *Beer in the Middle Ages*; Clark, *The English Alehouse*; Mathias, *Brewing Industry*; W. B. Stephens, 'English Wine Imports *c.*1603–40, with Special Reference to the Devon Ports' in Todd Gray et al., *Tudor and Stuart Devon* (Exeter, 1992), 114; L. M. Cullen, *The Brandy Trade Under the Ancient Regime: Regional Specialisation in the Charente* (Cambridge, 1998); Phil Withington, 'Intoxicants and Society in Early Modern England', *The Historical Journal*, 54:3 (2011), 631–40.

[52] Patrick Dillon, *The Much-Lamented Death of Madam Geneva: The Eighteenth-Century Gin Craze* (London, 2002); Jessica Warner, *Craze: Gin and Debauchery in an Age of Reason* (London, 2003); Charles Ludington, *The Politics of Wine in Britain: A New Cultural History* (Basingstoke, 2013).

[53] Thomas Brennan, *Burgundy to Champagne: the Wine Trade in Early Modern France* (Baltimore, 1997); Hancock, *Oceans of Wine*, especially Part Two.

per annum in 1574 to 146 million litres by 1600, the rise of the trade signalled by two classic early modern indicators of economic success: women were excluded from the business and brewers started becoming aldermen and mayors.[54] In the meantime Dutch merchants also galvanized the wine trade by connecting the markets of southern and north-western Europe, revitalizing traffic in other countries as they did so.

The jolt was remarkable. In an early modern city like York, the volume of wine imported by city merchants rose from 5.6 litres per capita of the urban population in 1609 to 118.3 litres per capita by 1639, the wine merchants establishing a tight and longstanding grip on civic power as a result.[55] The tremors have reverberated ever since. Business analysts predict that the global alcoholic drinks industry is expected to be worth more than $1 trillion per annum in 2014. On current trends beer will be the largest commodity, worth an expected $497 billion per annum, and spirits should exceed $306 billion per annum. In the meantime it is expected that the world wine market will exceed 26 billion litres per annum in 2015. The European Union constitutes 57 per cent of this enormous business.[56] In the United Kingdom alone, data collated by the Wine and Spirit Trade Association suggests that consumers spend between £37 billion and £40.7 billion per annum on alcoholic drinks, and that the alcoholic drinks industry pay between £15 billion and £16 billion per annum in excise duty.[57] The World Health Organization *Report on the Global Tobacco Epidemic 2011* claims that there are 1.1 billion smokers of tobacco globally in 2011 and that this figure is set to rise to 1.6 billion smokers by 2025.[58]

The *World Drug Report*, published by the United Nations Office on Drugs and Crime in 2012, estimates that 230 million people between the ages of 15 and 64 (i.e. 5 per cent of the world's adults) used an 'illicit drug' at least once in 2010, and that 'problem drug users' amounted to 27 million adults (0.6 per cent).[59] The prevalence of 'illicit drugs'—cannabis, opioids (heroin, opium,

[54] Lien Bich Luu, *Immigrants and the Industries of London, 1500–1700* (Aldershot, 2005), 259–62, 267; Bennett, *Ale, Beer, and Brewsters in England.*

[55] Phil Withington, 'Intoxicants and the Early Modern City', in Steve Hindle, Alexandra Shepard, and John Walter (eds), *Remaking English Society. Social Reations and Social Change in Early Modern England* (Woodbridge, 2013), 150–1.

[56] Information available at www.reportLinker.com/ci02014/Alcoholic-Drink [accessed 10 September 2012].

[57] Information available at www.wsta.co.uk/facts-and-figures [accessed 10 September 2012].

[58] WHO *Report on the Global Tobacco Epidemic* 2011. It is available at http://www.who.int/tobacco/global_report/2011/en.

[59] UNODC, *World Drug Report 2012* (United Nations Publications, Sales No. E.12.XI.1), iii.

non-medical opioids), opiates (synthesized opioids), cocaine, amphetamines, and ecstasy—is shown in Table 1.[60] In terms of their consumption by nationality, it is the developed economies of the USA and Australasia that top every category of drug except one (opiates), with the UK and The Netherlands not too far behind.[61]

Very much in the vanguard of capitalism, therefore, intoxicants have remained a barometer of economic practice thereafter. In this respect the alternating and relative fortunes of particular commodities is less significant than the capacity of producers and traders to organize themselves according to contemporary conventions and adapt to and exploit changing markets and circumstances. As Matthew Hilton has shown, cigarettes became the popular symbol of modern life *par excellence* not by accident, but because of an orchestrated campaign by businesses that took full advantage of available advertising techniques and technology—a campaign now being repeated in the developing and industrializing worlds by global organizations using, once again, available marketing techniques.[62] Yet while under capitalism intoxicants have always found mass markets, it is deeply misleading to argue, with Courtwright, that intoxication was and remains primarily the distraction or solace of the subordinate classes. There have always been intoxicants to suit most tastes and budgets—for every pack of 'Players' there is a 'Cohiba' luxury Cuban cigar—and while a drag, toke, or dram can certainly be consolatory, economists generally read expenditure on intoxicants as an index of affluence rather than impoverishment.[63] Friedrich Engels, more sensitive than most to the workings of capitalism, personifies the point. Engels wrote powerfully about the propensity for working class drinking in both Germany and England, in one instance recalling how in the Lower Rhine in the 1820s

> the mass of the great working population fell victim to drink. From nine in the evening, in great crowds and arm in arm, taking up the whole width of the street, the soused men tottered their way, bawling discordantly, from one inn to the other and finally back home.[64]

[60] See Appendix.

[61] *World Drug Report 2012*, 8–12.

[62] Matthew Hilton, *Smoking in British Popular Culture, 1800–2000: Perfect Pleasures* (Manchester, 2000), especially 83–115.

[63] Sander L. Gilman and Zhou Xun (eds), *Smoke. A Global History of Smoking* (London, 2004); John Chartres, 'No English Calvados?, 324; Avner Offer, *The Challenge of Affluence: Self-Control and Well-Being in the United States and Britain Since 1950* (Oxford, 2006), 60.

[64] Tristram Hunt, *Marx's General. The Revolutionary Life of Friedrich Engels* (New York, 2009), 37.

Table 1. Annual Prevalence and Number of Illicit Drug Users at the Global Level, 2010

	Prevalence (%)		Number (000s)	
	Low	High	Low	High
Cannabis	2.6	5.0	119420	224490
Opioids	0.6	0.8	26380	36120
Opiates	0.3	0.5	12980	20990
Cocaine	0.3	0.4	13200	19510
Amphetamine	0.3	1.2	14340	52540
'Ecstasy'	0.2	0.6	10480	28120
Any illicit drug	3.4	6.6	153000	300000

Source: UNODC, *World Drug Report 2012* (United Nations Publications, Sales No. E.12.XI.1), 1.

But as Tristram Hunt's biography makes clear, this does not mean Engels shied away from drunkenness himself. As a young bourgeois merchant he boasted in a letter to his sister, Marie, 'We now have a complete stock of beer in the office; under the table, behind the stove, behind the cupboard, everywhere are beer bottles'.[65] Later in Berlin, ostensibly training for the artillery, he fell in with university students to engage in extremely conspicuous and ritualized public drinking and ribaldry.[66] Even his life-long friendship with Marx was forged 'over ten beer-soaked days' in Paris. In later life heavy drinking sessions could leave Marx incapacitated for weeks at a time while Engels reported punctually to work.[67]

Engels's engagement with intoxication, whether as a journalist and political activist writing for the press, or as a young man keeping conspicuously drunken company in Berlin's alehouses and wineshops, points to a second structuring feature of modern intoxication. This is the long history of the 'public sphere' and 'culture industry'. These appellations are used here not as they were originally coined, as terms of Marxist critique.[68] Rather they simply describe at once organized forms of mediated communication such as printed and scribal texts, visual and performative media, and electronic technology, and also instances of public discussion and dialogue pertaining to

[65] Ibid., 27.

[66] Ibid., 55–6.

[67] Ibid., 115.

[68] Jürgen Habermas, *The Structural Transformation of the Public Sphere. An Enquiry into a Category of Bourgeois Society*, translated by Thomas Berger (Cambridge, 1989); Theodor W. Adorno, *The Culture Industry. Selected Essays on Mass Culture*, ed. and introduced by J. M. Berstein (London, 2001).

public life that are located outside the household or the state.[69] Just as intoxicants are an embedded feature of modern economic development, so they are well nigh inextricable from discursive and cultural practices that have proliferated globally since the sixteenth century. This is true in at least two respects. First, intoxication is closely associated with the act of cultural production at once metaphorically, mythically, and quite often literally.[70] Indeed the phenomenon of 'narcotic modernity', which takes drugs as its fulcrum, is only the latest variant on the long history of intoxicants epitomizing and fuelling the creative process.[71] The conflation of intoxication and the muse pre-dates the printing press, of course; for Islamic poets and Gaelic bards alike, intoxication was the crucible of their craft (see Matthee's chapter below).[72] The public sphere marks, as such, not the inception of a tendency so much as its proliferation and diversification: from the first generations of 'wits' in Elizabethan England to the newest pop sensation, the history of 'culture' is also the history of intoxication. This is even more apparent if, as cultural historians now insist, the sociable aspects of cultural production are recognized. Engels and his philosophical milieu were by no means original in thinking and writing publicly and collaboratively, in alehouses and wine-shops. From the taverns of 1590s London to the salons in eighteenth-century Paris to the cafés in fin-de-siècle Vienna to the bars of Greenwich Village, intoxicants have lubricated the more general public discourse out of which (for example) Elizabethan theatre, Voltaire's dictionary, Benjamin's journalism, and Dylan's songs emerged.[73]

69 J. B. Thompson, *The Media and Modernity. A Social Theory of the Media* (Cambridge, 1995).

70 Michelle O'Callaghan, *The English Wits: Literature and Sociability in Early Modern England* (Cambridge, 2007); James Nicholls and Susan J. Owen (eds), *A Babel of Bottles: Drink, Drinkers and Drinking Places in Literature* (Sheffield, 2000). The classic account is Malcolm Lowry, *Under the Volcano: A Casebook*, ed. Gordon Bowker (Basingstoke, 1987). For a recent treatment, see Olivia Laing, *The Trip to Echo Spring. Why Writers Drink* (London, 2013).

71 Phil Withington, '"Tumbled into the Dirt": Wit and Incivility in Early Modern England', *Journal of Historical Pragmatics*, 12:1–2 (2011), 156–77.

72 R. A. Dodgshon, '"Pretense of blud" and "place of their duelling": The Nature of Scottish Clans, 1500–1754' in R. A. Houston and I. D. Whyte (eds), *Scottish Society, 1500–1800* (Cambridge, 1989), 169–98; Jane H. Ohlmeyer, '"Civilizinge of those rude partes": Colonization within Britain and Ireland, 1580s–1640s' in Nicholas Canny, *The Origins of Empire* (Oxford, 1998), 128–30. See Rudi Matthee's chapter below.

73 O'Callaghan, *English Wits*; Steven D. Kale, *French Salons: High Society and Political Sociability from the Old Regime to the Revolution of 1848* (Baltimore, 2004); Charlotte

This points to a second interconnection between intoxication and the public sphere. Since the printing press at least, emergent forms of public discourse have been an important place to make and contest claims about intoxicants and their consumption—about the qualities, functions, and dangers of particular intoxicants, the rights and wrongs of different behaviours, appropriate or deviant modes of consumption, and so on.[74] As such the changing genres and technologies of public discourse – whether in the form of printed sermons, tabloid newspapers, political economies, Hollywood movies, Renaissance portraiture, or blogs – have an important role in determining attitudes and policies. In most instances this makes for a contingent and contested realm that is very different to Jürgen Habermas's idealization of a bourgeois sphere of rational and disinterested debate intended to establish truth; or, indeed, the analyses of historians who like to generalise about (for example) attitudes towards drunkenness at a specific moment in time. Not only is there conflict between the different claims and the epistemologies and worldviews they represent – between, for example, those who celebrated drunkenness in the seventeenth century and those who abhorred it, or between American proponents of the 'psychedelic revolution' and ideologues of the 'war on drugs'. There is also a politics inherent to the sociology of the public sphere itself: for example, of authorship and who can claim what and how; of the genres and technologies available to make those claims; of the kinds of audience so addressed; of the rules and procedures of censorship.[75] That a further layer of complexity is posed by the problem of how particular authorial statements are then appropriated and understood by audiences indicates just how unstable and variegated meanings of intoxication can be.[76]

Ashby, Tag Gronberg, and Simon Shaw Miller (eds), *The Viennese Café and Fin-de-Siècle Culture* (Oxford, 2013); John Strausbaugh, *The Village* (New York, 2013).

74 Nicholls, *The Politics of Alcohol*; James Nicholls, 'Vinum Britannicum: the Drink Question in Early Modern England', *Social History of Alcohol and Drugs*, 22:2 (2008), 190–208; Hilton, *Smoking*, 202–24. A nice case-study is Jonathon White, '"The Slow but sure Poison": the Representation of Gin and its Drinkers, 1736–1751', *Journal of British Studies*, 42 (2003), 35–64.

75 Thompson, *Media and Modernity*; J. B. Thompson, *Merchants of Culture: The Publishing Business in the Twenty-First Century*, 2nd edn (Cambridge, 2012); Phil Withington, 'Renaissance Drinking Cultures and Popular Print' in Herring et al., *Intoxication and Society*, 139–49.

76 Roger Chartier, *The Cultural Uses of Print in Early Modern France. Cultural History* (Oxford, 1987); Roger Chartier, 'Texts, Printings, Readings' in Lynn Hunt, ed., *The New Cultural History* (Berkeley, 1989), 168–71.

Modern intoxication is structured, thirdly, by major transformations in the organization of political and corporate power since *circa* 1500. This includes, of course, the formation of sovereign states and empires, the growth of which were in large part fuelled by taxes on intoxicants.[77] For example, by the second half of the eighteenth century two thirds of the revenue of the British state depended on the immanent and purposeful intoxication of the populace, and for a whole host of reasons it is no coincidence that tea became a symbol of Bostonians' resistance to the British.[78] But these developments also include the kind of associations and corporations that, while usually under the jurisdiction of sovereign authority, nevertheless provide its members with significant degrees of collective identity and agency. In the case of the Boston Tea Party, for example, the British government riled colonists by supporting at their expense the interests of the East India Company, an immensely powerful corporation that, due largely to profits from its monopoly of intoxicants, had acquired many of the attributes of a state in its own right.[79] While the genealogy of modern states and empires is fairly well established, that of modern corporatism, or what might be defined as the capacity for purposeful and voluntary association on the part of members, remains to be told. Such a genealogy would probably encompass the long tradition of medieval guilds, fraternities, and urban corporations; the emergence alongside these traditions in the early modern era of new kinds of company and civil society (including the formation of independent churches, which were important in disseminating the nomenclature); the proliferation of clubs, voluntary societies, and associational life after 1700; and the rise of national and global non-government organizations in the twentieth century.[80] What is

[77] John Brewer, *The Sinews of Power. War, Money, and the English State* (Harvard, 1990), 91–101; William Answorth, *Customs and Excise. Trade, Production and Consumption in England* (Oxford, 2003), especially chapter 12; Jacob M. Price, 'Tobacco Use and Tobacco Taxation: A Battle of Interests in Early Modern Europe' in Goodman et al., *Consuming Habits*, 158–77; Benjamin Woods Labaree, *The Boston Tea Party* (Oxford, 1964); T. H. Breen, *Marketplace of Revolution. How Consumer Politics Shaped American Independence* (Oxford, 2004).

[78] Patrick K. O'Brien, 'The Political Economy of British Taxation, 1660–1815', *Economic History Review*, 41 (1988), 11.

[79] Philip J. Stern, *The Company-State: Corporate Sovereignty and The Early Modern Origins of the British Empire in India* (Oxford, 2011).

[80] George Unwin, *Industrial Organization in the Sixteenth and Seventeenth Centuries*, introduced by T. S. Ashton (London, 1957); Phil Withington, *Society in Early Modern England. The Vernacular Origins of a Powerful Idea* (Cambridge, Polity, 2010); Peter Clark, *British Clubs and Societies 1580–1800: the Origins of an Associational World* (Oxford, 2000); Matthew Hilton, Nick Crowson, Jean Francois Mouhot, and James Mackay (eds),

clear is that how political and corporate power is organized, accessed, and used is quite as integral to theories and practices of intoxication as capitalism and the public sphere.

This is perhaps more obvious for states than corporations. Modern polities have always depended fiscally on intoxicants, raising revenue through taxes, monopolies, and licences. Likewise policing intoxication is a legitimate—and sometimes legitimizing—function of state power. In early modern England, parliamentary statutes against drunkenness were centrepieces of the Edwardian and Jacobean Reformation and facilitated unprecedented levels of communal policing and prosecutions.[81] In this volume Rebecca Earle and Hung Bin Hsu demonstrate the importance that colonial governments as different as the Spanish and Japanese nevertheless attached to intoxicants, and how the reform and control of indigenous practices was integral to colonial rule. But corporations and associations also play a vital role in shaping and defining modern cultures of intoxication. Most obviously, as groupings often predicated on principles of fellowship and sociability, the proliferation of associations, clubs, and societies since the sixteenth century has massively expanded the public sites and contexts of intoxication, both purposeful and immanent. As the webpage 'How to be an effective AA coffee person' notes, because 'Alcoholics Anonymous meetings are almost synonymous with coffee pots and coffee drinking, the coffee person plays an integral part in the organization of the meeting'.[82] More importantly, it is by forming associations and acting collectively that individuals with an agenda are best able to make their claims, introduce new practices, and influence the state and public sphere. Thus one of the busiest and publicly visible societies at the start of the eighteenth century was the Society for the Reformation of Manners, a national amalgam of local associations that took the intoxicating habits of the populace as its focus.[83] Thereafter a range of associations—from friendly societies, insurance societies, temperance groups, and churches, to the World Health Organization or British Medical Association—have all

A Historical Guide to NGOs in Britain: Charities, Civil Society, and the Voluntary Sector since 1945 (Basingstoke, 2012); Matthew Hilton and James Mackay (eds), *The Ages of Voluntarism: How We Got to the Big Society* (Oxford, 2013); Matthew Hilton and Rana Mitter (eds), *Transnationalism and Contemporary Global History* (Oxford, 2013).

[81] Wrightson, 'Alehouses'; Wrightson, *English Society, 1580–1680* (London, 1982), 167–9;

[82] http://voices.yahoo.com/how-effective-aa-meeting-coffee-person-7722426.html [accessed 22 September 2013].

[83] Martin Ingram, 'Reformation of Manners in Early Modern England' in Adam Fox, Paul Griffiths, and Steve Hindle (eds), *The Experience of Authority in Early Modern England* (Basingstoke, 1996).

campaigned for behavioural change.[84] These can be contrasted with groups taking contrary positions—whether the drinking fraternities and clubs of the early modern era, the hippy collectives of the 1960s, or consumer groups like CAMRA.[85]

The changing tenor and epistemology of these reformatory campaigns points, finally, to perhaps the single most important shift in how intoxication is conceived and practised in the modern world. Until the late nineteenth century the traditional sources for thinking about intoxication, at least from a western perspective, were the complex legacies of the ancient classical world on the one hand and Christian teachings on the other hand. As a number of chapters in this volume demonstrate, the lessons to be learned from these traditions were ambiguous and often contradictory, the manner in which they were disseminated and appropriated equally complicated. While the era of Renaissance and Reformation spawned or reaffirmed classical and Christian notions of temperance, moderation, morality, and self-control, it also fetishized the dangers, exhilaration, solidarities, and transcendent power of excessive consumption.[86] These legacies certainly pulled the great social theorist Max Weber in different directions. On the one hand, Weber is known for identifying the cultural and economic ramifications of Reformation puritanism and the emergence of what he famously termed the Protestant work ethic, upon which the accumulative and industrious power of modern capitalism rests. On the other hand, his most recent biographer, Joachim Radkau, relates that as a young professor Weber 'suffered from obsessional thoughts and, especially after nights of drinking, sometimes imagined for the whole day that he was Jumbo the elephant and lived in a zoo'.[87] This was fairly often,

[84] James Kneale and Shaun French, 'The Relations of Inebriety to Insurance': Geographies of Medicine, Insurance and Alcohol in Britain, 1840–1911' in Herring et al., *Intoxication and Society*, 87–109.

[85] Timothy Raylor, *Cavaliers, Clubs, and Literary Culture: Sir John Mennes, James Smith, and the Order of the Fancy* (Newark, 1994).

[86] Norbert Elias, *The Civilizing Process*, trans. Edmund Jephcott (Oxford, 2000); Anna Bryson, *From Courtesy to Civility: Changing Codes of Conduct in Early Modern England* (Oxford, 1996), 10–11; Mark Hailwood, 'Sociability, Work, and Labouring Identity in Seventeenth-Century England', *Cultural and Social History* 8:1 (2011); Angela McShane, 'Roaring Royalists and Ranting Brewers: The Politicisation of Drink and Drunkenness in Political Broadside Ballads from 1640–1689' in Adam Smyth (ed.), *A Pleasinge Sinne. Drink and Conviviality in Seventeenth-Century England* (Woodbridge, 2004); idem., 'The Extraordinary Case of the Flesh Eating and Blood Drinking Cavaliers' in Angela McShane and Garthine Walker (eds), *The Extraordinary and the Everyday in Early Modern England* (Basingstoke, 2010); Withington, 'Renaissance Drinking Cultures'.

[87] Joachim Radkau, *Max Weber: A Biography* (Cambridge, 2009), 46.

because 'alcohol-tinged male company, even without deeper friendships, seems to have been what excited him par excellence'.[88] According to those who knew him best there was 'a quite elemental kind of sociability in Weber: he was a buddy with all his soul, a buddy for the moment thought capable of creating happiness; a drinking pal, a song mate, an accomplice in furious story-telling and boasting'.[89] Radkau goes as far as to argue that 'Weber felt the delight of this male company as a primal social experience and a key to the earliest processes of human socialization'; that he remained, in fact, an archetypal German university student who 'intoxicated by alcohol, growling and laughing. . . feels indeed like primeval man'.[90]

Since the later nineteenth century this nebulous and variegated ideological framework has been supplemented and, in some quarters, superseded by advances in scientific knowledge and the medicalization of much public policy and debate. The enormous ideological baggage now placed on 'drug' is one consequence of this shift, the identification of substances as 'intoxicants'—that is, chemically and so inherently intoxicating—is another. Indeed so vociferous and politically adept are the proponents of a medically reductionist view of intoxication, a view nevertheless laced with the moral assumptions of early modernity, that it is unsurprising that an archaeologist like Sherratt should regard this new language as synonymous with modernity. It is important to remember, therefore, that these epistemological and technological changes, however significant, are nevertheless located in the much larger institutional field defined by the developments cursorily outlined above. They are not, that is, somehow above or beyond the history and anthropology of intoxication. Rather they are one more aspect of an ongoing and extraordinarily complex set of historical processes.

Cultures of intoxication

The chapters that follow reflect the major preoccupations and issues outlined above. The volume begins with two studies that focus expressly on the experiential dimensions of intoxication itself. In something of a methodological *tour de force*, Robin Osborne uses poetry, imagery, and pottery in order to try and reconstruct what it meant and even felt like to get drunk at an ancient Greek symposium. In addition, he pinpoints the paradox that has characterized the historiographical treatment of not only the symposium but also Europe's classical inheritance more generally. As perhaps the single most iconic institution of the ancient world, the symposium was also an intensive

[88] Ibid., 37.

[89] Ibid. Radkau is quoting Weber's nephew, Eduard Baumgarten.

[90] Ibid., 37–8.

and deeply ritualized drinking bout. However, until very recently the drunkenness that was so integral to its sociability and, indeed, philosophy has received no serious academic treatment. Moving the analysis forward 2000 years, Karen Joe-Laidler, Geoffrey Hunt, and Molly Moloney deploy social surveying techniques to fathom the feelings and perceptions of ecstasy and ketamine users in the San Francisco and Hong Kong dance scenes. Echoing Osborne they note that while there are plenty of studies treating youth culture and its excesses as a societal problem, the perceptions and motivations of the users themselves are rarely considered. In this instance the lacunae is easier to address. Clearly enormous structural differences separate the symposium, as the fulcrum of classical civil life, and the nightclub, an institution symptomatic of global capitalism and the culture industry. The studies accordingly point to the particular material and sociological contexts that frame and help to define the intoxicating moment. However, they also suggest remarkable parallels in consciousness and experience: its transformative power, its spiritual depth, and the prospect of belonging.

The next three chapters turn from the synchronic to the diachronic, telling stories about drunkenness in Spanish colonial America, the Islamic Near East, and South and West Africa. Rebecca Earle traces how government characterizations and explanations of south Amerindian drunkenness have changed from early settlement to the present day. She highlights the varieties and ambiguities of early Christian discourse and the difficulties of knowing the nature of Amerindian practices and motivations beyond the colonial texts. She also demonstrates how, over time, the paradigms of governance have changed according to epistemological developments in western thought more generally—from the Christian humanist (and self-serving) emphases of imperial rule to the bio-political preoccupations of the post-colonial republic to the prospect of genetic determinism raised by contemporary science. Matthee provides a more conventional and synoptic narrative of Islamic drinking from the medieval era to the present day. His points are many and varied: that alcohol has always been present in states and cultures that ostensibly proscribe it; that its consumption is inextricably linked to masculine identity and sovereign power; that in Islamic culture it is a lubricant of the private rather than public spheres, which are dominated by coffee and tobacco; that its public retail is an expressly modern, urban, and cosmopolitan affair; that, indeed, it is alcohol as well as 'drugs' that can signify modernity. Similar strains of ambiguity and ambivalence characterize Paul Nugent's rich and comparative study of intoxication in Africa. The chapter has two primary concerns: to show the importance of spatial and social context in making for different kinds of African drinking since the nineteenth century; and to argue that there is no straightforward story to tell about the relationship between drinking and modernity—or indeed 'tradition'—within Africa. Especially striking in the light of the 'modernizing' connotations of Iranian and Egyptian drinking is Nugent's identification of powerful Muslim modernity in Senegal—an ideology that expressly rejected 'tradition' not by identification with individualism, affluence, and intoxicants but by abstinence, decorum, and membership 'of a global Muslim community'.

Following these compelling narratives the volume turns to representations and ideologies of intoxication in the early modern and modern eras. Tom Nichols looks at depictions of drinking in Renaissance art. He sets out to test whether the stereotypical distinction between a reformatory and 'realist' northern tradition of painting and a more benign, celebratory, and 'classical' southern tradition holds true. The answer is that it does not. Although Bacchus is certainly idealized as an elevating figure by Italian painters and sculptors, his sinister and satirical undertones are never far away. And while more straightforwardly positive and proscriptive representations characterize Dutch renditions, Nichols claims that the most complex and ambiguous representations of the entire era are by Pieter Bruegel the Elder. Similar nuances are found by Jennifer Richards in her analysis of early modern conduct books—in particular their advice on how to partake in expressly 'civil conversation' while imbibing drink and enjoying mirth. It transpires that what might be assumed to be archetypal lessons in asceticism and restraint are in practice much more humane and pragmatic texts. Richards argues that early modern readers, both female and male, would have learned that the key to civility in the relentless face of immanent intoxication was not abstinence or denial. Rather it was an attuned and reflective sense of self that could establish in any given context when 'enough' was, indeed, enough: recognition, that is, of the personal thresholds of capacity beyond which social and bodily disorder could ensue. The essential ambiguity of early modern symbolism and discourse contrasts with the much more polarized positions taken in modern USA culture. At one side of the divide Sarah Shortall deconstructs the ideology of 'experience' espoused by Timothy Leary and his hippy milieu during the 'psychedelic revolution' of the 1960s. At the other end of the spectrum, Tim Hickman unpacks the semiotics of fMRI brain scans used by US government agencies to justify a 'war on drugs' in the first decade of the twenty-first century. The tricks and inconsistencies of both positions become clear. Shortall dwells on the contradictions between an ideology of communal and 'authentic' transcendence that nevertheless depended on artificial synthetics—LSD—inducing largely incommunicable and interiorized shifts in consciousness. She also suggests that ideals of collective and personal liberation were always mediated by more familiar inequalities of race, gender, and class. In the meantime, Hickman demonstrates how representational techniques applied to otherwise inconclusive scientific data transformed cautious hypotheses about the neurological impact of drugs into redoubtable and incontrovertible 'facts'. He also suggests that in the context of global terrorism, the aggressive lexicon of bio-politics melds all too easily into the language of the military industrial complex.

This concern with the relationship between intoxication and political power continues into the final three chapters. Their focus is on practice. Like Hickman, Hung Bin Hsu examines the activities of the state, in this instance showing how the Japanese wrested control of the Taiwanese opium market during their period of colonial rule. So important did the Japanese perceive the trade to be that they established scientific laboratories to make and refine the drug and created a state monopoly to control supply. So ingrained and discerning were local tastes, however, that the scientists were also forced to employ Taiwanese tasters to grade and verify the opium they produced. In this way Japanese scientists learned from and eventually superseded local aficionados as the local arbiters of taste and production. Angela McShane moves attention backwards to the ideological and political ferment of seventeenth-century England. Focusing on the material culture of drinking, she traces the development of two quintessential early modern practices: the secularization of Protestant Communion, whereby everyday cups and drinking implements were incorporated into the holy sacrament; and the sacralization of politics, whereby toasts of loyalty to the monarch or state converted alehouses and taverns into sacred spaces. McShane points out that in both instances, the 'willingness to drink alcohol' became a prerequisite of the socialized subject. Finally Karin Sennefelt examines political drinking practices a century later. Focusing on the Swedish diet in Stockholm, she shows at once the absolute centrality of drinking to the working of the four estates as well as its ambiguity and dangers. At the heart of Sweden's political culture, drinking created and maintained loyalties, encouraged camaraderie and signified hierarchy, affected patriotism and embodied corruption, levelled men by intoxicating them and obligated them through conventions of reciprocity. Indeed so ubiquitous was alcohol that it determined for much of the time the political judgement and subjectivity of Sweden's political deputies. Here, then, was the perfect mix of immanent and purposeful intoxication—a scenario that the animals of Manor Farm, looking in through the window, would no doubt have recognized.

Intoxication and Sociality: The Symposium in the Ancient Greek World

Robin Osborne

It is a persistent feature of stories about Dionysos, the god associated by the Greeks with wine, that with him, as with wine and other alcoholic drinks, you never quite know what you are getting.[1] Men fail to recognize him for what he is, and in consequence are transformed.[2] Hardly present at all in the *Iliad* and *Odyssey*, and not much more prominent in Hesiod's *Theogony* and *Works and Days*, Dionysos is properly introduced to us in *Homeric Hymn* 7, written a generation or two later.[3] The hymn tells how youthful Dionysos stands, handsome and well-dressed, on the seashore, and is promptly spotted and captured by pirates. The pirates take him to be some ruler's son—except for the helmsman, who is convinced that he is a god. But once they get out to sea amazing things begin to happen—the sea turns to wine, a vine grows round the mast, heavy with grapes, Dionysos becomes a lion, and the sailors, leaping into the sea, become dolphins—except for the helmsman, to whom Dionysos identifies himself. Few recognize Dionysos as a god, this hymn seems to tell us, and only those who do retain their humanity.

Shortly after the middle of the sixth century the most extraordinary painter of pots in Athens, a painter whose contemporaries were as struck by his work as modern scholars have been, painted a response to this story on the only cup we know him to have painted (Figure 1a). The manner and technique that

[1] I am grateful to Caroline Vout and to the editors for reading and improving an earlier draft. I have also benefited from discussions of this paper in Cambridge, Oxford and at Yale, and am grateful to those audiences. The following abbreviations are used: *ABV*: John D. Beazley, *Attic Black-Figure Vase-Painters* (Oxford, 1956); *ARV*: John D. Beazley, *Attic Red-Figure Vase-Painters*, 2nd edn (Oxford, 1963).

[2] For the classic instance of this, see Euripides' *Bacchae*. For a discussion of the trope of Dionysos' revenge see Park McGinty, 'Dionysos's Revenge and the Validation of the Hellenic World-View', *Harvard Theological Review*, 71 (1978), 77–94.

[3] 'It may tentatively be dated within the seventh century', Richard Janko, *Homer, Hesiod, and the Hymns* (Cambridge, 1982), 184.

 © The Past and Present Society

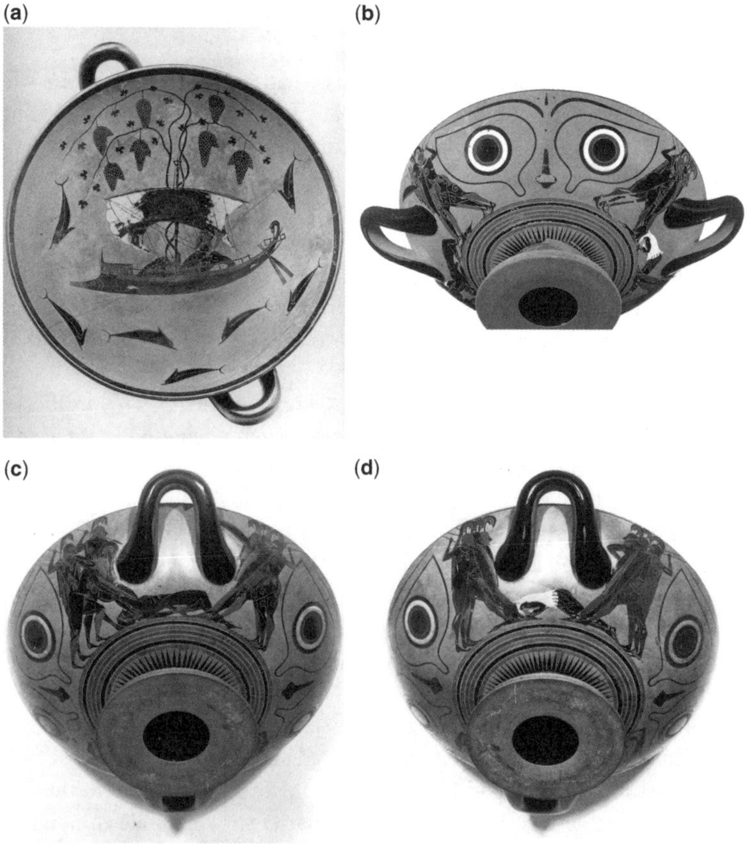

Figure 1. Attic black-figure kylix, Exekias, Munich 2044. Staatliche Antikensammlungen und Glyptothek München. Photograph by Renate Kühling. **a**) Interior featuring Dionysos in a ship with dolphins; **b**) exterior featuring decoration between the handles consisting of two large eyes, eyebrow and nose; **c**) and **d**) exterior handles feature scenes of men fighting over the body of a fallen comrade.

Exekias, who signed this cup on its foot as potter, chose to employ to decorate the interior were unusual—the scene filled the entire bowl and was executed in the coral-red slip that he seems to have invented.[4] And the scene he chose is one we know no previous artist to have attempted: Dionysos in a ship, its mast

[4] For the technique see Beth Cohen, *The Colors of Clay: Special Techniques in Athenian Vases* (Los Angeles, 2006), 45–6; for the cup in general the classic description remains John D. Beazley, *The Development of Attic Black-Figure* (Berkeley, 1951), 67–8. The cup is Munich 2044, *ABV* 146.21.

encircled by a vine with great clusters of grapes, sailing through a sea in which dolphins sport.[5]

The Homeric hymn stresses Dionysos is an attractive figure but one who turns men wild. The pirates, not realizing with whom they are dealing, find, on close encounter, strange things happening before their eyes, and themselves become creatures at sea. The hymn has no interest in sociality, no interest in the context in which men consume wine, simply in wine's deceptive attractions, as something that appears worldly, like the son of a ruler, but turns out to be other-worldly, subjecting men to animal forces. The only indication that there may be an alternative to Dionysos' turning men wild comes from the helmsman, who alone recognizes the god and retains his humanity.

In his refrain to the *Hymn*, however, Exekias presents us with a different image of Dionysos. The ship sails once more through a 'wine-dark' sea of ruby red, and a vine climbs round the mast; dolphins may play around the ship but on board is no lion, rather the bearded god, reclining with drinking horn in hand. The drinker who swirls his wine around in this cup sees before him a choice of roles: will he bob around like the dolphins, gently but giddily circling like part of a synchronized swimming team? Or will he hold his hand and head steady on the couch like this god, propped on his elbow, reclining in the attitude that was the trademark of the Greek *symposion*, the *banquet couché*?

Dionysos appeared in this guise on a late sixth-century temple pediment on Corfu and on a number of pots from that date and after. He comes to be shown like this with the god Hephaistos and with Herakles, but at the time Exekias painted he was shown like this primarily with a female companion, normally identified by scholars (although she is never in fact named) as the Ariadne whom he picked up abandoned by Theseus on Naxos.[6] The god who in the *Hymn* presents the power of intoxication to break down the barriers between human and animal is here pictured like a symposiast waiting for his girl. In this instance intoxicants have broken inter-personal barriers, lubricating social intercourse.

Along with everything else that is novel about Exekias' cup, it has a new shape. Earlier Athenian cups had been relatively small and delicate, often on a high foot, and their decoration had been made up of a single motif or a frieze.

[5] Two other black-figure scenes of Dionysos at sea are known, see *Lexicon Iconographicum Classicae Mythologiae s.v.* Dionysos nos 789 and 790 (Exekias' cup is no. 788).

[6] On what is at stake in the name Ariadne see Simon Goldhill and Robin Osborne, 'Introduction' in Simon Goldhill and Robin Osborne (eds), *Art and Text in Ancient Greek Culture* (Cambridge, 1994).

This cup is large, 30 cm in diameter, and on the exterior the decoration between the handles consists of two large eyes, complete with eyebrows, separated by a nose (Figure 1b). The drinker who lifts the cup to his lips, most elegantly by holding the foot rather than the handles, acquires a mask of which the handles are the ears and the foot the large round mouth (though if he holds the handles he finds the ship sailing directly into his throat). The mask gives the drinker a fixed stare, but is it the stare of stupefaction or the stare of madness?[7] He, for so he is gendered by this as by most sympotic imagery, is transformed into a curious monster, but not any sort of recognized animal. Indeed the scenes under the handles (Figures 1c and 1d) insist that we have not left the world of men: relegated to the margins, but not out of mind, are two scenes of battle in which men fight over the body of a fallen comrade. Dionysian sociality is highlighted by this reminder of the alternative forms of human society with which it is at the same time compared and contrasted. What is further from the *symposion* than the world of battle? Yet the encounter with wine has laid more men flat than enemies in battle, despoiling them of the arms and the clothing that marks them out as part of a world of culture. Coming face-to-face with Dionysos is quite as daunting as encountering enemy troops. Every drinker puts on this mask, in that every drinker is compelled to push the unpleasant realities of the world to the edges, but in exactly how they wear this mask each reveals his true identity.

This cup had an immediate effect on other potters. Exekias' great contemporary and rival, the Amasis painter, took up the shape and the scheme, and transformed it in scurrilous fashion.[8] In place of two eyes he painted, on one side, a single eye as the body of a siren (Figure 2a) (other painters would take up this conceit). A mask with a single eye suggests winking, and the left arm of the siren stretches forward to turn the viewer's attention round the cup. Around the cup, on the other side, we find not one figure, but two, who transform the hoplite fighters of Exekias, with eyes behind them, into the bearded heads of revellers with their bodies stretched out towards each other, one or both knees tucked up, masturbating (Figure 2b). And under the handles themselves, where Exekias has a corpse, the Amasis painter sites a dog, defecating. Where Exekias uses added white for the sail and coral red for the sea, the Amasis painter uses added red not just for the face and stripes on the wing and tail of the siren but for the penises of both revellers and the excrement of both dogs. If Exekias offered an image of sympotic sociality in which Dionysos promised pleasure and distraction from the world of politics, the

[7] Compare [Aristotle] *Problems*, (trans. E. S. Forster), Book 2, Problem 16, 873a22–3: 'Why has wine the effect both of stupefying and of driving to frenzy those who drink it?'

[8] Boston Museum of Fine Arts 10.651 (Gift of E. P. Warren), *ABV* 157.86.

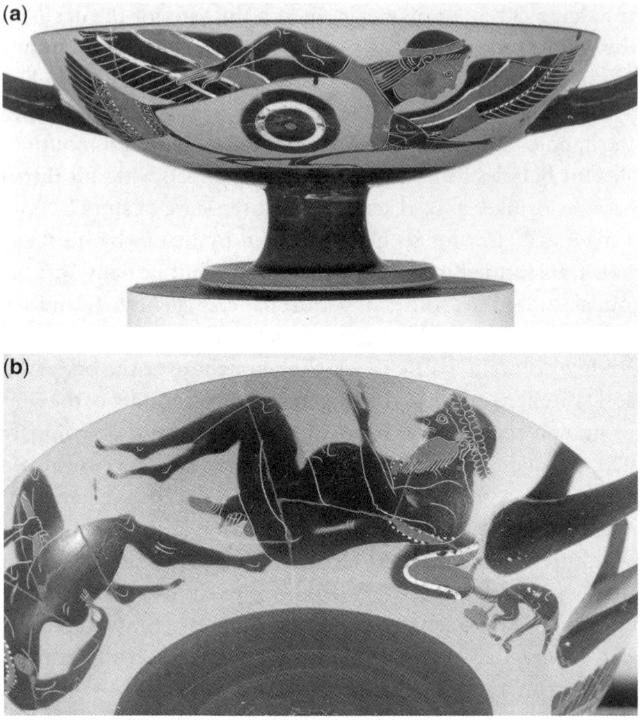

Figure 2. Black-figure drinking cup (*kylix*) ascribed to the Amasis Painter, Boston 10.651. Photograph © 2014 Museum of Fine Arts, Boston. **a**) exterior featuring a single eye as the body of a siren; **b**) exterior featuring bearded heads of revellers masturbating.

Amasis painter offers an image of sympotic sociality in which Dionysos lifts all inhibitions and rules: the boundary between man and beast cannot be overcome simply by adopting the conventions of the banqueting couch, discarded by these two men. At this drinking party we find men from whom wine elicits winking, misbehaviour and talking dirty.

We know more about how the ancient Greeks, and particularly the ancient Athenians, conceived of their drinking parties (*symposia*) than we know about almost any other aspect of their lives. We know more about their drinking parties than about their meals, their political meetings, or their military life either on or off the battlefield.[9] We know so much because Athenian and other Greek writers wrote descriptions of (not necessarily

[9] For food see Peter Garnsey, *Food and Society in Classical Antiquity* (Cambridge 1999); Andrew Dalby, *Siren Feasts: A History of Food and Gastronomy in Greece* (London, 1996).

typical) drinking parties and because Athenian and other Greek painters painted images of drinking parties on pots. But we also know so much because we have poetry that was written more or less certainly for, although not about, drinking parties and we have pottery, like these cups, that was painted for use at, though not directly illustrating, drinking parties.

There can be little surprise, therefore, that a great deal of modern scholarship has been concerned with the drinking party, treating it, indeed, as a key to Greek social intercourse. The only surprise is that scholarly attention turned to the drinking party so recently. As Oswyn Murray observed in 1990, before the 1970s the symposium had attracted very little attention.[10] For all the long-standing fascination with Plato's *Symposion*, few scholars had been concerned with the institution it explores and exploits, and the mass of ancient poetry now accepted to have been composed for *symposia* was studied without reference to its performance context. Even when attention did turn to the *symposion* as an institution little attention was paid to intoxication; even a volume devoted entirely to wine looked at almost every aspect of wine consumption before looking at drunkenness.[11] It has been left to those working on images of the *symposion* to devote attention to intoxication.[12]

[10] Oswyn Murray 'Sympotic History', in Oswyn Murray (ed.), *Sympotica. A Symposium on the Symposion* (Oxford 1990), 7.

[11] Oswyn Murray (ed.), *Sympotica*; William J. Slater, *Dining in a Classical Context* (Ann Arbor, 1991); Oswyn Murray and Manuela Tecusan (eds), *In Vino Veritas* (London, 1995). Note also the source collection Massimo Montanari, *Convivio: Storia e cultura dei piaceri della tavola* (Rome, 1989).

[12] François Lissarrague, *Un Flot d'images: une esthétique du banquet grec* (Paris 1987), translated by Andrew Szegedy-Maszak as *The Aesthetics of the Greek Banquet* (Princeton, 1990). Lissarrague discusses Exekias' cup at 116–18. See also Jean-Louis Durand, Françoise Frontisi-Ducroux and François Lissarrague, 'L'entre-deux-vins', in Claude Bérard et al. (eds), *La Cité des images: religion et société en grèce antique* (Lausanne 1984), 117–25 (translated by Deborah Lyons as *The City of Images: Iconography and Society in Ancient Greece* (Princeton, 1989)), and Robin Osborne, 'Projecting Identities in the Greek Symposion', in Joanna Sofaer (ed.), *Material Identities* (Malden, Mass., 2007), 31–52. Remarkably the index to Kathryn Topper, *The Imagery of the Athenian Symposium* (Cambridge, 2012), has no entry for intoxication, drunkenness, or even wine. The one aspect of intoxication in texts that has been discussed is the link between drinking and being at sea, well explored by William J. Slater, 'Symposium at Sea', *Harvard Studies in Classical Philology* 80 (1976), 161–70 and Malcolm Davies, 'Sailing, Rowing, and Sporting in one's Cups on the Wine-dark Sea' in William A. P. Childs (ed.), *Athens Comes of Age: From Solon to Salamis*, (Princeton, 1978), 72–95.

In turning the symposion into a sober institution, scholars have lost sight of the way in which the encounter with wine was also an encounter with the gods. These images were not simply consumed by those for whom Dionysos was a god and who in an important sense believed in the myths represented.[13] Used by people who were drinking, who were experiencing the effects of the god Dionysos upon them, the images were viewed in the context of intoxication. This paper explores the significance of this insight. The physiological effects of drinking wine in antiquity are likely to have been similar to those experienced today. We can therefore ask what difference it makes to seeing the images on these pots when one is drunk. The question is important because the symposion wasn't just a place where people happened to become intoxicated. Rather it was an occasion on which they consciously, deliberately, and in a carefully controlled and observed way experienced inebriation. To see Greek sympotic pottery through the eyes of its users we must look at it through inebriated eyes. And if to do so is to see these scenes subjectively, that is the necessary cost of recapturing a subjective experience.

The concerns explored in the *Homeric Hym*n and in the cups of Exekias and Amasis are the central concerns of the *symposion*: how is the god Dionysos to be managed? The question of how much to drink and whether drinking can be controlled is raised directly at the beginning of the *symposion* in Plato's *Symposium* (written in the early fourth century). Immediately the libations have been poured and a hymn sung, one of the party-goers, Pausanias, asks how they might drink 'most easily' in view of their having drunk heavily the night before. The others all agree that they were well 'soaked' the previous evening and do not have the strength to drink heavily, the doctor Eryximakhos adding that he thinks drunkenness is bad for people generally.[14] They agree to drink only for pleasure, with no compulsion applied (*Symp.* 176a3–e6). Later in the dialogue, the arrival of Alcibiades prompts again the question of drinking and its limits. Declaring them all to be sober, Alcibiades decides to drink a whole wine-cooler full of wine, and then passes it to Socrates (famously unaffected by drinking any amount of wine) for him to do the same, before Eryximakhos reasserts control and returns the party to an exchange of speeches (*Symp.* 213e–214c). The dialogue ends after a party of

[13] See Paul Veyne, *Les Grecs ont-ils cru à leurs mythes? Essai sur l'imagination constituante* (Paris, 1983), translated by Paula Wissing as *Did the Greeks Believe in their Myths? An Essay on the Constitutive Imagination* (Chicago, 1988).

[14] The question of the different effects on different bodies of different types of wine is a major theme in Book 2 of Aristotle's *Problems.*

revellers bursts in and forces everyone to drink large quantities of wine, in no order, causing some to leave and others to fall asleep (except Socrates) (*Symp.* 223b2–d11).

In Xenophon's *Symposium*, written more or less at the same time as Plato's dialogue, intoxication is again flagged as an issue. This drinking party opens with entertainment provided by a Syracusan with a young female pipe-player, a young female dancer and a young male lyre-player. But after one in the group joins in, and all are reduced to laughter, a call is made for a big cup of wine. Socrates declares that drinking wine is a good idea, since wine makes the soul damp, puts trouble to sleep, and wakes kindly feelings, but insists that drinking has to be done in small quantities so that the mind and body do not stumble but 'arrive at playfulness' (*Symp.* II.24–6). Kharmides picks up on Socrates' suggestion to claim that music does the same as wine, but says that music, rather than awake kindly feelings (*philophrosyne*), stimulates thoughts of sex (*aphrodisia*; *Symp.* III.1). At this point the dialogue turns to its centrepiece, a set of speeches by the party-goers about what each of them is most proud of, ending up with a beauty competition between the notoriously ugly Socrates, who defends his features on functionalist grounds, and the handsome Kritoboulos—which Kritoboulos wins (*Symp.* V).

The issue of intoxication returns when Socrates turns on Hermogenes, who has been distinguishing himself by not smiling at any of the fun, and asks him rather pointedly what *paroinia* (inebriation) is. This is a parody of the typical Socratic question, 'What is justice?' or 'What is virtue?' Hermogenes replies that he does not know what it is, which is plain enough from his behaviour, but that he thinks *paroinia* is annoying those one is with (*tous sunontas*) because one has drunk too much. Socrates uses this as a chance to accuse Hermogenes of annoying the company by being silent (*Symp.* VI.1–2). The point of this exchange is not simply to insist that partygoers need to be tipsy, but the parallel that will soon be drawn with sex. Insisting on the importance of love being for the soul and not merely for the body, Socrates specifically compares the boy who is loved by a man for only physical reasons to one who, sober, looks upon a man drunk with sexual passion (*Symp.* VIII.21). To be at a party and not intoxicated, on this version, is like having sex without feeling some spiritual attraction to the sexual partner. Not to be intoxicated, on this analogy, is the equivalent of being immature: intoxication and proper adult passion go together (cf. *Symp.* VIII.24).

The management of intoxication in the context of the drinking party which is so central an issue in these dialogues had been an issue from the earliest poetry written for sympotic performance. The term *paroinia* itself is one used to explore the behaviour of those who, while inebriated, are not totally drunk.[15] So too early lyrics explore the dangers that men who are 'fortified' by drink put themselves into: Theognis not only talks of 'gentle sleep' stealing over a person armed by drink, but claims that he will never be so fortified as to speak a hostile word about the person to whom the poem is addressed, and notes that although wine is in other respects a source of joy, in one respect it is not, when it arms someone and leads them to their enemy (Theognis 413, 470, 842). These different qualities of wine could be correlated with quantitative differences. In a fragment from his *Semele* or *Dionysos* the comic poet Euboulos had Dionysos declare that the first mixing bowl of wine is the crater of health, the second the crater of love, the third of sleep and fourth not Dionysos's at all but of insolence; (he goes on as far as the tenth crater, of madness).[16]

These literary texts certainly reveal an interest in what the effects of different degrees of intoxication might be, either generally or on a particular drinker. They also reveal a relatively sophisticated vocabulary in order to allow differentiated reference to the drunk and the merely tipsy. Did artists similarly register and explore degrees of intoxication?

Images that represent the *symposion* itself indicate intoxication by its effects. In the most dramatic examples, vomit indicates over-indulgence. The exterior of an early fifth-century cup attributed to the Foundry Painter shows five sympotic couches round the outside of the cup on which eight bearded men recline (Figure 3). Several variously hold up kylikes or pass them from one to another, one twirls a cup around his index finger in the dreg-throwing game called *kottabos*, one throws back his head to sing to the music of the pipes played by a naked female pipe-player, one holds a jug in one hand while extending the other to grope the pipe-player, and one turns his head down and vomits all over one of his shoes.[17] We can be confident here that vomiting is a sign of excess.[18] Should we think of the groping likewise? The relative

15 [Aristotle] *Problems* Book 3**; Book 2 Problem 27 at 875a1.

16 Quoted by Athenaeus 36b; Richard L. Hunter (ed.), *Eubulus: The Fragments* (Cambridge, 1983), *ad loc.* cites useful parallels.

17 Fitzwilliam Museum (on loan from Corpus Christi College) 103.18, *ARV* 402.12. For vomiting at the symposium see the tondo of a cup by Douris, Vatican 16561, *ARV* 427.2, and for vomiting at a post-sympotic revel the tondos of a cup in Berlin Staatliche Museen F2309, *Para* 372 IIbis, and of a cup attributed to Onesimos in St Petersburg, where the revel has turned violent, Hermitage B651/B2110, *Para* 511.

18 But not beyond learned discussion: [Aristotle] *Problems* Book 2 Problem 18, 873a24–5: 'Why is it that watery wine is more apt to cause vomiting than water and than unmixed wine?'

Figure 3. Red-figure cup attributed to the Foundry Painter, Loan Ant. 103.18, Lewis Collection. On loan to the Fitzwilliam Museum, Cambridge. Courtesy of Corpus Christi College and The Fitzwilliam Museum, Cambridge.

rarity of the motif, and the visual emphasis given to it when shown, encourage this reading.[19]]

The effects of intoxication may also be reckoned in question when the *symposion* turns violent. On a cup attributed to the Brygos Painter (Figure 4), a *symposion* attended by beardless youths is breaking up. Though one youth remains reclining on his couch and a female pipe player goes on playing, another youth bends over to display his anus and genitals to the viewer, a third kneels up on a couch, about to use a wineskin as a weapon against a fourth youth who is himself aiming a powerful kick at a fifth youth playing the pipes.[20]

It is not by showing wine consumption, however, that most of the visual imagery on the cups from which Athenians drink at *symposia* explores what it is to be intoxicated. As indicated by the Exekias and Amasis cups, drunkenness is explored by representing analogous experiences drawn from myth or other aspects of life. And because intoxication is always an encounter with the god Dionysos, the most prominent imagery depicts encounters, direct or indirect, with the gods.

[19] Compare New York Metropolitan Museum 07.286.47, *ARV* 175, name-vase of the Hegesiboulos Painter, where a bearded man turns an abnormally large head back to ogle a naked serving boy and reaches out to grope the boy's genitals. Reaching for genitals is, of course, much more commonly shown in scenes of homosexual foreplay, traditionally referred to by scholars as 'courtship' scenes (see Kenneth J. Dover, *Greek Homosexuality* (London 1978), 94–7)).

[20] London BM E71, *ARV* 372.29.

Figure 4. Red-figured cup, attributed to the Brygos Painter; British Museum 1866,0805.4. © The Trustees of the British Museum.

The single most common analogy is with the mythical satyr, a creature about whom there are almost no mythical narratives but who in painted pottery is, along with the female devotee referred to as the maenad ('raving one'), so regularly associated with Dionysos as to signal the Dionysiac world even when the god himself is not represented. Satyrs are men with the ears, tail, and in some early images, the legs and feet of horses, and they combine an ability to do anything that men do with an animal absence of inhibition. They are regularly pictured in a state of sexual excitement, pursue and molest young women, particularly young women asleep, are shown drinking or using drinking vessels in highly irregular ways, break the rules of sympotic mixing of wine and water by drinking directly from amphora or wineskin, and engage with wild animals such as leopards and snakes as if they were tame.

A cup attributed to the Brygos Painter will serve as an illustration (Figure 5a).[21] On the inside of the cup Dionysos stands between two satyrs. The god throws his head back, as singers characteristically do, and

[21] Cabinet de Médailles, Bibliothèque Nationale, Paris 576, *ARV* 371.14 (BA 203913).

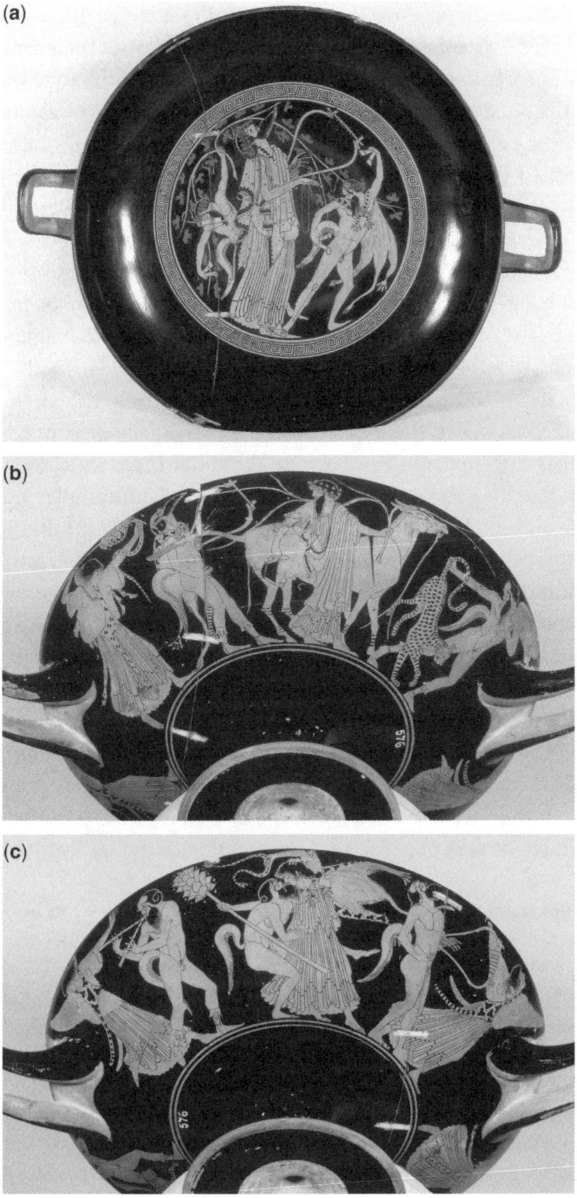

Figure 5. Cup attributed to the Brygos Painter, Paris, Bibl. Nat. 576. **a**) interior, Dionysos plays the *barbitos* and stands between two satyrs; **b**) exterior featuring Dionysos in front of a mule with satyrs and maenads in front of and behind him; **c**) exterior featuring dancing maenads and satyrs.

accompanies himself on the *barbitos*, a type of relatively light-weight lyre, of the sort used at *symposia*. The satyrs beside him throw out their arms in a wild dance, castanets and, in one case, a vine in one hand. Both satyrs wear animal skins. On the outside of the pot (Figure 5b) we find Dionysos again, this time himself holding a vine and standing in front of a mule, with a kantharos in his other hand. In front of him is a satyr holding a leopard by the tail and a wineskin over his shoulder. Behind him is another satyr, to whom Dionysos looks back, wearing an animal skin cloak and Thracian boots, carrying a barbitos and with his head thrown back in song. And behind the satyr is a maenad in baggy-sleeved chiton and animal skin, with thyrsos in one hand and snake in the other. Similar maenads dominate the other side of the cup (Figure 5c). At either end they dance, arms flung wide. In the middle a maenad is about to be lifted off her feet by an entirely naked and sexually excited satyr, on whom she looks down, not obviously discouraging the attention she is receiving, as she waves a snake above the satyr's head. On either side of this pair are satyrs, one with boots and one without, playing the pipes in one case and the *barbitos* in the other. No one actually drinks on this cup, but the intoxication of the *symposion* is its subject. Not just the intoxication of the wine, but the intoxicating music. These male and female figures are losing control, whether of their bodies, in extreme dancing, of the distinction between human and animal, or of the distinction between propriety and impropriety. These are figures who believe that all is in their power, offered to the gaze of the similarly tempted drinker.

Images of satyrs were most numerous on cups in the years immediately before and around 500.[22] Images of the *symposion* on cups were popular in the same period; they became popular in the last quarter or so of the sixth century, ceasing to be very popular after the second quarter of the fifth century.[23]

[22] There is no reason to think that the factors that have led to Greek pots being preserved (many of them in graves in Italy) have caused biases in the subjects represented: see Robin Osborne, 'Why did Athenian Pots Appeal to the Etruscans?', *World Archaeology*, 33:2 (2001), 277–95. A search of the Beazley Archive database for satyr(s) on cups on 5 August 2011 yielded 2500 results: Selected search criteria 'Cup and SATYR'; the number after the value indicates the number of results in the database: 400–300 (70); 425–375 (41); 450–400 (65); 475–425 (176); 500–450 (232); 525–475 (568); 550–500 (297); 575–525 (74); 600–550 (2); Cup and SATYRS: 400–300 (11); 425–375 (2); 450–400 (37); 475; 425 (88); 500–450 (128); 525–475 (246); 550–500 (259); 575–525 (70); 600–550 (2).

[23] A search of the Beazley Archive database for symposion scenes on cups on 5 August 2011 yielded 1044 results, which are given in overlapping periods and reverse chronological order: Selected search criteria 'Cup and SYMPOSIUM': 400–300 (1); 425–375 (1); 450–400 (64); 475–425 (210); 500–450 (324); 525–475 (262); 550–500 (76); 575–525 (61); 600–550 (7).

But for all their prominence in modern discussions of the *symposion*, sympotic scenes and scenes involving satyrs do not appear on more than 15 per cent of Athenian cups.[24] Most of those who used Athenian pottery from which to drink intoxicating liquor did not contemplate their intoxication through these mirrors. In the rest of this paper I take four cups, one painted in each half of the sixth century and one in each half of the fifth, in order to show how those who drank from Athenian cups were made to think about intoxication in relation to a range of myths and life experiences.

Broadly speaking, the black-figure pots of sixth century BC Athens, where figures are reduced to flat silhouettes, are dominated by direct allusions to the world of myth; the red-figure pots that begin to be popular around 520 and dominate production in the fifth century, where the figures begin to occupy space, are concerned far more with the world of life.[25] At a *symposion* in the sixth century one became intoxicated in a world of heroic endeavour, at a *symposion* in the fifth century one became intoxicated in the world familiar from day to day.

Something of what it meant to become intoxicated in the world of heroic endeavour emerges from looking at a famous band cup signed by both Glaukytes and Arhikles (Figure 6a).[26] Although the cup itself is not small (it has a diameter of 26.5 cm), like other band cups its decoration is miniature.

These results have to be read against the overall distribution of the 22,341 cups in the database, which a search of 5 August 2011 revealed to be: Selected search criteria 'Cup': 400–300 (564); 425–375 (392); 450–400 (1325); 475–425 (3236); 500–450 (3752); 525–475 (3676); 550–500 (3425); 575–525 (2189); 600–550 (246); 625–575 (1); 675–625 (1).

[24] Since there are several hundred pots that are counted as showing a satyr and as showing satyrs, the number produced by adding the two figures together is not strictly the number of separate pots. Other subjects that appear more than 1000 times on cups in the database are: athlete (1095), athletes (1021), eyes (1308), komos (1432), maenad(s) (1396); warrior(s) (1973); woman/women (3789); youth(s) (8587). The same pot may be counted twice in the cases of athlete and athletes, warrior and warriors, etc.

[25] This is true of imagery on painted pottery generally, not simply of imagery on cups: the disproportion between black-figure and red-figure for the full range of 'daily life' scenes is well brought out by the lists in Thomas B. L. Webster, *Potter and Patron in Classical Athens* (London, 1972). Many pots other than cups were also made for sympotic use, including drinking vessels of other shapes (e.g. skyphoi), containers for wine (amphoras), water (hydriai), for mixing the two (kraters, dinoi) and for dispensing from the mixing bowl (jugs, ladles).

[26] Munich Museum Antiker Kleinkunst 2243, *ABV* 163.2. For a helpful description see Paolo Enrico Arias, Max Hirmer and B. B. Shefton, *A History of Greek Vase Painting* (London, 1962), 295.

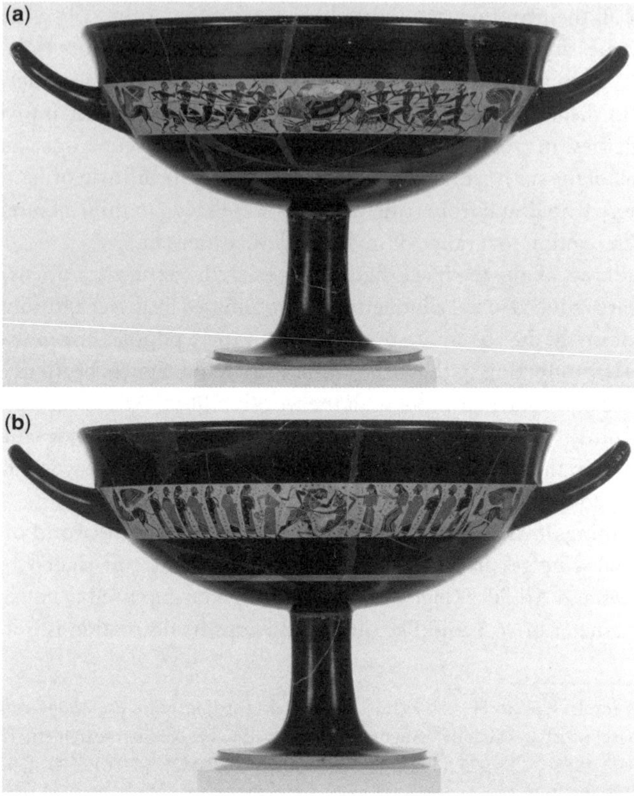

Figure 6. Band cup signed by both Glaukytes and Arhikles, Munich 2243. **a**) exterior featuring Calydonian boar hunt; **b**) exterior featuring Theseus and the Minotaur.

Unlike other band cups, however, it crowds its band with figures. On each side there is a central incident, surrounded by a number of figures who are flanked by outward-facing sphinxes. On one side the central incident is the killing of the Calydonian boar, which is shown attacked from above by a white hound and trampling over a supine hound that it has dispatched into the spears of a hunter named Kastor. Further hunters, spears at the ready and individually named, rush forward behind Kastor, or chase the boar from behind. On the other side (Figure 6b) the central incident is the despatch of the Minotaur by Theseus, who is backed up by Athena (carrying a lyre with which to celebrate his success) and watched on each side by a set of named young men and women—plus one bearded man named Simon, just possibly intended to be Minos.

Here is intoxication as macho encounter in the homosocial world of the hunt.[27] The hunters of the Calydonian boar knew that they were attempting to come to grips with an animal sent by the goddess Artemis to ravage Calydon because its king had not offered her appropriate worship. Theseus went to Crete to encounter the product of a sexual union brought about by Aphrodite between Pasiphae, wife of King Minos of Crete, and a bull provided by Poseidon after Minos decided not to sacrifice that bull. Theseus knew that all the young men previously sent from Athens had been killed by the Minotaur. These are such good stories precisely because they involve not the successful negotiation of the everyday chances that come a hero's way, but the decision to deal with a known danger.

The cup presents intoxication as a challenge not merely to reveal one's mettle among companions, but to show one's mettle to the gods. Can the drinker survive the encounter with what the gods have sent his way? Drinkers go out to face what has already laid many out flat, as the hound Podes is laid flat. The Calydonian boar hunt demanded solidarity from the hunters; for all that they each individually faced the danger, that danger was lessened for all of them by a united approach just as the co-ordinated approach to sympotic drinking may serve to keep all safe or lay all out—something explicit in Plato's *Symposium*. By contrast, dealing with the Minotaur was for the individual; at the end of the day personal capacity determines who is left standing in the *symposion*—and who gets the girl, as Theseus got Minos' daughter Ariadne (only to abandon her on Naxos for Dionysos to rescue). That individual test is undergone before the eyes of everyone else who is gathered, men and women alike, and men and women who know that individual and who are known to him, including the servants who are supposed to look up to him, like the nurse named here (*trophos*)—and also before the eyes of the gods. Can he face up to the challenge and still play the lyre? Not only is life at stake here, but love: winning the girl (or the boy) requires being seen to be facing up to the full challenge and living to tell the tale.

The encounters of myth offer the reassurance of closure. The Calydonian boar did not destroy the best men of Greece but was successfully hunted down; Theseus was able to defeat the Minotaur. But life isn't like that; no closure can be assured. Insofar as the encounters of life are concerned, scenes

[27] The hunt as a homosocial milieu is most famously explored in Euripides' *Hippolytos*. For the contrast between the heroic milieu of black-figure hunts and the more domestic context of red-figure hunts see Alain Schnapp, 'Eros the Hunter', in Claude Bérard et al., *A City of Images: Iconography and Society in Ancient Greece* (Princeton, 1989), ch. 5. Alain Schnapp, *Le chasseur et la cité: chasse et érotique en Grèce ancienne* (Paris, 1997). See also Judith M. Barringer, *The Hunt in Ancient Greece* (Baltimore, 2001).

that lock into no known story have their advantages, recapturing the thrill of life as it is lived. That sense of uncertain expectation comes out strongly in scenes showing warriors either preparing for action or in action. A cup attributed to the Colmar painter provides a nice example (Figure 7a).[28] Very similar in size to the band cup (diam. 24.3 cm), unlike that cup this has a painted interior tondo. The tondo shows a long-haired, beardless youth in a helmet, short chiton, and Thracian cloak running, head down, to the left, carrying spear and crescent-shaped light shield (*pelta*). The shield is decorated with two eyes, separated by a band of geometric decoration. We know these eyes: not for nothing are the frontal head of the gorgon and disembodied eyes motifs shared by warriors' shields and by drinking cups. In the *symposion*, as in war, confrontation cannot be avoided, confrontation that is in the public gaze and for which the stakes are the highest. Whether one will be able to sustain the gaze of others in future depends on what true self is revealed in this encounter today. This young man is smartly turned-out, with all that he properly needs for his task; but when the cup is drained will the young drinker still be quite so smart as this young soldier?

On the exterior of the cup (Figures 7b and 7c), three young warriors crouch expectantly on each side, spears at the ready and hoplite shields angled to deflect that attack; naked, but for their helmets, their defences rest in their shields. Not for nothing are Greek words for 'shield' also used to refer to cups, and Greek words for cups to refer to shields.[29] How the drinker carries his cup is quite as crucial as how the hoplite carries his shield. Will this drinker manage only the light cup, or can he handle the hoplite's *aspis*? When the drinker holds up his cup, what do we see—the tripod of victory, like that borne by one of these warriors? Or a proud horse, its tail held high? Is this drinker already reeling, like the wheel that leads the shield-devices on one side?[30] Or has he become the image of the bull that leads the shield devices on the other? No one facing this cup can avoid these questions since the shields

[28] London BM GR 1897.10–28.1, *ARV* 354.24. Full description by Dyfri Williams in *Corpus Vasorum Antiquorum*, Great Britain Fascicle 17, The British Museum Fascicle 9 (London, 1993), 27–8.

[29] For *sakos* (shield) as cup, see Aeschylus, *Seven Against Thebes*, 190; for *aspis* (shield) as cup see Aristophon, 13 K–A; Aristotle, *Poetics*, 1457b21; Aristotle, *Rhetoric*, 1407b16; for *phiale* (cup/bowl) as shield see ML 36.1 (Pausanias, 5.10.4); Athenaeus, 433c.

[30] Compare [Aristotle] *Problems*, Book 2, no. 9, 872a19–21: 'Why is it that to those who are very drunk everything seems to revolve in a circle, and as soon as the wine takes hold of them they cannot see objects at a distance, and so this is used by some as a test of drunkenness?' The same question, except reading 'count objects', rather than 'see objects', appears with a different answer, as no. 20, 874a5–7.

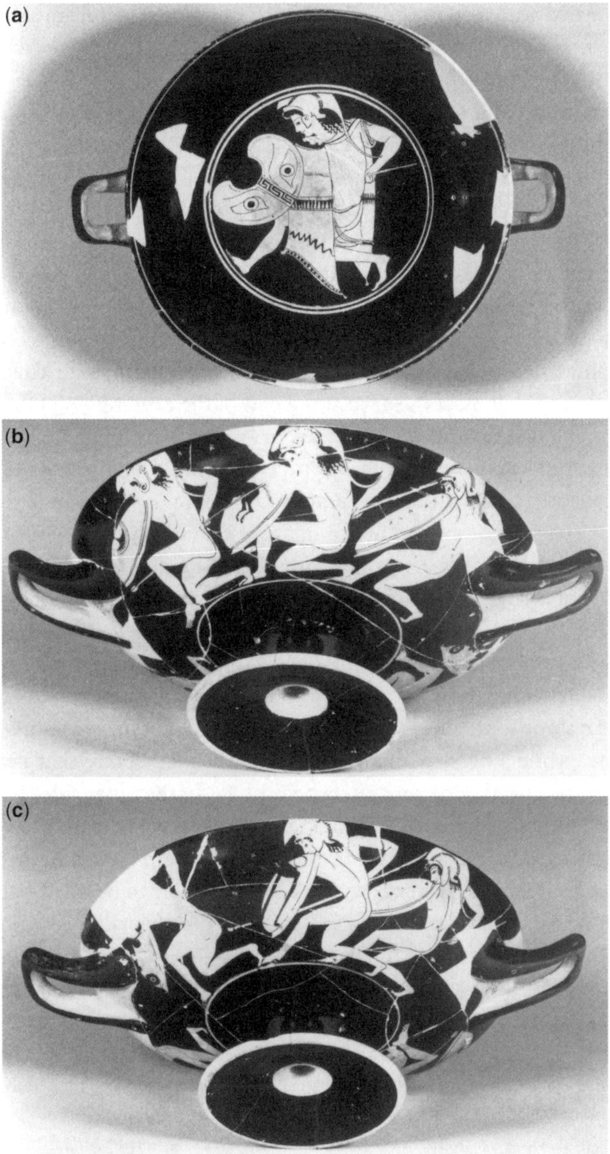

Figure 7. Red-figured cup attributed to the Colmar Painter, British Museum 1897,1028.1. © The Trustees of the British Museum. **a**) tondo featuring youth in a helmet, short chiton and Thracian cloak running and carrying spear and shield (*pelta*); **b**) exterior featuring three young warriors with *Leagros* inscribed on shield; **c**) exterior featuring three young warriors with *kalos* inscribed on shield.

that bring up the rear are inscribed, not with words that belong to a shield, but with the homoerotic greeting that belongs to a cup: *Leagros* we read on one shield, *kalos* we read on the other (and in case this particular viewer is ignorant of the most common of all *kalos* acclamations, *Leagros kalos* ('Leagros is handsome') is written again in the field behind the warriors).[31]

Like the wine, the interior and exterior scenes of this pot simply get a story going; some story is going to be told when young men run off to war or settle themselves down in ambush. Some story is going to be told at the end of the evening when a young man comes in dressed up and ready to party, or strips off to face the serious business behind his cup. The story will involve competition—at every symposion someone wins the trophy—and it will involve cutting a fine figure that will have missed its mark if it draws no acclamation. But whose eyes will meet the gaze at the end of the evening? Will the drinker have straightened up and walked away, or will he be rolling?

So much of what went on at a symposion pitted one partygoer against another that the competition to maintain control in the face of intoxication is bound always to figure large in the imagery on cups. But how intoxication affects perceptions of the world is, for the individual drinker, equally an omnipresent issue. Take the famous name vase of the Foundry Painter (Figure 8a).[32] The exterior shows, on one side, a furnace, with a boy working the bellows behind, and a crouching figure in a hat heating something at the end of a rod. Behind these figures are a collection of plaques and similar items, along with some tools and a pair of feet. On the right of them a youth leans on a hammer while a bearded man works on a headless body that lies on the ground, with a head lying separately behind it. On the other side (Figure 8b) two bearded figures dressed in himatia lean on sticks, apparently watching what is going on in a structure in the centre, where a striding figure of a warrior with helmet and shield wields a spear while two bearded figures half his size, one naked and one bare to the waist, scrape down his legs with strigils. Various other tools hang in the background.

How, this cup asks, can a drinker ever know what sort of a thing it is that he is looking at?[33] Presented with an image full of images—the votive plaques

[31] For *kalos* inscriptions on Athenian pottery see François Lissarrague, 'Publicity and Performance. Kalos Inscriptions in Attic Vase-painting', in Simon Goldhill and Robin Osborne (eds), *Performance Culture and Athenian Democracy* (Cambridge 1999), 359–73.

[32] Berlin Staatliche Museen F2294; *ARV* 400.1; see Richard T. Neer, *Style and Politics in Athenian Vase-Painting* (Cambridge, 2002), 78–81.

[33] Cf. Neer, *Style and Politics*, 78: 'this whole ensemble is in some way "about" image-making'.

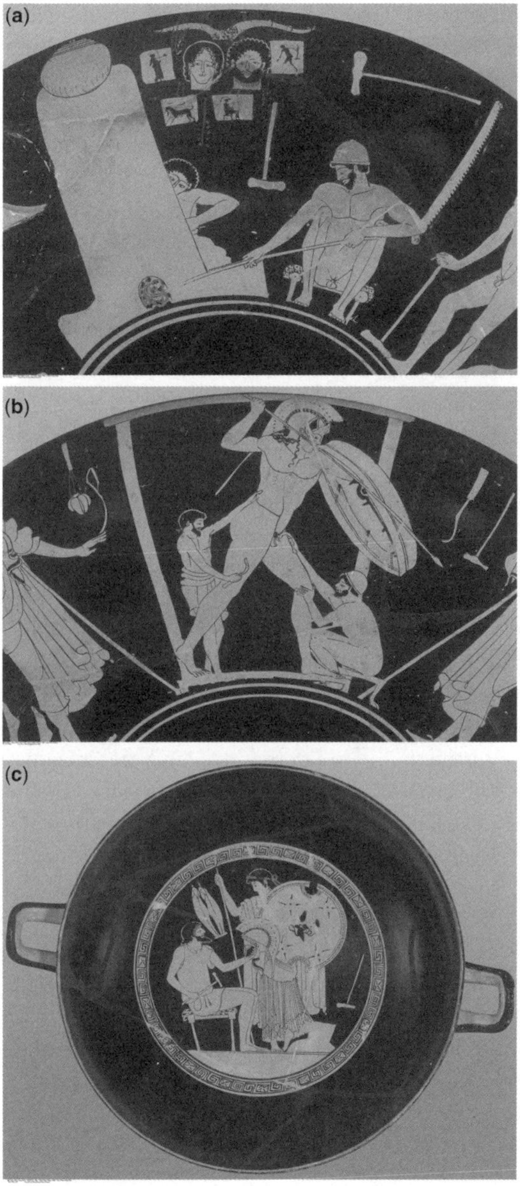

Figure 8. Cup from which the Foundry Painter is named, Berlin Staatliche Museen F 2294. **a**) exterior showing a furnace, with a boy working the bellows behind and a crouching figure in a hat; **b**) exterior featuring two figures dressed in himatia leaning on sticks watching the central figure of a warrior while two bearded figures half his size scrape down his legs with strigils; **c**) tondo showing a bearded man in a short chiton seated on a stool with a hammer in one hand and holding out a helmet in another to a woman, supporting herself on a spear and carrying a shield.

and heads, the headless statue—we are repeatedly challenged as to what we are looking at. Given the size of those working on the striding warrior, the striding warrior should be getting on for twice life-sized, in which case shouldn't he be a god? But should we not take the large spectating figures to be statues too, if the warrior is a statue? But those onlookers aren't dressed at all like gods. Again, if the warrior is a statue, why are the two smaller workers scraping his legs down with a strigil? If the onlookers are statues, why are the aryballoi that hang behind them in scale with them? But if the onlookers are real men, how come the two workers are tiny? Why are they so much tinier than the man at the furnace? The image defies the possibility of the viewer making consistent assumptions, and in doing so draws attention back to its own status as an image and to the way in which viewers constantly have to ask themselves a series of questions in order to ascertain the ontological status of what they observe—as here it is not having a base, supporting himself on a hammer, and adopting a casual pose not paralleled in sculpture that makes us think that the youth standing next to the saw is a person and not a statue. Or is he a unique sort of statue?

Intoxication heightens the imagination and weakens the grip on reality.[34] This is something famously celebrated in the story told by Athenaeus (37b–d) from Timaeus of Tauromenium (*FGrH*566F149), where young men who get drunk at a symposium come to suppose that the house they are in is a trireme in rough weather, and they then throw out the furniture to lighten the ship. The sense given by the Foundry Painter's cup of an impossible struggle to keep clear the distinction between the 'real' and the 'imaginary', to distinguish ontological levels, is exactly the sense experienced by those becoming intoxicated. But it is also fundamental to the worship of the gods: ritual clothing and washing of statues treats them just as the workers treat this statue—as if it were real.[35] We might neither be surprised if drunken men take a strigil to a statue, nor if that happened as part of a cult. And if it is the drunkards who experience parts of their own bodies as separate, as hands and feet cease to report sensations in the way a sober man expects, it is to the gods that separate body parts are dedicated.

This difficulty of the intoxicated in keeping different ontological levels apart is further explored in the tondo of the cup (Figure 8c). Here we meet

[34] Compare also [Aristotle] *Problems* Book 2, Problem 10, 872b4–5: 'Why is it that to those who are drunk one thing at which they are looking sometimes appears to be many?' and the very similar Problem 30 (875b9–10) 'Why is it that drunkards when looking at a single object sometimes see several objects?'

[35] Classic on this is Richard L. Gordon, 'The Real and the Imaginary: Production and Religion in the Graeco-Roman World', *Art History*, 2 (1979), 5–34.

a bearded man in a short chiton seated on a stool with a hammer in one hand and holding out a helmet with the other to a woman who stands before him, supporting herself on a spear and carrying a shield on which are represented four star-bursts and a bird of prey with a snake. In the background is a pair of greaves and a hammer. Are we still in the foundry shown on the exterior (the only inscription reads *ho pais kalos*—'What a handsome boy!')? Women on Athenian pots are frequently shown handing over elements of armour to departing warriors, so why not pick them up from the armourer? Armourers and sculptors were indeed closely linked—though primarily through the sculpted cuirass, which is the one element of the panoply not shown here.[36] Or are we instead in Hephaistos' forge on Olympos, and seeing the visit of Thetis to fetch new armour for Achilles? Achilles' shield too shows the heavens and their stars (*Iliad* 18.485–9); but if this is Achilles' shield, where are the two cities that are so much larger a part of the description in the *Iliad*? Eagles with snakes are notorious omens in epic poetry (especially *Iliad* 12.195–250 where Hector ignores such an omen) to the extent that Aristophanes parodies it (*Knights* 197–8). But does allusion to an epic omen on a shield mean that we are in the world of epic, or that we are not in the world of epic? In this image, as in the image of the foundry on the outside, ontological status proves impossible to fix, but here the issue is whether we are in the world of men or of gods, of history or of story.

Just as an intoxicated person fails to be able to distinguish between what was said to them and what happened, so here it proves impossible to keep reality and imagination apart. But the bird and snake refer to the condition of intoxication in another way too. Omens are a form of material riddle, not a matter of words whose reference is unclear but a matter of things which may or may not carry a message. To see an eagle with a snake means that there are eagles and snakes around, but does it mean more? How does one interpret the actions of the company one is with? Is one observing people throwing the dregs of their wine, or is one observing a move in a game of seduction? Does the fact that one is a little bit tipsy mean that one is over-inclined to find significance, or over-inclined to ignore the sign? Does inebriation make people more likely to do things without significance, or more likely to reveal the significance of what they do?

If the early history of red-figure painting tended to be dominated by scenes whose first reference was to life, later red-figure cups tend rather to return to the world of myth, but it is a world of different myths. Dionysiac myths remain a major theme, but the satyrs and maenads have become a little

[36] Cf. the discussion with the armourer Pistias in Xenophon, *Memorabilia*, 3.10 coming immediately after the discussions with the painter Parrhasios and the sculptor Kleiton.

more playful. Unusual myths, their identification presenting something of a challenge to the drinker, appear more often (for example, Linos and Mousaios on a cup by the Eretria Painter, *ARV* 1254.80), and many of the myths chosen have a notable element of feminine interest. I choose the name vase of the Painter of Berlin 2536 for my exploration (Figure 9a): it has a scene of the judgement of Paris on one side and of Paris and Helen on the other.[37] Scenes of Paris and Helen were not, of course, unparalleled earlier, but Paris and Helen continued to attract the attention of painters when other subjects ceased to be identified for sympotic contemplation.[38]

A large and almost naked Paris is shown on one side of the pot sitting on a dais between ionic columns and holding a sceptre in one hand and a lyre in the other (Figure 9a). In front of him is Hermes, carrying the staff known as the *caduceus* and wearing a winged hat. Hermes looks back at three goddesses, Aphrodite, veiled, holding out a winged Eros who offers a garland to Paris, and glancing back at Athena, who holds out a helmet, her aegis appearing beneath her chiton, and Hera, veiled and crowned, with a lion in one arm and a sceptre in the other hand. On the other side (Figure 9b), three men cluster at one end, two of them youths with the hunter's/ traveller's equipment of short cloak (*chlamys*), travelling hat (*petasos*), and two spears, and one bearded man in a himation and carrying a sceptre. The young man in the middle looks back at his fellow-traveller, but in doing so he uses his arm gently to ease the older man out of the way. At the other end a woman wearing a chiton and with silver leaves in her hair sits, resting her arm on the back of a chair, her head on her hand, looking back. She has a box on her knees. In front of her stands a woman in a peplos, holding up a mirror to look at her face as she adjusts her hair or her hairband. At the feet of the seated woman kneels a naked young male sporting extravagantly large feathered wings. There are no inscriptions on the cup of any kind.

No Greek viewer will have found the identification of the judgement of Paris difficult. The goddesses are each individually identifiable, as is Hermes, and their identity makes the naked young man with his sceptre undoubtedly Paris. There is an iconographic joke here in as far as columns are frequently used to indicate temples, and a seated figure on a raised platform between columns would normally be taken to be a cult statue of a god, so that the procession coming towards the seated figure would be a procession of

[37] Berlin Staatliche Museen F2536, *ARV* 1287.1.

[38] For Paris on cups the Beazley Archive on 6 August 2011 gives (in the usual reverse order): 450–400 (4); 475–425 (4); 500–450 (12); 525–475 (2); 575–525 (2); 600–550 (1). For Helen on cups it gives on 6 August 2011: 450–400 (3); 475–425 (2); 500–450 (9); 525–475 (6); 550–500 (4); 575–525 (3).

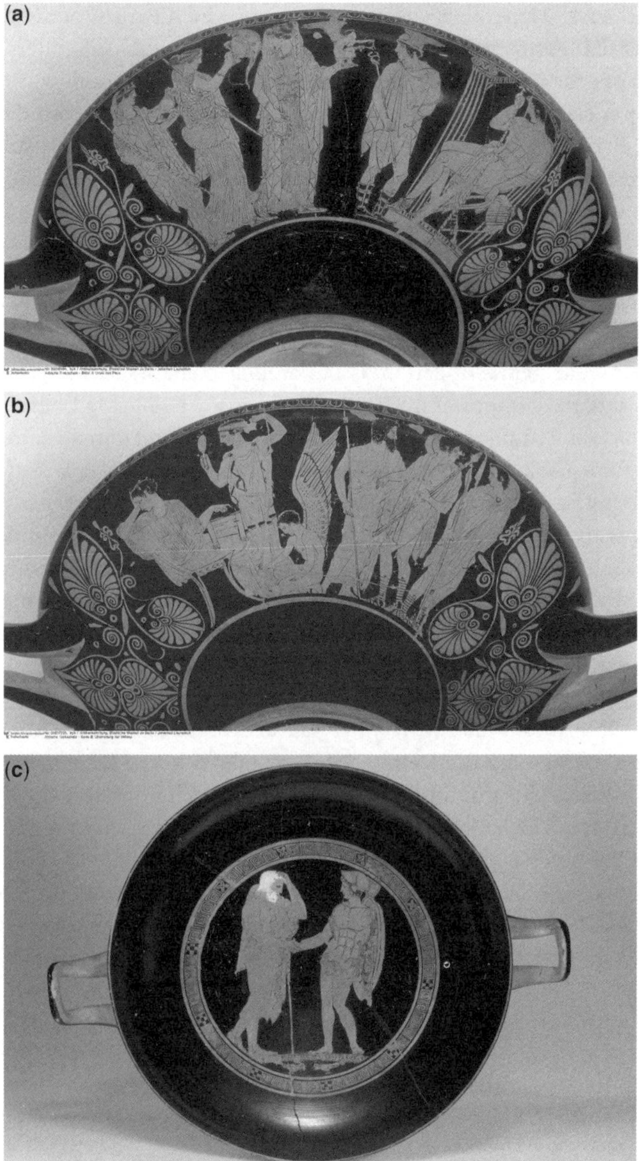

Figure 9. Name vase of the Painter of Berlin 2536 Berlin, Staatliche Museen zu Berlin, Antikensammlung, F 2536. **a**) exterior showing the judgement of Paris; **b**) exterior showing Helen seated as Paris arrives and is greeted by Menelaos (bearded figure with staff); **c**) interior showing youthful warrior taking leave of an old man who leans on a staff.

worshippers.[39] Here the peculiar position into which Paris is put is strongly emphasized by this role reversal. The scene on the other side offers rather more scope for debate. We should, I think, reckon the two young travellers to be Paris and a companion, and the brooding woman can hardly be other than Helen. Paris is, it seems, just arriving and being greeted by Menelaos, the bearded figure with a staff. Eros has already landed and done his job. The elegant woman with the mirror, reminiscent of Pandora, the woman created to be irresistible to men, draws attention to the issue of beauty, sexual attraction, and its consequences.

That the explicit eroticism of these scenes—Eros himself is portrayed—makes them appropriate for a pot used at a symposium is plain. But more is at issue here than gentle titillation. Issues of judgement, issues of personal relations and, most importantly, issues of passion are highlighted. Alcohol and desire have very similar effects in warming the heart, and intoxication makes people more liable to become passionate.[40] The *symposion* is a place of heightened emotions, where choices are made: how to prevent the party-goers leaving with the feeling that one of them has been especially favoured; how to negotiate talking too intently with the favourite of another; whether those who appear beautiful this evening will seem the same in the morning; and how to negotiate all of this with the gods, who inspire passions but see themselves as being judged by one's actions.

When the drinker drained this cup what he saw were two male figures (Figure 9c). An old man with white hair and beard and leaning on a stick raises one hand to his head while shaking hands with a young armed man in armour. Below the ground-line two cocks meet each other to fight. So who have we here? The handshake makes us expect a parting, and the old man's hand to his head suggests that he has some premonition that the coming war may not go well. The cocks point to bitter rivalry over masculinity.[41] Should we see Paris here, shaking hands with Priam? Young men put their masculinity on the line when they take part in the *symposion*,[42] but they also take a

[39] Compare, for example, from a very similar date to this cup, the scene on the crater in Ferrara (Mus. Naz. T 128) attributed to the Group of Polygnotos (*ARV* 1052.25). A naked figure with a lyre in a temple might, of course, be expected to be Apollo.

[40] Compare also [Aristotle] *Problems*, Book 2, Problem 24, 874b8: 'Why are the drunken more easily moved to tears?'

[41] On the cock fight see Herbert Hoffmann, 'Hahnenkampf in Athen. Zur Ikonologie einer attischen Bildformel', *Revue Archéologique* (1974), 195–220.

[42] Compare [Aristotle] *Problems*, Book 2, Problem 11, 872b15–16: 'Why is it that those who are drunk are incapable of having sexual intercourse?' The same question appears at Problem 33, 875b39–876a12.

step into the unknown where the fate that meets them lies in the hands of the gods. As intoxication takes hold, it is manliness or its absence that is on show. Inebriation loosens tongues and sharpens tempers, it causes men to say more than they intended and to stumble over what they mean to say;[43] drunken men see slights more readily and take offence more personally. How now does one negotiate the offers of power, military prowess, or love? One might as well be going off to war. One *is* going off to war. But the war isn't just with other men.

That when Greeks drank at the *symposion* they also thought about what they did when they drank at the *symposion* was, essentially, the message of Lissarrague's *Un Flot d'images.* Lissarrague concludes his book by noting that 'Les peintres de vases travaillent dans un milieu où le vin, la musique, l'image sont complémentaires et construisent, des uns aux autres, tout un réseau de correspondances; à tous niveaux métaphores et métamorphoses se développent sous le regard de Dionysos, maître de l'illusion'.[44] In this paper I have tried to show that this is true as well for the words spoken at the *symposion,* strangely unmentioned by Lissarrague here, as for the images, to show some of the various ways in which the images explored intoxication, and to suggest that different ways of thinking about what intoxication meant for the drinker were differently prominent at different times.

Whatever the physiological effects of alcohol on brain and body, intoxication is not one single thing, it is a phenomenon created and shaped by cultural practices and expectations. We have only a tenuous grasp of the changing cultural expectations in this case, since although changes in iconography are certainly not limited to scenes viewed at the symposium, the precise combination of artistic, technical, social, economic, and political factors that brought

[43] Compare [Aristotle] *Problems,* Book 2, Problem 31, 875b19: 'Why is it that the tongue of those who are drunk stumbles'.

[44] Lissarrague *Flot* 136 = *Aesthetics* 143: 'The vase painters are working in a setting in which wine, music, and image are complementary and, in their ties to one another, form a whole web of interrelations; at every level, metaphors and metamorphoses grow under the spell of Dionysos, master of illusion'; compare also *Flot* 12, = *Aesthetics* 8 and *Flot* 13, = *Aesthetics* 9.

[45] The story of the development of Athenian painted pottery has been dominated by accounts interested almost exclusively in artists' changing technical capacities (as in John D. Beazley's classic *The Development of Attic Black-Figure Pottery* (Berkeley, 1951). In reaction to that recent work interested in iconography has sometimes ignored change over time, as in Claude Bérard et al., *A City of Images* (Princeton, 1989), with Robin Osborne, 'Whose Image and Superscription is this?', *Arion,* 3rd series 1:2 (1991), 255–75. I devoted my unpublished Martin Classical Lectures at Oberlin College in 2007 to questions of changing imagery from 520 to 450 BC.

about the changes is still poorly understood.[45] Similarly, we have only a partial understanding of cultural practices, with debate still live about whether or not the symposium was a purely élite phenomenon.[46]

But intoxication is not simply created and shaped by cultural practices and expectations; it also creates and shapes them. In ignoring intoxication scholars have chosen to ignore something which, if not the basis of life (like nutrition) nevertheless played a crucial role in transforming that life and opening up worlds of possibility that were not grounded in daily toil or determined by physiological necessity.[47] We have seen that intoxication was not something merely tolerated in others because of the pleasures it gave to the self. Intoxication also both revealed the true individual, and bonded the group. The intoxicated both put on and took off their mask, they faced up to how they ordered the world and where they belonged in that world; those who would fight, and die, together established their trust in each other by daring to let wine reveal who they were and what they valued.

Mythology and literature alike (not to mention some ancient historians) make clear the impact of intoxication on society. The imagery in dialogue with which Greeks chose to become inebriated provides direct evidence for the ways in which intoxication was socially recuperated. In Greek cultural practices to become intoxicated was always to enter the world of the gods, as well as to find new roles in the world of men. The *symposion* was the place in which the Greeks determined and re-determined what it was to be intoxicated, and the history of the *symposion* is the history of what they made of intoxication—a history of the anthropology of Greek theology.

[46] See James N. Davidson, *Courtesans and Fishcakes: The Consuming Passions of Classical Athens* (London, 1995), 222–7 versus Richard T. Neer, *Style and Politics in Classical Athens: The Craft of Democracy c.530–460* BCE (Cambridge, 2002), ch. 3.

[47] On food and society see Peter Garnsey, *Food and Society in Classical Antiquity* (Cambridge, 1999).

'Tuned Out or Tuned In': Spirituality and Youth Drug Use in Global Times

Karen Joe-Laidler, Geoffrey Hunt, and Molly Moloney

> I would tell my friends, 'let's go to dance!' I could dance for the whole night and not return to my seat . . . I would get this feeling that I even forgot that I'm in fact a human being. Everything I saw was beautiful. That was weird . . .. When it's time to leave, you don't feel like you've taken drugs but would have a feeling of being really free. (Man, Chinese male in Hong Kong, age 18)

> The first time I tried ecstasy . . . I just really wanted to dance and after a while, I danced quicker to the beat. I was with friends chilling . . . I became more loose and wanted to hug people . . . I was really awake. It feels better than alcohol . . . if you're drunk you don't know what you're saying and it really feels bad . . . and you feel full. But having ecstasy, you won't feel full . . . The feeling I had was happy . . . Once I lose that explosion feeling, I still feel very excited and dance wildly. (Kitty, Chinese female in HK, age 26)

> When I'm on ecstasy, I wanna dance, and it's about being with friends. It's about me and my friends having a good time and losing ourselves for a few hours. And then not having the effects of alcohol. I get tired of wasting a Sunday recovering from alcohol, whereas with E, I get to sleep and then I'm fine. (Leticia, Hispanic female in San Francisco, age 20)

> At a rave . . . people are just there to have fun, meet other people . . . it's a good environment to do ecstasy in, because it's kind of the same way the drug is. It just makes you wanna do all those things anyway (James, white male in SF, age 21)

At first glance these narratives might simply suggest youthful abandonment —pleasure derived from friends, dancing, a night out, and psychoactive drugs. However, that young persons living in locales as different as Hong

 © The Past and Present Society

Kong and San Francisco should share similar emotions and perspectives suggests other forces at work. First, the accounts attest to the modern emergence of a global phenomenon—the youth dance drug scene.[1] Starting in London and New York in the 1980s, a distinctive culture of dress, music, setting, and drug use spread from Europe to the Americas, and so to Australia and Asia, throughout the 1990s and into the 2000s. Second, while this culture appears to be distinctively modern, its valorization of intoxication echoes other times and places.[2] This is hardly surprising. A perennial feature of intoxicants is the pleasure associated with their consumption and experience—the chemical and physiological reactions and the users' interaction with others in particular milieus.[3] Yet this pleasure imperative has received relatively little attention from academics and other commentators.[4] Whether in Ancient Greece or Enlightenment Europe, the governing principles of reason and rationality have privileged moderation and control. [5] As such, intoxication for pleasure evidences the absence of self-restraint and the need for government regulation.

I

The recent history of psychedelics exemplifies the tension between the desire for altered states and the rational dictates of moderation. Psychedelics have long been revered for their religious, medical, and social associations in Aztec, Toltec, Navajo and many other native cultures.[6] Wild and cultivated substances like cannabis and magic mushrooms are seen as mood and emotional enhancers, though more so than stimulants or depressants the effects are dependent on the emotional state of the user, the dosage, and the context.[7]

[1] Geoffrey Hunt et al., 'Dance Drug Scenes: A Global Perspective', in Geoffrey Hunt, Maitena Milhet, and Henri Bergeron (eds), *Drugs and Culture: Knowledge, Consumption, and Policy* (Surrey, 2011).

[2] Richard Rudgley, *The Alchemy of Culture: Intoxicants in Society* (London, 1993); Stuart Walton, *Out of It: A Cultural History of Intoxication* (London, 2001), 22.

[3] Rudgley, *The Alchemy of Culture.*

[4] P. O'Malley and M. Valverde, 'Pleasure, Freedom and Drugs: The Uses of "Pleasure" in Liberal Governance of Drug and Alcohol Consumption', *Sociology*, xxxviii (2004).

[5] Michel Foucault, *The Use of Pleasure* (New York, 1990); O'Malley and Valverde, 'Pleasure, Freedom and Drugs' ; G. Zajdow, ' "It Blasted Me into Space": Intoxication and an Ethics of Pleasure', *Health Sociology Review*, xix (2010).

[6] Marlene Dobkin De Rios, *Hallucinogens: Cross-Cultural Perspectives* (Prospect Heights, Ill., 1990); Darryl S. Inaba and William E. Cohen, *Uppers, Downers, All Arounders: Physical and Mental Effects of Psychoactive Drugs* (Ashland, Ore., 2000); Charles S. Grob (ed.) *Hallucinogens: A Reader* (New York, 2002).

[7] Inaba and Cohen, *Uppers, Downers, All Arounders.*

From the 1950s scientists developed a range of synthetic psychedelics in the hope that drugs like LSD and MDMA could be used therapeutically, in controlled settings, to unravel the spiritual self.[8] As the 1960s progressed LSD became increasingly available. A vociferous proponent was Timothy Leary, who encouraged, first in his work with students in the Harvard Psychedelic Research Project and later (after losing his academic post) the hippie generation to 'turn on, tune in, and drop out'. For Leary intoxication was not only about pleasure but also the spiritual awakening of self and society:

> 'Turn on' means to contact the ancient energies and wisdoms that are built into your nervous system. They provide unspeakable pleasure and revelation. 'Tune in' means to harness and communicate these new perspectives in a harmonious dance with the external world. 'Drop out' means to detach yourself from the tribal game . . . In every generation of human history, thoughtful men have turned on and dropped out of the tribal game, and thus stimulated the larger society to lurch ahead.[9]

This call to 'turn on, tune in, and drop out' spoke to the younger generation's political restiveness about capitalism, war, community, peace, and the nature of the modern self. Yet even as the hippie generation looked to LSD for pleasure, moral condemnation followed: by 1967 prohibitory laws banned the possession of LSD in several American states, and later nationally.

Leary's plea for intoxication is an important framework for understanding more recent youth narratives about raves and dance drug culture. The diffusion of dance drug culture to which these narratives refer has been through a variety of institutions, from alternative and spiritually orientated events like raves, free festivals, and underground events through to commercial fee-paying parties and permanent licensed discos, clubs, and lounges. This diversification, while partly a reaction to government, has also involved corporate enterprise and the creation of homogenized and domesticated dance music settings with chrome furnishings, sophisticated sound systems, and well accessorized attendees.[10] The resulting 'pleasure prisons'—with their regulations, licences, security systems, and behaviour codes—have enabled the state to contain, control, and shape the hedonism of youth (not always

[8] David Lenson, *On Drugs* (Minneapolis, 1995).

[9] Timothy Leary, *Leary on Drugs: Writings and Lectures from Timothy Leary (1970–1996)* (San Francisco, 2008).

[10] Paul Chatterton and Robert Hollands, *Urban Nightscapes: Youth Cultures, Pleasure Spaces, and Corporate Power* (New York, 2003).

successfully).[11] The dance drug scene has accordingly become accessible to a larger audience. But along with diversity have come social distinctions.[12] Raves and free festivals reflected a youth-driven ideal where solidarity and social inclusion were paramount.[13] Those who experienced the 'real' and 'authentic' rave spirit of PLUR—peace, love, unity, and respect—found themselves distanced from the younger generation. From the perspective of 'original' ravers, newcomers to the dance drug scene were driven less by a spiritual aesthetic and more by corporate entrepreneurialism and 'mainstream' values. These cultural distinctions have been further reinforced by the spatial segregation of venues, doormen and security, and costly entrance and beverage fees.[14]

Although social scientists have examined social exclusion and youth culture in a global perspective, drug researchers have largely restricted their enquiries to single cultures and locales.[15] Nor have they examined the importance of pleasure to practices of intoxication.[16] In the meantime religious

[11] Simon Reynolds, *Energy Flash* (London, 1998).

[12] M. Salasuo and P. Seppala, 'Drug Use within the Finnish Club Culture as Marks of Distinction', *Contemporary Drug Problems*, xxxi (2004); Dina Perrone, *The High Life: Club Kids, Harm and Drug Policy* (New York, 2009); Silvia Rief, *Club Cultures: Boundaries, Identities, and Otherness* (New York, 2009); C. Siokou, D. Moore, and H. Lee, '"Muzzas" and "Old Skool Ravers": Ethnicity, Drugs, and the Changing Face of Melbourne's Dance Party/Club Scene', *Health Sociology Review*, xix (2010).

[13] F. Measham and K. Moore, 'Repertoires of Distinction: Exploring Patterns of Weekend Polydrug Use within Local Leisure Scenes across the English Night Time Economy', *Criminology and Criminal Justice* ix (2009); Geoffrey Hunt, Molly Moloney and Kristin Evans, *Youth, Drugs, and Nightlife* (London, 2010).

[14] Chatterton and Hollands, *Urban Nightscapes;* R. Macdonald and T. Shildrick, 'Street Corner Society: Leisure Careers, Youth (Sub)Culture, and Social Exclusion', *Leisure Studies*, xxvi (2007); F. Measham and P. Hadfield, 'Everything Starts with an "E": Exclusion, Ethnicity, and Elite Formation in Contemporary English Clubland', *Adicciones*, xxi (2009).

[15] Hilary Pilkington, 'The Dark Side of the Moon?: Global and Local Horizons', in Hilary Pilkington, et al. (eds), *Looking West?: Cultural Globalization and Russian Youth Cultures* (Pennsylvania, 2002); George Lipsitz, 'Midnight's Children: Youth Culture in the Age of Globalization', in Sunaina Maira and Elisabeth Soep (eds), *Youthscapes: The Popular, the National, the Global* (Philadelphia, 2005); Sunaina Maira and Elisabeth Soep (eds), *Youthscapes: The Popular, the National, the Global* (Philadelphia, 2005); Pam Nilan and Carles Feixa (eds), *Global Youth?: Hybrid Identities, Plural Worlds* (New York, 2006).

[16] Exceptions include Amador Calafat et al., *Risk and Control in the Recreational Drug Culture: SONAR Project* (Palma de Mallorca, 2001); M. Agar and H. S. Reisinger, 'Going for the Global: The Case of Ecstasy', *Human Organization* lxii (2003); Anthony D'andrea, *Global Nomads: Techno and New Age as Transnational Countercultures in Ibiza and Goa* (New York, 2007); Hunt et al., *Youth, Drugs, and Nightlife.*

scholars have interpreted raves, free festivals, and conscious partying movements as sites for spiritual transformation.[17] They raise the question whether dance music culture, specifically in its 'authentic' form, serves as a source of spirituality for modern young people. Some studies view these events as facilitating a sense of community and transcendence for ravers. Others see it as the youthful pursuit of a re-enchanted world in which private concerns are shared through a collective identity to counter the modern social imperatives of independence and responsibility.[18] Spiritual narratives certainly feature prominently among rave goers, as expressions of personal growth, acceptance, communality, oneness, energy, and immediacy.[19] Importantly, these narratives are articulated in relation to the pleasure of intoxication as well as the collective event. Yet other settings, such as the commercialized club scene, also attract young people, begging the question what kind of pleasure does commercialized intoxication offer? Does spirituality also play a role within the commercialized club scene?

It is with these issues in mind that this chapter compares the experiences of party-goers in San Francisco and Hong Kong. The starting point is a striking divergence. In oral testimonies San Francisco dance party goers described how using their drug of choice, ecstasy (MDMA), at raves and other dance settings, encouraged emotional states reminiscent of Leary's 'tuning in'. Hong Kong dance party goers instead emphasized how their preferred drug, ketamine, enabled 'tuning out'. What follows considers how to account for these predilections for 'tuning out' and 'tuning in'. Are these two competing narratives of young people engaging in similar cultural practices? Are they solely related to pharmacological differences in ecstasy and ketamine? Are the narrated experiences dependent on the setting—the 'authentic' rave or the commercialized club? Are these different narratives connected to 'glocalization'—where global movements are articulated with differential effects

[17] Graham St John, 'The Difference Engine: Liberation and the Rave Imaginary', in Graham St John (ed.), *Rave Culture and Religion* (London, 2004); C. Partridge, 'The Spiritual and the Revolutionary: Alternative Spirituality, British Free Festivals, and the Emergence of Rave Culture', *Culture and Religion*, vii (2006); G. Beck and G. Lynch, ' "We Are All One, We Are All Gods": Negotiating Spirituality in the Conscious Partying Movement', *Journal of Contemporary Religion* xxiv (2009).

[18] Partridge, 'The Spiritual and the Revolutionary'; Beck and Lynch, "We Are All One, We Are All Gods".

[19] Melanie Takahashi, 'The "Natural High": Altered States, Flashbacks, and Neural Tuning at Raves', in Graham St John (ed.) *Rave Culture and Religion* (London, 2004); C. Partridge, 'The Spiritual and the Revolutionary'; Beck and Lynch, "We Are All One, We Are All Gods"; G. St John, 'Neotrance and the Psychedelic Festival', *Dancecult*, i (2009).

locally?[20] Or are these narratives expressing similar experiences but in culturally specific ways?

The data to answer these questions are drawn from interviews conducted in two parallel studies on club drug use: in San Francisco (2002–04) and in Hong Kong (2003–04).[21] The San Francisco sample comprised 300 young people, the Hong Kong sample 100 young people. Both studies had comparable inclusion criteria, involving recent attendance at a dance club or rave and use of illicit drugs in the past six months. The interview documented respondents' life histories, initiation, rationales and problems with alcohol and drug consumption, involvement in drug sales, and experiences in different dance venues. Although there were some minor differences in the interview schedules, the protocols were developed in tandem to allow for comparison between the two sets of interviews. We examined the interaction of young people and the meanings they ascribe to drug use in particular settings, focusing on their narratives of pleasure through intoxication and its connection to spirituality. It transpired that the pleasure derived from intoxication involves not only a physiological reaction but also an opportunity to transcend normal everyday routines. In this process of stepping outside of oneself, one may develop a spiritual awareness—a heightened sense of self, of others, and of oneness with the collective. We accordingly suggest that 'tuning in' and 'tuning out' are culturally comparative notions and that spirituality lies at the core of the experiences of young people in both San Francisco and Hong Kong. In doing so, we move beyond functional explanations about drug use to focus on the interaction of the pharmacological effects of particular drugs with the cultural meaning of altered consciousness.[22] To make this argument

[20] Diana Crane, 'Culture and Globalization: Theoretical Models and Emerging Trends', in Diana Crane, Nobuko Kawashima, and Ken'ichi Kawasaki (eds), *Global Culture: Media, Arts, Policy, and Globalization* (New York, 2002).

[21] The San Francisco interviews were conducted in English and the Hong Kong interviews were mainly conducted in Cantonese, the local Chinese dialect, and translated into English. Respondents were recruited from dance venues, advertisements, contacts from prior studies, and chain referrals from respondents. Interviews took place in various settings, from the respondent's or peer's home to public parks, coffee shops, fast food outlets, bars, quiet lounges, and at a university office. The methodology is explained in Hunt et al., *Youth, Drugs, and Nightlife* and K. Joe-Laidler and G. Hunt, 'Sit Down to Float: The Cultural Meaning of Ketamine Use in Hong Kong', *Addiction Research and Theory* xvi (2008).

[22] Functionalist accounts generally emphasize the functions of drinking or getting high to group rituals, sociability, or individual rationales. P. Sulkunen, 'Between Culture and Nature: Intoxication in Cultural Studies of Alcohol and Drug Use,' *Contemporary Drug Problems*, 29 (2002) 253, rightly argues that there are two competing tendencies in

the chapter first sketches the development of the dance scenes in each locale before exploring the recollections of intoxication recorded in the interviews.

II

San Francisco and Hong Kong share a similar vibrant nightlife. Intoxicants have long been a feature of San Francisco, with the hippie generation's psychedelic habits informing, from the 1960s, a sociologically eclectic disco culture. An urban populace consumed cocaine, alcohol, and sometimes tranquilizers at high energy discos, dance palaces, and organized mega-parties. Described by some contemporaries as uncontained hedonism, others noted the spiritualism of party-goers and disc jockeys alike.[23] By contrast, Hong Kong's nightlife until the 1990s involved alcohol consumption in a range of settings: among sophisticates in the Central district, working men in the pubs in Wan Chai, and working-class kids in public parks and housing estates. With the exception of heroin (associated with older male consumers) and limited amounts of marijuana, other intoxicants were not readily available or in demand in Hong Kong. Certainly psychedelic use was rare, perhaps because its hallucinogenic effects were linked locally to mental illness, and cocaine was restricted to the wealthy.[24]

Despite these differences the influence of British rave culture in the 1990s encouraged the appropriation of ecstasy in both locales. In San Francisco this happened at 'underground' parties and then more regular venues where ecstasy was encouraged and alcohol banned. The rave emphasis on spirituality made San Francisco distinctive from other US cities. In 1991 a group of British ravers formed the promotional company ToonTown. Noted for their techno-sophisticated psychedelic lighting and shaman-like disc jockeys,

---

functionalist explanations. One view assumes that the effects of drinking are related to specific cultural contexts without reference to more universal dimensions of the human experience nor the pharmacology of substances. The second tendency is to illuminate the universal and pharmacological effects of drink and drugs while ignoring the cultural context and meaning. Intoxication, however, must be understood as an interaction between the pharmacological and the cultural. M. Kiyaani and T. Csordas, 'On the peyote road', *Natural History*, 106 (1997), 47, illustrate this interaction in the spiritual practices of the traditional Navajo's peyote religion. The effects of peyote combined with the spiritual chants of prayer songs, rituals between healer and patient, and visual symbols produce an altered consciousness connecting individuals, in community with nature.

[23] David Diebold, *Tribal Rites: San Francisco's Dance Music Phenomenon 1978–1988* (Northridge, Calif., 1988).

[24] Y. W. Cheung and J. M. N. Ch'ien, 'Drug Use and Drug Policy in Hong Kong: Changing Patterns and New Challenges', *Substance Use and Misuse*, xxxi (1996).

they attracted thousands of San Francisco ravers with a sensory experience of ecstasy and dance. ToonTown inculcated the city's distinctive look—children's clothing, detachable wings, psychedelic colours, wrap-around glasses. In the meantime 'Wicked', the British music collective committed to nature worship and neo-Pagan rituals, attracted thousands to Full Moon Raves at the beach.[25] The style spread to other events and mainstream clubs, though from the mid-1990s tensions between promoters and supporters, conflicting musical tastes, and police raids meant fewer, more suburban events. Thereafter underground events were superseded by massive commercial raves. These attracted large numbers of young people from the Bay Area and were highly publicized, expensive, and involved big-production values. The burst of the dot com bubble in 2001 affected this night-time economy, but by 2005 a new scene had emerged offering smaller, 'mellower' venues.[26] Although many 'club drugs' remain popular today, alcohol also appears to be resurgent, with many nightlife operators worrying less about drugs in the clubs and more about violence.[27]

Hong Kong was a British colony until 1997 and it was British expatriates, with their North American counterparts, who organized raves as occasional events as early as 1993. Organized events in large open spaces became more popular from the mid-1990s and local middle-class and later working-class youth joined the party. Ecstasy was consumed from the start and became more popular thereafter. This scene was relatively short-lived compared to other cities, including San Francisco. Space was one factor, as were rigorous policing, the enforcement of stringent health and safety requirements, and the fallout of the SARS public health crisis.[28] Moreover, Hong Kong entrepreneurs took to converting karaoke bars and restaurants into permanent venues for dancing and clubbing for expatriate and local patrons. In the early 1990s rave music was typically from the UK and North America and without lyrics. By the later 1990s, permanent venues also played local Cantonese pop music.

[25] Simon Reynolds, *Generation Ecstasy: Into the World of Techno and Rave Culture* (New York, 1999).

[26] N. Chonin, 'The Beat Goes On', *San Francisco Chronicle*, 10 Mar. 2002 <http://www.sfgate.com/cgi-bin/article.cgi?file=/c/a/2002/03/10/PK183434.DTL>; C. Zinko, 'Club Scene Grows Up', *San Francisco Chronicle*, 2 Dec. 2005 <http://www.sfgate.com/cgi-bin/article.cgi?file=/c/a/2005/12/02/MNGSNG1SQH1.DTL>.

[27] Molly Moloney et al., 'New Forms of Regulating the Night-Time Economy—the Case of San Francisco', in Phil Hadfield (ed.) *Nightlife and Crime: Social Order and Governance in International Perspective* (Oxford, 2009).

[28] Karen Joe-Laidler, 'Globalization and the Illicit Drugs Trade in Hong Kong', in Colin Sumner (ed.) *The Blackwell Companion to Criminology* (Malden, Mass., 2004).

Raves were sites which encouraged high levels of anonymity and experimentation; in discos and clubs the commercial logic was to cater for different types of consumer. They ranged from exclusive membership clubs featuring local celebrities to large scale discos with private VIP rooms to no-frills dance rooms without liquor licences.[29] Despite the different clientèles, lifestyles, and budgets associated with these venues ecstasy became ubiquitous and integral to a 'night out'. However, ecstasy's prominence in Hong Kong was short-lived. A new drug, ketamine, was first used as a supplement to 'top up' and shift the high from ecstasy before becoming popular in its own right. Ketamine was accessible, affordable (between $6–12 per packet), and less adulterated than ecstasy. Unlike ecstasy, Hong Kong youth took ketamine in other recreational contexts.[30] The rapid rise of ketamine use among young people in Hong Kong is possibly unmatched internationally: within three years of its introduction it became the primary drug of choice among 21 year-olds and under.[31]

While ecstasy linked the dance scenes of both San Francisco and Hong Kong, ketamine subsequently distinguished them. Interviews show that while marijuana and ecstasy were nearly universally used by respondents in both locales, ketamine use was much less common in San Francisco. While the rates of ecstasy use in both locales are comparable, the use of most other intoxicants like cocaine, methamphetamines, mushrooms and GHB are relatively rare in Hong Kong. Hong Kong respondents reported significantly lower rates of drug experimentation; more than half of Hong Kong respondents had used three or fewer drugs in their lifetimes versus less than a quarter of San Francisco respondents. While there were relatively few differences in the ages at which club drug users tended to start using drugs, Hong Kong respondents tended to start using cocaine, LSD, and mushrooms later than respondents from San Francisco, but started using ketamine at a significantly earlier age.

All of which begs the question, why did ketamine come to dominate the youth dance drug scene in Hong Kong and spill over into use in other recreational settings? Answering this question requires looking not just at the

[29] K. A. Joe-Laidler, 'The Rise of Club Drugs in a Heroin Society: The Case of Hong Kong', *Substance Use and Misuse*, xl (2005).

[30] Joe-Laidler and Hunt, 'Sit Down to Float'.

[31] Karen Joe-Laidler, Jeffrey Day, and David Hodson, *A Study on the Psychotropic Drug Abuse Problem in Hong Kong. Final Report to the Action Committee against Narcotics, Narcotics Division, Hong Kong Government* (Hong Kong, 2001); Joe-Laidler and Hunt, 'Sit Down to Float'.

effects of each drug on individuals but also the meanings that young people in each place attributed to them.

III

Although our study was never designed to be representative (and our samples clearly cannot speak for all dance attendees in San Francisco or Hong Kong) the patterns to emerge are interesting nonetheless. While the age and gender breakdown of our samples are somewhat similar, our respondents' social class backgrounds are strikingly different. In San Francisco, 60 per cent of respondents come from middle-class backgrounds (based on their father's occupations and own educational background). About 65 per cent of respondents' fathers hold professional or white-collar jobs ranging from bank vice presidents and engineers to small business owners and insurance salesmen to musicians, teachers, lawyers, and doctors. Overall the sample is well-educated, with 60 per cent of them either currently or previously having pursued a post-high school education, ranging from vocational training to graduate school. Few respondents have dropped out of high school. Sixty per cent of respondents are employed at the time of the interview, mostly in white-collar business or clerical jobs, education or non-profit fields, or in retail and service. Few work in skilled trade or labour jobs. Of those working, 59 per cent of them work part-time, but over 65 per cent of the part-time workers are also students.

In contrast about 75 per cent of Hong Kong respondents come from lower-class or working-class families. The majority of employed respondents work in the service industries or in trade occupations, 33 per cent of whom are employed in trade jobs or at the lower end of the service industry, and less than 30 per cent earn the equivalent of more than USD 1,000 per month. The most common occupations are hair stylists, cosmetologists, sales clerks, decorators, tele-marketers, servers at restaurants and discos, and construction workers. Thirty-three per cent of the respondents are unemployed at the time of the interview, some of whom are students. Forty per cent receive 'pocket money' from their families every month, and for over 25 per cent this is their only source of income. Ten per cent supplement their income through various illegal activities, such as selling or delivering pirated videodiscs and selling drugs.

Social class may provide a partial explanation for ketamine's popularity: despite its initial association with celebrity culture in Hong Kong it later became linked to working-class venues.[32] Ketamine's working-class connections are due to a number of factors, affordability, accessibility, and greater

[32] Joe-Laidler and Hunt, 'Sit Down to Float'.

acceptability of ketamine-related behaviours in low budget venues. Ketamine's link to working-class venues is also related to young people searching for what they call the 'K ride'. Blackouts and physical and cognitive impairment are not encouraged in low-end discos. However, respondents describe witnessing or experiencing such states in these venues without restraint. Those on the 'K ride' are ignored, watched over by friends, or asked to leave. Behaviour associated with 'K rides' is not acceptable in upscale dance clubs.

While ketamine, like ecstasy, is easily purchased on or near the dance venue, ketamine is much less expensive. Moreover, the fact that ketamine tends to have considerably higher levels of purity in Hong Kong means that while an ecstasy tablet may be usually halved with one other person (depending on purity levels and length of use) ketamine is more likely to be shared with a group of friends. Users report that ketamine is the 'poor man's version of cocaine'. The majority of those using it either once or twice per month, or only at weekends, find ketamine an affordable and accessible option to supplement the high in order to continue dancing. In so doing they limit use to a few lines over the night.

If social class goes some way to explaining why ketamine is so popular in Hong Kong, it is also important to consider how intoxicants are perceived locally. Interviewees in San Francisco talked a lot about pleasure. But what is pleasure in this youthful context? The pleasure of ecstasy is defined in relation to fun, happiness, energy, and the ability to let go, to momentarily lose oneself. 'Fun' is important to San Francisco youth. When asked what they like about using ecstasy, participants repeatedly utilized the word to describe their experiences: 'To me E is like the funnest drug. It's the funnest. It's so much fun. And like the high was great' (Christina, white female, age 22). The centrality of fun is not surprising given ecstasy's association with dance parties, raves, and clubs and the juxtaposition of these places against the grind of work and school. Young people frequently describe how ecstasy, especially when used within the dance-event setting, allows them not just to have a good time but also to experience a uniquely superlative level of fun. For some, pleasure is centred around enjoying an exciting night out and the immediate physical effects of an increase in energy and a heightening of the senses, while for others the pleasures of ecstasy are described as life-changing, leading them to become more open, sociable, or even spiritual in their daily lives, even when not on the drug. The pleasures of ecstasy's physical effects are often tied to the social context within which they used the drug. Unsurprisingly (given its use while dancing) interviewees noted a connection between the drug and their enjoyment of music and dancing. 'The energy . . . I mean, you wanna go out and you wanna dance. You wanna meet people. I think mainly it's the social thing.

Lights . . . trance music. It's pretty much like a big . . . it's pretty much the only place you can go and be in a large social gathering' (Brian, white male, age 19).

Many ecstasy users describe a deeper enjoyment of music and dancing while on the drug; the music sounds 'better' or they could 'feel' the music, and they could dance for longer periods. The fact that this effect is communal—shared by hundreds of others dancing on ecstasy at the rave—intensifies the pleasure of the experience. Other interviewees focus on other sensory effects of ecstasy: visual pleasures and the heightened sense of touch. Other pleasurable effects relate to their emotions and sense of well-being. Participants are drawn to ecstasy because it makes them feel 'good', 'happy' and 'relaxed'. They describe a sense of freedom that allows them to behave in a less self-conscious or self-critical way. They feel free to act openly and authentically, to dance without worrying about whether they are 'good', and generally to express themselves without fearing what others might think. 'You just feel happy and really open, it's like you're in another world . . . away from danger and all. You just feel like . . . you're safe. No one's going to hurt you and you feel happy, you don't feel depressed or sad . . . you feel really alive. It's just a good feeling' (Antonia, Hispanic female, age 20).

> All your inhibitions are free, and you just like . . . all of a sudden you feel like you can do anything. That's the positive I guess . . . cuz it can . . . show you that, oh, yeah . . . You come to that whole epiphany of like, 'Oh, I can do this'. Or you know, I can talk to people. And then, I guess your self-esteem somehow rises. And . . . I mean, yeah, like the whole atmosphere, like everyone's . . . letting go. And like I said, you know, they're not trying to put up their guard. Everyone's guard is down, you know. It's like . . . very trusting, you know, and people will . . . you'll talk to people, it doesn't matter. Like you'll talk to people that you usually don't talk to. (Ling, Asian American female, age 19)

According to their narratives, ecstasy helps them open up, trust others, and achieve emotional connections that are difficult or impossible otherwise. Ecstasy's impact on people's physical and emotional state, its enhanced sociability, combined with a meaningful social context, fosters interactions with others that make users feel the pleasure of ecstasy goes beyond simple physical and mental effects.

Hong Kong respondents report similar effects: ecstasy allows them to express their emotions and to feel connected to others: 'You can express your deepest sentiments and feelings at the time. After that experience, my view in seeing the world changed' (Harry, Chinese male, age 23). Ecstasy's hallucinogenic effects, often described as illusions, are perceived as positive attributes of the drug. Ecstasy also allows users to feel disinhibited, to be more open and free without the restraints of everyday life: 'Dancing is kind of like drinking. Getting high on ecstasy is also like drinking. You don't think so much. I'm a very shy person and don't dance much, and I wasn't very good at it . . . but after drinking or taking ecstasy, I don't care about these things anymore' (Ray, Chinese male, age 29).

The meaning of pleasure so expressed—the euphoria, the energy, the emotion, the liberation to lose oneself—is trans-cultural; as other studies have shown, it may represent a global experience.[33] The immediate pleasure, for some, has a lasting impact—not in the physical sense, but in a greater awareness of self in everyday life. In San Francisco and Hong Kong, some occasional users experiment not with different drugs, but with different settings in which to consume ecstasy, hoping that new venues with alternative music and social groups will enhance their sense of pleasure. For many more seasoned users the pursuit of pleasure is redefined as they combine different drugs to extend, prolong, or alter the pleasures of ecstasy.[34]

In San Francisco, respondents report using substances such as marijuana or GHB 'to bring back up' the experience of being high. In such cases they use one drug to extend the effects of another. Alternatively certain drugs intensify the effects of others, particularly ecstasy (a point noted by other researchers).[35] Marijuana is frequently cited as enhancing an existing drug experience, in some cases by making it more intense, in others by nicely mellowing it. One young male describes combining marijuana and mushrooms: 'When you're peaking you smoke a bowl and you peak a little harder . . . Definitely marijuana just intensifies any drug. Whatever it is, it all intensifies the situation. And . . . you know, I would say with every drug I usually always put weed in with it' (Cary, white male, age 19). Another respondent noted:

> I used to smoke marijuana more for the effects it would give you on E. Because most of the time when you're on E, you're coming down

[33] Bill Sanders (ed.) *Drugs, Clubs, and Young People: Sociological and Public Health Perspectives* (Burlington, VT, 2006); Matthew Collin, *Altered States: The Story of Ecstasy Culture and Acid House* (London, 2009).

[34] G. Hunt et al., 'Combining Different Substances in the Dance Scene: Enhancing Pleasure, Managing Risk, and Timing Effects', *Journal of Drug Issues* xxxix (2009).

[35] N. Solowij, W. Hall, and N. Lee, 'Recreational MDMA use in Sydney: A Profile of "Ecstasy" Users and their Experiences with the Drug', *British Journal of Addiction*, lxxxvii (1992); A. J. M. Forsyth, 'Places and Patterns of Drug Use in the Scottish Dance Scene', *Addiction*, xci (1996); R. Hammersley et al., 'Patterns of Ecstasy Use by Drug Users', *British Journal of Criminology*, xxxix (1999); Hunt et al., 'Combining Different Substances'.

> on E and you need that little boost, and marijuana kind of . . . it wasn't too intense . . . It brought it back a little bit. Made you feel better. (Jay, Filipino/African American male, age 30)

Other drug combinations are believed to intensify not merely the ecstasy experience but transform the experience completely. Hallucinogens were believed to enhance the ecstasy high by adding visuals.

In Hong Kong ketamine becomes a booster to speed up and heighten the liberating sensations from ecstasy and dancing. Moreover, as an affordable 'top up' ketamine redirects and shifts the euphoric effects of ecstasy.[36] Based on hearing from and observing their peers, interviewees expect and are not disappointed by the reaction time and the shift in their high from shaking to the music on ecstasy to floating and flying on ketamine. With one or two lines, most users are able to continue to enjoy the dance environment. An additional attraction of ketamine is that while ecstasy took 20 minutes to take effect, ketamine works much more quickly:

> After taking E, you can dance more and it last longer. For K, it comes into effect very fast, it just takes about five minutes. And then I become dizzy so I may not always be able to dance. But it depends on the quality of the drugs . . . If I just take E, I feel full of spirit . . . If I take K, it feels like my eyes can't open very wide. People call this the K eye, and I feel higher. (Kiki, Chinese female, age 24)

> The first time was at a disco with my friend, after we had some ecstasy. We snorted it in the toilet. I saw people snorting heavy doses, but I told myself try only a little first . . . I had one line. It was very bitter and felt strange. It made me feel faint, confused, like floating in the air. The floating feeling is like when you listen to music, you feel like you're physically oppressed, and when you dance, you feel you are releasing this oppression, it feels very pleasant. I will only use K after ecstasy because once I had only K at a rave and the feeling was just faint. I didn't get that feeling of oppression and that sensation of a release and floating feeling that I felt before. (Sini, Chinese female, age 25)

Ketamine is used in conjunction with ecstasy to improve or transform the ecstasy experience. While ecstasy facilitates dancing and socializing,

[36] K. A. Joe-Laidler, 'The Rise of Club Drugs in a Heroin Society: The Case of Hong Kong', *Substance Use and Misuse*, xl (2005).

ketamine moves the high in a different direction, producing dizziness, floating, and release. This floating sensation is reported without the use of ecstasy.

> The first time going to a disco I didn't know what to do . . . standing in a group staring at others . . . then a friend suggested taking drugs, he had two packets [ketamine]. After taking it, my friends and I stood there, waiting, smoking, and suddenly, not knowing why . . . it seemed that someone was pulling me . . . suddenly I was out on the dance floor . . . I was floating and floating . . . it seemed that I could see myself floating but I wasn't really. All around me things are inclined this way and that . . . moving up and down . . . (Choi, Chinese male, age 16)

Participants in both San Francisco and Hong Kong use drugs in the pursuit of pleasure. This could involve a combination of drugs. While in San Francisco the preferred supplementary drug is either marijuana or GHB, in Hong Kong it is ketamine.

The shared pursuit of pleasure involves more subtle differences. While San Francisco respondents describe ecstasy accentuating 'being in the moment', Hong Kong respondents feel ketamine helps 'transcend the moment'. Losing control is an attractive feature of ketamine as told in Hong Kong narratives. Participants describe 'free floating or winging', becoming 'vague', 'blurry', or in a state of confusion.[37] If continuously snorted during the course of an evening it can make users physically immobile. This loss of control, the inability to move, is paradoxically connected to a sense of freedom. What they emphasize are the physical experiences of ketamine which they found to be particularly attractive. Ketamine enables respondents to relax and transcend the stress, conflict, and, in particular, the boredom of everyday life.[38] About ten per cent of the respondents describe the 'K ride' experience as exhilarating and frightening. Effects are understood positively and negatively both physically (confusion, numbness, dizziness) and metaphysically (out of control, out-of-body, flying). Although respondents sometimes describe their ketamine experiences as frightening to the point of near-death they also observe the experience as 'amazing'.

[37] Joe-Laidler and Hunt, 'Sit Down to Float'.

[38] For boredom see B. Anderson, 'Time-Stilled Space-Slowed: How Boredom Matters', *Geoforum*, xxxv (2004); Elizabeth S. Goodstein, *Experience without Qualities: Boredom and Modernity* (Stanford, Calif., 2005); Y. Musharbash, 'Boredom, Time, and Modernity: An Example from Aboriginal Australia', *American Anthropologist*, cix (2007).

> My greatest experience with K was when I nearly found myself dying. . . On that night, I had some money and took some ketamine and ecstasy. I got a pack of ketamine and people around me kept spooning it to me so I snorted a lot. While I was snorting the ketamine, I remembered I still had a packet in my pocket. I took it out and gave it to my friends, and they spooned to me again . . . After that, I went out to the stage and dance. I found I couldn't control myself. I just stopped there with my opened eyes. I saw many people in stripes. When the music was low in sound, I saw everything shaking. Then I asked my friends to take me back to sit down . . . I could not control myself and I thought I would probably die. I was really afraid of this . . . I wanted to move but I couldn't. I wanted to hold up my hand but I couldn't. How could this be? I was definitely afraid of that . . . I called to my friend, and my eyes had already turned over. I didn't know what was going on . . . They shouldered me to the toilet. At the time, I dimly saw people dancing in a slow pace with slow actions . . . I felt hard and the effect came again. They took me to the toilet to help me vomit . . . I sat at a side and I didn't know why it seemed that something was going back to my body. I did not know whether it belonged to me or not. Yes, maybe my soul did come back. I found myself becoming clearer. I came back to the world, came back to Hong Kong. I felt I was awake . . . I was very afraid. I didn't know whether it was a rebirth, but yes, you could say this. At least I understand the feeling which was nearly death. (Kai, Chinese male, age 23)

Ketamine's popularity for Hong Kong respondents may stem from its ability to transcend youthful boredom and stress and enable both corporeal and mental freedom. This state could be achieved in a variety of social spaces: an attractive quality in a society where freedom is undergoing especial contestation. Viewed in these terms, 'tuning out' is not so much about excluding surroundings as liberating, however momentarily, body and self.

Experiencing the moment is also noted by respondents in San Francisco, ecstasy changing the ordinary and the familiar into something that is 'out-of-the-ordinary'. This operates not only to disrupt or break the routine of life but also to transform mundane activities and interactions into ones that are deeply pleasurable, satisfying, and exciting.[39] Going beyond the everyday removes the ecstasy user 'from the "normal" times, spaces and social relations

[39] Stanley Cohen and Laurie Taylor, *Escape Attempts: The Theory and Practice of Resistance to Everyday Life* (New York, 1992), 45.

of their everyday lives'.[40] Transforming the everyday, 'transgressing boundaries', and inspiring 'pleasure, excitement, exhilaration and desire' are central and fundamental features of ecstasy's appeal.[41] The ecstasy experience of 'tuning in' is not so dissimilar to ketamine's 'tuning out'—both facilitate the transcendence of the everyday and spiritual quest for liberation (albeit ecstasy has been found to become routinized and mundane, perhaps encouraging the use of supplementary intoxicants).[42]

San Francisco interviewees find ecstasy attractive because it accentuates the moment. Their Hong Kong equivalents did not describe ketamine in the same ways. This suggests that drugs are meaningful according to context. Although the San Francisco respondents echo the effects of ketamine as floating, many of them do not like the specific physical experiences that are so attractive for young people in Hong Kong. Besides noting that their experiences of using ketamine are 'bad', they also complain of feeling ill, nauseous, dizzy, and jittery: 'It was . . . just really dizziness . . . I just wanted to like lie there, and get over the dizziness. It was never euphoric or felt good' (Theo, Filipino American male, age 30). These physical experiences convince some respondents that taking ketamine is not fun.

> I mean, that's just not my idea of fun. I don't like drugs like that. I like ones that make me either like happy, singing, dancing, or something like that . . . I think it's just preference, if they really wanna . . . tune out and . . . block everything out, be oblivious, if you're into that, then that's the drug for you. (Sarah, white female, age 28)

Moreover, the loss of control so attractive for young people in Hong Kong is described in San Francisco as too debilitating. Losing control on drugs is most commonly described as a state—even *the* state—to be most avoided. While the San Francisco respondents often privileged intoxication, they are generally in search of what Fiona Measham refers to as a 'controlled loss of control'.[43] Finally, using ketamine on its own, without ecstasy, is viewed by one respondent as an empty experience. 'I didn't like doing Ketamine without

[40] Ben Malbon, *Clubbing: Dancing, Ecstasy and Vitality* (New York, 1999), 83.

[41] Deborah Lupton (ed.) *Risk and Sociocultural Theory: New Directions and Perspectives* (New York, 1999), 167.

[42] D. Shewan, P. Dalgarno and G. Reith, 'Perceived Risk and Risk Reduction among Ecstasy Users: The Role of Drug, Set, and Setting', *International Journal of Drug Policy*, x (2000); Gerda Reith, 'On the Edge: Drugs and the Consumption of Risk in Late Modernity', in Stephen Lyng (ed.) *Edgework: The Sociology of Risk-Taking* (New York, 2005).

[43] Fiona Measham, '"Doing Gender" - "Doing Drugs": Conceptualising the Gendering of Drugs Cultures', *Contemporary Drug Problems*, xxix (2002).

being on E, 'cause the high was kind of empty' (David, white male, age 25). This may reflect a tendency of San Francisco respondents to emphasize the social element of ecstasy. Taking ketamine on its own provides no social element precisely because the drug's effect is so debilitating that it is impossible to relate to others.

The transitory and immediate effects of intoxication are not the only concerns of interviewees in San Francisco. They also emphasize the more enduring and even permanent benefits in using club drugs, especially ecstasy—a tendency which never figures in Hong Kong accounts. Participants in San Francisco describe how ecstasy produces changes both in their sense of themselves and in their interactions with others. While they look to transcend the mundane, at least for an evening, they also seek more. Some ecstasy users contend that its effects are ephemeral and limited to the moment of intoxication. Other users seek to build on and draw from their experiences by integrating intoxication into their everyday lives. The pleasures of ecstasy are thus associated with a longer-lasting positive experience: the recreation of some of the positive and pleasurable experiences of ecstasy on the dance floor into daily life. As respondents often noted their 'drug selves' could influence and bring happiness to their 'everyday selves'. They claimed ecstasy encouraged their self-confidence or self-esteem, their ability to interact with others, and their ability to connect with their emotions. For others this took on a metaphysical or spiritual undertone in which ecstasy was seen to have revealed a greater purpose or meaning in life.[44] Ecstasy's life-changing ability, and the new consciousness it engendered, was often tied to a process of self-discovery. While most had started using ecstasy for more mundane reasons, primarily for fun, some said this shifted over time, as ecstasy enabled a transformation in how they perceived themselves.

An emphasis on these more lasting changes—the self awareness, the prospect of a new emergent self, the forging of communal relations beyond the dance-drug setting—may be one reason why ketamine has very limited attraction to our San Francisco respondents. Although 37 per cent of them had tried ketamine, less than 25 per cent had used it in the last year, and only two per cent had used it in the last month. For those who used it in a measured and controlled manner, the ketamine experience was novel—watery legs and

[44] Feeling that one now understands the meaning of life is not unusual for drug users. E.g., Huxley (1954) Coleridge (1956), and De Quincy (1971) all described similar effects for mind altering drugs. See Marcus Boon, *The Road of Excess: A History of Writers on Drugs* (Cambridge, Mass., 2002); Aldous Huxley, *The Doors of Perception and Heaven and Hell* (New York, 1954); Samuel Taylor Coleridge, *Collected Letters, 2 vols* (Oxford, 1956); Thomas De Quincey, *Confessions of an English Opium Eater* (London, 1971).

Table 1. Lifetime drug-use rates, by location

Drug (%)	San Francisco (300 young people)	Hong Kong (100 young people)
Marijuana	97	89
Ecstasy	92	88
Ketamine	37	85
LSD	59	8
Mushrooms	78	9
Methamphetamine	55	31
GHB	25	3
Cocaine (powder)	60	32
Crack cocaine	11	0
MDA	14	0
Nitrous Oxide	62	0
Poppers	12	0

arms, walking in a dreamy and cloudy state and slight numbness. But most San Francisco respondents were aware, from friends and reading, of the potential negative effects of ketamine, such as confusion, numbness, loss of control. It was not seen in general as a pleasurable substance or consistent with the forging of a new self.

While we are not suggesting that our Hong Kong respondents did not experience any of these life-changing experiences, their accounts of ketamine tend to omit any such discussions. Nevertheless, in spite of these cultural variations, we would still suggest that their narratives of 'tuning out' are similar to 'tuning in' but articulated in culturally different ways. It was precisely the ability to lose control and become immediately and momentarily immobile that attracted young people in Hong Kong. But beyond this immediacy lies the pursuit and longing for freedom and liberation from the everyday and the spiritual enrichment of the self.

IV

Research in many locales around the world suggests that intoxicants have become embedded in a global youth dance drug culture. Ecstasy in particular has been integral to the scene even as users experiment and make cocktails with non-prescription drugs, hallucinogens, cocaine, and crystal methamphetamine in the pursuit of new heights of pleasure and altered consciousness. Ecstasy and other intoxicants have remained important aspects of this shared global youth culture despite the shift from grass roots raves to commercialized venues in cities across the world. With the emergence of a highly commercialized and segmented dance drug scene researchers have been left wondering if the original motives of rave-induced intoxication—that of emotionality and spirituality—have been lost in transition. Largely absent from discussions about the local and global youth dance drug culture are the different meanings associated with drug use in particular locales. The objective here has been to begin to fill this lacuna. In this respect intoxication understood as the pursuit of pleasure is a useful framework of comparative analysis. It is an integral feature of the modern condition, both experientially and in terms of the structural conditions in which people seek altered consciousness. It also provides a crucial link between the present and the past.

But what does youthful intoxication mean in modern times? This discussion has suggested that Leary's 1960s call to 'turn on, tune in, and drop out' in a spiritual and hallucinogenic search for the self illuminates the more recent attempt by ravers and the club generation to 'tune out' or 'tune in' through ketamine or ecstasy. Although the scenes in Hong Kong and San Francisco are defined in culturally and class specific ways, young people in both locales give similar meanings to their respective drugs of choice. On the one hand, they seek pleasure through intoxication in rave and dance settings. Pleasure is articulated as fun, happiness, euphoria, energy, liberation, and the losing of one's self to or beyond the moment. There are also intimations of finding and awakening the self in spiritual terms. This awakening, however, differs for young people in San Francisco who prefer ecstasy and those in Hong Kong who prefer ketamine. San Francisco youngsters describe ecstasy's role communally and with permanent ramifications. Hong Kong youth describe the isolated but also flying and liberating experience of the ketamine ride, intoxication providing a transitory and momentary tonic to the routine of everyday life. In both instances intoxication helps position young people within modern states—states in which they are paradoxically held accountable as responsible individuals and inured into habits of prolonged adolescent dependency.

Indians and Drunkenness in Spanish America

Rebecca Earle

In a sixteenth-century report into the treatment of Amerindians in its new world colonies, the Spanish Council of the Indies noted that 'all Indians are inclined to vice and drunkenness and laziness, never applying themselves willingly to any sort of labour'.[1] Indians, a Spanish physician concurred, were 'given to wine and drunkenness'.[2] A few decades earlier a colonial account of pre-conquest indigenous culture in Peru similarly concluded that 'drunkenness and intemperance in drinking was a characteristic passion of these people'.[3] In the late eighteenth century a priest in colonial Mexico commented that 'everyone knows the Indians' predisposition to drunkenness'.[4] One could easily cite a stream of comments spanning the intervening two hundred years, and from across Spanish America, that make the same observation about Amerindians and their tendency to get drunk. Proclivity to drunkenness, in short, was one of the criticisms most frequently levelled against Spanish America's native peoples during the colonial era.[5]

[1] 'Consulta del consejo de las indias sobre los servicios personales de los indios', 15 Aug. 1596, *Colección de documentos para la historia de la formación social de Hispanoamérica*, ed. Richard Konetzke (Madrid, 1953), II, 45.

[2] Francisco Hernández, *Antigüedades de la Nueva España*, ed. Ascensión H. de León-Portilla (Madrid, 1986 [*c.*1574]), 71, 97 (quote).

[3] Anon, 'Relación de las costumbres antiguas de los naturales del Pirú', *c.*1550, *Crónicas peruanas de interés indígena*, ed. Francisco Esteve Barba (Madrid, 1968), 174.

[4] Christine Eber, *Women and Alcohol in a Highland Maya Town* (Austin, 2001), 21–2.

[5] For example, Gonzalo Fernández de Oviedo, *Historia general y natural de las Indias*, ed. Juan Pérez de Tudela Bueso (Madrid, 1959 [1535–1557]), I, 136; Toribio Motolinía, *Motolinía's History of the Indians of New Spain* (Berkeley, 1950 [1541]), 45, 244; Diego de Landa, *Relación de las cosas de Yucatan*, ed. Angel María Garibay (Mexico, 1973 [1574]), 37, 84; Lope de Atienza, *Compendio historial del estado de los indios del Peru*, 1583, in *La Religión del imperio de los Incas*, ed. J. Jijón y Caamaño (Quito, 1931), 73–4, 163–8; Esteban de Salazar, *Veinte discursos sobre el credo* (Seville, 1586), 200; José de Acosta, *De procuranda indorum salute*, trans. L. Pereña, V. Abril, C. Baciero, A. García, D. Ramos, J. Barrientos, and F. Maseda (Madrid, 1984 [1588]), I, 545–73; José de Acosta,

 © The Past and Present Society

This chapter interprets the enduring assertion that Amerindians are peculiarly prone to drunkenness. Drawing on a range of colonial sources, as well as the substantial body of research into indigenous drinking practices produced by historians and anthropologists, it explores the role of alcohol consumption in a number of different indigenous cultures and reviews the varied meanings that the drinking Indian held for Europeans, creoles, and other colonial actors.[6] It further considers the drinking Indian's persistent vitality within the imagination of Spanish American elites. Complaints and hand-wringing about the propensity of Amerindians to get drunk endured long after the end of colonial rule. Nineteenth- and twentieth-century writers often asserted, much as had their colonial antecedents, that—in the words of one Ecuadorian scholar—drunkenness was 'innate in the [indigenous] race and constitutes one of the most pronounced features of its moral physiognomy'.[7] The conclusions that elite writers drew from such observations, however, changed significantly over time, for the meanings ascribed to indigenous drunkenness mirror the larger place of the indigenous population within the colonial or national project. Most of Spanish America achieved independence from metropolitan rule in the early nineteenth century. Although nationalist ideologues were deeply concerned with fomenting a sense of national identity and forming cohesive republican societies, the indigenous population continued to occupy an equivocal position within the new republics, just as they had under colonialism. The nature of the threat Amerindians were believed to pose to the body politic nonetheless underwent significant transformation from the early colonial period to the nineteenth century.

Natural and Moral History of the Indies, trans. Frances López-Morillas (Durham, 2002 [1590]), 143–4, 199; Alonso de Ovalle, *An Historical Relation of the Kingdom of Chile*, 1646 (London, 1703), 73; Bernabé Cobo, *Historia del Nuevo Mundo*, 1653, *Obras*, ed. Francisco Mateos (Madrid, 1956), II, 16–24; Alonso de la Peña Montenegro, *Itinerario para parrochos de indios* (Madrid, 1668), 202–11; Carlos de Sigüenza y Góngora, *Alboroto y motín de los indios de México*, 1692, in *Teatro de virtudes políticos y Alboroto y motín* (Mexico, 1986), 197, 215–16; Francisco Javier Clavijero, *Historia antigua de México* (Mexico City, 1958 [1780]), I, 138–9; Pedro Ignacio de Elguera, 'Diario Histórico', Chuquibamba, 30 Dec. 1781, Archivo General de Indias [henceforth AGI], Audiencia de Cuzco 29; and *Recopilación de leyes de los reynos de las Indias* (Madrid, 1943 [1791]), II, 197–8, 304.

[6] 'Creoles' are people of European heritage born in the Americas.

[7] Federico González Suárez, *Historia general de la República del Ecuador* (Quito, 1969 [1890]), I, 226 (quote); and Rebecca Earle, 'Algunos pensamientos sobre "el indio borracho" en el imaginario criollo', *Revista de Estudios Sociales*, 29 (2008).

Post-colonial writers often viewed drunkenness in indigenous communities as the death throe of a moribund culture. Colonial writers, in contrast, generally regarded indigenous drinking practices as evidence that native peoples were a dangerous and all too vibrant part of Spain's colonial world. The essay concludes with a discussion of recent medical research suggesting that Amerindians possess a genetic predisposition towards alcoholism, which offers another powerful but ambiguous framework for interpreting the figure of the indigenous drinker.

I

Drunken Indians did not exist before the Spanish conquest of the Americas in the late fifteenth and early sixteenth centuries because 'Indians' are a colonial creation; the term imposes an artificial unity on the many disparate groups that inhabited the Americas prior to the arrival of Europeans. Nonetheless, people in pre-conquest Spanish America—unlike the native peoples in the regions further north later colonized by the British—possessed many forms of alcohol and the production, distribution, and consumption of fermented beverages often served both social and ritual purposes. The anthropologist Tom Cummins, for example, has argued that in Inca culture drinking was a central element of the periodic feasts that bound Andean society together. Through the provision of corn beer local rulers manifested their authority to call forth communal labours at the same time as they honoured village deities; such festivals, Cummins writes, conflated 'all relationships into one celebration that conceded as natural the interdependence and alliance between all entities'.[8] The decorations on Incaic drinking vessels therefore allude to the symbolic importance of such communal acts. Beyond mere consumption, intoxication, whether induced by alcohol or other means, sometimes played an important role in pre-conquest religious celebrations. For example, many of the Maya festivals described by the sixteenth-century friar Diego de Landa apparently concluded with acts of group intoxication.[9] It is worth noting that both Spanish commentators and Amerindians believed that drunkenness could result from activities other than the consumption of alcohol. Spanish chroniclers detailed the many substances that native people ingested in their quest for what the Spanish called *borrachera*, or drunkenness, while the Maya regarded as comparable the mental states induced by alcohol, hot chocolate,

[8] Thomas Cummins, *Toasts with the Inca: Andean Abstraction and Colonial Images on Quero Vessels* (Ann Arbor, 2002), 43; and Catherine Allen, *The Hold Life Has: Coca and Cultural Identity in an Andean Community* (Washington, 1988), 137–50.

[9] Landa, *Relación*, 70, 72, 76, 79, 84, 94, 96, 100.

and bloodletting.[10] We should therefore not view drunkenness as a phenomenon linked solely to what we have come to call alcohol. After all, as anthropologists and social scientists have reminded us, 'drunkenness' is as much a socially conditioned response as it is a physiological process.[11]

In any event, in the pre-colonial world the powerful forces unleashed by drunkenness were often subject to controls. Among the Meso-American Nahua drunkenness outside of ritual contexts was thought to disturb the body's equilibrium, and was therefore considered dangerous and unhealthy.[12] A number of early colonial sources stress that for this reason Mexica rulers sought to limit alcohol consumption. The Dominican priest Bernardino de Sahagún's late sixteenth-century history of the Mexica reports, for example, that on their enthronement rulers informed their people:

> What I principally command is that you shun drunkenness, that you do not drink *pulque*, because it is like henbane which removes man from his reason.... This *pulque* and drunkenness is the cause of all discord and dissention, and of all the revolts and unrest among the towns and kingdoms; it is like a whirlwind that upsets and disturbs everything; it is like an infernal storm that brings with it all possible evils.[13]

[10] See, e.g., Fernández de Oviedo, *Historia general*, I, 116; Nicolás Monardes, *Historia medicinal de las cosas que se traen de nuestras Indias Occidentales* (Sevilla, 1580), 93v; Bernardino de Sahagún, *Historia general de las cosas de Nueva España*, ed. Alfredo López Austin and Josefina García Quintana (Mexico, 1982 [1577]), II, 575, 578; Acosta, *De procuranda*, I, 549, 551; and Juan de Cárdenas, *Problemas y secretos maravillosos de las Indias* (Madrid, 1945 [1591]), 245–6. Sin, noted the Franciscan Gaspar de Recarte, induced a state of 'drunkenness' much worse than that caused by alcohol: 'Tratado del servicio personal y repartimiento de los indios de Nueva España', 3 Oct. 1584, *Documentos inéditos del siglo XVI para la historia de México*, ed. Mariano Cuevas (Mexico, 1914), 363.

[11] The classic work is Mary Douglas (ed.), *Constructive Drinking: Perspectives on Drink from Anthropology* (Cambridge, 1987). See also Dwight Heath, 'Cultural Variations Among Drinking Patterns', *Drinking Patterns and their Consequences*, ed. Marcus Grant and Jorge Litvak (Philadelphia, 1998).

[12] On Nahua concepts of moderation see Louise Burkhart, *The Slippery Earth: Nahua-Christian Moral Dialogue in Sixteenth-Century Mexico* (Arizona, 1989), esp. 159–68.

[13] Sahagún, *Historia general*, I, 267 (quote), II, 486–7; Bartolomé de las Casas, *Apologética histórica*, c.1550, in *Obras escogidas* (Madrid, 1958), III, 117–19, IV, 268–9; and Hernández, *Antigüedades de la Nueva España*, 72. *Pulque* is a low-alcohol beer made from agave sap.

Similar accounts emerged from Peru, where, colonial chroniclers maintained, the Inca state had also regulated alcohol consumption. The indigenous Peruvian writer Felipe Guaman Poma de Ayala for example insisted in his early seventeenth-century chronicle that drunkenness had been unknown during Inca rule. 'In the time of the Inca', he claimed, 'there was no drunkenness (although they drank and had festivals), and it was especially prohibited. . . The drunkard was put to death under the Inca's law'.[14]

There thus exist a variety of early colonial sources that insist that drinking was strictly regulated in the pre-colonial world, in contrast to the unrestrained drinking said to characterize the indigenous universe after the advent of colonialism. To some extent these assertions match what we know about the moral universe of pre-conquest peoples such as the Mexica. At the same time, these sources cannot be separated from the context in which they were produced. Early colonial histories of pre-conquest life, which were often the outcome of complex interactions between scholarly clerics and members of the former indigenous elite, reveal as much about the new norms introduced with Spanish rule as they do about pre-colonial customs. For example, in labelling drunkenness a European innovation Guaman Poma not only provided an idealized image of life in pre-conquest Peru—indeed, to do this was one of his principal goals—but he also reflected the profound alterations colonialism imposed on the cultural and religious contexts in which drinking occurred, since Guaman Poma's account of Inca sobriety reflects very clearly his own interactions with colonial Christianity.

Felipe Guaman Poma de Ayala, the descendent of a privileged subsection of Andean society, was born in the mid-sixteenth century, during the Spanish conquest of Peru. In the last years of his life—around 1615—he composed a lengthy chronicle, called *The First New Chronicle and Good Government*, which he sent to the reigning Spanish monarch Philip III. The text, which runs to over 1200 pages and includes some 400 illustrations, comprises a history of the Inca Empire, together with an extended account of the destructive impact of colonialism on Peru and its peoples. Guaman Poma's purpose in writing his chronicle appears to have been to defend the integrity and legitimacy of the Inca state and to alert the Spanish monarchy to the abuses being perpetrated against the Andean population. His dissatisfaction with Spanish rule notwithstanding, he was a devout Christian and his attitudes

[14] Felipe Guaman Poma de Ayala, *El primer nueva corónica y buen gobierno*, 1615–16, fol. 863 [877], http://www.kb.dk/elib/mss/poma; Cummins, *Toasts with the Inca*, 225; and also Garcilaso de la Vega, *Royal Commentaries of the Incas and General History of Peru*, ed. Harold Livermore (Austin, 1966 [1616–17]), I, 499.

towards drunkenness reveal clearly the impact of Christian teaching on his retrospective vision of the Inca Empire.

The arrival of European colonisers, which provoked catastrophic transformations of indigenous societies, also introduced the distinctive Spanish-Catholic understanding of alcohol. Early modern Catholicism did not advocate total abstinence. Wine, after all, was the substance miraculously converted into the very blood of Christ during the Mass and hence was redolent of Christianity itself.[15] In early modern Iberia, moreover, wine acquired a particularly Catholic resonance since Islamic teaching specifically forbade its consumption. Medical opinion also endorsed the daily consumption of moderate quantities of wine, which was considered a supremely healthful and nourishing drink suitable for virtually all complexions.[16] Far from being a menace to health, it was a medical necessity. 'To deprive an old man or a youth of a little wine', observed one Spanish writer, 'is to send him straight to the grave'.[17]

Getting drunk was another matter. Drunkenness was not only a sin, as Thomas Aquinas had insisted, but it was also dishonourable, for it entailed the loss of reason and judgement.[18] Masculine identity in particular required the ability to drink without becoming drunk. 'There is no greater insult among them than to call someone a drunkard', noted one seventeenth-century French traveller of Spanish men.[19] As Thomas Nichols suggests in his chapter, this attitude is perhaps reflected in Diego Velázquez's critical portrayal of drunkenness in *Los Borrachos*. Iberian writers often contrasted

[15] See, e.g., Antonio de Leon Pinelo, *Question moral si el chocolate quebranta el ayuno eclesiástico* (Madrid, 1638), 46–7; Juan de Solórzano Pereira, *Política indiana* (Madrid, 1736 [1647]), I, 99; and Peña Montenegro, *Itinerario*, 349.

[16] See, e.g., Pedro Mexía, *Silva de varia lección*, ed. Antonio Castro (Madrid, 1989 [1540]), II, 104; Luis Lobera de Avila, *Vergel de sanidad* (Alcalá de Henares, 1542), xxr; and Ken Albala, *Eating Right in the Renaissance* (Berkeley, 2002), 74, 121.

[17] Carta de Tomás López Medel, 25 March 1551, AGI, Audiencia de Guatemala 9A, R. 18, n. 77, fol. 1.

[18] Thomas Aquinas, *Summa Theologica*, second part of the second part, question 150, http://www.newadvent.org; Diego Durán, *Historia de las Indias de Nueva España* (Mexico, 1967 [1570]), I, 201–2; and Real Academia Española, *Diccionario de autoridades* (Madrid, 1963 [1726]), I, 654, II, 391; 1.

[19] Francisco Nuñez de Oria, *Regimiento y aviso de sanidad* (Medina del Campo, 1586), 16v, 19r; Mme. D'Aulnoy, *Relation du voyage d'Espagne* (La Haya, 1692), II, 116–117 (quote); James Wadsworth, *The Present Estate of Spayne* (London, 1630), 74; Amadé Frezier, *A Voyage to the South-Seas* (London, 1717), 251, 253; and Jean-Louis Flandrin, 'La diversité des gouts et des pratiques alimentaires en Europe du XVIe au XVIIIe siècle', *Revue d'Histoire Moderne et Contemporaine*, 30 (1983), 68.

the moderation they considered characteristic of Spain and Italy with the norms they believed to be prevalent in Germany and the Low Countries, where, astonished travellers claimed, men appeared drunk in public without shame.[20]

By insisting that drunkenness—even in ritual contexts—was unknown in Inca times, Guaman Poma implicitly endorsed this Spanish-Catholic view of drunkenness as an undesirable, immoral state, even as he condemned the Spanish for its introduction. Indeed, his claim that sobriety reigned even at Inca festivals probably reflects a familiarity with the specifically post-Tridentine condemnation of the drunken commemoration of saints and relics more than the actual nature of pre-conquest festivals.[21] His insistence that drinking but not drunkenness was common to Inca society ('they drank and had festivals') similarly reflects his absorption of the Spanish view that drinking, but not drunkenness, was an honourable, manly activity. Guaman Poma attempted to defend the Inca empire against accusations of incivility by inscribing it within the norms endorsed by colonial culture. Attitudes towards drunkenness in other words serve as windows into the complex interactions between indigenous and European cultural norms that created Spanish American colonial culture. They reveal something of the extent, and limits, of transculturation.

Many early colonial sources—not only those composed by native peoples but also those written by settlers—contrast the unrestrained drinking of the colonized population with the social controls that had reportedly prevailed before the advent of colonialism, but they do not all share Guaman Poma's distinctively transcultured optic. Clerical writers often stressed that uncontrolled drinking was a colonial phenomenon. The sixteenth-century Franciscan scholar Gerónimo de Mendieta for example insisted that pre-conquest Indians had condemned drunkenness 'as we Spaniards do'. He reported that Indians in colonial Mexico, on the other hand, routinely drank themselves into drunken stupors, 'which was not the case in the time of their gentility'. His explanation for this phenomenon, however, had nothing to do with vindicating the pre-conquest order. On the contrary, Mendieta saw contemporary drunkenness as evidence for the epic battle for indigenous souls in which he and his fellow clerics were engaged. Prior to the arrival of the Christian friars, the new world was in Mendieta's view less the domain of Satan than a land as yet untouched by the word of God. Only with the advent of evangelization did the devil truly show his hand. The devil—in Mendieta's

[20] Recarte, 'Tratado del servicio personal', 363; and Nuñez de Oria, *Regimiento*, 9r.

[21] *The Canons and Decrees of the Sacred and Oecumenical Council of Trent*, ed. J. Waterworth (London, 1848), 24th session, 3–4 Dec. 1563.

interpretation—therefore provoked the indigenous population to drunkenness, 'so that they thereby cease to be true Christians'.[22] Colonial drunkenness thus revealed the Spanish colony to be a site of struggle between the forces of good and evil. Restrained pre-colonial drinking patterns, in turn, simply indicated that the region had not yet begun to occupy this momentous role. Thus although their sobriety did not reflect particularly positively on them, pre-conquest peoples were moderate drinkers, in Mendieta's view.

Not all colonial writers agreed with this interpretation and many seventeenth-century commentators, both religious and secular, insisted that pre-colonial society was plagued by demoniacally inspired drunkenness. 'Through the sowing and cultivation of maguey [from which *pulque* is made] the astute Enemy has introduced and set ever so firmly in place among these Indians the vice of drunkenness', observed a priest in early seventeenth-century Mexico.[23] It is certain, wrote a landowner in Colombia in the same years, 'that before this Kingdom entered into the word of God the devil ruled'. This, he believed, was why all pre-conquest social gatherings had degenerated into drunken orgies.[24] To counter this demonic force sermons and catechisms aimed at Amerindians elaborated on the evils of drink and stressed their particular sensitivity to its lure.[25] Thus whether it was believed to have originated in the pre-conquest or in the colonial world, indigenous drunkenness was seen by European and creole writers as evidence for demonic activity.

Because of its links to the demonic colonial officials were convinced that drunkenness among Amerindians was a key factor in the persistence of pre-conquest religious beliefs. As the Second Council of Lima, which met in the late 1560s to implement the resolutions of the Council of Trent, explained, 'the vice of drunkenness . . . is the root of infidelity'.[26] Uncontrolled drinking

[22] Gerónimo de Mendieta, *Historia eclesiástica indiana* (Mexico, 1971 [*c.*1596]), 139 (both quotations).

[23] Hernando Ruíz de Alarcón, *Treatise on the Heathen Superstitions that Today Live Among the Indians Native to this New Spain,* 1629, ed. J. Richard Andrews and Ross Hassig (Norman, 1984).

[24] Juan Rodríguez Freyle, *Conquista y descubrimiento del Nuevo Reino de Granada* (Madrid, 1986 [1638]), 82.

[25] *Confessionario para los curas de indios* (Lima, 1585), 26; Diego de Torres Rubio, *Arte de la lengua aymara* (Lima, 1616), 71; Bartolomé de Alva, *A Guide to Confession Large and Small in the Mexican Language, 1634,* ed. Barry Sell and John F. Schwaller (Norman, 1999), 93–7, 106, 118; and Diego de Nagera Yanguas, *Doctrina y enseñanza en la lengua maçahua de cosas muy utiles y provechosos* (Mexico, 1637), 25–6, 65.

[26] Cummins, *Toasts with the Inca,* 149 (quote), 224; Durán, *Historia de las Indias,* I, 200–4; Rodríguez Freyle, *Conquista y descubrimiento,* 69, 74, 81–2; *Recopilación de leyes,* II,

among Amerindians was thus fundamentally incompatible with Christianity, whose introduction into the Americas was the principal justification of Spain's colonial endeavour. In other words, indigenous drinking needed to be eliminated for Indians to become true Christians and colonial officials were convinced that this would best be accomplished through the imposition of colonial rule: indigenous drunkenness demonstrated the need for a colonial presence. The sixteenth-century Jesuit chronicler José de Acosta thus maintained that the debauchery he believed was typical of traditional Andean feasts would be eliminated if such events took place under Spanish supervision. 'If done in this way', he noted, 'there is no fear that great drunkenness will proliferate so much, since they will be watched over and punished'.[27] Indigenous drinking demonstrated the need for colonialism's civilizing gaze.

Spanish and creole writers thus viewed drunkenness as a sign that the devil was at work in the new world, which in turn indicated the need for a colonial presence. And drunkenness, understood as a sinful condition reflecting loss of honour, turned out to be a condition to which native peoples were particularly prone, along with cannibalism, dishonesty, and myriad other faults that revealed a fundamental lack of civilization. Colonial commentary on indigenous drinking practices thus reveals something of the *imaginario*, or mental universe, of Spanish settlers, and reflects the place they accorded Amerindians within the colonial system.

II

Can we say anything more than this? Can we move from a discussion of how colonial discourse reveals the attitudes of colonial writers to any consideration of actual indigenous behaviour? In particular, given the considerable interest in the origins of alcohol abuse among the contemporary Native American population, can we shed any light on whether—as some colonial writers claimed—native peoples did drink more during the colonial era? As we saw, writers such as Mendieta ascribed the purported post-conquest increase in indigenous drinking to demonic intervention. Mendieta saw no correlation between the widespread indigenous drunkenness that he reported and the profound social dislocation caused by conquest.

197–8; Benito de Peñaloza y Mondragón, *Libro de las cinco excelencias del español* (Pamplona, 1629), 125; and Charles Gibson, *The Aztecs under Spanish Rule: A History of the Indians of the Valley of Mexico, 1519–1810* (Stanford, 1964), 150.

[27] Acosta, *De procuranda*, I, 553–79, 591 (quote); and Cummins, *Toasts with the Inca*, 309.

This, however, is precisely what more recent scholars have seen in such reports. They view post-conquest indigenous drinking as an indication of cultural trauma, a sign of the widespread social anomie induced by the destructive forces of colonialism. Since the mid-nineteenth century many analysts have argued that the cultural dislocation caused by the conquest, together with the collapse of regulatory social mechanisms that had previously governed consumption practices, produced societies awash with drunken, demoralized Indians whose descent into alcoholism reflected, in the words of one twentieth-century scholar, 'the bitterness of a defeated race'.[28] The historian Peter Mancall, for example, speculates that during the colonial era North American native peoples drank 'because the world they knew was crashing down around them'.[29] Many Native Americans themselves maintain that 'the loss of their culture is the primary cause of many of their existing social problems, especially those associated with alcohol'.[30]

This interpretation is strengthened by the fact that Spanish settlement introduced Amerindians to an entirely new set of high-alcohol intoxicants: distilled liquors. Pre-conquest cultures elaborated many fermented beverages, but they did not develop distillation. Fermentation alone cannot produce drinks of greater than about 16 per cent alcohol. Common pre-conquest drinks such as *pulque* and *chicha* range from 1 to 4 per cent alcohol. With the arrival of Spanish colonizers came not only wines (8–13 per cent) but also distilled liquors (up to 80 per cent). In particular, the rise of sugar cultivation led to the development of rum, *aguardiente* and other distilled sugar-cane based spirits. In addition, both the state alcohol monopolies established by the Spanish crown and the growing commercialization of alcohol sales helped sever the regulatory systems that had linked alcohol consumption to religious

[28] Pío Jaramillo Alvarado, *El indio ecuatoriano. Contribución al estudio de la sociología nacional* (Quito, 1925), I, 230–1. See also Gibson, *The Aztecs under Spanish Rule*, 7, 150, 409; William Madsen and Claudia Madsen, 'The Cultural Structure of Mexican Drinking Behaviour', *Contemporary Cultures and Societies of Latin America*, ed. Dwight Heath (New York, 1974), 439; Serge Gruzinski, *The Conquest of Mexico: the Incorporation of Indian Societies into the Western World, 16th-18th Centuries* (Cambridge, 1993), 203; and Eber, *Women and Alcohol*, 6.

[29] Peter Mancall, *Deadly Medicine: Indians and Alcohol in Early America* (Ithaca, 1995), 7–8.

[30] Fred Beauvais, 'American Indians and Alcohol', *Alcohol Health & Research World* (henceforth *AHRW*) 22:4 (1998), 256 (quote); and Teresa Milbrodt, 'Breaking the Cycle of Alcohol Problems Among Native Americans: Culturally Sensitive Treatment in the Lakota Community', *Alcoholism Treatment Quarterly*, 20:1 (2002), 25–32.

ritual in the pre-colonial world. The historian Serge Gruzinski thus speaks of the progressive 'secularization' of alcohol in the seventeenth century.[31] Post-conquest indigenous cultures therefore had at their disposal a powerful set of intoxicants whose sale directly benefited both state revenues and individual vendors. This is reflected in the distinction some indigenous cultures make to this day between traditional fermented alcohols and distilled spirits. The twentieth-century Maya community studied by the anthropologist Christine Eber, for example, considered maize beer, or *chicha*, a beneficial drink, while rum was viewed as a symbol of white domination.[32] These factors have encouraged many scholars to argue that post-conquest Amerindians suffered from what we can anachronistically call alcoholism, and to view widespread alcohol abuse as an indication of the traumatic impact of colonialism.[33]

This interpretation persists despite the challenges to it posed by William Taylor, who argued in a now-classic study published in 1979 that colonial reports of widespread indigenous drinking should not be taken at face value. He suggested that these reports reflect not an indigenous descent into alcoholism but rather different Spanish and indigenous understandings of moderation. In his view one of the reasons that Spaniards commented so often on Indian drunkenness was not that Amerindians drank more than Spaniards, but that (at least in the case of Mexico) they drank differently. For indigenous Mexicans, Taylor argued, moderation consisted in drinking on the right occasions, and in the right company: 'solitary, daily drinking was generally condemned'.[34] But when they drank, Taylor argued, they drank to get drunk. 'Periodic heavy drinking in ritual situations, often to complete saturation, was accepted as the standard of moderation—not considered behaviour that brought ridicule or shame to the drinker.'[35] In the words of one seventeenth-century Spanish friar, 'the Indian uses [*pulque*] to get drunk and unless he is intoxicated he doesn't believe that he has been drinking'.[36]

31 Gruzinski, *The Conquest of Mexico*, 277.

32 Eber, *Women and Alcohol*, 33.

33 The conversion of drunkenness from a moral to a medical condition is reflected in the late nineteenth-century invention of a new vocabulary to discuss excessive drinking; *alcoholismo*, which entered the Spanish lexicon in the 1890s, was an illness, not a sin: Real Academia Española, *Diccionario histórico de la lengua española* (Madrid, 1992), II, 204.

34 Taylor, *Drinking, Homicide, and Rebellion*, 41.

35 Ibid., 42.

36 Ibid., 43. Indians, insisted the sixteenth-century chronicler Gonzalo Fernández de Oviedo, 'drink until they collapse, if they are given the chance': *Historia general y natural*, II, 120.

In Taylor's view this was probably a continuation of pre-conquest patterns, when 'on ritual occasions when drinking was permitted, adult male participants could apparently drink themselves into a stupor without shame'.[37] In contrast Spanish culture endorsed the daily consumption of smaller quantities of alcohol and expressly condemned public displays of drunkenness. What the Spanish saw as disgusting drunkenness, Taylor argued, in fact revealed a different concept of moderation and a different sense of what drinking was supposed to look like.

Taylor's analysis described indigenous drinking patterns in selected parts of colonial Mexico. Nonetheless, the conviction that drinking should induce the dramatic loss of bodily control—that the drinker should collapse, vomit, pass out—and that this loss of self-control is positive, indeed beneficial, is reported in a number of more recent ethnographic studies from other parts of Spanish America. Mary Weismantel, for example, argued that such drunkenness was a central feature of celebrations in the Ecuadorian community of Zumbagua, which she studied in the 1980s. Villagers there maintained that eating or drinking to overflowing allows worshippers to transmit food to others (in particular, the dead): vomiting as a consequence of drinking feeds the dead. Consumption of *chicha* therefore plays an important role in indigenous ritual.[38] Studies of the contemporary Maya world reveal similar links between intoxication and religious devotion. Describing her observations of a Maya community in Chiapas in the 1980s Christine Eber commented that:

> from the symbolic perspective, ritual drinking to intoxication, but not to the point of passing out, appeared to me as one way [villagers] try to connect an interior opening-up within themselves to an exterior flowering in the universe. Drinking in service to their Gods empowers individual drinkers, unites the group, and carries on ancestral values and beliefs.[39]

Overall, this research suggests that 'drunkenness' might serve to transport the drinker to a liminal position between the sacred and the worldly. Far from being a symptom of trauma it was, in the words of the historian David McCreery, 'pleasing to the saints and a satisfying social affair'.[40] Such communal drinking was a mark of affirmation, not cultural devastation.

[37] Taylor, *Drinking, Homicide and Rebellion*, 30.

[38] M. J. Weismantel, 'Maize Beer and Andean Social Transformations: Drunken Indians, Bread Babies, and Chosen Women', *MLN* 106 (1991).

[39] Eber, *Women and Alcohol*, 243.

[40] David McCreery, *Rural Guatemala, 1760–1940* (Stanford, 1994), 87.

III

Writers have thus been evaluating the indigenous drinker since the early colonial era. Into this already crowded interpretative field has stridden a new analytical force armed with one of our era's most powerful discourses: genetics. Could genetic make-up play any role in shaping indigenous responses to alcohol? Scientists have known for decades that sensitivity to alcohol has a genetic component. Alcohol abuse can run in families and twin studies show that genetics plays an important role in determining the risk of alcoholism.[41] Ascertaining precisely which genes are at work has proved more difficult and scientists now suspect that multiple genes are involved. Some evidence also suggests that certain population groups possess distinctive genes that affect sensitivity to alcohol. Nonetheless, the link between genetics and drinking practices remains murky and a number of studies have found no significant genetic factors that might explain variations in drinking patterns among different communities.[42] Scientists moreover acknowledge that, whatever the role of genetics, individual drinking patterns can change as a result of social forces. Mexicans who migrate to the USA, for example, 'modify their consumption patterns by adopting the more frequent drinking patterns preferred by Americans'.[43]

Is there any evidence that Amerindian responses to alcohol have a genetic component? In particular, might some indigenous groups possess a greater genetic susceptibility to alcohol abuse? Although there is scant analysis of the links between genetics and alcohol consumption among native peoples in contemporary Latin America, there is a growing body of literature dedicated to exploring these links among Native Americans in the USA. In the eyes of geneticists there is little genetic diversity between different Native American populations (one study found that the Pima of the American Southwest and self-identified Quechua Indians in Peru share a similar genome), which raises the possibility that genetic studies of indigenous groups in the USA might

[41] Mary Koss and David Goldman, 'Genetic Factors and Alcoholism', *American Journal of Public Health*, 90:11 (2000), 1799; Mary-Anne Enoch and David Goldman, 'The Genetics of Alcoholism and Alcohol Abuse', *Current Psychiatry Reports*, 3 (2001); and 'Alcohol and Minorities: An Update', *Alcohol Alert*, 55 (January 2002).

[42] See, e.g., Elena Doudoladova Korir, David Ochieng, and Douglas Ndiritu, 'Comparative Genetics of Alcoholism in the Kenyan Populations', *African Journal of Biotechnology*, 3:2 (2004), 154.

[43] Linda Bennett, Carlos Campillo, C. R. Chandrashekar, and Oye Gureje, 'Alcoholic Beverage Consumption in India, Mexico, and Nigeria: A Cross-Cultural Comparison', *AHRW*, 22:4 (1998), 252 (quote); and 'Alcohol and Minorities: An Update'.

illuminate the genetics of alcohol response among native peoples elsewhere in the Americas.[44]

Some genetic evidence suggests that certain Native Americans are *less* vulnerable to alcohol abuse than people of European descent. For example, a 1992 study showed that, like many people from Japan and China, Native Alaskans eliminate ethanol from their systems faster than individuals of European origin.[45] As the speedy elimination of ethanol among many Japanese is often cited as a trait that protects against alcohol abuse, this research implies that Native Alaskans are less likely than Europeans to suffer from alcoholism. Mary-Anne Enoch, a research physician at the US National Institute on Alcohol Abuse and Alcoholism, has moreover found that some Plains Indians possess a genotype that seems to protect against alcoholism, although when expressed in Finnish men the same genotype is associated with a tendency towards alcoholism.[46] In her view 'there is little evidence that Native Americans have a genetic background that makes them more vulnerable to the effects of alcohol or to the development of alcoholism. The fact that most aboriginal groups have such high rates of alcohol abuse can most likely be attributed to historical and current trauma and deprivation'.[47] This opinion is echoed by a number of other scientists. 'Cultural dimensions of Native American drinking must be considered far more important than the notion that Native Americans' propensity for heavy and dependent drinking is primarily genetic', insisted three scholars in the *American Journal of Public Health* in 2000.[48]

Not all scientists however share this view. Some argue that evidence is still lacking as to the precise role of genetics in shaping indigenous responses to alcohol. Others maintain that there is increasingly clear genetic evidence that Native Americans have a higher tolerance for alcohol than do Europeans, which means that they can drink more without feeling the effects

[44] Heather Collins-Schramm et al, 'Mexican American Ancestry-Informative Markers: Examination of Population Structure and Marker Characteristics in European Americans, Mexican Americans, Amerindians and Asians', *Human Genetics*, 114:3 (2004), 263.

[45] Bernard Segal and Lawrence Duffy, 'Ethanol Elimination Among Different Racial Groups', *Alcohol*, 9:3 (1992).

[46] Caroline Cross, 'Genes and Alcoholism', 1 June 2004, Welcome Trust, http://www.wellcome.ac.uk/en/genome/genesandbody/hg06f013.html.

[47] Mary-Anne Enoch, Personal communication, August 2005.

[48] J. W. Frank, R. S. Moore, and G. H. Ames, 'Historical and Cultural Roots of Drinking Problems among American Indians', *American Journal of Public Health*, 89 (2000), 350.

of drunkenness. This trait is associated with increased risk of alcohol abuse.[49] In addition, several studies show that certain genes known to reduce the risk of alcohol addiction are generally absent in the Native American population.[50] There is thus disagreement among scientists as to the role played by genetics in shaping indigenous responses to alcohol.

Despite the lack of consensus this body of work poses challenges to historians. The first concerns the concept of 'racial' groups. Many scholars working in the humanities regard race as a social, cultural, and at times legal construct; Latin Americanists, in particular, have long noted the imprecise and mutable nature of racial classifications.[51] Many scientists, too, are dissatisfied with the category of race, and ethnicity often replaces race as a classificatory concept within scientific studies.[52] At the same time, discussions of genetics inevitably invoke a concept of difference—racial or otherwise—that is embedded in the body, rather than the ambient culture. Yet if the category of 'Indian' is essentially social or cultural, what does it mean to speak of the role of genetics in

[49] Consuelo Garcia-Andrade, Tamara Wall, and Cindy Ehlers, 'The Firewater Myth and Response to Alcohol in Mission Indians', *American Journal of Psychiatry*, 154:7 (1997), 983.

[50] 'Genetic Influences on Alcohol Drinking and Alcoholism', *Research & Creative Activity*, 17:3 (Indiana University, 1995); 'Alcohol and Minorities: An Update'; Tamara Wall, Lucinda Carr, and Cindy Ehlers, 'Protective Association of Genetic Variation in Alcohol Dehydrogenase with Alcohol Dependence in Native American Mission Indians', *American Journal of Psychiatry*, 160:1 (2003); and Connie Mulligan et al., 'Allelic Variation at Alcohol Metabolism Genes (*ADH1B*, *ADH1C*, *ALDH2*) and Alcohol Dependence in an American Indian Population', *Human Genetics*, 113 (2003), 325–336, 333.

[51] See, e.g., Richard Graham (ed.), *The Idea of Race in Latin America, 1870–1940* (Austin, 1990); Peter Wade, *Blackness and Race Mixture: the Dynamics of Racial Identity in Colombia* (Baltimore, 1993); Douglas Cope, *The Limits of Racial Domination: Plebeian Society in Colonial Mexico City, 1660–1720* (Madison, 1994); and Nancy Appelbaum, Anne Macpherson, and Karin Alejandra Rosemblatt (eds), *Race and Nation in Modern Latin America* (Chapel Hill, 2003).

[52] But see Jean Phinney, 'When We Talk about American Ethnic Groups, What Do We Mean?', *American Psychologist*, 31:9 (1996); Alan Templeton, 'Human Races: A Genetic and Evolutionary Perspective', *American Anthropologist*, 100:3 (1999); Saif Rathore and Harlan Krumholz, 'Race, Ethnic Group, and Clinical Research: Implications of Incorporating Race and Ethnicity into Trials Go Beyond Ethical Issues', *British Medical Journal*, 327 (2003), 7418; and Michael Montoya, 'Bioethnic Conscription: Genes, Race, and Mexicana/o Ethnicity in Diabetes Research', *Cultural Anthropology*, 22:1 (2007).

shaping *indigenous* responses to alcohol?[53] Research into whether Native Americans possess particular genetic variants assumes that the concept of 'Native American' exists outside the realm of culture and law, yet few scientific studies define this term in a robust way.

It appears that in most cases participants in medical experiments self-identify as to race or ethnicity, which can produce culturally meaningful but scientifically confusing classifications. The Peruvian anthropologist Marisol de la Cadena has described an illuminating example of the subjective nature of this process. Shortly after her arrival in the USA, she met a man whom she immediately classified as a mestizo—a man of mixed indigenous and European ancestry. He informed her that he was instead a Native American, and asked her, 'Aren't you a Peruvian Indian too?' She writes: 'I answered that I was not—and my explanation confused him. Although my skin is brown, and I have some "Indian looking" features, in Peru most people consider me to be white. Perhaps some would accept it if I self-identify as "mestiza", but everybody would laugh at me if I claimed to be "Indian".'[54] As De la Cadena makes clear, these categories are the outcome of historical processes, and have quite different meanings in different parts of the hemisphere. One wonders whether De la Cadena would be classified as Peruvian Indian, white, or perhaps 'Hispanic' if she participated in a medical study in the USA. Although in general Native Americans in the USA can claim tribal status only if they are able to demonstrate a familial link to an indigenous ancestor, the required degree of affinity varies among different tribal groups from one grandparent to one great-grandparent. It is moreover difficult to make sense of scientific studies that purport to contrast the DNA of 'Mexican Indians' with that of 'Hispanics'.[55] 'Ancestry', traceable through the presence of geographically specific genomic markers, certainly offers the possibility of constructing individual and group genetic histories, but ancestry is not synonymous with race. As a number of Brazilian studies of 'colour' and genomic

[53] For the intersection of genomics and race see Jenny Reardon, *Race to the Finish: Identity and Governance in an Age of Genomics* (Princeton, 2005); Montoya, 'Bioethnic Conscription'; Barbara Keonig, Sandra Soo-Jin Lee, and Sarah Richardson (eds), *Revisiting Race in a Genomic Age* (New Brunswick, 2008); Ian Whitmarsh and David Jones (eds), *What's the Use of Race: Modern Governance and the Biology of Difference* (Cambridge, 2010); and Peter Wade, 'Blackness, Indigeneity, Multiculturalism, and Genomics in Brazil, Colombia, and Mexico', *Journal of Latin American Studies*, 45:2 (2013).

[54] Marisol de la Cadena, 'Are Mestizos Hybrids? The Conceptual Politics of Andean Identities', *Journal of Latin American Studies*, 37:2 (2005), 261.

[55] See, e.g., Collins-Schramm et al., 'Mexican American Ancestry-Informative Markers'.

ancestry demonstrate, physical appearance alone is a poor predictor for ancestral origin.[56] In the view of some scientists, the poorly defined nature of ethnic or racial classification threatens to undermine much research into drinking patterns.[57]

It is also clear that different cultures define 'problem' drinking in different ways. Just as different understandings of moderation underpinned William Taylor's interpretation of indigenous drinking in colonial Mexico, so a comparative study of drinking patterns in Mexico City, Ibadan, and Bangalore in 1998 showed that 'thresholds for a diagnosis of alcohol dependence or addiction as defined by heavy drinkers, their family members, and health care professionals differed widely'.[58] Problem drinking is sometimes defined in absolute terms (more than a certain number of units of alcohol per day), and sometimes through more qualitative criteria such as those developed by the World Health Organization, which consider not only the quantity of alcohol ingested but also the larger patterns of consumption.[59] As the biochemist Howard Edenberg notes, this lack of uniformity in symptoms of alcoholism 'complicates genetic analyses'.[60] In other words, it is not clear whether alcohol abuse can be robustly defined in cross-cultural terms, and even assuming that it can, there is no agreement on whether Native Americans are genetically more disposed to it than anyone else.

IV

It is therefore difficult to determine whether colonial accounts of widespread indigenous drinking reveal a traumatized Amerindian population struggling to cope with the onslaught of colonialism, a vibrant and resilient indigenous

56 Flavia Parra, Roberto Amado, José Lambertucci, Jorge Rocha, Carlos Antunes, and Sérgio Pena, 'Color and Genomic Ancestry in Brazilians', *Proceedings of the National Academy of Science*, 100:1 (2003); and S. D. J. Pena, L. Bastos-Rodrigues, J. R. Pimenta and S. P. Bydlowski, 'DNA Tests Probe the Genomic Ancestry of Brazilians', *Brazilian Journal of Medical and Biological Research*, 42:10 (2009).

57 Dwight Heath, 'Uses and Misuses of the Concept of Ethnicity in Alcohol Studies: An Essay in Deconstruction', *International Journal of the Addictions*, 25:5A and 6A (1990–1); Raul Caetano, Catherine Clark, and Tammy Tam, 'Alcohol Consumption among Racial/ Ethnic Minorities', *AHRW*, 22:4 (1998), 234; and Raul Caetano, Catherine Clark, and Tammy Tam, 'Methodological Approaches for Implementing Research among Ethnic Minorities', *AHRW*, 22:4 (1998), 239.

58 Bennett et al., 'Alcoholic Beverage Consumption', 251.

59 'Diagnostic Criteria for Alcohol Abuse and Dependence', *Alcohol Alert*, 30 (October 1995).

60 Howard Edenberg, 'The Collaborative Study on the Genetics of Alcoholism: An Update', *Alcohol Research & Health*, 26:3 (2002), 216.

world that resisted the imposition of Spanish norms and persisted in its pre-conquest drinking culture, or a genetically vulnerable ethnic cohort. Between the views, on the one hand, that indigenous drinking is the result of genetics or cultural trauma and, on the other hand, that it reflects indigenous resistance, there is a space, an emptiness, somewhat equivalent to that identified by Gayatri Chakravorty Spivak in her discussion of *sati*, or widow sacrifice, in India. As Spivak notes, British imperialists presented *sati* as evidence of Hindu barbarism, whereby innocent women were cruelly sacrificed, whereas Indian nationalists celebrated it as a meaningful, autochthonous tradition supported by the women themselves. For Spivak the subaltern woman is caught in an endless 'shuttling' between the view that 'white men are saving brown women from brown men' and that 'the women actually wanted to die'. In Spivak's view, there is no opening between 'patriarchy and imperialism . . . tradition and modernization' for the voice of the subaltern woman herself.[61] The indigenous drinker, similarly, is positioned between the view that 'colonialism [or genetics] has driven the Indians to drink', and 'the Indians actually wanted to drink'. Excessive drinking is perhaps an illustration of the evils of colonialism, or perhaps a sign of the distinctive vitality of indigenous culture. Since Spivak cautions against attempting to speak for the subaltern I will, by way of conclusion, leave the 'indigenous drinker' shuttling back and forth between these interpretative poles and comment only on what the 'Indians are drunks' discourse reveals about elite understandings of the place of indigenous peoples within the larger body politic.

Early colonial elite writers tended to view indigenous drunkenness as proof of the devil's ceaseless efforts to undermine human salvation. At the same time, such views reflected very clearly the belief that native peoples could not possibly be left to their own devices, unable as they were to resist the devil's blandishments. Native peoples, in other words, were a vibrant but dangerous part of the colonial world. By the late colonial era the 'demonic' interpretation had been largely replaced with a proto-racial vision that viewed drunkenness as evidence for the backward and uncivilized nature of indigenous culture more broadly. Hispanic racial thinking tended to embed race in the ambient culture. By the late eighteenth century drunkenness was widely considered a key feature of indigenous culture. Recall the priest who insisted in 1796 that 'everyone knows the innate predisposition of Indians to drunkenness'. Early colonial concerns about the close links between drunkenness and idolatry thus gave way to anxieties about the weak minds and vulnerable

[61] Gayatri Chakravorty Spivak, 'Can the Subaltern Speak?', *Marxism and the Interpretation of Culture*, ed. Cary Nelson and Lawrence Grossberg (Houndmills, 1988), 297, 306.

bodies of the crown's indigenous subjects, who needed to be improved by state projects and strict regulation. By the mid-nineteenth century, when republicanism had replaced colonialism across the American mainland, indigenous drunkenness was viewed primarily as a bio-political issue. As an emblem of the barbarous, the drunken Indian personified the fears of nineteenth-century Spanish American elites that their nations were so inextricably mired in the indigenous as to be incapable of progress. Spanish American elites' dreams of progress were haunted by the spectres of degeneration, represented powerfully by 'backward' and 'archaic' native peoples who rejected the allure of the modern. An indigenous culture mired in alcohol prevented progress. Strong alcohol, lamented the Peruvian writer José de la Riva-Agüero in 1915, 'poisons the Indians, and produces thereby the degeneration of their race and *consequently the decadence of Peru*'.[62]

The meanings ascribed to indigenous drunkenness thus mirror the larger place of the indigenous population within the colonial or national project. Early colonial writers did not insist that indigenous drinking revealed the fundamentally obsolete or degenerate nature of indigenous culture. On the contrary, it indicated its alarming vitality and potential to challenge the colonial state. In the republican era, when scholars across the Americas united in condemning indigenous culture as an obstacle to progress and modernity, elite writers viewed drunkenness as proof of the Indian's essential obsolescence. It was a sign, to quote again the Ecuadorian scholar Pío Jaramillo, of the 'bitterness of a defeated race'. Attitudes towards indigenous drunkenness illuminate both indigenous cultures and colonial and postcolonial mentalities. Perhaps drunkenness, to mis-cite Levi Strauss, can be good to think.

[62] José de la Riva-Agüero, *Paisajes Peruanos* (Lima, 1955), 45 (my emphasis); Nancy Stepan, *'The Hour of Eugenics': Race, Gender and Nation in Latin America* (Ithaca, 1991), 75, 92–4; Michael Aronna, *'Pueblos Enfermos': The Discourse of Illness in the Turn-of-the-Century Spanish and Latin American Essay* (Chapel Hill, 1999), 182–5; and Rebecca Earle, *The Return of the Native: Indians and Mythmaking in Spanish America* (Durham, 2008).

Alcohol in the Islamic Middle East: Ambivalence and Ambiguity

Rudi Matthee

> Wine (khamr) has flowed in my veins like blood
> Learn to be dissolute; be kind—this is far better than
> To be a beast that won't drink wine and can't become a man.
> (Hafez of Shiraz (14th c.))

> Great is the difference between the Turks and the Persians, for the Turks, being by law prohibited, abstain from wine yet drink it covertly, but the Persians, now, as of old, drink openly and with excess.
> (Thomas Herbert, 1627)

This essay starts with—and builds its main argument on—a paradox. Historically, most people, and certainly Muslims, inhabiting the world where Islam spread and became the dominant faith, did not drink. This was in accordance with Islam's formal proscription of the consumption of alcohol and the draconian punishment for violators of the ban—eighty lashes; forty for women and slaves.[1] Water has always been their main beverage, women as a rule never drank, and fermented or distilled drinks were generally not readily available, least of all in the respectable public sphere. Throughout Islamic history, radical prohibition of drinking has often followed the rise to power of puritanical regimes—the North African Almoravids and Almohads in eleventh- and thirteenth-century Spain, respectively; the Wahhabis who haunted the Arabian Peninsula and Iraq in the early nineteenth century; more recently the clerics of the Islamic Republic of Iran and the Taliban in Afghanistan. Yet alcohol has always played a surprisingly important role in male elite circles in the Islamic Middle East. The very word alcohol is Arabic in origin, deriving from *al-kohl*, pulverized antimony used to darken the eye lines, and Muslim alchemists, most notably the Iranian Zakariya al-Razi (865–925; better known

[1] Felicitas Opwis, 'Shifting Legal Authority from the Ruler to the 'Ulamā for Drinking Wine during the Saljūq Period', *Der Islam*, 86 (2009), 66–7, 77–8.

 © The Past and Present Society

under his Latin name Rhazes) are credited with the invention of the process of distillation. Throughout history, Muslim rulers and their courtiers have consumed alcohol, often in huge quantities and sometimes in public view; the examples of ordinary Muslims violating their religion's ban on drinking are too numerous to count; and, while alcohol is strictly forbidden in many modern Muslim countries, quite a few, from Tunisia and Turkey to Syria, Egypt—except during Ramadan—and Indonesia, allow for its (restricted) sale and consumption.

The Islamic world is far too large and complex for generalizations to have any validity, yet one is struck by the similarities throughout its history and across the lands where it came to prevail, in the manifestations of drinking and in the ambivalent approach to alcohol, most clearly expressed in attempts to keep up the appearance of sobriety in the face of reality. The first part of this essay will discuss some of these similarities, the customs and traditions that transcend geography and time to form cultural patterns. The second part will focus on the central lands where Islam became the dominant faith after its great conquests of the seventh and eighth centuries. Within that zone I will single out two early modern states, Safavid Iran and the Ottoman Empire, with the aim of comparing and contrasting their respective drinking customs in order to identify the extent to which these conformed to traditions carried over from earlier times and to what extent these reveal new, 'early modern' consumption patterns. The third part, focusing on the nineteenth-century Ottoman state and Qajar Iran, will explore the effects on alcohol consumption resulting from the intrusion of trade-based capitalism and the concomitant adoption of western-style modernization by these countries' elites. The essay concludes with a survey of the divergent trajectories with regard to drinking taken by the two modern countries that emerged from these states, Turkey and Iran.

I

The Islamic proscription of alcohol was a gradual, almost reluctant process, one that reveals itself as relative despite its apparent absoluteness, providing loopholes, allowing for subterfuge, and leaving open the chance of having one's guilt absolved. In the Abrahamic tradition the vine and wine have been linked from the outset, and wine has been connected with drunkenness and impudence as early as the story about Noah in the Book of Genesis 9, 20–21.[2] That the early Muslims knew about alcohol is clear from the references in pre-Islamic poetry about the existence of a trade in wine, supplied by Christian and Jewish merchants to the monasteries that dotted the Arabian

[2] François Clément (ed.), *Les vins d'Orient. 4000 ans d'ivresse* (Nantes, 2008), introd., 8.

Peninsula.[3] This familiarity is also reflected in the Koran, which is ambiguous about alcohol, evincing a 'progressively negative sequence' in a series of 'discreet, evocative statements', with regard to its properties and its consumption, clearly 'in response to a particular set of human circumstances'.[4] It praises wine as God's gift and recognizes it as a source of enjoyment, but 'etherealizes' it by giving it a place in paradise. Presumably reflecting the problems Mohammad and the first few caliphs had with drunkenness among their followers, Islam's sacred text (5:90–1) ultimately condemns grape wine (*khamr*) for its effect, intoxication, which interferes with the clear-headedness needed for the proper execution of its religious commands.

There is also relief of a different kind for those who transgress. Most importantly, those who cannot resist drinking in contravention of the Holy Law can find comfort in the Islamic notion that sin can be expiated through repentance. Sin in Islam is the wilful act of turning one's back to God, which means that the act can be reversed. Drinking alcohol thus is a transgression for which atonement or a specific punishment is prescribed. Drinking is bad, but the act as such does not turn the actor into a heretic, excluding him irrevocably from the community of believers. It is heretical, rather, to consider it permissible to drink alcohol.[5] It also helps if the alcohol one consumes is manufactured by a non-Muslim, for this absolves the person who drinks at least to some extent from the intentionality or the premeditated nature of the offence.[6]

Shifting the focus from sin to shame, the imbiber is offered a place of refuge of sorts in the form of the respect Islam has always evinced for the privacy of the inner home, the sanctuary of the family and its honour. In an approach that favours procedure over substance, a strong Islamic, prophetically underwritten injunction about the impermissibility of prying into people's private lives for hidden sin—so as not to bring shame on them—has often provided some kind of legal shelter against the intrusion of the state by way of a morality police.[7] In other words, since social solidarity is an important virtue in traditional Islamic culture, as long as drinking and other proscribed activities

[3] Kathryn Kueny, *The Rhetoric of Sobriety: Wine in Early Islam* (Albany, NY, 2001), 89ff.

[4] Ibid., 66.

[5] Devin J. Stewart, *Islamic Legal Orthodoxy. Twelver Shiite Response to the Sunni Legal System* (Salt Lake City, 1998), 47.

[6] Ker Porter, *Travels in Georgia, Persia, Armenia, and Ancient Babylonia, etc. etc. during the Years, 1817, 1818, 1819, and 1820* (London, 1821–2), 347–8.

[7] Michael Cook, *Commanding Right and Forbidding Wrong in Islamic Thought* (Princeton, 2000), 481–2.

remained confined to the private sphere, the community tended to 'keep up appearances' by pretending that no infringement was taking place.

From the sixteenth century onward foreign observers have commented on the tendency among Muslims to drink to excess, linking the formal ban on drinking to heavy drinking. As the Flemish Ogier Ghiselin de Busbecq, Austrian envoy to Istanbul in the mid-sixteenth century, put it, the 'drinking of wine is regarded by the Turks as a serious crime, especially by the older men; the younger men can commit the sin with greater hope of pardon and excuse. They think, however, that the punishment which they will suffer in future life will be just as heavy whether they drink much or little, and so, if they taste wine, they drink deep'.[8] Reinhold Lubenau, who in 1587 visited Istanbul as a pharmacist attached to an Austrian mission, similarly reports how Muslim Turks, invited to his house, would burst into loud shrieking before putting the glass to their lips, in hopes that their soul might move elsewhere while they engaged in drinking, so as not to become tainted by this sin. He claimed that, since the transgression was thought to be punishable regardless of the volume of the intake, people would keep drinking until they 'collapsed on the floor'.[9] Jean Chardin, the most astute outside observer of seventeenth-century Iran, insisted that to get drunk fast was the purpose of drinking for Iranians, which is why they appreciated strong wines. Echoing Lubenau's comments, he also recounts how Iranians would recoil while drinking, treating alcohol like a medicine to be swallowed rather than enjoyed.[10]

That quick inebriation was often the point of drinking relates to the fact that alcohol in Islamic culture was not synonymous with sociability. Given its status as a forbidden substance, alcohol in a Muslim environment could never become fully integrated into the idea of good living. In the Greek symposium tradition, alcohol might enliven court sessions, and it was taken for granted as part of the lifestyle of the elite, but it remained a forbidden fruit, and thus could not escape furtive embrace amid public disavowal. Unacknowledged, alcohol in the Islamic world never became an accompaniment to food, enhancing the convivial atmosphere of the meal, the way it did in Mediterranean and Christian/European culture. As foreign visitors noted, meals in the Islamic Middle East were typically taken in silence and rather

[8] Ogier Ghiselin de Busbecq, *The Turkish Letters of Ogier Ghiselin de Busbecq*, trans. Edward Seymour Forster (Oxford, 1927), 9–10.

[9] Reinhold Lubenau, *Beschreibung der Reisen des Reinhold Lubenau*, ed. W. Sahm, 2 vols. (Königsberg, 1914, repr. Frankfurt a/M, 1995), 1, 260.

[10] Jean Chardin, *Voyages du chevalier Chardin en Perse et en autres lieux de l'Orient*, ed. L. Langlès, 10 vols. and atlas (Paris, 1810–11), III, 218; IV, 69–70.

quickly, to be concluded with a glass of water. Only afterwards would the (male) host and his guests engage in discussion—over coffee or tea and with the enjoyment of the water pipe, and often in a different room.[11]

Class played a role as well in the consumption of alcohol. Those who drank in the Middle East hailed predominantly from the high end of the social spectrum. Piousness and with it, abstemiousness, was most prevalent among the middling classes. The upper classes drank from a sense of entitlement, enjoying alcohol as a 'right', one of the privileges traditionally granted to the elite, *khass*, in Islamic lands. Abstention was something for commoners, the *'avvam*, unable to restrain themselves. The lower classes tended to use other drugs, especially opium—which is not explicitly condemned in either the Koran or the Prophetic Traditions—to while away boredom, to find oblivion from miserable lives and, above all, as a form of self-medication. To the extent that commoners drank it was part of a subculture of subterfuge and furtiveness, with people sneaking off to taverns located in back alleys in the non-Muslim quarters of town, run by Jews, Armenians, or Greeks. Taverns in Islamic lands remained disreputable, associated with the seamy side of life, and the tavern owner occupied 'roughly the same place on the social scale as the prostitute, the overt homosexual, and the itinerant entertainer'.[12] In these conditions drinking remained hidden, 'invisible', even though it took place in 'full view'. Drinking, after all, was common in court circles and among the elite, and Muslims frequented taverns. But since alcohol was formally outlawed, it could not be linked to reality, so that wine became a metaphor for the ardent feelings of the lover for the beloved in the imaginary world of (mystical) poetry. Unlike coffee, religiously controversial for being stimulating and distracting, alcohol could never become the subject of a public discourse, just as the tavern, operating in the shadows, could never become part of a quasi-public sphere, unlike the often open and airy coffee house, a communal extension of the private home and the basis for political action.

II

In the Arabian Peninsula, where wine was hardly indigenous, Islam's formal ban on alcohol was of little consequence. Elsewhere, the spread of new faith hardly interrupted a long tradition of alcohol consumption. This is certainly true for two vast areas that were initially conquered and that were also among

[11] See Hélène Desmet-Grégoire, *Cuisine et modernité: Á travers l'exemple de la Turquie. La migration des saisons* (Istanbul, 2012), 137–8.

[12] Ralph Hattox, *Coffee and Coffeehouses. The Origins of a Social Beverage in the Medieval Near East* (Seattle, 1985), 78.

the world's oldest wine-growing and wine-drinking cultures—the Mediterranean basin and 'greater Iran', encompassing Mesopotamia, the Iranian plateau, the Caucasus, as well as Central Asia as far as the Oxus (Amu Darya) River. The Mediterranean tradition of viniculture is so well known as not to need any elaboration, yet the world's earliest wine culture, going back some 9,000 years, has been located rather farther to the east, in the eastern Taurus, the Caucasus, and the northern Zagros Mountains of Iran.[13] Pre-Islamic Mesopotamia was the land of wine-soaked royal banquets, of alcohol-induced divination, and of prophecy inspired by intoxicating drinks.[14] In Zoroastrianism, wine symbolized liquid gold and the flowing fire of the radiant sun, and as such had a ritual function, being part of a libation ritual, in which it substituted for blood. Ancient and late antique Iranian elite history could be written as the history of *razm va bazm* (fighting and feasting), with wine at the centre.

As a result, many (newly converted) Muslims continued to consume alcohol, and especially wine, with an alacrity barely dimmed by a guilty conscience. Pre-Islamic poets had drawn their inspiration from wine, and the *khamriyya*, a form of Bacchic poetry, survived the Islamic proscription to thrive in the eighth-century Omayyad state.[15] Wine also retained the various medical benefits ascribed to it by physicians in pre-Islamic times.[16] Drinking was ubiquitous at the secular-minded Abbasid court of Baghdad, to the point where the caliph carousing with his boon companions came to represent a topos.[17] Then, as later, anti-alcohol measures tended to target public consumption, seeking to avoid public scandal in the form of disturbances and brawls, rather than private drinking. The authorities typically tolerated semi-public drinking, and only curbed it when it overstepped its implicitly accepted boundaries of privacy and led to urban unrest. Violators were typically fined or, rather rarely, flogged or paraded in public.[18]

[13] Patrick McGovern, *Uncorking the Past: The Quest for Wine, Beer, and Other Alcoholic Beverages* (Berkeley, 2009), 82.

[14] Jean Bottéro, 'Boisson, banquet, et vie sociale'. In L. Milano (ed.), *Drinking in Ancient Societies: History and Culture in the Ancient Near East* (Padua, 1994), 1–13.

[15] Edgar Weber, 'Le vin dans la tradition arabo-musulmane', in Clément (ed.), *Les vins d'Orient*, 54–83.

[16] See P. A. Norrie, 'The History of Wine as a Medicine', in Merton Sandler and Roger Pinder (eds), *Wine. A Scientific Exploration* (London and New York, 2003), 21–55, esp. 35–6.

[17] Ibid., 64.

[18] Christiane Lange, *Justice, Punishment, and the Medieval Muslim Imagination* (Cambridge, 2008), 56, 82, 185, 227.

From Andalusia in the far west to Khorasan on the eastern marches of the Islamic empire, wine drinking flourished in the classical age of Islam. Spain, with a climate and soil that allow the grape to grow almost everywhere, had a viticulture going back to the sixth century BCE.[19] The Omayyad rulers of Spain, including the most famous one, ʻAbd Al-Rahman III (r. 912–61), were known for their fondness of wine. The eleventh-century king of Grenada, Badis, remained in his palace, engaged in drinking, for such a long time that people thought he had died. And the last of the so-called Party Kings of Seville (in reference to their divisiveness, not their lifestyle) Muhammad ibn ʻAbbad al-Muʻtamid (r. 1069–91), ruler as well as poet, sought oblivion in wine as the invading Almoravids stood at the gates of his city.[20] In North Africa Islam managed to erase virtually all traces of Christianity, yet proved unable to eradicate a long-standing tradition of viniculture and viticulture. Medieval Arab authors describing the region mention the production of wine made of dates, of honey and dry raisins. As elsewhere, Jews were often the ones who engaged in the trade of all kinds of fermented drinks.[21]

In the eastern half of the empire, encompassing modern Iran and Afghanistan, matters were little different. The rulers of the Saffarid and Samanid dynasties, the first to seek autonomy from their Abbasid overlords, are known for the gusto with which they and their entourage indulged in wine-drinking.[22] Modern Persian poetry, which originated at the courts of these rulers, is replete with vivid references to wine bibbing, its rituals and its symbols. Mystical (Sufi) poetry, much of it written in Persian as well, is even more drenched in wine. Its wine-related metaphors, most powerfully expressed by Hafez of Shiraz, include the handsome cupbearer as the object of desire, the refraction of the ruby red wine in the goblet as a symbol of divine radiance, the wine shop, *meykhaneh*, standing for the ʻrealm of angelsʼ, and the libertine image of the free-spirited Sufi drunk who spills wine on the payer mat to show his contempt for clerical bigotry and hypocrisy. It is not always easy to distinguish between the metaphorical use of wine and references to the real thing, yet often ʻthe literal meaning seems to be the only plausible oneʼ.[23]

[19] François Clément, ʻVignes et vins dans l'Espagne musulmaneʼ, in Clément (ed.), *Les vins d'Orient*, 87.

[20] Heine, *Weinstudien*, 127.

[21] Hildebert Isnard, *La vigne en Algérie. Étude géographique*, 2 vols (Paris, 1947), I, 261–2, 265.

[22] Ehsan Yarshater, ʻThe Theme of Wine-Drinking and the Concept of the Beloved in Early Persian Poetryʼ, *Studia Islamica* 13 (1960), 43.

[23] Dick Davis, ʻWine and Persian Poetryʼ, in Najmieh Batmangelij, *From Persia to Napa. Wine at the Persian Table* (Washington DC, 2006), 62.

The many hallucinatory images of swaying rocks and undulating landscapes in Persian miniatures depicting Sufis certainly point in that direction.[24] And although some poets hint at a sense of unease endorsing a practice at variance with the Islamic law, there is in fact little suggestion in any of their works that wine is intrinsically sinful.[25] The bon viveur image of the cultured courtier included not just the actual quaffing of wine, but presupposed knowledge about when and how to serve and consume it, and, of course, how to come to terms with the fact that it is formally forbidden in Islam. All this is reflected in the medieval Persianate *Adab* and *Nasihat*, Mirror for Princes literature, which includes advice involving hospitality and etiquette with regard to royal drinking parties in its guidelines for proper conduct.[26]

III

The rulers of the dynasties that came to rule the Middle East from the tenth century were either ethnic Turks or Mongols hailing from the steppes of Central Asia. Both groups were known for their bibulousness—albeit mostly involving *kumiss*, fermented mare's milk, in the case of the Mongols.[27] Their drinking patterns, combined with the Islamic tradition already in place, were carried over into Safavid Iran, named after the dynasty, the Safavids, which ruled the country between 1501 and 1722, and to a lesser extent, the Ottoman Empire, which expanded from its fourteenth-century western Anatolian origins to become the largest, most powerful and longest-lasting Muslim state in the early modern period.

The early Safavids exemplify a type of pre-modern elite drinking combining ancient pre-Islamic traditions with the customs of the Central Asian steppes and, following the introduction of numerous Georgians and Armenians as slave soldiers and bureaucrats, the rites and rituals of Christianity. The head of a wild tribal warrior band, revered by his followers as an incarnation of the divine, and espousing a form of Twelve Shiʿism suffused with pre-Islamic semi-pagan customs and rituals, the first Safavid shah, Shah Ismaʿil (r. 1501–24), drank copiously, in public, banquet-style,

[24] See Nina Ergin, 'Rock Faces: Opium and Wine. Speculations on the Original Viewing Context of Persian Manuscripts', *Der Islam* 90:1 (2013), 65–99.

[25] Davis, 'Wine and Persian Poetry', 59.

[26] See Kay Kavus ibn Iskandar ibn Qabus, *A Mirror for Princes. The Qābūs nāma*, trans. Reuben Levy (New York, 1951), 57–60; and Nizam al-Mulk, *The Book of Government or Rules for Kings. The Siyar al-Muluk or Siyasat-nama*, trans. Hubert Darke (Richmond, Surrey, 1960, repr. 2002), 119.

[27] For Mongol drinking, see Antti Ruotsala, *Europeans and Mongols in the Middle of the Thirteenth Century. Encountering the Other* (Helsinki, 2001), 110–29.

surrounded by his warriors, who feasted as hard as they fought—before and after going into battle. Paradoxically, the shah's hard drinking did nothing to detract from his aura, indeed augmented it. By drinking in public Isma'il projected the image of a ruler who inhabited his own moral universe, beyond the strictures of religion, and drinking copiously marked him as a tribal chief, a big man able to hold his liquor.[28]

The dynasty lost some of its divine aura with the terrible defeat Shah Isma'il suffered against the Ottomans on the battlefield of Chalderan in 1514. Turning inward, his successor, Shah Tahmasb (r. 1524–76), sought salvation through repentance, and abstained from intoxicating substances for life. Yet most shahs who came after him drank again, and some drank in excess. With the exception of Shah Isma'il all Safavid shahs declared bans on drinking at one point or another during their reign. At the same time, most continued to tipple themselves, and several are known, or are likely, to have died from overconsumption. Many high officials and even some high-ranking clerics appear to have been heavy drinkers as well. Shah 'Abbas I (r. 1587–1629), the greatest of the Safavid kings, was an exception for drinking in moderation, surrounded by his courtiers and quite often foreign guests, who were allowed to quaff from his own gold goblet. Shah 'Abbas was also heir to a long tradition of Iranian rulers, going all the way back to the Achaemenids, who used alcohol to loosen lips among his courtiers.[29]

Shah 'Abbas's grandson and successor, Safi I (r. 1629–42) declared a ban on alcohol upon coming to power. Yet, advised by his physicians to treat a cold that his opium use had caused with alcohol, he soon succumbed to hard drinking, to die from dipsomania in 1642.[30] His successor, Shah 'Abbas II, proclaimed a ban on drinking when he acceded to the throne at the tender age of nine in 1642.[31] Seven years later, still in his teens, he took up the cup during a triumphant return from a campaign that had gained him mastery over Qandahar. The chronicler who narrates the events justifies the shah's

[28] For more on alcohol in the Safavid period and, in general, in Iranian history, see Rudi Matthee, *The Pursuit of Pleasure; Drugs and Stimulants in Iranian History, 1500–1900* (Princeton, 2005), chs. 2, 3, and 6; and Rudi Matthee, 'The Ambiguities of Wine in Iranian History: Between Excess and Abstention', in Florian Schwarz, Ralph Kauz, and Bert Fragner (eds), *Wine in Iranian History* (Vienna, 2014), 1–30.

[29] Pietro della Valle, *Viaggi di Pietro della Valle*, 2 vols, ed. Gancia (Brighton, 1845), I, 668.

[30] Abu'l Mafakher b. Fazl Allah al-Hoseyni Savaneh-negar Tafreshi, *Tarikh-e Shah Safi*, ed. Mohsen Bahramnezhad (Tehran, 1388/2010), 22–3; and Matthee, *The Pursuit of Pleasure*, 52–3.

[31] J.-B. Tavernier, *Les six voyages de Jean Baptiste Tavernier en Turquie, en Perse et en Indes* (Paris, 1678), 579; Fasa'i, *Farsnameh-ye Naseri*, 2 vols paginated as one (Tehran, 1367/1988), 477.

change of heart by referring to an old adage also proffered in the Mirror of Princes literature, according to which God and the law both permit happiness and pleasure, especially in youth. In this reasoning, the shah in particular enjoys the right to unbounded pleasure as long as he does not neglect his realm and his subjects.[32] Like his great grandfather, Shah 'Abbas I, Shah 'Abbas II showed a remarkable bonhomie toward his foreign guests, inviting them to his frequent drinking sessions.[33] The relaxed mood was interrupted when in 1653 the sheikh al-islam of Isfahan urged the shah to foreswear wine as a way to prevent the Mughals from retaking Qandahar. In customary fashion, the ban became moot within a year; life returned to its normal state of ambiguity, and the shah resumed his previous lifestyle, drinking lustily until his death in 1666.[34]

Exemplifying the shift the Safavid state had undergone in the century and a half since its inception—from tribal dispensation to agrarian-based urban-centred polity—the last two shahs of the dynasty, Soleyman (r. 1666–94) and Soltan Hoseyn (r. 1694–1722), no longer ruled as warrior kings, patrolling their realm and engaged in endless campaigns. Instead, they reigned as stationary monarchs, ensconced in their palace, where they engaged in 'lust and play', as the Persian sources call it. They, too, issued bans on the consumption of alcohol. Indeed, the inauguration ceremony of the exceedingly pious Soltan Hoseyn included a ban on frivolous pastimes such as kite-flying, on the public appearance of women unaccompanied by male relatives, and on the use of intoxicants. Six thousand bottles of wine were taken from the royal cellar and demonstratively poured out on Isfahan's main square. Yet, the proscription lapsed less than two years after the shah's accession, removed at the behest of his great-aunt who, herself addicted, persuaded the king to take up the bottle.[35]

The Ottoman Empire was different. True to their semi-nomadic background, its early rulers were ambulant warriors, too. Yet with the conquest of Constantinople in 1453, Ottoman rulers prematurely came to preside over an urban-based stationary court. Henceforth the sultan reigned from the privacy of the Topkapı palace, and his drinking thus remained hidden from view. Some sultans were notorious tipplers; others are known to have been teetotallers. Süleyman the Magnificent (r. 1520–66), in Busbecq's words, lived modestly and was never seduced by wine (or by pederasty, a common

[32] Mohammad-Yusof Valeh Esfahani, *Khold-e barin. Iran dar zaman-e Shah Safi wa Shah 'Abbas-devvom*, ed. M. Naseri (Tehran, 1380/2001), 480.

[33] Tavernier, *Les six voyages*, 544.

[34] Matthee, *The Pursuit of Pleasure*, 85–90.

[35] Ibid., 92–4.

indulgence in the Ottoman Empire as much as in Iran).[36] The German chaplain Franciscus de Billerberg (Franz Billerbeck), who spent time in Istanbul in the 1580s, called Murad III (r. 1574–95) a teetotaller as well.[37] He also contradicts Busbecq, who attributed the good order in the sultan's military to an absence of intoxicating drinks in the regular army.[38] The troops of Murad's father, Selim II (r. 1566–74), De Billerberg insists, could not be 'compelled to abstain from wine'.[39] Indeed, alcohol consumption seems to have been rife among the Ottoman soldiery, most notably in the ranks of the notoriously unruly Janissaries.[40]

Other than consumption by dervishes, about which we have limited information, and with the exception of conditions in the Balkans and Greece, the use of alcohol in the Ottoman Empire among civilians was largely confined to the cities. In the Balkans the old tradition of wine drinking continued with little noticeable abatement, even in the countryside, with the interesting twist that Muslims in Bosnia seem to have obeyed the wine prohibition prescribed by the Sharia while considering raki, an anise-flavoured spirit distilled from grapes, to be permitted by Islam. Sarajevo was home to twenty-one taverns in the second half of the eighteenth century.[41]

But even in urban centres, the nature of drinking was determined by the type of inhabitants. The Ottoman Empire was fundamentally different from Iran in that a large percentage of its originally Christian population never converted to Islam. This was particularly true in the Balkans and on Aegean islands such as Naxos and Mytilini (Lesbos) and Chios, which supplied most of the wine consumed in Ottoman lands, but also in the port cities such as Istanbul and Izmir. Since dhimmis were officially exempt from liquor laws, alcohol might be obtained wherever they dwelled. Hence taverns, *meyhanehs*, watering holes tucked away in side alleys and run by indigenous Greeks, Armenians, or Jews, were predominantly found in port cities and invariably located in the Christian part of town.[42] In 1829 all of the 554 taverns in

[36] Busbecq, *The Turkish Letters.*

[37] Franciscus de Billerberg, *[Most Rare and Straunge Discourses, of Amurathe the Turkish Emperor that now is with the Warres betweene Him and the Persians: The Turkish Triumph, Lately Had at Constantinople.] (1584)* (London?, 1584), unpag. (2).

[38] Metin And, *Istanbul in the 16th Century. The City. The Palace, Daily Life* (Istanbul, 1994), 187.

[39] De Billerberg, [*Most Rare and Straunge Discourses*], unpag. (2).

[40] See James Grehan, *Everyday Life and Consumer Culture in 18th-Century Damascus* (Seattle, 2007), 134.

[41] Jelena Mrgić, 'Wine or *Raki*—The Interplay of Climate and Society in Early Modern Ottoman Bosnia', *Environment and History*, 17 (2011), 633.

[42] Busbecq, *The Turkish Letters*, 19.

Istanbul were run by non-Muslims.[43] The availability of wine and other pleasures gave the city's Christian quarters across the Golden Horn, Galata and, later, Pera, an image of 'otherness', eliciting a reaction part abhorrence part envy from Ottoman commentators.[44] In eighteenth-century Smyrna (modern Izmir) the non-Muslim community kept its taverns 'open all Hours, Day and Night'.[45] In Aleppo greater restrictions applied. There, Ottoman officials and Janissaries were known tipplers, and drinking by Sufis seeking ecstasy was generally tolerated, but, beyond private dwellings, the consumption of alcohol was confined to the *Han al-gümrük*, the 'customs hostel' where (foreign) merchants were lodged.[46] In nineteenth-century Egypt, the Coptic population distilled arak from dates, while local Greeks produced *tafia*, a sweet beverage of poor quality made with molasses and sugar cane.[47] Boza, a beer-like drink made of fermented millet and of low alcoholic content, was consumed in Egypt, too, as it was elsewhere in the Ottoman Empire, mostly by members of the lower classes whiling away time in *bozahanehs*, establishments of a distinctly disreputable fame.[48]

Muslims would only frequent these establishments stealthily, fearful of the punishment that awaited those who were caught. Meanwhile most people, Muslims and the 'People of the Book' alike, drank in the privacy of their homes. In seventeenth-century Aleppo, people, Muslims as well as Jews and Christians, would buy enormous amounts of grapes, to turn these into wine at home.[49] As in Iran, Ottoman authorities periodically issued bans on alcohol consumption while turning a blind eye to Christian drinking, or indeed to the

[43] François Georgeon, 'Ottomans and Drinkers: The Consumption of Alcohol in Istanbul in the Nineteenth Century', in Eugene Rogan (ed.), *Outside In: On the Margins of the Modern Middle East* (London and New York, 2002), 12.

[44] Edhem Eldem, 'Istanbul: From Imperial to Peripheralized Capital', in Edhem Eldem, Daniel Goffman, and Bruce Masters (eds), *The Ottoman City between East and West. Aleppo, Izmir, and Istanbul* (Cambridge, 1999), 150.

[45] Daniel Goffman, 'Izmir: From Village to Colonial Port City', in Eldem, Goffman, and Masters (eds), *The Ottoman City*, 94, quoting the French botanist Joseph Pitton de Tournefort.

[46] Grehan, *Everyday Life and Consumer Culture*, 134; and James Mather, *Pashas. Traders and Travellers in the Islamic World* (New Haven and London, 2009), 78.

[47] Jean-Jacques Luth, *La vie quotidienne en Égypte au temps des Khédives* (Paris, 1998), 180.

[48] Edward Lane, *The Manners and Customs of the Modern Egyptians* (New York, 1908; repr. 1966), 96; Ebru Boyar and Kate Fleet, *A Social History of Ottoman Istanbul* (Cambridge, 2010), 189.

[49] Laurent d'Arvieux, 'Mémoires du Chevalier d'Arvieux', in Hussein I. El-Mudarris and Oliver Salmon (eds), *Le consulat de France à Alep au XVIIe siècle* (Damascus, 2009), 344.

boozing of the Janissaries, taking bribes to allow the latter to indulge.[50] Most sultans proscribed alcohol and, with it, controversial consumables such as coffee and tobacco at one point or another during their reign, whether upon acceding to the throne, or in order to propitiate the heavens during natural disaster or on the eve of a military campaign, motivated by religious fervour, pressured by the ulama, mindful of the approach of old age and the reckoning in the hereafter, or, simply seeking to maintain public order. Süleyman thus forbade the public sale of wine in the 1540s, making it difficult even for non-Muslims to obtain any.[51] Similar bans were issued by his successors, Selim II (1566–74), Murad III (1574–95), Mehmed III (r. 1595–1603), Ahmed I (r. 1603–17), and Murad IV (1623–40). The latter, an alcoholic himself, was particularly severe in his reaction to public drinking, killing violators encountered during incognito nocturnal outings with his own hand. The ban on drinking issued during his reign was part of a larger offensive known as the Kadızadeli movement. Named after Kadızade Mehmed (1582–1635), a preacher from the provinces who in 1631 rose to become the highest religious state official, the Kadızadeli movement long after its founder's death continued to exert pressure on the state to act against improper practices associated with its main target, Sufism, not just drinking but smoking and music-making as well. In 1662, following a terrible fire in Istanbul and an outbreak of pestilence, disasters that the ulama blamed on unislamic practices, the sale of wine was prohibited within the walls of Istanbul, comprising the Muslim quarter of the city. Eight years later, the ban was tightened by being extended, first to any neighbourhood that housed a mosque, and next to private use even among non-Muslims.[52] Naturally, such bans proved unenforceable, and soon wine-drinking and selling resumed.

The frequency and sequential nature of these decrees indeed suggest that they were largely incantatory. The ban Sultan Selim III (r. 1789–1808) decreed upon his accession to power in 1789 foundered in the face of creative circumvention—with Muslim males disguised as non-Muslim women sneaking drinks into their homes—but failed above all for economic reasons. The people of the Aegean islands, deprived of income, filed numerous petitions protesting their loss of livelihood. Most important was the loss in much

50 And, *Istanbul in the 16th Century*, 188; Boyar and Fleet, *A Social History of Istanbul*, 195.

51 Özlem Kumrular, 'The Role of Wine in Ottoman Society. A Collective Vice: Restrictions and Disobedience to the Laws', in Özlem Kumrular, *The Ottoman World, Europe and the Mediterranean* (Istanbul, 2012), 188; and Suraiya Faroqhi, *Subjects of the Sultan: Culture and Daily Life in the Ottoman Empire* (London and New York, 2000), 215.

52 Madeline C. Zilfi, *The Politics of Piety: The Ottoman Ulema in the Postclassical Age (1600–1800)* (Minneapolis, 1988), 129ff.

needed state revenue. Spirits taxes were a problematic issue, for to impose them was to acknowledge, indeed, encourage the use of alcohol, which is why they were abolished soon after being introduced in the seventeenth century. Drinking proved to be too lucrative a source of income for the state, though, and by the late eighteenth century the (reinstated) tax on alcoholic beverages was a major source of revenue for the Ottoman state. Pragmatism, in other words, tended to prevail: people, and certainly dhimmis, were left alone in their drinking as long the public order was not disturbed, and rulers often effectively stimulated consumption for the tax revenue it yielded, even if they would never advertise this inclination.[53]

IV

Alcohol and the venues where it was consumed could never be agents of change in the Islamic world. Taverns fundamentally differed from coffeehouses because wine was fundamentally different from coffee (and tobacco), both of which conquered the world long after the emergence of Islam. When they were first introduced, coffee and tobacco sparked lively debates about their commensurability with religious norms and values, in Islam as much as in Christianity. Eighteenth-century European coffeehouses (and taverns), venues where commercial transactions took place and news was collected and distributed, were incubators of capitalism and modern politics. Over time, coffeehouses in the Middle East played a similar 'modernizing' role in the sense that they contributed to the creation of a cultural public sphere separate from the mosque.[54] Taverns, however, never assumed that function, could not assume that function. They 'had no chance to nourish their own distinct social life', for their raison d'être, drinking, invited just denial and repression, or at most connivance.[55]

53 Cengiz Kirli, "The Struggle over Space: Coffeehouses of Ottoman Istanbul, 1780–1845' (Ph.D. dissertation, State University of New York at Binghamton, 2000), 58–62.

54 For the Ottoman case, see, besides Kirli, "The Struggle over Space'; Ilay Örs, 'Coffeehouses, Cosmopolitanism, and Pluralizing Modernity in Istanbul,' *Journal of Mediterranean Studies*, 12 (2002), 119–45; Selam Akyazici Özkoçak, 'Coffeehouses: Rethinking the Public and Private in Early Modern Istanbul', *Journal of Urban History* 33 (2007), 965–86; and, arguing that the Ottoman coffeehouse was a 'heterotopic' space rather than a public venue conforming to Habermas's model, Alan Mikhail, 'The Heart's Desire: Gender, Urban Space, and the Ottoman Coffee House', in Dana Sajdi (ed.), *Ottoman Tulips, Ottoman Coffee. Leisure and Lifestyle in the Eighteenth Century* (London, 2007), 133–70.

55 James Grehan, 'Smoking and "Early Modern" Sociability: The Great Tobacco Debate in the Ottoman Middle East (Seventeenth and Eighteenth Centuries)', *American Historical Review*, 111 (2006), 1375.

This does not mean that the onset of the modern age in the form of a creeping growth of European influence on the lifestyle of the elite classes did not help change drinking practices in the nineteenth-century Ottoman Empire and in Qajar Iran; it did—albeit in different ways.

As elsewhere in the Muslim world, in the Ottoman Empire water remained the customary drink of the Anatolian heartland, and any changes that occurred in consumption patterns left most parts of the empire, especially Arabia, totally unaffected. The availability of alcohol in port cities such as Istanbul, Alexandria, and Izmir increased with the growth of the expatriate European population in the nineteenth century. Expanding trade relations and the signing of commercial treaties with European powers brought in new western drinks, such as rum and champagne, enabling non-Ottoman subjects to open up taverns as well. The modernizing Sultan Mahmud II (r. 1808–39) set the tone for more open elite consumption of alcoholic beverages. Robert Walsh, Irish chaplain to the British embassy in Istanbul in 1820–27, observed how under this ruler the former curtailing practices had become 'restrained', and how 'the sultan himself, though formerly a very temperate man, [had] adopted the use of wine as one of the European customs to which he has made such approximations'. He called Mahmud 'particularly fond of champagne', adding that a bottle was 'set beside him every day at dinner', and noted that Ottoman officials 'drank as freely as any of the company' during receptions given by European ambassadors, always preferring a large goblet and never mixing their drinks with water.[56] A preference for European spirits thus became a marker of modernity for the upper classes taking their cue from the palace. Mahmud II's successor, Sultan Abdulmecid (r. 1839–61), a 'gentle sybarite', would visit representatives of the Christian community of Izmir, occasions where alcohol was served in a semi-public fashion, and was sometimes too drunk to stay on his horse.[57] It was mostly French wines, especially Bordeaux, which gained some popularity in the late nineteenth century, even if its clientele was mostly limited to foreign residents and rich Ottoman citizens—who were said not to like French wine and only to put it on the tables to show off their sophistication.[58] Wine, meanwhile, never caught on in the Turkish heartland—despite the fact that at the turn of the twentieth century

[56] Robert Walsh, *Residence at Constantinople during the Period including the Commencement, Progress, and Termination of the Greek and Turkish Revolutions*, 2 vols (London, 1836), vol. 2, 275–6.

[57] Philip Mansel, *Levant: Splendour and Catastrophe on the Mediterranean* (New Haven and London, 2011), 54, 168.

[58] Ibid.; and Yavuz Köse, *Westlicher Konsum am Bosporus: Warenhäuser, Nestlé & Co. im späten Osmanischen Reich (1855–1923)* (Munich, 2010), 164–5.

the Ottoman sheikh al-islam declared it legal for Muslims to consume it if they thought it beneficial for their health.[59] Locally produced brands were (and are) mediocre, especially the white variety—Istanbul's francophone Bulletin of the Chamber of Commerce in 1902 called it 'simplement horrible'—and were mainly consumed by Greeks.[60]

Beer, first introduced by German immigrants in the 1830s, made inroads from the middle of the nineteenth century, first in Izmir and later in Istanbul.[61] Izmir was home to two breweries by the 1860s. By the turn of the century, beer had become the second most favoured alcoholic drink in Ottomans lands—after raki. Izmir especially, the most Levantine of Ottoman cities, by then had developed a sophisticated drinking culture, with many brasseries and beer gardens that encountered little opposition, in part because there was no religious stigma attached to beer.[62] In Istanbul matters appear to have been less relaxed. Initially, the beer houses of Pera, small, unregulated and ephemeral, catered mostly to travellers, expatriates, and sailors. In the 1890s, drinking moved to the district near Taksim Square, which became the centre of a newly developing middle class leisure culture, with brasseries, cafés chantants, and casinos run by Greeks crowding out the traditional *meyhanes* and *şaraphanes*.

By far the most popular alcoholic drink became mastik, distilled with anis, and especially raki, mastic without the resin. Imported from Chios, raki became a popular aperitif in the late nineteenth century—consumed by everyone, Christians, Jews and, above all, it was said, by Muslims. Taken with mezze, light snacks that increased thirst and helped digest the alcohol, raki at the turn of the twentieth century became known as Turkey's national drink.[63] In 1903, the annual consumption in Istanbul alone was estimated at 37,000 hectolitres.[64]

Beer, mostly consumed in a solitary rather than a sociable ambiance, long remained associated with foreignness and superficial modernization—especially in the last days of the Ottoman Empire, as the Young Turk

[59] *Revue Commerciale du Levant. Bulletin Mensuel de la Chambre de Commerce Française de Constantinople*, 261, 'Vins et spiritueux' (31 Dec. 1908), 807 and 322–7, 'Vins et spiritueux' (1914, first semester), 83.

[60] *Revue Commerciale du Levant*, 261, 'Vins et spiritueux' (31 Dec. 1908), 808.

[61] Malte Furhman, 'Beer, the Drink of a Changing World. Beer Consumption and Production on the Shores of the Aegean in the 19th Century', *Turcica*, 45 (2013, forthcoming 2014); quoting Anna Forneris, *Schicksale und Erelebnisse einer Kärntnerin während ihrer Reisen in verschieden Ländern* (Laibach, 1849; repr. Klagenfurt, 1985), 56–64.

[62] Fuhrman, 'Beer, the Drink of a Changing World'; and *Revue Commerciale du Levant*, 322–7, 'Vins et spiritueux' (1914, 1st semester), 96.

[63] *Revue Commerciale du Levant*, 322–7, 78.

[64] *Revue Commerciale du Levant*, 196–201, 'Raki et apéritifs' (1903, 2nd semester), 119.

government came to emphasize patriotism. Raki, by contrast, was to gain a status as indigenous, more authentic, 'patriotically accepted'. Raki also won out over imported and increasingly popular fare such as cognac (and knock-off substitutes), either because it was cheaper or because it allowed Muslims to circumvent the Koranic prohibition, which did not explicitly target a drink of relatively recent vintage like raki.[65] This beer–raki controversy gained in poignancy during the First Balkan War, and Ataturk, a life-long raki aficionado, following the Turkish capture of Smyrna in 1922 famously ordered a raki upon entering the city.[66]

These developments remained confined to port cities, including Salonica and Beirut. Even so, there was clerical opposition to the relaxation of the strictures on drinking in public, and the imposition of a uniform spirits tax in the Tanzimat period. Such resistance seems to have quieted in the later part of the century, and especially with the onset of the Public Debt Administration, which made taxes, including the excise on alcohol, a matter of paying debt, lending it an aura of legitimacy. Henceforth, the authorities navigated an ambivalent course between licensing and wariness.[67]

Nineteenth-century Iran underwent various changes in its drinking culture as well. Some of these were similar in nature, even if they typically occurred later than in the better connected western Ottoman lands; others were different, reflecting different circumstances. Farther away from European influence, with a much smaller non-Muslim population, and without any major cosmopolitan ports, the country's relationship with alcohol had never been mediated by large numbers of Christians or European expatriates. In contrast to the Ottoman state, which expanded its military and administrative reach throughout the nineteenth century, the Qajar state was rather weak. Emerging as a tribal confederation in the late eighteenth century, Iran's rulers were perennially challenged by defiant tribes and obstreperous clerics. The latter especially had gained in power ever since the late Safavid period, taking advantage of the turmoil of the eighteenth century to take on the role of

[65] Köse, *Westlicher Konsum am Bosporus*, 164–5; Georgeon, 'Ottomans and Drinkers', 16–18; and Fuhrman, 'Beer, the Drink of a Changing World'.

[66] Mansell, *Levant*, 214; Giles Milton, *Paradise Lost: Smyrna 1922. The Destruction of a Christian City in the Islamic World* (New York, 2008), 284.

[67] Stanford Shaw, 'The Nineteenth-Century Ottoman Tax Reforms and Revenue System', *International Journal of Middle East Studies*, 6 (1975), 442–3; Köse, *Westlicher Konsum am Bosporus*, 151, and 170; and Fuhrmann, 'Beer, the Drink of a Changing World'. As late as 1903 the Ottoman authorities outlawed the consumption of alcohol for Muslims, causing the consumption of raki to drop by 40 per cent. See *Revue Commerciale du Levant*, 196–201, 'Raki et apéritifs' (1903, 2nd semester), 126.

the sole defenders of a rudderless population fleeced by a succession of rapacious rulers. Most importantly, the Qajars lacked the religious legitimacy of the Safavids, who had turned Iran into a Shiʿi country, or, for that matter of the Ottomans who, ruling over Mecca and Medina, boasted the title of protectors of Islam's two holy shrines.

As a result the Qajars, in order to establish their religious credentials, adopted sobriety or, at least, moved their drinking into the inner palace. Some, such as Mohammad Shah (r. 1834–48), may even have been teetotallers. In a reflection of how far Iranian kingship had moved away from the open-air bacchanals of the Safavids, Naser al-Din Shah, the longest ruling Qajar monarch (1848–96), liked to drink a glass or two of Bordeaux for dinner or, to calm his nerves, in anticipation of public executions.[68] By then, a public ceremony organized by the palace which included the distribution of soup had long replaced the raucous drinking fest of the Safavid Qizilbash.

This does not mean that the Qajar elite stopped boozing. Indeed, there is ample evidence that the ruling classes, especially in rural and tribal areas like Kurdistan and Khorasan, continued to drink with abandon.[69] Much of this was done in traditional fashion. Ritter von Riederer, an Austrian adviser who spent time in Iran in the 1870s, noted that an Iranian would observe religious rules as long as others watched him but do whatever appeared to him as comfortable and pleasurable as soon as he was in the privacy of his home. Drinking in private was among these activities. The state, Ritter von Riederer added, followed time-honoured conventions by punishing only those drunks who caused a public nuisance, and never bothered to intervene with indoor drinking parties, even if in the end 'all were lying about'.[70]

Much of Qajar drinking remained traditional, seeking to reconcile public censure and private craving by way of self-fashioning. The Russian S. Lomnitski, an engineer who resided in Iran at the turn of the twentieth century, includes an anecdote in his perceptive travelogue that is as amusing as it is informative in describing an example of such self-fashioning according to changeable circumstances. He recounts how he was among the guests at a drinking party at the residence of a wealthy Iranian where clerics were in attendance. Before bringing out alcohol, the owner of the house ordered

[68] Eʿtemad al-Saltaneh, *Ruznameh-ye khaterat-e Eʿtemad al-Saltaneh* (Tehran, 3rd edn, 1356/1977), 300 and 778; and, for the wider context, Matthee, *The Pursuit of Pleasure*, 179ff.

[69] Patricia Crone, *God's Rule: Government and Islam* (New York, 2004), 316–17.

[70] Anon. [Ritter von Riederer], *Aus Persien. Aufzeichnungen eines Oesterreichers der 40 Monate im Reiche der Sonne gelebt und gewirkt hat* (Vienna, 1882), 86.

'something and the hats to be brought in'. A tray filled with hats was brought in, and each of the clerics took one and put it on his head, declaring that he was now no longer a mullah but a private person, after which they set out to play Islamically forbidden games—checkers, chess, cards—while availing themselves of the 'something'; which turned out to be an array of alcoholic drinks, including vodka, cognac, wine, and liqueurs.[71]

Also traditional but with a new twist, was the defiance displayed by some drinkers, who in their taste for alcohol recall the libertine, anti-clerical attitude of traditional high-minded Sufis claiming a private moral sphere that is so powerfully articulated by Hafez and his fellow poets. New in the Qajar period was not so much the contempt these showed for the increasingly abrasive ulama who felt no longer restrained by a forceful ruler capable or willing to rein them in, as the self-conscious stridency with which they flouted the laws of the Prophet, exhibiting a 'modernizing', western inflected disposition. Flaunting one's drinking became an explicit political statement, displaying a 'modern' attitude by way of heaping scorn on obscurantist clerics and their cant, and as such it was part of a social ferment in nineteenth-century Iran that bred forms of radicalism such as the Babi movement as well.[72]

Among the ruling classes European liquors gained in popularity in the same process that affected the Ottoman Empire—that of a growing entwinement with the outside world by way of tastes and the imports that fed them. This includes the type of alcohol people consumed as well as the ambience in which it was enjoyed. The nineteenth century witnessed the introduction of new types of high-percentage alcoholic beverages into Iran—beyond Russian aquavit which had been known since Safavid times—as part of the country's ongoing incorporation into the global market.[73] A century and a half after Chardin, James Baillie Fraser pointed to an Iranian fondness for potent stuff, suggesting by way of explanation that the pleasure of drinking 'consists, not in the gradual exhilaration produced by wine and conversation among companions who meet to make merry, but in the feelings of intoxication itself; and therefor a Persian prefers brandy, and deep potations, because these soonest enable him to attain that felicity'.[74]

[71] S. Lomnitskii, *Persiia i Persy* (St. Petersburg, 1902), 121–2.

[72] For more on this, see Matthee, *The Pursuit of Pleasure*, 199–204.

[73] M. von Kotzbue, *Narrative of a Journey into Persia in the Suite of the Imperial Russian Embassy of 1817* (London, 1819), 122–3; J. A. Perkins, *A Residence of Eight Years, Among the Nestorian Christians with Notices of the Muhammedans* (Andover, 1843), 225.

[74] James Baillie Fraser, *Narrative of a Journey into Khorasan in the Years 1821 and 1822* (London, 1825), 422.

European wines, which seem to have entered the Iranian market quite a bit later, were still far from ubiquitous by mid-century. The British Resident Justin Sheil at that time called the Iranians 'extremely fond of European wines', yet added that, 'still none among them, even the richest, are willing to undergo the expense of its conveyance from Europe. They satisfy themselves with the thin growth of their own vineyards, quantity compensating for quality.'[75] In keeping with a trend among the Ottoman upper classes, a fairly large number of Iranians had meanwhile taken to the Russian habit of consuming *zakuska*, hors d'oeuvre, accompanied by vodka.

Russian influence was especially paramount in northern Iran, evolving around the time of the Constitutional Revolution (1905–11) into outright military occupation. In the late nineteenth century, as Russia's influence on Iran grew, the import and consumption of arak increased so that by century's end more was said to be consumed in Tabriz than in Tbilisi.[76] By the first decade of the twentieth century Russia's influence had made vodka quite common in the north.[77] A report about the latter province from the early 1920s, when Gilan was under Russian control, insists that alcoholism was rampant among the region's Armenian and Russian inhabitants and that a predilection for the best wines and spirits prompted a search for good French wines, cognacs, and liqueurs among the well-to-do classes.[78] The French consul in Rasht at the time added that much of the wine consumed in Gilan came from Russia and that alcohol was sold clandestinely in coffee houses in the province.[79] Cognac, too, entered Iran at the time, from India as well as from France and Greece. The other popular drink among upper-class Iranians was champagne. Fantastic prices were paid for this luxury item. French and German wines and liquors were imported for the same clientele. By now, beer, too, was consumed by the most affluent Iranians, but even more so by resident foreigners. In the north Russian beers were most common; German and English and even some American brands prevailed in the south.[80] In 1902 a total of 134,634 bottles entered the country, 121,130 of which originated in Russia.[81]

[75] Lady Sheil, *Glimpses of Life and Manners in Persia* (London, 1856), 157.

[76] Sayyed Hasan Taqizadeh, *Zendegi-ye tufani (khaterat)* (Tehran, 1379/2000), 45.

[77] Walther Kuss, *Handelsratgeber für Persien* (Berlin, 1911), 121.

[78] Archives des Affaires Etrangères (AAE, French National Archives, Paris), CP, n.s., Perse 49, 'Notes sur Guilan', fol. 57.

[79] Ibid., 'Notes sur les conséquences économiques de la guerre en Guilan', fols. 5 and 27.

[80] Kuss, *Handelsratgeber*, 121.

[81] AAE, Corr. Politique (CP), n.s., Perse 47, 'Rapport sur le mouvement commercial de l'année persane bars-il, 21 mars 1902 a 20 mars 1903'. For conditions in the Ottoman Empire in this period, see Georgeon, 'Ottomans and Drinkers'.

V

Rules and regulations concerning the sale and consumption of alcohol vary widely from country to country in the modern Islamic world, ranging from secular Syria, where alcohol is freely available, to Pakistan and Malaysia, where only non-Muslims can obtain alcohol by presenting proof of (religious) identification, to absolute interdiction in Saudi Arabia. The level of official secularism, that is, the degree to which the official religion does not inform the legal system, generally determines the availability of alcohol.

For most of the twentieth century Turkey and Iran followed the 'secular' model. In keeping with Ataturk's vision and preference, the republic of Turkey became not just a secular state but one in which religion was deliberately marginalized. In 1926 the sale and consumption of alcohol by Muslims was made legal, and for the remainder of the twentieth century no legal restrictions were imposed on either, so that drinking alcohol became socially accepted. Turkey nonetheless continued to be a nation of 'light' drinkers, and women by and large still abstained. The majority of Turks who do imbibe prefer beer, which accounts for some 60 per cent of total consumption, with the average person consuming 0.8 litres in 2005, or spirits, meaning raki, at 0.5 litres per person. Wine, by contrast, is hardly drunk at all.[82]

Things began to change with the coming to power of the Justice and Development Party (AKP for *Adalet ve Kalkınma Partisi*) in 2002. Since 2005 the government of Recep Tayyip Erdoğan has waged a campaign to limit the supply and consumption of alcohol. It has become much harder to obtain and renew liquor licences and, citing the 'need to protect family values', municipalities have outlawed drinking in government-owned hotels, restaurants and cafes.[83] Proposals have also been made to ban alcohol in city centres by limiting the sale and consumption to restricted areas, 'alcohol ghettoes', on the edge of towns. By 2005 alcohol bans were in place in 61 of Turkey's 81 provinces.[84] Proposed changes in labour legislation call for the right for companies to fire anyone who shows up having had anything to drink. In September 2012 a law took effect that bans the sale of alcohol and cigarettes 'by breaking its packaging or dividing them', which, critics say, effectively prohibits the sale by the glass in restaurants.[85] In April 2013 Erdoğan declared *ayran*, a salty mixture of yoghurt and water, rather than raki the national drink of Turkey, and a month later the Turkish parliament,

[82] http://www.turkishmuse.com/2011/01/war-against-alcohol-in-turkey.html

[83] *Asia Times*, 26 August 2009, 'Turkey's beer-swillers get hammered'.

[84] *The Guardian*, 23 Dec. 2005, 'Alcohol the battleground in east-west conflict'.

[85] *Hürriyet Daily News*, 23 Sept. 2012, 'Turkish AKP alcohol law raises question marks'.

citing public health reasons, passed a bill that would ban retail sales of alcohol between 10 p.m. and 6 a.m., halt all advertising and promotion of alcohol-related products, and forbid the sale of liquor within 100 metres of schools and houses of worship. In September 2013 the bill became law. Its restrictions quickly led to the emergence of an underground alcohol market in the form of late-night delivery services.[86]

The state has been most consistent in curbing availability by dramatically raising taxes. In 2002 the government instituted a special consumption tax (ÖTV) on alcohol, raising VAT on alcohol from the regular VAT rate of 18 to 48 per cent, with a further increase to 63 per cent in 2009. Severely criticized for this policy, the government in 2010 eliminated this impost on some alcoholic beverages, such as wine, only to add a lump-sum tax on each bottle. The tax on beer, meanwhile, went up by almost 800 per cent between 2002 and 2010. The price of raki, which remains the national tipple, in the same period has quadrupled to some 35 TL, or almost $20 for a 700 cl bottle.[87]

These tax hikes have made a glass of beer or raki exorbitantly expensive, on par with Scandinavian countries, and, taking into account the moderate purchasing power of most Turks, the most expensive in the world, putting alcohol out of reach for most. The result is that Turkey's per capita consumption, already very low by international standards, has dropped by one third in the last few years, and that the number of cafes and restaurants selling alcohol was reduced by 21 per cent between 2005 and 2008. This creeping social transformation has also pitted secular Turks who uphold the right of citizens to make their own lifestyle choices against their more traditional fellow-citizens who believe that drinking is a sin and should be outlawed by the state, reflecting a general debate in Turkish society about the role of religion in public life that in the late spring of 2013 erupted in confrontation and violence.[88]

Twentieth-century Iran evinces initial convergence with Turkish patterns followed by a sharp turn in policies with the establishment of the Islamic

86 *The Economist*, 1 June 2013, 'Alcohol in Turkey. Not so good for you'; *Hürriyet Daily News*, 9 Sept. 2013, 'Restrictions on alcohol sale go into effect today in Turkey', at http://www.hurriyetdailynews.com/restrictions-on-alcohol-sales-go-into-effect-today-in-turkey.aspx?PageID=238&NID=54074&NewsCatID=344; and Emre Kizilkaya, 'Turkey's new prohibitions lead to underground alcohol market', *al-Monitor*, 17 Sept. 2013.

87 *Hürriyet Daily News*, 10 May 2010, 'AKP, Alcohol and government-engineered change in Turkey'; Ibid., 29 Oct. 2010, 'Turkish consumers dazed by another alcohol tax increase'.

88 For the role drinking has assumed as a symbol of resistance for many secular Turks, see Tim Arango, 'Resisting by Raising a Glass', *New York Times*, 9 June 2013.

Republic in 1979. Anti-liquor campaigns, often following riots instigated by clerics and targeting Jewish property, would occur into the twentieth century. The early part of the same century saw several more attempts at restrictions on sale and consumption. In 1909, during the Constitutional Revolution, the police chief of Tehran sought to regulate alcohol by licensing the right to operate distilleries and awarding licences only to cabarets run by non-Muslims and foreign nationals.[89] The government that came into being following Reza Shah's coup of February 1921 at first experimented with prohibition. One of its first proclamations included a ban on the importation, and then the overall consumption of alcohol. The sale of liquor was outlawed and shops selling alcohol were closed. Presumably inspired by Sayyed Zia Tabataba'i, Reza Shah's fellow conspirator and a cleric, the measure was designed in part to forestall Bolshevik influence by way of strengthening Iran's religious profile.[90] Upon Tabataba'i's forced resignation in May 1921, liquor stores and alcohol-serving venues were allowed to open their doors again.[91] Within a year, the ban on foreign imports had been 'considerably diluted', largely for reasons of revenue, as the British resident in Tehran put it.[92] In 1924, all distilleries in Tehran were concentrated in five locations outside the city.[93] Late 1926 saw the proclamation of a new ban on the importation of luxury imports—items whose domestic manufacture should be encouraged—which included alcoholic beverages.[94] In 1926–27 tariffs on alcohol reached 100 per cent, putting it beyond the means of most people.[95] The result was a steep decline in imported liquor.[96]

Alongside continued religiously based opposition to (public) drinking at the turn of the century, one observes a growing medicalization in the evaluation of the use and abuse of alcohol. Seeking to curb and contain through admonition and exhortation, advocates of this new approach used medical, health-related arguments. Publicists now presented drinking as harmful, using

[89] Willem Floor, *A Fiscal History of Iran in the Safavid and Qajar Periods 1500–1925* (New York, 1998), 405–6.

[90] Hoseyn Makki, *Tarikh-e bist saleh-ye Iran. Kudeta-ye 1299*, 3 vols (Tehran, 1323/1944; repr. 1358/1979), I, 298–9; and Ja'far Shahri, *Tarikh-e ejtema'i-ye Tehran dar qarn-e sizdehom* (Tehran, 3rd edn, 1378/1999), vol. 4, 378–9.

[91] Shahri, *Tarikh-e ejtema'i-ye Tehran*, vol. 4, 380–1.

[92] National Archives, London, FO, E8057/8057/34, Ndeg314, 'Persia. Annual Report, 1922. XII - Medical Affairs. (2.) Sanitary and Allied Questions', 64.

[93] Floor, *A Fiscal History of Iran*, 407.

[94] AAE, Corr. Commerciale, Tehran to Paris, 8 Jan. and 10 Feb. 1927, fols. 65ff.

[95] AAE, CP, n.s. Perse 62, fol. 116.

[96] *Tableau générale du commerce avec les pays étrangères pendant l'année 1305* (Tehran, 1927), xi/2, 'Importations'.

arguments borrowed from European scientific research. This trend intensified in the 1920s, reflecting the new era represented by Reza Shah and the push for a modern, orderly and disciplined Iran that marked his political agenda.[97]

Yet neither interdiction nor admonition seems to have lowered the level of alcohol consumption; indeed, indications are that it went up, riding on an increase in relatively cheap, domestically produced alcohol.[98] Much of this was no doubt consumed indoors. Friedrich Rosen, a German diplomat stationed in Iran in the early twentieth century, observed that most Iranians did not drink and that Iran by and large was a 'dry country'. Yet, echoing earlier observers of life in Iran, Rosen also pointed to the propensity among those Iranians who drank to do so generally 'with the idea of getting totally intoxicated', since the 'sin [. . .] is anyhow committed, therefore it is advisable to make the best of it'.[99]

By the time Reza Shah was forced to abdicate, in 1941, Lalehzar Street had opened up. Originating as a garden, the Bagh-e Lalehzar, this famous street had been laid out in the 1870s at the orders of Naser al-Din Shah after his return from his first European trip. In the course of the twentieth century Lalehzar Street developed into the entertainment district of the capital, a symbol of modernity filled with cinemas, theatres, cabarets, and European-style restaurants and bars serving food and drink. Elsewhere in the city the western bar, *piyaleh-forushi*, made its entry as well in the late Qajar period. Substituting for the traditional speakeasies, the *kharabat* and *meykhanehs*, the *piyaleh-forushi* would become more common in the reign of Mohammad Reza Pahlavi (1941–79), first in Tehran and later in provincial cities as well.[100] The modern hotels that opened in the 1960s invariably had their own bars, catering to foreigners as well as to more westernized Iranians keen to flaunt their modern lifestyle by drinking gin-tonics and whiskey. Yet, overall, Iran continued to be, as it had always been, a 'most sober nation', where most people lived and died without ever tasting wine.[101]

This situation—in which alcohol was publicly available yet not common, its consumption limited, as before, to the lower classes and the haute

[97] *Peyk-e Sa'adat-e Nesvan* 1:3 (Esfand 1306/Ramazan 1346), repr., ed. Banafsheh Mas'udi and Naser Mohajer (Berkeley and Créteil, 2012), 4–6 (134–6 in new edn); and *Salnameh-ye Pars* 1314/1925, 88, 89.

[98] *Baladiyeh-ye Tehran. Devvomin salnameh-ye ehsa'iyeh-ye shahr-e Tehran/Deuxième annuaire statistique de la ville de Teheran*, 1925–1929 (Tehran, 1310/1930).

[99] Friedrich Rosen, *Oriental Memories of a German Diplomatist* (London, 1930), 139.

[100] http://www.darioush-shahbazi.com/index.php?option=com_content&task=view&id=314&Itemid=12

[101] Rosen, *Oriental Memories*, 139.

bourgeoisie—remained in place until the end of Pahlavi rule in 1979. The Islamic government which took over in that year moved against alcohol not, as its Turkish counterpart, by stealth but in full combat mode, outlawing both the sale and consumption for Muslims. (Armenian Christians are exempted from the ban and allowed to produce their own alcohol.) Iranians thus once again had to turn to the privacy of their homes to quench their alcoholic thirst. And by all accounts the thirst is greater than ever. According to a report issued in 2011 by the official Iranian news agency *Mehr News*, some 80 million litres of alcohol are currently bootlegged in the country each year. Much of this is smuggled into the country from abroad, especially from Iraqi Kurdistan, in an illicit trade reportedly facilitated by bribe-taking Revolutionary Guards and thus controlled by the very same authorities that occasionally mete out draconian punishment to boozers. Whether supplied with moonshine provided by local Armenian bootleggers or imbibing expensive imported liquor, modern Iranians drink for various reasons, to seek solace from the frustrations of daily life in the Islamic Republic, or to act out their part in the country's continuing 'culture wars'. In keeping with tradition, those who indulge tend to drink heavily and with great gusto, the intensity of the experience sharpened by the 'taboo' element, the fact that consuming alcohol, in addition to violating religious strictures, is decried by a regime loathed by many.[102] As one cleric, excoriating the rampant alcohol consumption in his country, intoned in 2011, 'Not even the Westerners drink alcohol like we do. They pour a neat glass of wine and sip it. We here pour a four-litre barrel of vodka on the floor and drink it until we go blind. . . . We are all the masters of excess and wastage.'[103] So rampant has alcohol abuse

[102] See BBC 'Illegal Alcohol Booming in Iran', 15 Sept. 2011, at http://www.bbc.co.uk/news/world-middle-east-14939866. Also see Frontline, Tehran Bureau, 10 April 2012, 'That Sweet Iranian Spirit', at http://www.pbs.org/wgbh/pages/frontline/tehranbureau/2012/04/dispatch-that-sweet-iranian-spirit.html; *Express Tribune*, 15 May 2012, 'Rising alcohol intake "worrying": minister'; Radio Free Europe, 'Iranian officials warn alcohol abuse on the rise', at http://www.rferl.org/content/iran-alcohol-abuse-on-the-rise/24617070.html; Omid Memarian, 'Death sentence marks Iran's latest battle in Iran's culture war', *The Daily Beast*, 27 June 2012, at http://www.thedailybeast.com/articles/2012/06/27/death-sentence-marks-latest-battle-in-iran-s-culture-war.html; Max Fisher, 'Forbidden Drink: Why alcoholism is soaring in officially booze-free Iran', *The Atlantic*, 28 June 2012, at http://www.theatlantic.com/international/archive/2012/06/forbidden-drink-why-alcoholism-is-soaring-in-officially-booze-free-iran/259120/ and *Los Angeles Times*, 7 July 2012, 'Iran confronts its alcohol problem', at http://www.latimes.com/news/nationworld/world/la-fg-iran-alcohol-20120707,0,5211937.story

[103] See BBC 15 Sept. 2011, 'Illegal alcohol booming in Iran', at http://www.bbc.co.uk/news/world-middle-east-14939866.

become that the authorities in 2013 bowed to reality by seeking religious permission for the opening of an alcohol rehab center with the argument that alcohol addiction is an illness not a sin.[104]

[104] Merhnaz Samimi, 'Iran opens first alcohol rehab center', *al-Monitor*, 25 Oct. 2013, at http://www.al-monitor.com/pulse/originals/2013/10/iran-alcohol-permit-rehab-center.html.

Modernity, Tradition, and Intoxication: Comparative Lessons from South Africa and West Africa

Paul Nugent[1]

As a transient state of being, intoxication is inherently elusive. The imbibing subject often experiences a sense of euphoria and clarity of insight that is never fully recaptured the morning after. In that sense, drinking is much like dreaming: residual traces of the experience remain, but almost always in an incomplete and discontinuous manner. Recapturing the subjective experience of intoxication poses an even greater challenge for historians, given that most of the evidence tends to come from observers whose relationship to the state in question may be less than sympathetic. This is true of colonial Africa, where administrators, missionaries, and employers, as well as African proponents of Islamic orthodoxy, framed a public discourse that was broadly opposed to alcohol and frowned on open displays of drunkenness. By continuing to indulge as they saw fit, Africans made a statement of sorts, but one that needs to be decoded with nuance. On the whole, we know far more about what Europeans thought of African consumption than what the drinkers themselves did.

How intoxication is experienced depends not just on what is drunk and in what quantities, but also on two other inter-related factors: namely, the social context and the spatial setting. The social context refers to the meaning that is bound up with the act of drinking. There is a wide spectrum covering the individual act of gratification at one end, and performative bouts of consumption, at the other end—with many gradations in between. The setting refers to the spatial configuration under which the act of drinking takes place: it may be just anywhere, it may be located in a clandestine location or channelled into approved and controlled spaces such as formally designated bars. Together, the context and the setting shape the overall experience of drinking and of being drunk. The issue of modernity is germane to both of these dimensions, because how and where drinking takes place is intimately bound up with ideas about the wider consequences of consumptive acts.

[1] The research for this article was partly funded by a Leverhulme Trust Fellowship. It was written up under a fellowship at the Stellenbosch Institute for Advanced Study (STIAS). The author wishes to express his gratitude to both.

 © The Past and Present Society

For example, during the first half of the twentieth-century the consumption of substantial quantities of wine in France, which started from a tender age, was validated by the close association with the family table. In that sense, wine was regarded positively as a sub-category of food and was considered distinct from mere alcohol, by which was meant a distilled product. It was only in the 1970s that the anti-alcohol lobby in France was able to make a serious dent in these underlying assumptions and to portray excessive wine consumption as a serious threat to public health.[2]

Across Africa, there has always been a clear sense of what intoxication is, but what it means—and hence what it really amounts to—has varied considerably. Popular understandings have been shaped by a wider discourse about 'tradition' and 'modernity' and the values attached to each. 'Tradition' has tended to be associated with the countryside, with ritual practices and with communal norms, whereas 'modernity' has been associated with the city, with consumption for its own sake and with individual self-expression. The constituent elements of the latter are not, in fact, so far removed from sociological understandings of what characterizes modernity: most notably a stress on individual subjectivity and experientialism, and a belief in progress located in the context of a 'mass' society (as opposed to face-to-face community). But the complicating factor is that ideas about 'tradition' are themselves a product of modernity, and are often positively valorized in response to the perceived erosion of social bonds. Hence while an opposition between modernity and tradition might appear to indicate a hard and fast division, in practice the lines have often been blurred. This is especially the case with respect to the consumption of alcohol, where what has been construed as 'traditional' has often embodied elements that might appear to be distinctly modern, most obviously in the sense of being manufactured and bottled for mass consumption.

In this chapter, which straddles the nineteenth and twentieth centuries, I will draw on two sets of examples from West Africa—from the Senegambia and Ghana—and two from South Africa—the Witwatersrand and the Western Cape—in order to tease out some conclusions about the ways states of intoxication have been framed by the interplay between context and setting. I am not primarily concerned with the individual experience of being drunk. The central argument is that there was no one-to-one correlation between drunkenness and sobriety, on the one hand, and ideas about tradition and modernity, on the other. It turns out that permutations were altogether more complex, and more interesting.

[2] Marion Demossier, *Wine Drinking Culture in France: A National Myth or a Modern Obsession?* (Cardiff, 2010).

Historically, African societies have made alcoholic drinks from a variety of resources at their disposal.[3] In Southern Africa and in the West African Sahel, beers have been made from a variety of grains, such as millet, sorghum and increasingly maize, which possessed some nutritional value in addition to their intoxicating effects.[4] In highland Ethiopia, *tej* was a kind of mead made from honey, the consumption of which was highly valued by the nobility. In the Great Lakes region, the use of plantain was common, while along the East and West African coastal zones palm-wine was tapped from different categories of palm trees, either as they stood or once felled. The product required no further processing, although the length of time between tapping and drinking had an important bearing on the strength and taste of the drink in question. Distillation was rare in Africa before the twentieth century—except at the Cape where brandy was made from grapes that were widely planted from the later seventeenth century onwards.

In most African societies, controlling access to alcohol was integral to the inscription of social hierarchies. In imperial Ethiopia, for example, the obligation to supply one's master with *tej* was part of what underpinned the relationship between the noble and the peasant. In general, certain categories of alcohol were reserved for the exclusive use of those who wielded power. In more decentralized African societies, daily access to alcohol was considered the preserve of elders, whereas young men, women, and slaves generally had more restricted access. However, alcohol was also regarded as providing the cement that bound communities together. Hence, there were occasions when alcohol was widely distributed and where drunkenness might be positively construed: one thinks of life-cycle events such as funerals and weddings, but also of particular moments in the agricultural cycle when the harvest or first fruits were celebrated. An example would be yam festivals that were common across West Africa, or so-called 'beer parties' in Southern Africa that peaked around harvest time.[5] These were documented by European observers in the nineteenth century and early twentieth centuries.

Alcohol was not to be taken lightly because in many societies it was also the means by which the living communicated with the ancestral spirits. This is true, for example, of the Akan peoples of southern Ghana and Côte d'Ivoire

[3] Justin Willis, *Potent Brews: A Social History of Alcohol in East Africa, 1850–1999* (Athens OH and Oxford, 2002); Emmanuel Akyeampong, *Drink, Power, and Cultural Change in Ghana c.1800 to the Present* (Portsmouth and Oxford, 1996), ch. 2.

[4] Patrick McAllister, *Xhosa Beer Drinking Rituals: Power, Practice, and Performance in the South African Rural Periphery* (Durham NC, 2006), 20–21.

[5] McAllister, *Xhosa Beer*; Patrick Harries, *Work, Culture, and Identity: Migrant Labourers in Southern Africa c.1860–1910* (London, 1994), 9.

and the Ewe/Fon peoples straddling the borders between what is now Ghana, Togo, and Benin. In the principal kingdoms of the Gold and Slave Coasts, notably in Asante and Dahomey, imported spirits became central to communication with royal ancestors. T. C. McCaskie has provided a detailed account of the manner in which the hegemonic aspirations of the Asante monarchy were structured around an annual political cycle that culminated in the Odwira festival, which required anyone of importance to converge on Kumasi to pay homage.[6] McCaskie focuses on the point where one cycle came to an end—at which moment there was a notional breakdown of social norms—before order was fully restored at the start of a fresh cycle. During this interstitial moment, commoners were furnished with alcohol in the streets of the capital. Successive European commentators bore witness to the drunken revelry that ensued. McCaskie quotes one such account dating from 1817:

> [the] king [Osei Tutu Kwame] ordered a large quantity of rum to be poured into brass pans, in various parts of the town; the crowd pressing around, and drinking like hogs; freemen and slaves, women and children, striking, kicking and trampling each other under foot, pushed head foremost into the pans, and spilling much more than they drank. In less than an hour, excepting the principal men, not a sober person was to be seen, parties of four reeling and rolling under the weight of another, whom they affected to be carrying home; strings of women covered with red paint, hand in hand, falling down like rows of cards; the commonest mechanics and slaves furiously declaiming on state palavers; the most discordant music; the most obscene songs, children of both sexes prostrate in insensibility. All wore their handsomest clothes, which they trailed after them to a great length, in a drunken emulation of extravagance and dirtiness.[7]

McCaskie also refers to an account by Basel missionaries held captive in Kumasi in 1870 which recorded that 400 large pots of palm-wine were left in the streets for public consumption.[8] Despite the appearance of anarchy, in which inebriated slaves and women were free to mimic their superiors, the events were closely stage-managed. The subliminal message in Asante's version of carnival was that this was what society might look like in the absence of

[6] T. C. McCaskie, *State and Society in Pre-Colonial Asante* (Cambridge, 1995).

[7] McCaskie, *State and Society*, 215.

[8] McCaskie, *State and Society*, 215–16.

the monarchy. The day after, normality was restored and displays of public drunkenness were severely punished.

What is noticeable in these descriptions is the lack of reference to spirits. However, in the eighteenth century, distilled alcohol became one of the most important imports into West Africa as a companion to the slave trade. In return for the right to trade, European merchants were generally expected to furnish African rulers with quantities of gin and rum, and much of what was sold by them consisted of the same products. As I have already indicated, alcohol performed an important role in communicating with royal ancestors. Through acts of pouring libation, one might say that it was the ancestral spirits who enjoyed the privileges of intoxication rather than the living. The Dutch gin that came to be so highly prized along the coast was manufactured in Europe for the African market and was sought after for its supposed purity (being clear) and strength. But the very alterity of the product was what imparted its importance in ritual functions that were quintessentially traditional. The more potent the substance, the greater its ability to serve as a lubricant with the spirit world: although palm-wine might suffice for a village chief, only the imported product was suitable for the king and his ancestors.

The fact that those who wielded power imbibed imported liquor is clear from countless European encounters with inebriated rulers with whom they were forced to negotiate trading privileges. Although European merchants often expressed their disapproval, open displays of royal intoxication made a statement about the nature of power. In a nutshell, the king was drunk not just because he could afford to be, but also because he knew how to manage the perils associated with alcohol. The drunken king is actually a recurring trope in many West African oral traditions and in the historical renditions of the praise-singers, or *jeli*, attached to ruling families across much of the Sahelian region.[9] But it was also one that could be turned on its head. In the nineteenth century, Islamic reformers who declared jihad against the Mandinka and Wolof states of the Senegambia treated royal drunkenness as a sign of moral debasement and as further evidence that the established lineages were no longer fit to govern. In the Wolof states to the north, alcohol became entrenched as a political as well as a religious marker. Whereas the royal soldiers, the *tyeddo*, allegedly drank before going into battle, their Muslim opponents were committed to eradicating alcohol. Further south, once Muslim reformers had triumphed over the Mandinka ruling houses, they turned their attention to neighbouring acephalous peoples, such as the

[9] See, e.g., David Conrad, *A State of Intrigue: Epic of Bamana Segu According to Tayeru Banbera* (Oxford, 1990).

Jola, whose fondness for palm-wine was regarded as evidence of their barbarous nature. Hence, alcohol provided a fresh marker of difference between Mandinka and Jola, which mapped neatly onto the distinction between Muslim and traditionalist 'unbeliever'.[10]

In most of Southern Africa, imported spirits commanded less of a role, although the dissemination thereof greatly expanded over the course of the nineteenth century. It was the brewing of beer by women that was the major source of alcohol. The ability to supply substantial quantities of beer for collective consumption made a clear statement about the location of power and wealth. Hence, Zulu kings from Shaka onward always had large supplies of beer to dispense in public, part of which was supplied to warriors because of its notional strengthening effects. McAllister also observes that in some Southern African societies beer was sprinkled on the graves, and that amongst the Xhosa it had an important ritual function that is rather obscured by the use of the terminology of the 'beer party'.[11] In Southern Africa, as much as in West Africa, power and the right to consume alcohol were closely interconnected.

At the turn of the twentieth century, there were dramatic shifts that affected the societies of West and Southern Africa in quite different ways. In South Africa itself, the discovery of diamonds at Kimberley, and subsequently gold on the Witwatersrand in 1886, had the most profound consequences. In the early days, Africans and whites from across the world rubbed shoulders at the mining camps and provided a ready market for locally produced 'rotgut' consumed in makeshift canteens.[12] With time, the social landscape around the mines became more regulated, and this included attempts to control access to liquor. At the same time, the autonomy of Africans was progressively circumscribed as the mining companies sought to marshal a captive labour force. Within relatively little time, the system of labour procurement spread well beyond the boundaries of South Africa. By the 1920s, segregationists imagined an ideal world in which Africans would remain tied to their rural homesteads, but would travel to the mines on short-term contracts—despite

[10] Paul Nugent, 'Putting the History back into Ethnicity: Enslavement, Religion and Cultural Brokerage in the Construction of Mandinka/Jola and Ewe/Agotime Identities in West Africa, *c.*1650–1930', *Comparative Studies in Society and History*, 50:4 (2008), 920–48.

[11] McAllister, *Xhosa Beer*, 20–5.

[12] Charles Van Onselen, *Studies in the Social and Economic History of the Witwatersrand, 1886–1914* (Johannesburg, 1982), 48–67.

the reality that significant numbers of Africans had already made the cities their own.[13]

Much of the incentive to enter the cycle of migrancy came from land pressures, especially after the 1913 Native Land Act that made it more difficult for Africans to reproduce themselves only by farming. The need to acquire cash to pay taxes was also an imperative in South Africa and in the Portuguese colonies that supplied much of the labour.[14] But it is equally clear that many Africans regarded migrancy as kind of rite of passage marking the progression from youth to adulthood. As David Coplan demonstrates in his study of *lifela*—the poems that Basotho migrants composed about themselves—the risk to life and the hardship involved in working on the gold mines also produced new bonds of solidarity and enabled young men to establish their identity as men.[15] The mines were fraught with danger, but they were also associated with the allure of modernity, embodied physically in new items of consumption. Miners hoped to return home with a package of material goods and the wherewithal to acquire a wife—often bypassing the elders who had hitherto controlled access to brideprice through ownership of cattle. In their rural homesteads, their dress and their ways of speaking singled the migrants out from those who had been too timid to travel.

It is in this context that attitudes towards drinking have to be understood. In the rural areas, the making of beer was typically a female pursuit, while the drinking of beer was largely the preserve of elder men. The emergent mining compounds initially attracted women who brewed beer in the customary manner, but as access to the compounds became increasingly restrictive, the continuities with rural forms of production and consumption became more attenuated. Mine managers sought to manage access to liquor, being worried about the incidence of absenteeism and fighting, but also dispensed 'kaffir beer' (made from sorghum) to their workers in order to keep them on the compound.[16] This came at the expense of African women's ability to earn money through brewing 'traditional' beer for the mining camps. African

[13] Harold Wolpe, 'Capitalism and Cheap Labour Power in South Africa: From Segregation to Apartheid', *Economy and Society*, 1:4 (1972), 425–56; Jonathan Crush, Alan Jeeves, and David Yudelman, *South Africa's Labor Empire: A History of Black Migrancy to the Gold Mines* (Boulder, 1991).

[14] Harries, *Work, Culture, and Identity.*

[15] David Coplan, *In the Time of Cannibals: Word Music of South Africa's Basotho Migrants* (Chicago, 1994).

[16] Julie Baker, 'Prohibition and Illicit Liquor on the Witwatersrand, 1902–1932', in Jonathan Crush and Charles Ambler (eds), *Liquor and Labor in Southern Africa* (Athens and Pietermaritzburg, 1992), 141.

miners, on the other hand, did everything in their power to assert their right to drink, often resorting to anything at their disposal to create alcoholic concoctions that had a far greater kick than 'traditional beer'. A case in point was *skokiaan*, which was made using a particular root, golden syrup and other ingredients that were smuggled in.[17] The right to consume stronger variants of alcohol was defended by miners as part of their ownership of their non-working hours, and at weekends there were bouts of collective drinking, often accompanied by the communal consumption of meat. This often involved people from the same ethnic group, but it was also the case that drinking circles crossed ethnic lines, with solidarities between work-mates, who worked alongside each other under the most hazardous conditions, providing the operative bond.[18]

The mine managers and police blamed excessive drinking at the weekend—often away from the compound—for the high absentee rates on Monday morning. Drink was also linked to the incidence of so-called faction fighting, which often followed ethnic lines.[19] But while the attempt to channel competition into the support for dance troupes and sport enjoyed some success, the attempt to instil the temperance message singularly failed. For African miners, the right to be drunk in the company of comrades was construed as an integral part of what it meant to become a man. To some extent, this drew on traditional norms—in which courting danger and demonstrating the capacity to fight were highly valued—but both the context and the setting were distinctly urban and, in that sense, modern. On the mining compounds, traditions mutated in ways that accommodated social change.[20]

Meanwhile in the informal settlements that grew up around the formal city, new possibilities for drinking emerged in the shape of shebeens. The response of the municipal authorities was to set up approved beer halls, initially in Durban and subsequently in other locations.[21] The beerhalls dispensed a locally manufactured beer that was supposed to imitate traditional

[17] T. Dunbar Moodie, *Going for Gold: Men, Mines, and Migration* (Johannesburg, 1994), 161–2, 169; Baker, 'Prohibition', 143.

[18] Dunbar Moodie, 'Alcohol and Resistance on the South African Gold Mines, 1903–1962', in Crush and Ambler, *Liquor and Labor*, 169.

[19] Moodie, *Going for Gold*, 180–210.

[20] A case in point is 'mine marriages' in which older men took younger migrants as 'wives'. This involved the performance of chores, but also sexual relations. The 'wife' would eventually become a man in his own right if he continued to migrate to the mines. Moodie, *Going for Gold*.

[21] Paul la Hausse, 'Drink and Cultural Innovation in Durban: The Origins of the Beerhall in South Africa, 1902–1916', in Crush and Ambler (eds), *Liquor and Labor*.

sorghum beer. However, the intention was also to cut women out of brewing altogether, provoking a furious response in Natal in the 1920s.[22] Moreover, a strict limit was placed on how much Africans could drink on any one visit to the beerhall. These soulless venues, which provided a healthy source of revenue for the white municipalities, found limited favour amongst Africans precisely because they were so tightly regulated and did not permit the freedom of expression associated with consumption. Hence, Africans continued to frequent illegal shebeens where it was possible to drink in an environment that was more conducive to conviviality amongst friends and where there was some possibility of engaging in the company of women. While women had lost their position in brewing, they generally owned the shebeens and therefore remained central to the liquor trade. Over time, the sheebeens evolved in ways that became more highly differentiated. From 1928, it had been illegal to sell wine, spirits, and bottled beer to Africans, and yet it was common knowledge that urban dwellers were finding ways to beat the system by means of shebeen 'runners' who ferried liquor from European bottle stores. By the 1950s, the liquor industry was doing a roaring trade in brandy, sherry, and cheap wines destined for the African market. The impossibility of effective enforcement led to a revision of the liquor laws in 1962, which permitted Africans to purchase liquor under controlled conditions. The Malan Commission, which had made the case for a change to the liquor laws, had done so not just on the grounds that restriction was ineffective, but also because it was impressed by the lack of any manifestations of public drunkenness in Lourenço Marques where Africans had been permitted to purchase Portuguese wines.[23]

The liquor companies perceived an opportunity with the ending of prohibition for Africans, and began a concerted campaign to target the urban African consumer. Interestingly, despite advertising campaigns designed to entice African drinkers, the sale of wine only climbed gradually. The great breakthrough was in the sale of bottled beer, both through approved bottle stores and in the shebeens. In the process, the image of the shebeen was rapidly transformed. In the 1950s, the association of the shebeen with violence and excess began to be replaced by images of urban chic, captured and

[22] Helen Bradford, '"We Women will Show Them": Beer Protests in the Natal Countryside, 1929', in Crush and Ambler (eds), *Liquor and Labor,* 208–16.

[23] *Report of the Commission of Enquiry on the General Distribution and Selling Prices of Liquor, May 1960* [Malan Commission], unofficial translation by the Western Province Bottle Store Keepers Association. The same observation had been made by members of the Wine Committee in 1931.

disseminated in the enormously popular photo-magazine, *Drum*. In the words of Anne Mager:

> Knowing what to do and how to do it in a respectable shebeen was part of what it meant to live in a city. Drinking was a smart thing to do; it demonstrated worldly familiarity and the power that came with it.[24]

In the 1970s, even more up-market shebeens emerged, which were tolerated by the authorities. The willingness of white commentators to take a fresh look at the shebeen phenomenon is apparent from a 1978 issue of the wine industry magazine, *Wynboer*, which portrayed them in an entirely new light. In place of the image of places of excess, white readers were assured that shebeens were actually sites of sociability. Here, it was said, friends shared bottles amongst themselves and consumed food with their drink:

> The Blacks were never, not even to this day, partial to the colonialistic habit of sundowner drinking. Drinking alone in front of the family or even with the wife has never been a happy circumstance among them. Unlike custom in Western civilization, the Black knows no set hours in which it is sociable to consume alcohol. By nature he is a sociable person and indeed a social drinker. He is inclined to want to drink in large groups sharing his liquor with easy-going gregarious company.[25]

The implication was that it was whites who were prone to lone drinking in the privacy of their homes and were more at risk of addiction. This inversion of racial stereotypes was driven in large part by self-interest, but it also has to be seen in the context of an emergent discourse about the relationship between food and drink. The defenders of the wine industry imported a European model of healthy drinking and purported to find evidence of such patterns in the urban African, although in this case it was beer and spirits rather than wine that predominated.

However, the romanticization of the shebeen was not universal. In the 1970s, many young Africans were of the view that excessive consumption was enervating, and during the Soweto disturbances it is significant that liquor outlets were specifically burned down. For radicalized youth, excessive alcohol consumption by their parents' generation posed a threat to liberation. In the 1980s, the National Union of Mineworkers (NUM) itself campaigned

[24] Anne Kelk Mager, *Beer, Sociability, and Masculinity in South Africa* (Bloomington, 2010), 14.

[25] 'Wine and Shebeens in Soweto', *Wynboer*, October 1978.

against excessive drinking which was held to weaken the solidarity of the labour movement.[26] For their part, the liquor companies imagined a world in which consumption might even bridge the racial divide. As ever, drinking was invested with a wider societal significance on all sides. Whereas the critique of drunkenness had hitherto tended to focus on deviation from (imagined) rural virtues of sobriety, the emphasis was increasingly placed on the modern African who belonged in the city and who understood the importance of moderation. In fact, by the 1980s, the South African rural population became ever more urban in its orientation—as is reflected in the spread of a discourse surrounding youth.[27]

In the Western Cape, a very different story unfolded. Although a weakness for alcohol was part of the repertoire of ethnic stereotypes across Africa, there was no single group as closely defined by its relationship to heavy drinking as the so-called Cape Coloured population. As one Commission baldly stated:

> The Cape Coloured people have certain psychological characteristics which have had an adverse influence on their power of resisting the temptation to over-indulge in liquor. They are intensely emotional and act on the spur of the moment. . . .[28]

The Coloured relationship with alcohol was not forged in the twentieth century, but was embedded in the history of slavery and emancipation at the Cape. During slavery, the forebears of those who are today called Coloured were supplied with cheap wine at various points in the working day. After emancipation, even if the possibility of former slaves finding alternative employment were limited, the provision of the so-called 'dop' or 'tot' served as one means of holding on to a scarce labour force—and in effect tying former slaves to the farm.[29] In fact, there was a tendency for successive generations descended from slaves to remain within the same valley.

In the twentieth century, the wine industry in the Western Cape depended upon the labour contributed by Coloured workers, but the latter also provided the principal outlet for the products of the vine. As indicated, Africans were legally debarred from consuming wine and spirits, while Afrikaners

[26] Moodie, *Going for Gold*, 160.

[27] This has mostly been viewed in political terms, but ideas surrounding what youth meant were also about consumption. See Ineke Van Kessel, *Beyond our Wildest Dreams: The United Democratic Front and the Transformation of South Africa* (Charlottesville, 1999).

[28] Union of South Africa, *Report of the Cape Coloured Liquor Commission of Inquiry* (Pretoria, 1945), 3.

[29] Pamela Scully, 'Liquor and Labor in the Western Cape, 1870–1900', in Crush and Ambler (eds), *Liquor and Labor*, 56–60.

drank relatively little, and then mostly brandy. Although Coloureds consumed brandy as well, the conditions of habitual drunkenness in rural districts hinged mostly on the consumption of cheap wines that could not otherwise find a marketable outlet. Just about every commission of enquiry into the liquor question over the course of the twentieth century recommended the legal proscription of the dop, but legislation to ban it was not forthcoming. The farmers had every reason to resist giving up the one instrument that gave them control over their workforce, but even the more enlightened employers noted that farm labourers insisted on their entitlement to consume the products of their own labour. This insistence on the right to be drunk—much like in the mines—could be regarded as a means of asserting limited autonomy in a highly regulated environment. As the Cape Coloured Liquor Commission of Enquiry stated in 1945:

> . . . the general opinion on the mind of the Commission is that amongst a very large section of the Coloured people the week-end 'drunk' is commonly regarded as the proper and eminently desirable reward for the labours and deprivals of the week—their one 'little bit of heaven' as one clerical witness described it—and that this attitude is shared by the women.[30]

Farms in the Western Cape were effectively closed institutions in which labourers were dependent upon their employers not just for work, but also for housing and for access to health care. A paradox resided precisely in the cohabitation between abject dependency on cheap wine, a certain refusal by labourers to be bound by the clock of the master/employer and outward signs of deference to the 'baas'. The rules of the game were forged in the context of emancipation in the 1830s and were still being worked out one hundred and fifty years later.

Farm workers would generally receive tots dispensed in 'empty beer or fish tins or plastic mugs, at least five or six times a day, totalling more than two-and-a-half litres'.[31] Hence much of the work was conducted in a semi-inebriated state. At the end of the day, it was also common for employers to provide additional wine to take home. Finally, at the weekends, it was normal for farm workers to buy wine from the nearest bottle store and to engage in binge drinking over the weekend, a pattern that remains deeply ingrained in the rural Western Cape today. This was drinking that involved

[30] *Report of the Cape Coloured Liquor Commission of Inquiry*, 7.

[31] 'Battle Against Drinking on Farms Partly Won', *Cape Argus*, 14, April 1981, contained in Cape Archives A1696 'Women's Christian Temperance Union', sub-file 'Coloured Affairs, 1961–1972'.

men and women and was entirely divorced from the intake of food and entertainment: indeed it could be considered a substitute for both of these. D. F. Malan, the later Prime Minister, who was a leading advocate of the temperance interest in Parliament in the 1920s, recalled that his eyes had been opened during his time as a minister in a rural congregation around Montagu, where drunkenness was as destructive as it was habitual. He wrote that:

> The other day a brother Minister wrote me that he had met someone who had travelled in other lands of low moral standards, who declared that nowhere in the world had he seen the drunkenness such he had seen in some of our villages on a Saturday afternoon . . .[32]

The liquor companies, most notably Stellenbosch Farmers Winery (SFW) and Distillers Corporation, regarded the Coloured market as essential for the profitability of their operations even as they sought to promote better quality wine for whites at higher price points. The marketing strategy was always racially differentiated.[33] For whites, there was an attempt to push wine as a lifestyle product for young people, especially couples, who might enjoy sharing a glass around the braai (barbecue). Wine advertising for the white market was sensitive to perceived shifts in consumer preferences, for example away from sweet wines and in the direction of drier white and red wines in the 1970s. In the case of wines targeted at the Coloured market, by contrast, the emphasis was placed on the lack of change. The minimalist advertising typically consisted of simple images of a bottle depicting bunches of grapes, a homestead, and/or some mountains. The labels and the contents hardly ever changed, in part because Coloured consumers were said to be resistant to it. Perhaps the most famous iconography surrounded Oom Tas (launched in 1952), which was a dark-coloured dry white wine that was sold in 4.5 litre kegs and had a very loyal consumer base amongst the Coloured population.

[32] 'Echo from the Past', Extract from an Address by the Hon. D. F. Malan, Stellenbosch 1912, Stellenbosch University Document Centre. On temperance in South Africa, see Paul Nugent, 'The Temperance Movement and Wine Farmers at the Cape: Collective Action, Racial Discourse, and Legislative Reform *c.*1890–1965', *Journal of African History*, 52 (2011), 341–63.

[33] For a more detailed account of the way the wine industry functioned, see Paul Nugent, 'Who Killed Innovation in the Cape Wine Industry? The Story of a Stuck Fermentation *c.*1930–1986', in Jan-Bart Gewald, André Leliveld, and Iva Pesa (eds), *Transforming Innovations in Africa: Explorative Studies on Appropriation in African Societies* (Leiden, 2012).

The label, which depicted an older (possibly Coloured) man set against the backdrop of a range of Cape mountains, continues to evoke feelings of familiarity to this day. Farmworkers were in the habit of buying a bottle of Oom Tas together and drinking half of the contents in turn. A printer's error on the label enabled the partners in drink to know where the halfway mark was. Legend has it that when someone in the SFW decided to correct the error and issued a replacement label, the result was complaints and even fighting between friends who could no longer agree on where the halfway mark was![34] The Coloured case therefore provides a complex configuration in which certain elements of the drinking dynamic were linked to a distinctly pre-modern pattern of work and leisure, at the same time as a strong brand loyalty pointed to the power of the market. Significantly, the one section of the Coloured population that was most opposed to drinking, namely the Cape Malays, was both urban and Muslim. For Cape Malays, a rejection of alcohol was a marker of their identity as a people set apart from their inebriated country cousins. It was also a statement about their modernity.

In West Africa, Africans retained a much greater say over the terms of the colonial relationship than in the south of the continent. The British and French administrations did not express particularly strong views on the alcohol question, despite the efforts of metropolitan temperance lobbies to secure prohibitionist legislation. Indeed, at the turn of the century, it is remarkable that Senegal was the third largest importer of bottled French claret.[35] In northern Senegal, the imposition of European rule had prevented the consolidation of jihadic states, but the authorities were broadly sympathetic to Muslim demands for restricting alcohol consumption. But in the Gambia and the Casamance region of Senegal to the south, periodic concern was expressed about the drinking habits of the Jola. As one Gambian official wrote in rather matter-of-fact terms in 1898:

> The country itself is much the same as usual, drinking bouts among the Jolahs with the usual drunken fights, which are bound to continue as long as there are palm trees in the country.[36]

[34] This episode is referred to in SFW's own official history. Romi van der Merwe, *A Magic Blend: SFW, 1925–2000* (Stellenbosch, 2000), 70.

[35] James Simpson, *Creating Wine: The Emergence of a World Industry, 1840–1914* (Princeton and Oxford, 2011), 124.

[36] National Archives of the Gambia, Banjul (NAGB) ARP 33/1 Reports on Kombo, Foni, and Kiang (1894–99), 'Report on Kommbo, Fogni, and Kiang Districts 1. and 2. for 1897–1898' by Sitwell, Travelling Commissioner (2 July 1898).

Again, a report from 1901 stated that:

> This part of the country is still very uncivilized, the Jolahs are a very wild people, their ideas rising little beyond palm wine & tobacco. . . . Crime in Fogni is excessive, the Jollahs [sic] they are continually committing murders & highway robberies. The hard part of a Commissioner's work in this District is his inability to make arrests, no Jolah will ever arrest another, & the Mandingos are afraid to; another point is that it is very hard indeed to get one Jolah to give evidence against another. Most of these murders are committed at funerals, when it is the custom to drink quantities of palm wine and rum & to fire off guns. I have myself heard over one hundred guns fired at a single funeral.[37]

Many of the same stereotypes attached to other non-Muslim populations of the southern Casamance such as the Balanta and the Karoninka, the latter of whom migrated into the Gambian border zone in significant numbers during the interwar years.

Although the French and British authorities saw it as their duty to discourage these populations from excess, in fact a fundamental social change was taking place beneath their noses. Having previously associated Islam with enslavement, the Jola converted rapidly to Islam in the interwar years, a process that was mediated by Mauritanian marabouts such as Cheikh Mahfoudz who were not tainted by any prior association with jihad. When the Jola converted, they changed their names, but also ceased tapping and indulging in palm-wine. The Karoninkas were slower to convert, and many migrants came to an arrangement with their Mandinka hosts whereby they were permitted to tap palm-wine for consumption and sale in Bathurst. A reputation for drunkenness continued to cling to the Karoninkas, and it is really only in the recent past that significant conversion has led to widespread abstention from alcohol. Crucially, the embrace of Islam was itself connected to ideas about modernity, but it was a distinctly Muslim modernity that was envisaged. The convert adopted an aesthetic that governed dress and deportment and valorized membership of a global Muslim community. The renunciation of alcohol was an integral part of what was construed as a personal voyage to redemption through a rejection of everything traditional—especially drink—and embracing a timeless truth associated with the teachings of the Prophet. This transformation owed nothing to Christian

[37] NAGB ARP 33/2 'Reports on Kombo, Foni, and Kiang (1900–01 and 1906–07)', Report from the Travelling Commissioner, Sangster, 26 September 1901.

missionaries or European officials and everything to a proliferation of religious networks that traversed colonial borders.

Finally, we come to the case of the Gold Coast where the production of homemade beers and palm-wine had co-existed with imported alcohol since the era of the slave trade. One of the peculiarities of the Gold Coast was that there was no system of direct taxation, while the European firms were opposed to duties levied on exports. In practical terms, therefore, the colony ran on the income derived from import duties, of which those levied on imported alcohol were by far the most significant. Although the development of gold mining did lead to the emergence of a migrant labour system, this was much less regimented than in Southern Africa. Moreover, the real driver of social change was the cocoa industry, in which large numbers of peasant producers in the southern part of the colony were able to earn a steady income through the sale of their cocoa beans and thereby to expand the range of their consumption. The list came to include snuff, tobacco, toiletries, and alcohol. To some extent, the booming economy of the 1920s was also conducive to the expansion of the cities: notably, Kumasi, which was located at the heart of the cocoa economy, Accra (the capital), and Takoradi, whose importance was as a coastal port. Together with the growth of urban centres came the expansion of the number of paid employees and the entrenchment of the concept of leisure time. The drinking bar as a distinct leisure space began as an urban phenomenon, but spread to even quite small towns as money circulated more widely.

In the 1920s, the consumer boom led to growing concern in some quarters about the threat to social order posed by the consumption of alcohol, and most especially Dutch gin. Protestant missionaries, chiefs, and some employers expressed concern about rising levels of gin imports and the impact upon public morals. Leading chiefs, in particular, alleged that the drinking of gin for pleasure was giving rise to a situation in which the youth refused to accept the authority of chiefs and elders. As the future Asantehene summed it up: 'When a person is drunk he loses his sense of respect for his superiors'.[38] It was even claimed that gin was impacting adversely on fertility. The chiefs were not in favour of a total ban on alcohol, and expressed the opinion that indigenous drinks like palm-wine (tapped by men) were not deleterious to health, but they were in favour of a complete ban on imported spirits. Police witnesses at the Newlands Commission of Enquiry expressed the view that there

[38] Evidence of Nana Agyeman Prempeh and statement presented to commission, contained in Enclosure No 1: 'Notes of Evidence Taken by the Commission of Inquiry Regarding the Consumption of Spirits in the Gold Coast', in Governor Slater to Lord Passfield (12 April, 1930), National Archives, Kew, CO 96/692/6.

was not a serious problem with drunkenness in the colony, while customs officials warned against doing anything that might create an incentive to engage in illicit distillation.[39] Although there was official scepticism about the need for action, the pressure from chiefs and missionaries was such that the authorities felt compelled to begin a process of phasing out gin imports over a ten-year period. As had been predicted, this led to the expansion of an indigenous distillation industry that was very difficult to put back in the bottle (as it were). A strong liquor called *akpeteshie*, popularly known as 'kill me quick' and later as 'DC-10', began to be made from palm-wine and other crops like sugar-cane, and much of this was sold through informal outlets. When the experiment was aborted by the government, this did not lead to a decline in illicit distillation. Instead there remained a thriving market for the local product that was considerably cheaper. As Emmanuel Akyeampong has indicated, the right to drink *akpeteshie* was a cause with which the Convention People's Party (CPP) associated itself in its attempt to mobilize opposition to British rule—providing a further illustration of the way in which alcohol could be politicized.[40] There was one further twist to this tale that is worth recounting here. Dmitri van den Bersselaar has examined the attempt by Dutch gin manufacturers to re-brand their product for a mass market after independence. This campaign to reorient gin as an everyday lifestyle drink failed miserably, as a result of which the Dutch manufacturers were forced to return to the association with tradition and especially with chieftaincy.[41]

In each of the cases we have considered, the major shift in consumption patterns from the early 1960s came with the rapid expansion of beer consumption. In South Africa, bottled beer became a drink of preference in the shebeens and amongst white consumers alike, although Coloureds remained loyal to wine. South African Breweries (SAB) managed to establish a monopoly over beer in the 1970s, and campaigned in an aggressive fashion amongst different segments of a racially divided beer market. For white consumers, male bonding around sport was an important advertising theme, while a different kind of male conviviality connected to football was sold to Africans.[42] Carling Black Label, which was alleged to be stronger than the

[39] For a more detailed account, see Paul Nugent, *Smugglers, Secessionists, and Loyal Citizens on the Ghana–Togo Frontier: The Lie of the Borderlands Since 1914* (Oxford, Athens, and Legon, 2002), 82–7.

[40] The right of women to drink was also insisted upon; see Akyeampong, *Drink*, 118–28.

[41] Dmitri van den Bersselaar, *The King of Drinks: Schnapps Gin from Modernity to Tradition* (Leiden, 2007).

[42] Mager, *Beer, Sociability, and Masculinity*, 47–65.

other SAB products, achieved a commanding position in the African consumer market by virtue of its association with virility. But SAB also pushed brands with advertising that emphasized a break with the past, a message designed to appeal to upwardly mobile young men.[43] Although South Africa lagged behind the leading beer consuming countries, drinking amongst young, urban males of all races certainly increased considerably in the 1970s and 1980s. Being drunk on bottled beer made a statement about belonging to an urban, cosmopolitan world, whereas the 'beer' associated with the beerhalls still harked back to the in-between existence of the migrant with one foot in the countryside.

In Ghana, the story was both the same and different. Two major breweries, one located in Accra and the other in Kumasi, competed for the loyalty of Ghanaian consumers. Drinkers tended to identify with ABC, Star, or Club beer. As a global brand, Guinness was sold as a drink that was conducive to good health, to the extent that Muslims in the north imbibed what came to be popularly known as 'zim tim' ('blood tonic'). Although people in the villages who had limited income would become drunk on *akpeteshie*, those who could afford it also embraced beer. In the early 1980s, an acute economic crisis meant that bottled beer became virtually unobtainable—or if the beer was there the bottles were not—which meant that people fell back on substitutes like palm-wine and *akpeteshie.* But when the good times returned in the mid-1980s, there was a return to bottled beer. Even relatively small villages typically had a number of drinking 'spots' where beer could be purchased and drunk against the backdrop of pounding music. At the weekends, small settlements swelled in numbers on account of the regular cycle of funerals where drinking was construed as part of the mourning process. Equally, the annual cycle of festivals, such as the yam festival in Ho or royal festivals in Kumasi and Kyebi, provided the occasion for public displays of drunkenness that counterbalanced the rather solemn official proceedings. Being drunk has not had a single, stable meaning in Ghana: it has depended very much on the occasion. Alcohol continues to have a role in public functions, because of its role in mediating with the world of the spirits, but it also possesses a recreational function. Inevitably during festivals and funerals, there is a blurring of the boundaries and it is not uncommon for arguments to break out about precisely what is appropriate behaviour on such occasions.

Let us now return to the precise relationship between modernity and drunkenness. In the African context, ideas about modernity have popularly been associated with the city and with distinctive patterns of consumption.

[43] Mager, *Beer, Sociability, and Masculinity*, 57. Women scarcely featured, except as an adornment. However, they were targeted in spirits advertising.

Inevitably the drinking of manufactured alcohol, whether gin, brandy, or bottled beer, was associated with new sources of income and emergent spaces for conviviality in the city and even in smaller towns. Moreover, in the later twentieth century, advertisers routinely bombarded their target audience with seductive images of the good life. In the context of social constraints, such as prevailed in apartheid South Africa, asserting the right to drink also provided a way of defending a semi-autonomous social space. However, what also emerges from the comparisons is a rather more complex story.

Firstly, in the Senegambia region, drunkenness came to be associated with traditional—and hence 'backward'—behaviour from the nineteenth century onwards. This meant that a premium was placed on converts to Islam actively renouncing alcohol. Although the alcoholic content was relatively low, palm-wine was construed as problematic precisely because it carried the stigma of being something traditional, and hence doubly opposed to the Muslim project of social reform. Secondly, in the Gold Coast/Ghana, Dutch gin was part of a global trade in alcohol since the slave trade, and particular brands—especially Henkes gin—came to be highly appreciated in the twentieth century. But gin could not shrug off its association with tradition despite being a product made specifically for the African market. Becoming intoxicated on spirits came to be associated much more with the consumption of *akpeteshie*, which afforded a means of getting drunk cheaply. *Akpeteshie* was not tagged with any particular conception of modernity, but was generally regarded as the recourse of those who were unable to afford something better. These days, palm-wine is construed as a product consumed by rural dwellers that does not provide an easy route to intoxication, even if it does produce a pleasant sensation.

Thirdly, Coloured drinking habits in rural South Africa were in large part a hangover of pre-industrial social relations between white masters and their slaves (later farm servants), in which alcohol was customarily dispensed as part of the work ration. Coloureds also became the principal consumers of cheap, bottled wine. Strikingly, such wine was not sold as a lifestyle product, but as almost a need. Wine afforded a means to get drunk at little cost, in exactly the same way each time. It is in bottled beer as well as in imported spirits like Scotch whisky that one can identify a clear-cut association between consumption and ideas associated with modernity. It is only now that an emergent Black middle class is beginning to discover the pleasures of wine—less as a means of getting drunk and rather more as a way of displaying wealth.

Fourthly, it is important to distinguish between drinking that is purely recreational and that which has a well-understood social function. When white university students in South Africa get drunk, they are often simply enjoying themselves. But during occasions such as Rag week or in fraternities, the context and the setting are highly structured and the meanings associated with collective drunkenness are well understood. Being drunk at a funeral in Ghana similarly involves a particular combination between the context and the setting. The pouring of libation is a direct propitiation of the ancestors, but being intoxicated during a wake is thought to bring the mourner closer to the spirit of the deceased person. This is part of the reason why individuals appear to become drunk on such occasions despite having consumed relatively little. It is not necessarily that they are pretending, but simply that drunkenness at a funeral represents a kind of altered state. At most wakes and burials, people will frequent the bars at the fringe of the main event and drink for its own sake, thus blurring the context at the margins. Within a single event, therefore, the meanings associated with intoxication may be very different.

Finally, as the parallel cases of the Senegambian Muslims and the Cape Malays clearly demonstrate, the conditions associated with modernity could certainly lead to increased drinking by virtue of the association with consumptive acts, but being urban, modern and connected to a global community of believers could also lead to an explicit renunciation of alcohol and a stigmatization of its side-effects. In that sense, there were competing visions of modernity that played themselves out in attitudes towards alcohol in West Africa and South Africa alike.

Double Vision: The Ambivalent Imagery of Drunkenness in Early Modern Europe

Tom Nichols

This essay explores two superficially opposed traditions showing drinking and drunkenness in visual art of the sixteenth and seventeenth centuries. Art history has long distinguished between an idealizing and narrative artistic tradition in Italy, and a realist or descriptive mode in northern countries such as Holland and Germany.[1] In accordance with this, it might be tempting to make a contrast between a classically inflected southern tradition, in which drinking is shown as socially and spiritually elevating, and a realist and satirical northern alternative, in which it is condemned as destructive and marginalizing. But the evidence suggests that visual depictions of drinking and drunkenness in this period were much more equivocal than this dichotomous model allows.

This ambiguity in visual imagery was, in part, a reflection of the unresolved or paradoxical status of social discourses on drinking in early modern Europe. Social historians have shown that hard drinking was understood as one means by which young men distinguished themselves from boys in seventeenth-century Holland, but also that it could be seen as unmanly or emasculating. In Germany, participation in drinking bouts likewise helped to enhance men's social status, but it was also proscribed by the authorities, and was strictly forbidden to women. The pros and cons of the consumption of brandy and gin were the cause of widespread controversy, and wine drinking was the subject of similarly conflicting discourses in Italy, where it was promoted for medicinal purposes while also being condemned as the cause of social disruption.[2]

[1] The *locus classicus* for the binary distinction between northern and southern traditions is Svetlana Alpers, *The Art of Describing: Dutch Art in the Seventeenth Century* (Chicago, 1983).

[2] See Ken Albala, 'To Your Health: Wine as Food and Medicine in Mid-Sixteenth Century Italy' in *Alcohol: A Social and Cultural History*, ed. Mack P. Holt (Oxford and New York, 2006), 11–23; B. Ann Tlusty, 'Water of Life, Water of Death: The Controversy Over Brandy and Gin in Early Modern Augsburg', *Central European History*, 31 March

 © The Past and Present Society

These contradictory social attitudes reflect more fundamental intellectual and religious tensions around intoxication by alcohol within early modern culture. Just as Renaissance classicism revived the idea that alcohol consumption might facilitate social elevation or even spiritual transformation, so this possibility was undermined by the intensifying strictures of reformed Christian morality which condemned it as a cardinal sin. In northern Europe, at least, this disapprobation may reflect the demand for personal control within expanding states that were, at least according to scholarly orthodoxy, increasingly work-orientated. But even if alcohol drinking often served as a marker of non-productivity or social failure, its meaning was reversed if it was consumed in moderation. Indeed, it was often promoted as the essential lubricant oiling the wheels of the business exchanges that secured inclusion within the new burgher elites.[3]

An ideal image? The imagery of Bacchus revived and reviled

Ambiguity is central to the revival of the imagery of Bacchus, god of wine, a newly popular subject matter reflecting the emergence of classicizing humanistic values among the social elite at the courts of Renaissance Italy.[4] Titian's influential *Bacchanal of the Andrians* of *c.*1523 (Figure 1) is wholly untroubled in its imagination of Bacchus's domain as a privileged and pleasurable one. It has been argued that Bacchus himself is rescued from direct association with drunkenness in Renaissance art.[5] This is the case in Titian's picture, where the effects of inebriation are carefully adumbrated but the god does not appear. We are, however, shown the recognisable appearances and behaviours of people under the influence of wine: the pot-bellied drinker on the left appears like a drunken peasant in a painting of everyday life, while others have taken

(1998), 1–30; B. Ann Tlusty, 'Gender and Alcohol Use in Early Modern Augsburg', *Social History/Histoire Social* (1994), 241–59; Benjamin Roberts, 'Drinking Like a Man: The Paradox of Excessive Drinking for Seventeenth-Century Dutch Youths', *Journal of Family History*, 29:3 July (2004), 237–52.

[3] See Simon Schama, *The Embarrassment of Riches: An Interpretation of Dutch Culture in the Golden Age* (London, 1991), 189–93, 195, 199–203, 208–12, 218–20; B. Ann Tlusty, *Bacchus and Civic Order: The Culture of Drink in Early Modern Germany* (Charlottesville and London, 2001); Adam Smyth (ed.), *A Pleasing Sinne: Drink and Conviviality in Seventeenth-Century England* (Cambridge, 2004).

[4] See Malcolm Bull, *The Mirror of the Gods* (Harmondsworth, 2005), 223–61.

[5] Bull, *The Mirror of the Gods*, 230–5, argues that the image of drunkenness settled on the ribald figure of his fat old follower Silenus, allowing Bacchus himself to maintain his god-like characteristics. For Titian's painting see Harold E. Wethey, *The Paintings of Titian* (London, 1971), vol. III, cat. 15, 151–3.

Figure 1. Titian, *The Andrians*, *c.*1523. Madrid, Museo del Prado. ©2013. Photo Scala, Florence.

to dancing.[6] The amorous nature of the conversation between the young women lying on the grass is suggested by the naked men who encircle them, who might be intended as visualizations of the girls' erotic fantasy. The physical effects of wine are also noted: the inability to stand up (the river god at the background right); the desire to sleep (foreground right nude) and, of course, to urinate. The cupid pissing on his mother's legs is, though, a classical motif which conforms to a well-established type of garden statuary and has symbolic associations with sexual fertility.[7]

The classicism of Titian's painting very thoroughly mediates these references to contemporary life insisting on a degree of separation from the

[6] The fat drinker might well be Silenus himself: see Wethey, *The Paintings of Titian*, III, 38.

[7] See, e.g., the figure of cupid urinating into his mother's lap in Lorenzo Lotto's *Venus and Cupid* (*c.*1540, New York, Metropolitan Museum of Art) which more overtly alludes to sexual union, probably within an epithalamic context. See Peter Humfrey, *Lorenzo Lotto* (New Haven and London, 1997) 139.

present. *The Andrians* was painted for one of Alfonso d'Este's *camerini d'alabastro* in the Ducal Palace at Ferrara, but the relation of the Duke's world to that shown by Titian is made a matter of inference. Titian depicts the story in Philostratus' *Imagines* recording the occasion when Bacchus turned the river on Andros into wine. But Alfonso was particularly famed for his vineyards and provision of fine wines, and the Andrians imbibe out of a range of early sixteenth-century drinking vessels from cut-glass to pewter and clay jugs.[8] More generally, perhaps, the golden-age that the inhabitants enjoy was intended as a reference to the ideal social conditions under the Duke's reign in Ferrara.

Titian's painting deliberately evokes an ancient classical frieze, and in literary terms, the Arcadian wooded groves between mountain and coast so familiar to readers of Latin and Greek pastoral poetry. It is Titian's adoption of the visual and poetic tropes of mythic antiquity that generates space for an image that insistently celebrates alcoholic inebriation: the message is encapsulated as a verbal synecdoche on the small *cartellino* in the foreground: 'he who drinks and does not drink again does not know what drinking is'.[9] Renaissance classicism could, of course, function in the service of humanistic and religious reform as it did, for example, in early sixteenth-century Florence and Rome. But at the court of Ferrara it served, rather, as an aristocratic motif of cultural displacement through which alternatives to the more circumscribed possibilities of the present are imagined and enjoyed. In Titian's Bacchanals, the imagery of reckless drunkenness offered an escape from the exigencies of the here and now that was especially palatable to an autocratic patron who was the guardian of social and moral order within his princely state.

The elite context of celebratory drinking may also explain the suggestion in Titian's painting that it has a sacred or divine dimension. The consumption of wine is pictured as sensually enervating: as in the Catholic Mass, wine functions in a transformative manner raising the intoxicant to a higher state of

[8] For the role of goblets in Venetian Renaissance paintings as tools of transformation within the 'civilizing process' see Pascale Rihouet, 'Veronese's Goblets: Glass Design and the Civilizing Process', *Journal of Design History*, online publication, 2012. For the classical literary sources and contemporary allusions in Titian's Bacchanals, including *The Andrians* see Paul Holberton, 'The Choice of Texts for the Camerino Pictures' in Görel Cavalli-Björkman (ed.), *Bacchanals by Titian and Rubens* (Stockholm, 1987), 57–66.

[9] From 'Qui boyt et ne reboy/Il ne scet que boyr soit'. It has been suggested that the music accompanying these words is part of a canon by the Flemish choirmaster of St. Mark's in Venice, Adrian Willaert, see Wethey, *The Paintings of Titian*, III, 39.

consciousness. At the peak of the main compositional pyramid a dancer pauses to hold aloft a glass chalice in which the wine is very clearly visible. His raising of the chalice heavenwards might echo the elevation of the wine at the Mass (the consecration of the chalice), as it must also the ecstatic gesture of Bacchus himself in many celebratory sculptures of the period (Figure 3). This association reflects the fashionable Renaissance idea that Bacchus's alcoholic intoxication represents one of Plato's four forms of divine madness.[10] In Titian's painting, nothing explicitly equivalent to the miracle of transubstantiation at the Catholic Mass is envisaged. But the Neo-Platonic synthesis nonetheless meant that depictions of the Bacchic rite allow a transcendent and creative dimension for drinking.

Such was the persistence of this kind of sacred association that visual artists in early modernity sometimes identified themselves directly with the god of wine, enacting Bacchic drinking rituals to express their creativity and to emphasize its sacred source. The so-called 'Bentvueghels' ('birds of a feather'), a group of Dutch artists working in seventeenth-century Rome, staged pageants in honour of Bacchus, their identification with the god offering further support for the prevalent idea of the *divino artista.*[11] But the Bentvueghels' identification was also half-ironic, a satirical side-swipe at the pomposity of academic Italian artists in Rome. And the positive imagery of Bacchus discussed so far was increasingly open to a contrary interpretation. Michelangelo's pioneering early sculpture of the mid-1490s, in which he sought to emulate a famous work of antiquity by Praxiteles, might appear to represent an idealizing sculptural equivalent to Titian's *Andrians* (Figure 2). It too was a private commission from an elite patron and art collector, Raffaelle Riario, a cardinal at the papal court in Rome. Riario was in close correspondence with Marsilio Ficino himself, chief philosophical propagator of the Neo-Platonic alliance between pagan and Christian values.[12]

[10] Edgar Wind, *Pagan Mysteries of the Renaissance* (New York, 1968), 177–90; Erwin Panofsky, *Studies in Iconology: Humanistic Themes in the Art of Renaissance* (New York, 1972) 129–69. For the overlap with sacramental imagery see Stephen Bann, *The True Vine: On Visual Representation and the Western Tradition* (Cambridge, 1989).

[11] T. J. Kren, 'Chi non vuol Baccho: Roeland van Laer's Burlesque Painting about Dutch Artists in Rome', *Simiolus* 11 (1980), 63–80. For the divinely-inspired artist see Ernst Kris and Otto Kurz, *Legend, Myth, and Magic in the Image of the Artist: A Historical Experiment* (New Haven and London, 1981).

[12] For Riario's friendship and correspondence with Marsilio Ficino see Bull, *Mirror of the Gods*, 230.

Figure 2. Michelangelo Buonarroti, *Bacchus*, 1496–7. Florence, Museo Nazionale del Bargello. ©2013. Photo Scala, Florence. Courtesy of the Ministero Beni e Att. Culturali.
Figure 3. Jacopo Sansovino, *Bacchus*, 1510–12. Florence, Museo del Bargello. ©2013. Photo Scala, Florence. Courtesy of the Ministero Beni e Att. Culturali.

But Michelangelo's Bacchus lurches to the left to subtly disorder the expected *all'antica* balance of the *contrapposto* pose and suggest a more sinister meaning. And by the mid-sixteenth century, the work was interpreted as a Christian allegory against drunkenness by the sculptor's follower Ascanio Condivi. Though the tiger skin held by the little satyr is a reference to Bacchus's sojourn in India, Condivi explains its presence as showing 'that he who loses himself in sensuality and the cravings for that fruit [grapes] and its liquor in the end loses his life'.[13] Michelangelo's work offers a telling contrast with those of followers such as Jacopo Sansovino (Figure 3). Although Sansovino maintained the little satyr and tiger skin, he also re-established the classical balance of Bacchus himself, re-orientating his gaze

[13] This translation is taken from Ascanio Condivi, 'Life of Michelangelo Buonarroti', in George Bull (ed.), *Michelangelo: Life, Letters and Poetry* (Oxford, 1987), 21. For Michelangelo's *Bacchus* see Charles De Tolnay, *The Youth of Michelangelo* (Princeton, 1943), cat. no. IV, 142–5; Michael Hirst, 'Michelangelo in Rome: An Altar-piece and the "Bacchus"', *The Burlington Magazine*, cxxiii (1981), 581–93; Michael Hirst and Jill Dunkerton, *Making and Meaning: The Young Michelangelo 1496–1501* (London, 1994), 29–35.

and gesture toward the heavens to emphasize his status as a god rather than a tottering drunk.[14]

It may be that Michelangelo—who played a formative role in the writing of Condivi's biography—wanted to make a pious re-interpretation of a sensuous early work from the perspective of the reformed mentality of his old-age.[15] But the moral interpretation of his *Bacchus* is nonetheless in keeping with a noticeable hardening of attitudes against the god as the sixteenth century advanced. Andrea Alciati had published an emblem entitled 'Vino prudentium auguri' (Figure 4) with a motto explaining that 'if an abstemious man hates wine, he'll have no help from the goddess [Pallas]'. But another of Alciati's emblems is entitled 'Prudentes vino abstinent', or 'wise men abstain from wine' (Figure 5). Alciati understood Michelangelo's model—the antique *Bacchus* by Praxiteles—as a moral allegory on the harmful effects of drink.[16] By the later years of the century a new literary genre dominated by German Lutherans had emerged, in which the intoxicated world of Bacchus and his followers is imagined as a threatening and absolute other to the established social and moral order.[17]

If the above examples have already shown that the early modern imagery of Bacchus was open to wide vicissitudes of meaning between ideal and ironic interpretation, it is also clear that these varying attitudes were not readily delimited by contrasting northern and southern visual traditions, or even by more immediate conditions of reception (patronage or audience). Thus Caravaggio's half-length depictions of the god from the 1590s were made with an elite courtly circle of patrons in Rome in mind, but nonetheless undermine the kind of ideal interpretation of 'courtly' works such as Titian's *Andrians.* In a very early painting, Caravaggio made a potentially

[14] Bruce Boucher, *The Sculpture of Jacoo Sansovino* (New Haven and London, 1992), vol. 2, cat. no. 6, 317. Boucher contrasts Sansovino's *Bacchus* with Michelangelo's noting that the latter's sculpture 'is more of a visual pun on drunkenness' (vol. 1, 13).

[15] Paul Barolsky, *Michelangelo's Nose: A Myth and its Maker* (Pennsylvania, 1990) for the artist's formative impact on Condivi's 'biography'. For Michelangelo's later disavowal of the allurements of visual art, see Alexander Nagel, *Michelangelo and the Reform of Art* (Cambridge, 2000).

[16] Andrea Alciati, This translation from *Emblematum Liber* (1550, Lyon), trans. Betty I. Knott (Aldershot, 1996) nos. 24 and 30. The motto in the voice of the tree of Wisdom (or Pallas Athena) reads: 'Branching vine, why do you trouble me? I am the tree of Pallas. Take your grapes away–this virgin shrinks from Bromius [Bacchus]'. For Alciati's moral interpretation of Praxiteles' sculpture see Bull, *The Mirror of the Gods*, 230.

[17] See, e.g., Nicolous Calenus, *In detestationem, originem et ritum Bacchanaliorum oratio* (Marburg, 1591) and Salomon Gesner, *Oratio de personis sive larvis . . .* (Wittenburg, 1600).

Figure 4. Andrea Alciati, 'Vino prudentium auguri'. Number 23 from the *Emblematum Liber* (1531). By permission of the University of Glasgow Library, Special Collections.
Figure 5. Andrea Alciati, 'Prudentes vino abstinent'. Number 24 from the *Emblematum Liber* (1531). By permission of the University of Glasgow Library, Special Collections.

elevating self-identification with Bacchus, but at the same time ironized the image by showing himself as sick (Figure 6). Fleshly discoloration and the clenched posture of the painter-god's body indicate his physical malady and, by extension, his moral corruption.[18]

In this painting, as in the more subtle work now in the Uffizi (Figure 7) Caravaggio's representation of Bacchus only superficially conforms to classicizing precedents, employing the imagery of realism to undercut ideal or sacred presentation. These half-lengths featuring a single figure set behind stone parapet-like structures recall Renaissance portraits, an association that is itself suggestive of Caravaggio's insistence on the real. The classicizing tradition had revived something of the integrity of the body in antique art and stood apart, in this regard, from the predominant mode in contemporary Christian art, where physical desecration or mutilation was thematically central.[19] In Caravaggio's Uffizi *Bacchus*, the collision of these two visual modes is made key to the meaning of the painting. If the heightened or supernatural

[18] Mia Cinotti and G. A. Dell'Acqua, *Michelangelo Merisi detto il Caravaggio* (Bergamo, 1983), cat. no. 52, 505–10. Other painters, such as Giovan Paolo Lomazzo and Hans von Aachen also showed themselves in the guise of Bacchus in this period, see Bull, *The Mirror of the Gods*, 253.

[19] For an examination of this division see Tom Nichols, 'Defining Genres: The Survival of Mythological Painting in Counter-Reformation Venice' in Abigail Brundin and Matthew Treherne, *Forms of Faith in Sixteenth-Century Italy* (Aldershot, 2009), 119–48.

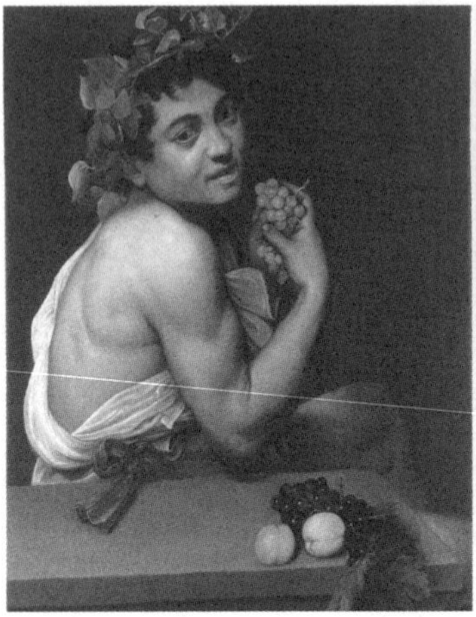

Figure 6. Caravaggio, *Sick Bacchus*, *c.*1593–4. Rome, Galleria Borghese. ©2013. Photo Scala, Florence. Courtesy of the Ministero Beni e Att. Culturali.
Figure 7. Caravaggio, *Bacchus*, *c.*1595–7. Florence, Galleria degli Uffizi. ©2013. Photo Scala, Florence. Courtesy of the Ministero Beni e Att. Culturali.

lighting of Bacchus's form, like the treatment of his drapery, recalls more ideal presentations, his fleshiness is undermining, as are the withered vine-leaves and rotting fruit. The 'sitter' is disturbingly youthful, appearing like one of Pasolini's *ragazzi di vita*, a full-lipped and heavy-lidded Roman street boy whose intimate yet compromising offer of a glass to the viewer immediately collapses the effect of classical distance maintained in earlier Italian representations (Figure 3). Bacchus is brought into the present moment with all its moral fragility in the Christian universe. The knowing directness of his sensuous gaze offers a challenge to the viewer: immediate sensual pleasure will be had by those who accept his glass, the sharing of wine a tissue-thin euphemism for the offer of sex. The substitution of Bacchus's classical thyrsus for a seventeenth-century love-knot suggests as much. But rather than removing earthly care, our acceptance of the boy-god's invitation will necessarily have dark consequences.

When Diego Velázquez turned to the Bacchic theme in a work made in Madrid in 1628–9, he revived the ambiguous mode of Caravaggio's Uffizi painting (Figure 8).[20] Spanish painters of the seventeenth century treated subjects from ancient mythology more rarely and with less ease or sympathy

[20] José López-Rey, *Velázquez: The Complete Works* (Cologne, 1997), cat no. 41, 259.

Figure 8. Diego Velázquez, *Los Borrachos*, 1628–9. Madrid, Museo del Prado. ©2013. Photo Scala, Florence. Culturali.

than the Italians, reflecting their physical and cultural distance from the classical heritage and relative ignorance of available models for imitation. In Velázquez's painting the language of ideal classicism which the painter had recently learned from the extensive art collections at the court of Philip IV in Madrid is referenced in the figure of the god and his two acolytes on the left.[21] As in Caravaggio's paintings, Bacchus' form possesses a supernatural light, his flesh taking on something of the heightened contrasts of an antique marble nude, while his classical drapery makes a bold contrast with the rough contemporary clothes worn by those to the right.[22] Likewise the direction of his gaze away from the ceremony he conducts suggests his otherworldly origin. And though he sits on a barrel his followers crouch or recline on a

[21] The painting was probably completed shortly before Velázquez's first visit to Italy between August 1629 and January 1631: López-Rey, *Velázquez: The Complete Works*, 65–71.

[22] For the idea that the painting is a *teoxenia* or visitation of god to men, based on an engraving of a Hellenistic relief known to Velázquez in Madrid see Delphine F. Darby, 'In the Train of the Vagrant Silenus', *Art In America*, 31 (1943), 140–8. But the limitations to this suggestion are evident enough from the discussion here.

snatched indication of a pastoral landscape that still suggests a measure of sacred or poetic otherness.

The more elevated portrayal granted to the god and his followers is juxtaposed with the coarse realism of the drinkers to the right, depicted by Velázquez in a manner that revives his earliest style as developed in Seville for his so-called *bodegón* paintings.[23] But the supposedly contrasting 'ideal' and 'real' sides of the painting are not shown in a hierarchical or opposing relation to one another, and are in fact only superficially distinct. It is the potential overlap between the ancient and modern worlds they reference that Velázquez is most interested in. Bacchus's skin is still more oily than that of Caravaggio's street boy (Figure 7) and his expression more definitely a leer, pointing up the complicity of his world with the grubby one to his left. And although the two reclining followers still recall the mythic innocent youths of the Arcadian groves, they are confined to the shadowy margins while the contemporary street drunks take centre stage as the god's true devotees.

If there is a contrast to be drawn in this painting, then it is not between Bacchus and the drunks, but rather between the secular pagan ceremony depicted and the sanctified Christian ritual of the Mass that the scene recalls. In many Counter-Reformation altarpieces pious worshippers kneel before the seated or enthroned sacred figures, with the implication that their spiritual lives are miraculously transformed through their participation in the ceremony.[24] But those enamoured of Bacchus are already and habitually drunk: the clumsy kneeling motion of the foreground drinker calls to mind its sacred alternative only in order to make the contrast. There will be no transformation or transcendence of the drinker's depraved reality. The god's crowning with vines is to this extent a degrading drunken mockery of pious church ritual. And the anti-Christian nature of the proceedings is indicated again by the all but forgotten figure of the beggar on the extreme right, whose plea for charity is apparently ignored by the intoxicated who huddle around Bacchus.[25]

[23] López-Rey, *Velázquez: The Complete Works*, cat nos. 1, 3, 6, 7, 16, 17 and 18. See also 34–8.

[24] López-Rey, *Velázquez: The Complete Works*, 68, notes that the kneeling reveller adopts a 'communion-like pose'. His posture is not so very far from that taken up by the pious pilgrims who kneel before the Virgin in Caravaggio's *Madonna of Loreto*, *c.*1604–5, Rome, S. Agostino: see Cinotti and Dell'Acqua, *Michelangelo Merisi detto il Caravaggio*, cat. no. 60, 524–5.

[25] López-Rey, *Velázquez: The Complete Works*, 68–9. Antonio Palomino, writing in 1724, understood the painting as a parody of Bacchus's own pretentions, describing it as 'The Triumph of Bacchus in Burlesque' (quoted in López-Rey, 65).

The didactic image of drinking in Dutch and Flemish art

Caravaggio was, of course, a controversial figure in seventeenth-century art, while Velázquez's powerful critique of the *all'antica* imagery of Bacchus reflects both the religiosity of Catholic culture in seventeenth-century Spain and its intensifying opposition to the classical-humanist cult of Renaissance Italy. It would be easy enough to find examples in which the more ideal aspects of this iconography are maintained, particularly in the field of allegory, where the god was very occasionally depicted as 'Liber' and thus as a personification of political freedom.[26] But it is nonetheless significant that such leading artists were inclined to dispute or undermine idealistic aspects in the Renaissance imagery of intoxication. This sceptical approach, similarly adopting a realist or genre mode of presentation had, in fact, a much longer history in the art of northern Europe, with its origins in the *grille* featured in the margins of medieval manuscripts and in subsequent didactic paintings and prints. In many such images from Germany and the Low Countries, beer is imbibed by debauched-looking contemporary-looking peasants or beggars, often in front of an ale house (Figure 9).[27]

Drinking is made the cause of 'Ira' in Hieronymus Bosch's didactic *Seven Deadly Sins* table top of *c.*1475, the placement of the fight outside an inn, like the jug brandished by one of the drunken protagonists, making the point succinctly enough (Figure 10).[28] In an etching/engraving published some thirty-five years later by Lucas van Leyden, alcohol is again made central to the interchanges between the ragged protagonists (Figure 11). The tattered clothing of these figures, who are barely shod, along with their staffs and (perhaps stolen) rosary beads identify them as false pilgrims or vagrant beggars, as does their placement within a harsh rocky landscape with a symbolic dead tree.[29] The walking figure passes a drinking bowl, probably containing

[26] Bull, *The Mirror of the Gods*, 249–52, for some painted and printed examples following Tintoretto's groundbreaking depiction of *Bacchus and Ariadne* as an allegory of the freedom of the Venetian Republic in 1578. But Bacchus was only very rarely used as a personification of the early modern state.

[27] Hans-Joachim Raupp, *Bauernsatiren: Enstehung und Entwicklung des bäuerlichen Genres in der deutschen und nierderländischen Kunst c.1470–1570* (Cologne, 1986); Alison Stewart, 'Taverns in Nuremberg Prints at the Time of the German Reformation' in Beat Kumin and B. Ann Tlusty (eds), *The World of the Tavern: Public Houses in Early Modern Europe* (Aldershot, 2002), 95–115.

[28] Charles De Tolnay, *Hieronymus Bosch*, trans. Michale Bullock and Henry Mins (London, 1965), cat. no. 2, 338–9 and 58–69.

[29] E. S. Jabobowitz and S. L. Stepanek (eds), *The Prints of Lucas van Leyden and His Contemporaries* (Princeton, 1983) cat. no. 23; Tom Nichols, *The Art of Poverty: Irony and Ideal in Sixteenth-Century Beggar Imagery* (Manchester, 2007), 194–5.

Figure 9. David Vinckboons, *Peasant Kermis*, *c.*1605. Dresden, Gemäldegalerie. ©2013. Photo Scala, Florence/BPK, Bildagentur fur Kunst, Kultur und Geschichte, Berlin.

Figure 10. Hieronymus Bosch, *Ira*. Detail from *The Seven Deadly Sins* tabletop, *c.*1475. Madrid, Museo del Prado. ©2013. Photo Scala, Florence.
Figure 11. Lucas van Leyden, *Beggars*, *c.*1509–10. Etching and engraving. Rijksprentenkabinet, Amsterdam. Photo: Courtesy of the Warburg Institute, London.

alcohol, to the seated one, almost casually suggesting one prominent cause of their degradation. The open vessel glimpsed between the legs of the woman seated nearby euphemistically suggests another consequence of intoxication, one that may already be implicit in the comically intimate and unintentional 'dance' enacted between the fighter and the 'restraining' woman in Bosch's

Ira (Figure 10). And dancing proper, considered as sinful by many early modern moralists, is more explicitly featured in David Vinckboons' painting in which drunken peasants cavort around in a wild *kermis* in front of an inn (Figure 9).[30]

Drinking in this representational context is allowed no elevating or learned associations with Bacchus or the classical world, functioning rather as an expression of a range of perceived contemporary vices among the lower classes.[31] The default position in the many low-life genre images produced in seventeenth-century Holland, for example, is to suggest that the abject social and moral position of those depicted is the result, not of the social and economic exclusions of the capitalist economy, but rather of their own abhorrent addictions. Many of these works serve to 'frame' those they depict in a punitive sense, making them wholly responsible for their actions, and showing them as the miscreant 'others' to the respectable middle classes who bought and enjoyed such images. It is likely that the new denizens of the Dutch towns would have gained pleasure precisely from the inverse relation this imagery insisted on: through the definition of low-life drinkers as poor, idle, ugly, mad and, above all, responsible for their own demise, the viewer could know himself to be the opposite: that is, an economically productive and morally respectable citizen in a justified social order.[32]

The Haarlem painter Frans Hals developed a particularly loose or painterly pictorial technique which signals the 'alterity' of his low-life subjects (Figure 12).[33] The words we might use to describe this brush work ('rough', 'loose', or perhaps even better, given the presiding presence of alcohol, 'fluid') tellingly match our sense of the unstable identities of the drinkers.[34] But such a technique also carries an implication of artistic sophistication and serves as a distancing sign to the middle-class viewer. Hals varied

[30] In 1494 the German moralist Sebastian Brant noted that dancing 'stirs up pride, immodestly/ And prompts man ever lewd to be': Sebastian Brant, *The Ship of Fools*, trans. E. Zeydel (New York, 1944), 205. His opinion was often restated in the centuries that followed: see Nichols, *The Art of Poverty*, 66–71.

[31] Immoderate drinking was frequently used to identify both peasants and beggars, whose imagery overlapped significantly in this period: see Nichols, *The Art of Poverty*, 49–57.

[32] See Paul Vandenbroeck (ed.), *Beeld van de andere, vertoog over het zelf: over wilden en narren, boeren en bedelaars* (Antwerp, 1987), 11, for this suggestion. But see also the very wide audience for genre prints suggested in Eddy de Jongh and Ger Luitjen, *Mirror of Everyday Life: Genreprints in the Netherlands 1550–1700*, trans. Michael Hoyle (Amsterdam, 1997), 9–41.

[33] Seymour Slive, *Frans Hals* (London,1970), vol. 1, 112–13.

[34] The term 'rouw' was already in use in the seventeenth century: See Seymour Slive, 'On the Meaning of Frans Hals' 'Malle Babbe', *The Burlington Magazine*, cv (1963), 432–6.

Figure 12. Frans Hals, *Malle Babbe, c.*1633–5, Berlin, Gemäldegalerie, Staatliche Museen, Berlin. Photo: Joerg P. Anders. ©2013. Photo Scala, Florence/BPK, Bildagentur fur Kunst, Kultur und Geschichte, Berlin.

his technique in accordance with the social status of his sitters, employing a relatively tight handling for commissioned portraits of Haarlem worthies, and a much rougher and sketchier one for those towards the bottom of the social hierarchy.[35] His *Malle Babbe* or 'Mad Barbara' was only a portrait in a

[35] Compare the *Malle Babbe* with near-contemporary commissioned works such as the *Portrait of a Man* (1630, London, Royal Collection) or *Pieter van den Broecke* (*c.*1633, London, Kenwood).

circumscribed sense (given that it was certainly not commissioned—or sanctioned—by the sitter herself). But Malle Babbe was nonetheless a real individual, a vagrant woman who was eventually imprisoned in the Haarlem house of correction in 1653—about twenty years after Hals had made his portrait.[36] One might wonder how these two incarcerations (the one pictorial, the other penal) relate to one another. Malle Babbe's sudden shriek, her drunken frenzy, is captured above all by the fluidity of Hals' handling of paint, the detached brush-marks capturing an uncontrolled outburst of emotion pictured as a sign of her social and moral ephemerality.

Hals' painting is not, in the first place, a critique of the terrors of drink: Malle Babbe's cackle may have its immediate cause in her present intoxication, but this in itself is made to reflect something deeper, symbolized by the owl perched uncertainly on her shoulder. Owls had long been associated with vagrants (the Flemish word 'scovuut' signified both 'owl' and 'beggar') and had come to symbolize their moral falsity.[37] The ancient identification of owls with Pallas Athena's wisdom covers their darker identification as birds of prey of the night, the time of shadowy deception, of potential thievery and wrongdoing. By placing an owl on Malle Babbe's shoulder, Hals revealed to the viewer her true moral identity as a false beggar and cheat. When the city authorities finally apprehended her a few decades later, they re-confirmed in the sphere of criminal justice what Hals' portrait had already shown in paint.[38]

The dialectic between satire and idealization that was noted above in the context of the imagery of Bacchus is apparent once again within Hals' own oeuvre. In a famous series of group portraits painted for the Haarlem militia companies the officers raise glasses to make a toast, and wine-drinking is central to the merriment of the occasion depicted and to its reading in a positive light (Figures 13 and 14).[39] These group portraits typically depict

[36] Seymour Slive (ed.), *Frans Hals* (London, 1989), cat. no. 37, 236 and doc. 94, 395.

[37] Owls were also associated with drunkenness; the phrase 'drunk as an owl' ('zoo beschonken als een uil') was already in use: see Slive (ed.), *Frans Hals*, 239. For further discussion of early modern owl-beggars see Nichols, *The Art of Poverty*, 38–40, 60, 187.

[38] The incarceration of Malle Babbe in 1653, as also the particularly negative representation of her in Hals' painting, was also a reflection of the distinction between male and female drinking in early modern Europe: see Tlusty, 'Gender and Alcohol Use in Early Modern Augsburg', 241–59. For the particular link between female drinking and sexual availability in early modernity see Lucas van Leyden's print discussed above (illus. 11) and also A. Lynn Martin, *Alcohol, Sex, and Gender in Late Medieval and Early Modern Europe* (Basingstoke and New York, 2001).

[39] Slive, *Frans Hals*. For the paintings illustrated here see Seymour Slive, *Frans Hals*, vol. 3 (London, 1973), cat. Nos. 7 and 46.

Figure 13. Frans Hals, *Banquet of the Officers of the St George Civic Guard*, 1616, Haarlem, Frans Hals Museum, Harlem. ©2013. White Images/Scala, Florence.
Figure 14. Frans Hals, *Banquet of the Officers of the St George Civic Guard*, *c.*1627, Haarlem, Frans Hals Museum, Harlem. ©2013. White Images/Scala, Florence.

merchants rather than soldiers, emphasizing the civic rather than military functions of the companies. Commercial business was readily conducted in the militia meeting hall in Haarlem where these paintings hang, with the proviso (inscribed in the chimney breast) that 'no commerce conducted in this hall can be held so binding that he who rues it may not revoke the agreement on the following day by paying for the wine'.[40] Drinking was central to business exchanges conducted within the militias, playing a vital part in the creation of social harmony and prosperity expressed in the group portraits. Hals pays particular attention to the fine glassware, and to the raising of a toast: in the 1616 painting of the officers of the St George Civic Guard, visual prominence is given to Nicolaes Woutersz van der Meer (*c.*1574–1637), the only figure seated in front of the table, who was a wealthy brewer, as if to emphasize the binding centrality of drink within the ruling class of Haarlem (Figure 13).[41]

Significantly, however, the militia companies are shown as merry rather than drunk: drinking is tolerated in the wider context of a feast, and despite the evident sociability and enjoyment of the company, each figure maintains the requisite measure of self-control expected for a commissioned group portrait. The hierarchical boundaries of acceptable drinking practices within the militia companies are also indicated by the fact that it is only the promoted officers who propose the toast.[42] In European portraiture as a whole, displays of expressive emotion were avoided, or circumscribed by considerations of social manners and rank. Though Hals' smiling militiamen are certainly a departure from the glum-faced late sixteenth-century depictions of the company by Cornelis Cornelisz van Haarlem, their expressions are still a far cry from Malle Babbe's uncontrolled drink-induced cackle.[43] The need for moderation is made explicit in the later depiction of this company, where Captain Michiel de Wael, also a leading brewer in Haarlem, is shown turning his glass upside down, as if to pour his drink away: his gesture intimates that temperance is a prerequisite of civic harmony (Figure 14).[44]

The prominence of brewers in these paintings of Haarlem high society, and more widely of drinking at civic feasts, tells us that alcohol was the essential commercial lubricant in the town, as in many others across early modern Europe. The inclusion of subtle indications of the need for temperance, and the way this might distinguish 'high' from 'low' social drinking, should not distract us from the quasi-baptismal role it enjoyed in secular society.

[40] Koos Levy-van Halm and Liesbeth Abraham, 'Frans Hals, Militiaman and Painter: The Civic Guard Portrait as an Historical Document', in Slive (ed.), *Frans Hals*, 93.

[41] Van der Meer was also an alderman and burgomaster of Haarlem.

[42] Levy-van Halm and Abraham, 'Frans Hals, Militiaman and Painter', 94.

[43] See footnote 38 above for the division of gender roles regarding drinking that would have encouraged Hals' positive image of the all-male militias and his negative one of a drunken old woman.

[44] Levy-van Halm and Abraham, 'Frans Hals, Militiaman and Painter', 93–4. Like Van der Meer, de Wael was also active in the civic administration of the city.

Through the frequent toasts raised by the officers in the Haarlem militia, the individual (so carefully delineated in Hals' group portraits) was bound into the wider social body, becoming properly part of the citizenry.

Double vision, or a reversible image of drinking

Analysis of Italian and Spanish images of Bacchus has already indicated the pitfalls of assuming a unitary or singular meaning for depictions of drinking in any one iconography or visual tradition in this period. The discussion above of the 'negative' and 'positive' representations of this activity in the work of a single artist—Frans Hals—has revealed a parallel kind of ambiguity in northern art. Analysis of Pieter Bruegel the Elder's famous painting of a *Peasant Dance* (Figure 15) will allow us to trace visual contradiction in such representations more closely still: within the domain of a single work.[45] At first sight Bruegel's painting seems merely to encapsulate the didactic and satirical tendencies visible in certain other Flemish and Dutch images of the period. It features carousing peasants in front of an inn: fuelled by alcohol, these crude and heavy-footed figures are governed by lustful impulses and desires, revealing their surrender of all mental control. But the moral distance that is central to effective visual satire is undermined by Bruegel's innovative pictorial composition. In Vinckboons' *Peasant Kermis* (Figure 9) the panoramic viewpoint insists that we 'look down on' those depicted, in a manner that is both literal and metaphorical. And this kind of constructed spatial discontinuity between viewer and image is in fact normative within the entire genre of peasant gatherings in the period, establishing in visual terms the distinction between 'high' viewer and 'low' subject. Bruegel's lowered viewpoint, on the other hand, challenges this implied social division between audience and actor.

Rather than distancing the viewer from the subject it makes the figural arrangement appear radically contingent. The mode of the painting challenges the usual comforting separation between image and reality, confusing our understanding of the painting as a pre-arranged composition.[46]

[45] F. Grossmann, *Bruegel: Complete Edition of the Paintings* (London, 1966), 201; Wolfgang Stechow, *Pieter Bruegel the Elder* (London, 1970), 130–3; Wilfried Seipel (ed.), *Pieter Bruegel the Elder at the Kunsthistorisches Museum in Vienna* (Milan, 1998), 138–47; Ethan Matt Kavaler, *Pieter Bruegel: Parables of Order and Enterprise* (Cambrdige, 1999), 184–211.

[46] Bruegel's learned circle of friends and supporters in Brussels might have given him access to contemporary humanist interests in 'the image made by chance': see H. W. Janson, '"The Image Made by Chance" in Renaissance Thought' in *De artibus opuscula XL: Essays in Honor of Erwin Panofsky*, ed. Millard Meiss (New York, 1961), 54–66.

Figure 15. Pieter Bruegel the Elder, *Peasant Dance*, *c.*1567, Vienna, Kunsthistorisches Museum. ©2013. Photo Art media/Heritage Images/Scala, Florence.

In accordance with this spontaneous effect, the peasants are not fully contained within the picture space, their forms cut off in seemingly arbitrary fashion at the picture's edges. The rapid and unexpected entry of the dancing couple from the right makes the image appear to encircle and absorb the viewer, generating a destabilizing 'wrap-around' effect, as if he must become another protagonist within the riotous scene. Moved up close to the peasants who argue, gesticulate, dance, grope, and drink, the viewer necessarily experiences something of the immediate sensate world they inhabit. Sound, smell, touch, and taste come to the fore, threatening to dethrone sight, widely accepted as the superior sense within early modern culture, and as the primary means of experiencing a work of art. And this new primacy allowed to the 'lower' senses is itself a further aspect of the denial of a clear and comprehensive 'viewpoint' of the entire scene from above.[47]

But it would nonetheless be a mistake to read Bruegel's image as a hearty folkloric endorsement of the vigour of peasant life. In many of his earlier paintings the high viewpoint, originally derived from Bosch, is apparent

[47] For the early modern hierarchy of the senses: David Summers, *The Judgement of Sense: Renaissance Naturalism and the Rise of Aesthetics* (Cambridge, 1990); Francois Quiviger, *The Sensory World of Italian Renaissance Art* (London, 2010).

enough, and the sins of those depicted are realized in their odd appearances and behaviours. Sixteenth-century images of peasants, and Bruegel's in particular, have been the subject of fierce disagreement, with scholars hamstrung between polarized 'positive' and 'negative' interpretations.[48] Part of the problem with this debate lies in the attempt to make the image a passive reflection of what comes before it, whether the determinative factor is imagined as the painter's personal attitude or as his more passive reflection of pre-existent social ideology. Whether the paintings are understood as satirical or otherwise, there is a shared assumption that they express an internally coherent meaning. And yet, in works such as the *Peasant Dance*, it is just this kind of 'clarity' or resolution that is circumvented by the particularity of the compositional arrangement.

Rather than tying such an image to a predetermined social viewpoint for or against peasants and their drinking habits, it may be more fruitful to note the contradictory or undecided possibilities contained or held within the image. Perhaps such a work even flirts with the taboo of non-meaning, offering a more unmediated kind of representation that did not follow a fixed or coherent position for or against drinking. This more unmediated kind of space was at least a necessary aspiration for a realist artist such as Bruegel. This is not, of course, to argue that all of Bruegel's paintings, or indeed many other early modern images of drunkenness, achieve this kind of blurring effect, or double-vision (to use that phrase advisedly in the context of a discussion of intoxication). But Bruegel's painting nonetheless exploits the special potentiality of the visual domain as a site of semantic contradiction or disturbance that perhaps parallels the disorientating effects of alcohol itself.

Instead of delimiting meaning, the visual imagery discussed in this paper may be seen to have opened or widened the possibility of a more discursive interpretation of drinking. The affirmation of one social attitude appears to have stimulated its alternative. Thus, in the southern European iconography of Bacchus, the idealization of drunkenness was quickly joined by an opposing narrative that stressed darker moral and satirical meanings. In northern art, where this kind of didactic meaning had long been more apparent, negative interpretation was also met by its opposite, with the development of

[48] For peasant imagery as satirical see Hessel Miedema, 'Realism and the Comic Mode: The Peasant', *Simiolus* 9 (1977), 205–19; Keith Moxey, *Peasants, Warriors, and Wives* (Chicago, 1989); Paul Vandenbroeck, 'Verbeeck's Peasant Weddings: A Study of Iconography and Social Function', *Simiolus* 14 (1984), 79–124. For the opposing view, see Svetlana Alpers, 'Bruegel's Festive Peasants', *Simiolus*, 6 (1972–3), 163–76; Margaret D. Carroll, 'Peasant Festivity and Political Identity in the Sixteenth Century', *Art History*, 10 (1987), 289–314.

imagery showing drinking as an essential means to social inclusion or elevation. In certain works, such as Bruegel's *Dancing Peasants*, the 'conversation' is played out in the arena of a single image in a way that overruns the narrower pre-determinations of a given position vis-à-vis the subject matter.

In sophisticated fashion Bruegel exploited the inherently ambiguous aesthetic of Renaissance illusionism to elucidate his equally ambiguous or debatable subject matter. His work acknowledges its status as a fiction, a deceiving illusion of three-dimensional reality on a two-dimensional surface that is knowingly not what it seems.[49] For this reason too, early modern visual art must be seen as particularly well-suited to register cultural ambiguities on its delusional surfaces. If Bruegel was unusual in his full exploitation of this withholding or mediating capacity, it may also be true that illusionistic visual art of the period always possessed a particular potential to express a more inclusive, if also more inconclusive, imagery of the contemporary cultures of drinking.

[49] For the special (and perhaps defining) illusionistic proclivities of artistic and literary culture in seventeenth-century Europe see José Antonio Maravall, *Culture of the Baroque: Analysis of a Historical Structure* (Minnesota, 1986).

Health, Intoxication, and Civil Conversation in Renaissance England*

Jennifer Richards

'He kept bottles of wine at his lodgeing, and many times he would drinke liberally by himselfe to refreshe his spirits, and exalt his muse.'[1] So records John Aubrey in his brief biography of the poet Andrew Marvell. The idea that alcohol lubricates the imagination is entrenched in Renaissance culture, and with good reason. As Shakespeare's figure of excess John Falstaff reliably explains, wine 'ascends me into the brain, dries me there all the foolish and dull and crudy vapours which environ it; makes it apprehensive, quick, forgetive, full of nimble, fiery, and delectable shapes, which delivered o'er to the voice, the tongue, which is the birth, becomes excellent wit.'[2]

Literary scholars have long recognized the good as well as bad effects of intoxication on the tongue and on wit; there are plenty of textual examples to attest to both. Recently, though, it has been the beneficial effects of hard drinking on voluble male communities that has caught our attention.[3] Michelle O'Callaghan reminds us that The Mermaid and The Mitre taverns were home to several convivial societies, the drinking activities of which helped to 'open an extemporised space for exploring the dimensions of laughter and pleasure', which in turn inspired literary composition, especially modes of ' "uninhibited discourse," from fantastical linguistic play to satires

* I would like thank the Leverhulme Trust who funded the research for this essay, and Phil Withington for his advice on earlier versions.

[1] John Aubrey, *'Brief Lives', chiefly of Contemporaries, set down by John Aubrey, between the Years 1669 and 1696*, vol. II, ed. Andrew Clark (Oxford, 1898), 54.

[2] William Shakespeare, *The Second Part of King Henry IV*, ed. A. R. Humphreys (London and New York, 1967, repr. 1987), 4. 3. 95–100.

[3] Michelle O'Callaghan, *The English Wits: Literature and Sociability in Early Modern England* (Cambridge, 2007); Joshua Scodel, *Excess and the Mean in Early Modern English Literature* (Princeton, 2002), 197–232; Adam Smyth, ' "It were far better be a *Toad*, or a *Serpant*, then a Drunkard": Writing about Drunkenness', in Smyth (ed.), *A Pleasing Sinne: Drink and Conviviality in Seventeenth-Century England* (Cambridge, 2004), 193–210.

 © The Past and Present Society

on the Church and State'.[4] Adam Smyth recalls that against a tide of moralizing, anti-drinking literature, John Cotgrave's *Wit's Interpreter* (1655, 1662, 1671) 'constructs a drunkard's discourse that is lexically rich'.[5] This literary intoxication not only lubricated the imagination but also freed the drinker to speak his mind. As Ben Jonson writes in 'Inviting a Friend to Supper': 'No simple word / That shall be uttered at our mirthful board / Shall make us sad next morning, or affright / The liberty that we'll enjoy to-night'.[6]

This literary scholarship contrasts with, and is increasingly being used to modify, a rather different and very well established historical narrative: that from 'the later sixteenth century . . . drunkenness began to attract much more moral criticism and governmental regulation', facilitated by the ' "revival" of "classical doctrine" ' with its emphasis on moderation.[7] One of the effects of this regulation, the argument goes, was that it reined in the elite, leaving the ' "meaner sorts of men" ' to indulge. Intoxicants became 'a source of solace and escape from material deprivations'.[8] These assumptions have been questioned most recently by Phil Withington, who has argued 'that Renaissance humanism could be used to valorize drunkenness and wit'—by which contemporaries meant either 'fancy' or 'discretion'—'as well as to idealize moderation and civility'.[9] Indeed, Withington makes use of literary scholars

4 O'Callaghan, *The English Wits*, 8.

5 Smyth, 'Writing about Drunkenness', 208.

6 Ben Jonson, *Poems*, ed. Ian Donaldson (Oxford, 1975), 56 (ll. 39–40). On this intoxicated liberty see Lorna Hutson, 'Civility and Virility in Ben Jonson', *Representations*, 78 (2002), 1–27.

7 Phil Withington, 'Intoxicants and Society in Early Modern England', *Historical Journal*, 54:3 (2011), 631–57, 633. For the scholarship that supports this emphasis on increased regulation see Beat Kumin, *Drinking Matters: Public Houses and Social Exchange in Early Modern Central Europe* (Basingstoke, 2007), 178–85; David Underdown, *Revel, Riot, and Rebellion: Popular Politics and Culture in England, 1603–1660* (Oxford, 1987), 44–72; Ronald Hutton, *The Rise and Fall of Merry England: The Ritual Year 1400–1700* (Oxford, 1996); Keith Wrightson, 'Alehouses, Order and Reformation in Rural England, 1590–1660' in Eileen Yeo and Stephen Yeo (eds), *Popular Culture and Class Conflict 1590–1914: Explorations in the History of Labour and Leisure* (Brighton, 1981). For a different perspective see B. Ann Tlusty, *Bacchus and Civic Order: The Culture of Drink in Early Modern Germany* (Charlottesville, 2001).

8 Ibid., 634, recalling David Courtwright, *Forces of Habit: Drugs and the Making of the Modern World* (Harvard, MA, 2001), 2, 59.

9 Withington, 'Intoxicants and Society', 635. On 'wit' as either 'fancy' or 'discretion' see this essay, 651, and Withington, 'Tumbled into the Dirt: Wit and Incivility in Early Modern England', *Journal of Historical Pragmatics*, 12 (2011), 156–77.

like O'Callaghan to identify educated milieus in which a 'capacity for "extraordinary fancy" and "hard drinking" went hand-in-hand'.[10]

This essay contributes further to this line of enquiry, exploring the interplay between intoxication and wit and the forms of civic expression it encouraged. However, whereas Withington focuses on wit as fancy, I am more interested in the interplay between intoxication and that other manifestation of wit, discretion; discretion goes hand in hand with light intoxication, not hard drinking. I will also be digging yet deeper into the moral narrative of intoxication. My sources are vernacular regimens and table philosophies, the advice of which tends to be viewed as prescriptive. Yet these books, I explain, simply offer food for thought: material for the exercise of discretion. Moreover, as the source I will keep until last, Stefano Guazzo's conduct book *La civil conversatione* (1575), makes clear, it is the 'turning' over of advice that exercises judgement and, at the table, interrupts drinking and paces intoxication. Guazzo may not champion the 'extraordinary fancy' of the English hard-drinkers that is favoured by many historians, but he does show how discretion—the 'subtil demands and serious alterations' of advice shared between tipsy dinner guests as they moderate their conversation and consumption of wine[11]—provides an opportunity to think fancifully about what civil company can be.

What does this mean exactly? Early modern discourses about intoxication acknowledge its social benefits as well as the moral dangers, as Withington explains. Yet how these benefits are represented, and the kinds of 'company' they give rise to, depends very much on the drink being quaffed, the manner and the context. The anonymous dialogue *Wine, beere, and ale, together by the eares* (1629; 1630), discussed by Withington, gives us one perspective: it reminds us how socially stratified drinking culture was in early modern England. Its all-male cast of characters includes 'Wine, A Gentleman', 'Beere, A Citizen', 'Ale, A Country-man', all of whom are contending for social precedence, and their servants, 'Nutmeg', 'Tost' etc. We find this social self-consciousness elsewhere. Sir William Cornwallis's essay 'Of Alehouses' resonates with his discomfort on finding himself in an urban space not meant for his sort:

> I write this in an Alehouse, into which I am driuen by night, which would not giue me leaue to finde out an honester harbour. I am without any Company but Inke, and Paper, and them I vse in stead

[10] Withington, *Intoxicants and Society*, 652.

[11] Stefano Guazzo, *The Ciuile Conuersation of M. Stephen Guazzo*, trans. George Pettie (I-III) and Bartholomew Young (IV) (London, 1586), 4. 176^{v}.

> of talking to my selfe: my Hoste hath already giuen me his knowledge, but I am little bettered, I am now trying whether my selfe be his better in discretion.[12]

However, the English translation of Guazzo's *La civil conversatione* achieves something different. It introduces a new way of thinking about how to enjoy an imported drink—wine[13]—to sustain the give and take of 'civil conversation', and it invites us to think again about who with. While the context depicted in this book is aristocratic, its readership was not; it included educated, self-improving, middling sort of men like the Cambridge humanist Gabriel Harvey, son of a Saffron Walden rope-maker.[14] Finally, the domestic context represented admits some chatty drinking companions who are largely ignored in drinking literature, except as the object of toasts or drunken jests: women.

It should be clear by now that in returning to so-called moralistic sources this essay is also questioning the dichotomy of excess and restraint that has dominated our understanding of Renaissance culture since Norbert Elias's *The Civilizing Process* was translated into English in 1969.[15] Elias's argument is that sixteenth-century conduct books inculcate and signal increased levels of embarrassment and self-surveillance which grew out of, and enabled, the centralization of government. Although his thesis has come under pressure in recent years, historians and literary critics still tend to reinforce the restraint/excess dichotomy by privileging moments when civil restraint is breached.[16] Moreover, food historians who take regimens and table philosophies as guides to early modern eating and drinking remain somewhat in Elias's thrall.[17]

[12] William Cornwallis, *Essayes* (London, 1600–1601), $M5^{v}$–$M6^{r}$.

[13] W. B. Stevens, 'English Wine Imports *c.*1603–1640, with special reference to Devon ports', in Todd Gray et al., *Tudor and Stuart Devon* (Exeter, 1992); see also Withington, ibid.

[14] Harvey owned an Italian edition (1581), which he heavily annotated (now held at The British Library), and the 1582 English translation of Books I–III, which he lightly annotated (now held at the Newberry library, Chicago). Virginia F. Stern, *Gabriel Harvey: His Life, Marginalia, and Library* (Oxford, 1979), 217–18.

[15] Norbert Elias, *The Civilizing Process: Sociogenetic and Psychogenetic Investigations,* trans. Edmund Jephcott (Oxford, 2000).

[16] O'Callaghan, *The English Wits*, 6–7; Anna Bryson, *From Courtesy to Civility: Changing Codes of Conduct in Early Modern England* (Oxford, 1998), 193–7. See also Robert Appelbaum, *Aguecheek's Beef, Belch's Hiccup, and Other Gastronomic Interjections: Literature, Culture, and Food among the Early Moderns* (Chicago, 2006), 208–11.

[17] Ken Albala, *Eating Right in the Renaissance* (Berkeley, 2002), 26, 209, 217–18; Appelbaum, *Aguecheek's Beef*, xvi, 13, 206–7, 211, 222, 228–30.

This essay argues, in contrast, that the preoccupation with restraint and excess has left the conviviality of moderate intoxication, light-headedness, and its rhetorical practice—the witty adaptation of sayings—overlooked and undervalued. I study the same textual sources that were central to Elias's *Civilizing Process*, but I read against the grain of his argument, exploring them as rhetorical works that address the process of managing intoxication so as to give voice to different views.

I

Vernacular regimens digest medical advice on healthy lifestyle for the benefit of a lay readership and physicians without Latin. The medicine they represent is broadly Galenic. Maintaining health is understood as a constant process of balancing the humours: blood, phlegm, black and yellow bile. Cures for disease involve purgation, but also diet. Food is ascribed 'qualities'—degrees of hotness, coldness, moistness, dryness—that help a reader to see what works best with his or her complexion. A range of foods are described, and this also includes potables: wine, beer, ale, mead, milk etc. In *Castel of Helth* (1539), the ur-text of the genre in England, Thomas Elyot conventionally notes that 'wyne heateth and moysteth the body', conserving 'nature'.[18] Wine is invariably described as hot in the second degree, although, as the physician Thomas Cogan points out in *Haven of Health* (1584), different kinds of wine have different temperatures: 'who doeth not knowe that Sacke is hotter than white Wine or Claret, and Malmsey or muskadell hotter than Sacke, and wine of Madera or Canary to be hottest of all?'[19]

Vernacular regimens have been a resource for historians of medicine concerned with the dissemination of medical knowledge to lay readers.[20] They have also, unsurprisingly given their focus on food and drink, attracted the attention of historians of diet and gastronomy. Yet, for this second group of historians and literary scholars it is not the presumed physiological effects of eating and drinking that is of primary interest, but the implications of medical

[18] Thomas Elyot, *The Castel of Helth* (London, 1539), E2ᵛ.

[19] Thomas Cogan, *The Haven of Health* (London, 1596), N7ᵛ. All references from this edition.

[20] See in particular Paul Slack, 'Mirrors of Health and Treasures of Poor Men: The Uses of Vernacular Medical Literature in Tudor England', in Charles Webster (ed.), *Health, Medicine, and Mortality in the Sixteenth Century* (Cambridge, 1979); Charles Webster, *The Great Instauration: Science, Medicine, and Reform 1626–1660* (Bern, 1975, repr. 2002); Andrew Wear, *Knowledge and Practice in English Medicine, 1550–1680* (Cambridge, 2000); Margaret Healy *Fictions of Disease in Early Modern England: Bodies, Plague, and Politics* (Basingstoke, 2001).

description for the evaluation of lifestyle and diet. Regimens are categorized as moral treatises. Ken Albala regards them as 'one among many forms of self-government', noting that 'It is no coincidence that the words *regime* and *regimen* share a common root with the Latin *regere*, to rule'.[21] For Robert Appelbaum regimens 'encouraged their readers to be finicky eaters' and 'to adopt a system of self-monitoring through which they internalized the discipline of regimented, "civilized" behaviour as a whole',[22] while Michel Jeanneret argues that books dedicated to dietetics contribute to the 'normalization of the meal'. He complains that 'Medical science counters gluttony with the need for a sensible diet: it prescribes rational control over one's eating for those with undisciplined brute appetites'.[23]

There is good reason for this suspicion. When medical writers are not fussing over the qualities of foodstuffs, they are collecting wise sayings from the Bible, moral philosophers, and Roman writers. Advice on drinking is invariably accompanied by the caveat 'measurably', and it is often backed up with moral examples. For example, in *Haven of Health* Thomas Cogan follows Hippocrates in applying the term 'Mediocre' to all five aspects of health (labour, meat, drink, sleep, and 'Venus'). Let the 'quantitie of the meate be such, as may be well digested in the stomacke', he advises, and 'according to the nature of him that eateth, & not always according to appetite' (L4^{r}). Cogan may understand measure medically, yet the example he offers in his preface of a healthy man is the philosopher Socrates, the defender of temperance (¶3^{r}–4^{r}). Socrates—or rather his student Plato—is also Jeanneret's repressor of 'base appetite'.[24] At the same time, health writers delight in offering admonitory examples of excessive drinking. In a chapter entitled 'Of drinke' Cogan dismisses men who choose to 'carouse lustily' at the end of a meal by drinking 'a whole pynt or a quart of Wine, Ale, or Beere' all in one go (N4^{v}). He also laments the degeneracy of Cicero's son. Despite his privileged education in Rome and Greece, Marcus was known as 'such a tosspot, as would quaffe or carouse a galon or two at a time' (O2^{r}).

Less is more; or so the authors of health books argue. Sometimes, they recognize, it is the moralist rather than the physician who knows best. In his

[21] Albala, *Eating Right*, 218.

[22] Appelbaum, *Aguecheek's Beef*, 42.

[23] Michel Jeanneret, *A Feast of Words: Banquets and Table Talk in the Renaissance*, trans. Jeremy Whiteley and Emma Hughes (Chicago, 1991), 73. For a different emphasis again see Craig Muldrew, *Food, Energy, and the Creation of Industriousness: Work and Material Culture in Agrarian England, 1550–1780* (Cambridge, 2011), 31–45. Muldrew focuses on what is deemed healthy for labourers.

[24] Muldrew, *Food, Energy, and the Creation of Industriousness*, 79.

Treatise of Temperance and Sobrietie, translated from the Italian by the poet and clergyman George Herbert, the eighty-three year old Luigi Cornaro explains how his spare diet has kept him healthy. He recounts how he was persuaded by his physicians to add to his diet because they thought 'that old age could not be sustained with so little meat and drink'.[25] Cornaro says he tried to resist his physicians by reminding them of two Italian proverbs: 'He that will eat much, let him eat little' and 'The meat which remaineth, profits more than that which is eaten'. But, he admits, this had no effect. So, to avoid the accusation of 'obstinacie' and to 'gratifie my friends', he 'yeelded, and permitted the quantitie of meat to be increased, yet but two ounces onely', and 'the measure' of his 'drink, which before was foureteen ounces' he 'made now sixteen'. The result is that after ten days he became 'melancholy and cholerick'. On the twelfth day he developed a pain in his side and shortly after this a fever 'which continued thirtie five dayes and nights', whereupon he wisely abandoned the extra ounces ($L2^{v}$–$L3^{v}$).

The view that regimens defend joyless banqueting puts them into the same moral category as table philosophies, another genre that aims to domesticate appetite and prescribe rules for the dinner table. According to Jeanneret, table philosophies codify the manners appropriate to the table, providing 'ready-made formulae for use in meal-time conversation'.[26] Thus, *Philosophica Mensa*, translated by the physician Thomas Twyne as *The Schoolemaster, or Teacher of Table Philosophie* (1576), is a 'compilation of clichés drawn from the great authors'; these are organized 'to help the diners adapt their discourse to their interlocutor', according to his 'social class'.[27]

Furthermore, many of the clichés listed in *The Schoolemaster* are medical as well as philosophical, and the implication is that discussing them at the table helps diners 'to moderate and gouerne themselues'.[28] The first book of *The Schoolemaster* is a regimen; it describes the qualities and effects of food, including intoxicating beverages. Readers learn that the ninth-century Arab physician Rhazes claims that mead engenders red choler, that strong or 'double Ale' 'maketh the head to ake, filleth the bodie with winde, but it provoketh vrine, and represseth the heate which cummeth of drukennesse', and that wine, if taken in moderation, 'heateth colde bodies, and cooleth hot'. It also 'moistneth the drie, and drieth the moist. And many times it quencheth

[25] Luigi Cornaro, *Treatise of Temperance and Sobrietie,* trans. George Herbert, printed in Leonard Lessius, *Hygiasticon: Or, The right course of preserving Life and Health unto extream old Age* (Cambridge, 1634), $L2^{r}$.

[26] Jeanneret, *Feast of Words*, 95.

[27] Ibid., 96–7.

[28] Thomas Twyne, *The Schoolemaster, or Teacher of Table Philosophie* (London, 1576), $A4^{r}$.

the thirst more than water'. While 'Wine also maketh the soule merrie'; however, 'if it bee immoderately taken' then 'it hurteth the Liuer, braine, and Sinewes' (B3^{r-v}).

Jeanneret regards this 'scientific' advice—the leaking of medical information at the dinner table—inappropriate for a feast. It spoils the party.[29] Yet there were plenty of health writers who deemed medico-moral advice suitable for the dinner table. Elyot not only published *Castel of Helth* but also a table philosophy, *The Bankette of Sapience* (1539). Some of the advice he offers in this book overlaps with his regimen, especially under the heading 'Drvnkennes':

> Howe suffycyent vnto a lerned man is a smal quantite of wyne? for therwith whan thou slepest thou shalt not be troubled, nor fele any peyne.

> wine inordinatly taken, troubleth mans reason, maketh dulle vnderstandynge, inflebeth remembraunce, sendeth in forgetfulnesse, powreth in errours, and bryngethe forthe sluggyshenes.[30]

William Basse's *A Helpe to Memory and Discovrse: with Table-Talke as Musicke to a Banquet of Wine* (1620) advises on the kind of regimen that aids memory and table talk, while also providing material for discussion at the table. Thus, 'fuming drinks, strong Wine, and Ale, or any broths made of unwholesome water' should be avoided.[31] Likewise:

> Late Suppers, the too much vse of Tobacco, meates that ingender grosse humors, too much woman, too much surfetting and costly fulnesse; all bad for Memory, ill for the purse, and worse for the health: for the rich Prodigall or wealthy vnthrift is like a powder-master, that hath prouision against an enemy, but is in danger of being blowne vp himselfe. (B2^{r})

The greatest party pooper of them all, though, is surely Henry Buttes, the author of *Dyets Dry Dinner* (1599), an advice book that explicitly connects the genres of the regimen and the table philosophy. On the verso of each page Buttes describes the qualities and physiological effects of a different food or beverage. For example, we learn that milk is moist in the second degree 'and temperately hot'; and that it is to be avoided by those with 'feuers, headaches,

[29] Jeanneret, *Feast of Words*, 96.

[30] Thomas Elyot, *The Bankette of Sapience* (London, 1539), C6^{r}.

[31] William Basse, *A Helpe to Memory and Discovrse: with Table-Talke as Musicke to a Banquet of Wine* (London, 1630), A8^{v}.

sore eyes, distillations of rume, diseased reynes, obstructions, the teeth, the gummes, olde folkes'.[32] On the recto, he offers stories 'for Table-talke'. In the case of Milk we find the following:

> Eate no more Milke, then you can well digest: though it seemeth to be soft and easie meat, fit for children and milkesops, yet it is not so. Vse no violence after it, nor drinke wine, afore you feele it throughly decocted. (N3^{r})

The contrast is typographically expressed: the verso uses black letter, the recto, Roman type.

Moreover, *Dyets Dry Dinner* is literally a 'dry' book. Buttes invites the reader to a feast 'without Wine', or any other 'drinke' (A5^{r}), although he does reluctantly allow one intoxicant at the end of his meal—tobacco—following an epigram warning against its 'wanton, and excessiue vse' (P3^{v}). On the verso Buttes provides medical information: tobacco is 'hot and dry in the second [degree]' (P5^{v}); when used moderately this herb 'cureth any griefe, dolour, opilation, impostume, or obstruction, proceeding of cold or winde; especially in the head or breast'. In addition:

> the leaues are good against the Migram, cold stomackes, sick kidnies, tooth-ache, fits of the moother, naughty breath, scaldings or burnings: 4. ounces of the iuyce drunk, purgeth vp and downe: cleanseth the eyes, being outwardly applied. (P4^{v})

On the recto Buttes lists stories about tobacco that one can share with companions at the table: stories about the origins of this herb 'among the Indians, and especially those of *America* or new *Spain*'. The 'Indians', for example, honour this herb: 'when the Priests are consulting in matters of importance, they [...] smoak [tobacco] through a Cane, till they fall downe dead-drunke', and then, after 'reuiuing againe, they giue answeres according to the phantasmies and visions, which appeared to them in their sleepe' (P5^{r}, P6^{r}).

All of which begs the question whether medical advice really was discussed at the dinner table? In the dedicatory epistle to *The Schoolemaster*, Twyne recalls feasts presided over by his dedicatee, Alexander Nowell, Dean of St Paul's Cathedral, at which interlocutors ponder the 'qualities of meats, or their vsages in forrain contries' (A3^{v}). Meanwhile, the compilers of other types of medical book which touch on taboo subjects worry instead that their advice will furnish only ribald table talk.[33]

[32] Henry Buttes, *Dyets Dry Dinner* (London, 1599), N2^{v}.

[33] Eucharius Rösslin, *The byrth of Mankynde*, trans. Richard Jonas (London, 1540), AB1^{v}.

It is perhaps unsurprising that we typically celebrate the 'uninhibited discourse' of those works that represent bacchanalian excess rather than cliché-ridden 'normative' advice. Yet dismissal of the advice books is based on a basic misunderstanding: that they are prescriptive. It is true that moderation is the key to personal and social health in both regimens and table philosophies, and that it is described as a virtue. But the virtue of moderation depends not on following a rule but on working out what constitutes 'enough'. Moreover, the process of doing so is understood as a social practice. To dismiss the regimens and table philosophies as cultural tools of social constraint, reflecting and enabling the encroachment of the state in personal lives, is to overlook both their defence of intoxication as convivial light-headedness (rather than drunkenness) and of the value of talk in the healthy commonwealth. In the next section I will offer a different reading of the same sources to understand the benefits of mild intoxication.

II

It is unsurprising that table philosophies and regimens should be understood as didactic texts. After all, they offer advice, much of which comes in the form of quotations—wise sayings—that are surely meant to be followed, such as the aforementioned:

> wine inordinatly taken, troubleth mans reason, maketh dulle vnderstandynge, inflebeth remembraunce, sendeth in forgetfulnesse, powreth in errours, and bryngethe forthe sluggyshenes.

This is both a statement of fact and also sensible advice. Yet, often it is difficult to know what instruction is being given, so vague or contradictory is the advice. This is especially the case when health writers urge moderation since this is almost never quantified. (Cornaro is an exception). Thus, in *A New Almanack and Prognostication* (1643), the astrologer Thomas Langley conventionally advises that his readers 'take measure, and no more; for in measure resteth health and vertue'.[34] This is good advice, of course, but it is meaningless if you do not know what the measure is. That Langley does not try to quantify this is odd given his preoccupation with weights and measures: in his yearly almanacs he often includes tables for useful calculations, which explain different measures, including for alcohol.[35]

[34] Thomas Langley, *A New Almanack and Prognostication* (London, 1643), C2^{v}, also cited in Louise Hill Curth and Tanya M. Cassidy, '"Health, Strength, and Happiness": Medical Constructions of Wine and Beer in Early Modern England', in Smyth (ed.), *A Pleasing Sinne*, 143–59, 152.

[35] E.g., Thomas Langley, *A New Almanacke and Prognostication* (London, 1635), C3^{r-v}.

The same conundrum faces the reader of regimens. Elyot opens Book II of *Castel of Helth* with the chapter 'Of quantitie', yet gives no quantities. The reader is advised that labouring men and men with 'very cholerike stomackes' can eat a '*greate* quantitie' of 'grosse meats', while the 'temperate bodye is beste nouryshed with a *lyttell* quantitie of grosse meates' (my italics). How much 'drynke' should be consumed? Elyot advises this be 'moderated, [so] that it excede not, nor be equalle vnto the quantitie of meate' (B8^{v}-C1^{r}). In a chapter on 'quantities of meates', Cogan recalls that one man 'who was before verie grosse and fat', made himself slender 'within a yeare or two' 'by feeding uppon one dish onely at one meale, and drinking thereto but small drinke' ('small' meaning weak rather than a little) (L5^{r}).

Working out 'enough' is all the more difficult given that it is not sobriety (in our sense of the word) that is being advised. While early modern physicians understood that excessive drinking caused illness, they also supposed 'the same' was 'true of not drinking enough wine, ale or beer'.[36] Indeed, mild inebriation is described as healthy in just about all vernacular regimens. Elyot emphasizes that 'wyne moderately drunke, norysheth and co[m]forteth, as well the body, as the spirites of man' (E2^{v}). Cogan argues that 'Wine measurably drunken & in time, bringeth gladnesse and cheerfulnesse to the mind', and he explains the phrase 'a dogges dinner' as 'where there is no wine at dinner or supper' (N8^{r-v}). Levine Lemnius, translated by Thomas Newton, writes eloquently of the benefits of intoxication in *The Touchstone of Complexions* (1576). Wine serves as a simile for the fluidity of the body. Just as wine can be mixed and adulterated, 'so humours in a man being eyther of themselves euil or meeting wyth others of other quality, are through theyr com[m]ixtion therewith, qualifyed and waxe milder, and leauing theyr owne naturall qualitie are altered into an other'.[37] Wine drunk in moderation helps this process, qualifying and transforming evil humours. Lemnius cites the transformative effects of wine-drinking on the 'churlish, sterne & frowning' Cato, the hero of Roman republican restraint. [Y]et did wyne so much driue away his naturall seueritye and grimme countenaunce' he became 'a pleasaunte companion, and of manners very gentle and familiar' (A6^{r}).

Just because these books do not quantify 'enough' did not mean they have no practical advice on moderation to offer. Rather 'measure' is more usually understood as the pacing of drinking rather than a quantifiable term. In John Hales's translation of *The preceptes of the excellent clerke & graue philosopher*

[36] Curth and Cassidy, '"Health, Strength and Happiness"', 153.

[37] Levine Lemnius, *The Touchstone of Complexions, Generallye appliable, expedient and profitable for all such, as be desirous and carefull of their bodylye health*, trans. Thomas Newton (London, 1576), A4^{v}.

Plutarche for the preseruation of good Healthe (1543), the reader is told that wine 'is a drynke muche profitable, a medycine mooste pleasaunte, a meate leaste of all hurtyng, yf it be vsed temperately, and receiued by *lytle and lytle* at ones, rather by it self, then alayed with water' (my italics).[38] Drinking water between draughts is also helpful, and Hale advises two or three cups of water a day (E1^{r}). Even Cogan, who thinks 'a draught of Sacke or good wine' is better after strenuous labour than a glass of water (N7^{r}), still recommends that 'drink' should 'be mixt with the meate by sundry little draughtes, than by one great draught at the end of the meale' (N4^{v}).

Eating is one way in which heavy drinking can be interrupted. However, it is also helpful to share food-for-thought; and here the link with table philosophies emerges again. Plutarch is often thought of as the progenitor of table philosophy, and it is perhaps to be expected that talk should feature as healthy in his medical advice book. Wine-drinking, he suggests, can be managed by 'callyng the mynde from meate, and tournyng it to studye'. The 'rude Scythian', his speaker recalls, was 'not ashamed in the myddest of his drynkyng oftentymes to drawe his bowe, and when it is unbent, to syng, by this meanes kepyng hym selfe from drounkennesse' (E3^{r-v}). The same applies to table talk. He acknowledges that disputation at the table may cause a headache, and there is a tendency to suppose that the mind should not be troubled after supper (E4^{v}-E5^{r}). However, there are many topics that are suitable: for example, 'narracions [. . .] that concerne good maners, wherin some thing is worthye to bee consydered and weighed, uoid from all contention and stryfe, and yet mixed with suche pleasures as maye coumforte and delite the mynde' (E5^{v}).

Moral and medical sentences are suitable for discussion, too. Indeed, the usefulness of the regimens, I would suggest, rested as much on the material they provided for reflection and discussion as on the practical advice they gave. Or, to put this differently, the regimens invite various styles of reading: information gathering, practical application, and rumination.[39] After all, the regimens are kinds of commonplace book; they gather opinions—proverbs, aphorisms, *sententiae*, quotations—from diverse sources which can be applied and, as Elyot put it, 'wel masticate' at table.[40]

This is understood by the compilers of table philosophies, many of whom were practising physicians. Thus, the first book of Twyne's *The Schoolemaster*

[38] Plutarch, *The preceptes of the excellent clerke & graue philosopher Plutarche for the preseruation of good Healthe*, trans. John Hales (London, 1543), D8^{v}.

[39] See Jennifer Richards, 'Useful Books: Reading Vernacular Regimens in Sixteenth-Century England', *Journal of the History of Ideas*, 73 (2012), 247–71.

[40] Elyot, *Bankette*, A3^{r}.

is a regimen which describes the qualities of different foods, including wine (it 'moistneth the drie, and drieth the moist. And many times it quencheth the thirst more than water' etc.). As in regimens for students and physicians, Twyne presents alternative perspectives for debate. On the question whether 'it be good once in a month to be drunken with wine?' he recounts that while Avicenna and Rhazes agree, Averroes takes a different view (M2^{r-v}). He also provides questions 'to be propounded while wee be at meate, or at any other time' (K2^{r}) similar to those that medical students and their tutors disputed at university (K2^{v}–K3^{r}). The only difference is that this is material for table talk, not medical debate.

The Schoolemaster offers a dizzying range of perspectives on intoxication for discussion at table, and it collects stories that reflect differently on the experience of drunkenness. In one story, King Pyrrhus recalls that 'certen Tarentines had talked of him very broade, and undutifull language at a banket', and when he asks one of their company 'whether they had sutch talke' the frank response turns 'the Kinges wrath into laughter' and so saves their lives: 'yea truly said hee, wee had so indeede, and unles our wine had fayled vs these had bin but trifles in respect of that we would haue spoken' (F1^{r-v}). In another story, a fondness for wine keeps a 'good woorkeman' poor. The man's priest, perceiving that he is 'giuen mutch to drinkinge', enjoined him to this penance: 'that hee should not drinke aboue a certen measure of wine at a meale' unless he had bought or sold something that day. At dinner that night he drinks 'his measure of wine' but finds he is still thirsty, so his wife offers him this counsel: 'I will sel you a cow & then you may drink more by couenant, and you shal sell her to me againe'. In this way, the tale concludes, the man 'could neuer bee ritch' (Q2^{r}). The reader might apply these as he sees fit: as warnings, or as jokes for merry conversation, or as topics to be debated. The point is that it is their rumination that helps the reader 'to moderate and gouerne' himself (A4^{r}).

Thus while regimens and table philosophies share precepts on healthy consumption, emphasizing the importance of moderation, they are not prescriptive in any straightforward fashion. Rather, they offer material for discussion and debate. Indeed, table philosophies and even regimens might be read alongside the language study aids of the sixteenth century which aim to facilitate *copia* in everyday situations as well as instil proper decorum: colloquies like Erasmus's *The Profane Feast* (1518), which gives schoolboys formulae for talking about eating and drinking in Latin, while reinforcing the principle that ' "There are as many opinions as men," ' and a variety of tastes.[41] Or Claudius

[41] Desiderius Erasmus, *The Colloquies of Erasmus*, trans. Craig R. Thompson (Chicago, 1965), 599.

Hollybande's bilingual teaching aid, *The French Schoolemaister* (1573), which shares sentences likely to prove useful in domestic settings: 'Rince the glasse, that I may taste of it: how like you this wine?' Or 'Rinces le verre, & que i'en gouste: que vous semble de ce vin?'; 'Geeue mee drinke in that Goblet' or 'Donnnez moy a boire dans ce goblet'.[42] Their emphasis, moreover, is on variation, not reiteration. They are not 'static collections of materials' but rather 'a dynamic method' to achieve a copious style that is 'rooted in generative principles' and encourages transformation.[43] How variation and transformation was aided by wine-drinking, how intoxication was checked by 'rumination', and finally, who this civil company included are nicely illustrated by my last example.

III

Stefano Guazzo's *La civil conversatione* (1575) is a conduct manual organized as a fictional dialogue in four books between two characters, William, the author's brother, and a physician, Annibale Magnocavelli, a friend and neighbour. It aims to explain how to behave in company, but it also doubles as a medical book of sorts: Guazzo explains in his proem that his brother is suffering from melancholy and needs the company of friends and family as well as the 'aduice and counsell of some good Phisitian' ($A1^v$). Annibale's counsel takes the form of a dialogue in which he digests with William many different moral commonplaces. This helps William by enabling him to understand that 'moderation' entails flexibility rather than absolute restraint; for example, he is taught not to judge others too harshly or quickly. However, the cure is not complete until the final book, when William announces that he has been cured 'by meanes' of Annibale's 'sweet companie'. 'I doe sensiblie feele', he declares, 'all the superfluous humours (engendred by solitarinesse) consumed quite, & spent in mee' (4. 176^r). Annibale is quick to respond: 'not by the meanes of my discourse onelie', he clarifies, 'but by the uertue especiallie of your subtil demands and serious alterations, the causes & grounds of Ciuill Conuersation' (176^v).

Book IV completes William's cure by moving from a private conference between William and Annibale to a banquet in mixed company in Casale, at which stories and sayings are 'ruminated', thereby pacing the meal. In this respect, this final book is also an example of table philosophy 'in action', as at least one English reader recognized. Gabriel Harvey clearly marked the stages

[42] Claudius Hollybande's *The French Schoolemaister* (London, 1573), $H8^v$, $I1^v$.

[43] Terence Cave, *The Cornucopian Text: Problems of Writing in the French Renaissance* (Oxford, 1979, repr. 2002), 11.

of the meal in his copy of the Italian text: '1. Avanti la cena.' (227^{v}); '2. La cena. (235^{r}); '3. Dopo la cena.' (251^{r}).[44]

Book IV, printed in an English translation by Bartholomew Young in 1586, provides a fitting conclusion to this essay not only because it brings together table philosophies and regimens but also because it dramatizes the argument I have been exploring: that the sharing of moral and medical advice—the talking about and disputing of it—paces intoxication, and that this in turn provides the model for conversation in the healthy body politic. It also does more than this, dramatizing the importance of light intoxication to conversation, which is conceived, in this dialogue at least, as inclusive rather than dominated by a single speaker (180^{v}). Moreover, unlike the restrictively homo-social symposiastic tradition that the regimens and table philosophies represent, Guazzo's banquet includes noble women as well as men (recalling Castiglione's *Il libro del cortegiano* (1528)). Indeed, much is made at the start of book IV of the election of a 'Queene' to oversee the banquet, a woman who is 'able enough to haue gouerned a Monachie' (179^{v}).

Pacing is all-important in this banquet. This dialogue marks the different stages of the meal. The table is laid and wine is poured and shared in a cup in the shape of a ship. The diners pause to taste the wine and savour the food, and also to comment on them. When someone observes that he seems to be 'eating' his wine, he cites a proverb in his defence: 'Three things are ill handled, Byrdes in boyes hands, Young men in olde mens hands, And wine in Germains hands, who doe not drinke it, but swallow it down at a gulp' (188^{r}).

The stages of the meal interrupt and pace the conversation, keeping it civil. '[W]hile they were thus arguing', Annibale relates, 'the table cloathes wer spread & furnished the sundrie sorts of Viandes' (185^{r}). By the same token, conversation interrupts and paces consumption too, especially since the topics the diners choose, such as wine-tasting, are relevant to this activity. Another topic the diners take up is the question how much is 'inough' (185^{v}). 'Ther was in times past', one speaker offers, 'a certain Poet, who amongst the chiefest felicities of mans life, set downe a light banquet for one'. This story leads the diners to reflect on what is meant by a light banquet and different opinions are offered: a banquet is light if it is easy on the purse or easy to prepare, or if it includes the kind of 'meats, which put not the teeth to anie paine in grinding them, but are easilie swallowed down, as good Potage, tarts, Milke, Honie, whitepots, grated cheese, iellies, & such like'. Another

[44] Stefano Guazzo, *La Civil Conversatione del S. Stefano Guazzo* (Venice, 1581). Gabriel Harvey also writes in his copy: 'mensa philosophicae aulica exornatio. Symposiorum Idea', 229^{r}, inner margin.

discussant adds, it might be 'light' because of 'the qualitie of the stomacke, which receiuing but a little meate, makes easie & speedy digestion' (185^{v}-186^{r}). Finally, others relate this to their experience. 'I haue kept and nourished this naturall heat within me, more with a spare and temperate diet, than with great & copious fare', one interlocutor boasts, supporting this with a proverb we have already encountered in Cornaro, 'the lesse one eates, the more he eates', which he glosses thus: 'I meane he liueth longer to eat more' (186^{r}).

It is easy to feel impatient with these interlocutors, wishing them to stop talking and just enjoy the feast. Jeanneret complains that Guazzo 'tells us nothing of the menu or the quality of the food, for pleasure derived from food is vulgar'. 'The meal is so sanitized', he explains, 'that it does not nourish, but rather provides the guests with a suitable setting and pretext to show off the elegance of their manners and the distinguished nature of their language'.[45] He is right: eating and imbibing are metaphors in this dialogue for talking, thinking, and assimilating knowledge and ideas, and this is deemed as pleasurable as the act of consumption itself (181^{v}). But Guazzo has concerns other than the menu, one of which is to explore a practice of sociability that allows different interlocutors to have their say and to be heard. Indeed, book IV represents a new style of dialogue. There is no dominant speaker. It is structured, not by question and answer (so familiar to readers of Renaissance dialogues) but by 'subtil demands and serious alterations'. Interlocutors—both men and women—are asked to share their views, and this is also reflected in the frame dialogue between Annibale and Guazzo: 'Now Sir, tell mee what you thinke of this Philosophers sentence [. . .]' (177^{r}); 'But tell mee now, (I pray you Sir) to what purpose you haue alleadged this opinion' (177^{v}).

Moreover, intoxication is integral to this banquet: this is no dry feast in the manner of Buttes. As the cup of wine is passed around, one of the ladies is asked whether she 'will not imitate now the auncient custome of those noble Romaines, who as Dant[e] saith, Were content, of water for to drink'. Her response is unequivocal; she repeats the saying that is also recycled in Cogan's *Haven of Health*: 'Nay [. . .] I will leaue water for Dogs to drinke' (188^{r}). Another shares this familiar 'sentence': 'that [Julius] Caesar being sober, did ruinate and destroie the common wealth' (189^{r}).

Wine is good for one's health. It is noted, for example, that physicians hold that wine 'doth greatlie helpe and comfort the melancolicke humours' and 'doe[s] reuiue and dissolue (as soueraigne remedie) the drowsie and congealed spirits with in' (192^{v}). But it is also good for the health of the 'common wealth'. The cup is communal; the diners take it in turns to share it, just as

[45] Jeanneret, *Feast of Words*, 47.

they take it in turns to share their opinions. One of the company is teased for calling for 'his Wine with a privie becke'. He is told (half-jokingly) that he disrespects the 'companie', which is 'priuiledged for euerie one to speake freelie what he thinketh, and to call for franklie what he lacketh' (194^{r}). Wine also makes the diners fluent and easy-going in their merry-making. The drinking begins after one of the speakers makes a linguistic slip, mispronouncing Aristippus 'Aripistus'. 'I know not how my tongue went a wrye', he quips, 'my lippes hauing not as yet, once saluted the Cup'. The 'Queene', joining the joke, then 'commanded that a Goblet of wine should be filled for him, to set his tongue in his right bias againe' (187^{v}–188^{r}).

It is not hard to see why wine-drinking is good for this little commonwealth; sharing the cup is a bonding experience. However, it is also a healthy social practice for another reason: this banquet is a supportive setting in which the interlocutors can express opinions, share their views, agree and disagree. The diners talk about the different effects of wine on young and old men, and of different habits of drinking: do you 'eat' the wine, swilling it in your mouth, or gulp it down? But most importantly, as they drink and talk they share different ways of interpreting received wisdom, especially as it is condensed into proverbs and *sententiae.* This happens increasingly as the banquet proceeds, so that no authority is left unquestioned. It also means not only that authority in the dialogue is shared but also that it is attributed to interlocutors who would not usually possess it, like the women drinkers. To be sure, Guazzo's diners are not talking politics. They are sharing and swapping stories about drinking, eating, falling in love. Nonetheless, we need to take this seriously: the give and take of their talk represents the process of civil contestation and the healthiness of debate.

Intoxication facilitates this process. After several drinking rounds, a diner supposes that they must have finished, to which one of the ladies responds 'Not too hastie [. . .] I meane to giue you a peece of an eager Tart to drawe on one cup of wine more'. The diner believes that he has had too much already, and in response he recalls a saying familiar from Erasmus's *Adages*: 'I feare me then I shall drinke of the cup of foolishnesse'. He elaborates thus: the first cup of wine quenches thirst, the second induces merriness, the third is for temptation and the fourth, proposed by his hostess, is for 'foolishnesse'. However, he is corrected by this lady who refuses to 'allow of these distinctions', and argues against a literal interpretation of the saying. She first speculates that 'follie and dronkennesse' are perhaps 'gotten not by the number of the pots, but by the quantitie of wine [i.e. the size of the pots]',[46] then she wonders

[46] Young is offering a literal translation: 'l'ubriacchezza non s'acquistano col numero de'bicchieri, ma con la quantità del vino', Guazzo, *Civil Conversatione,* 1581, 245^{v}.

whether 'their pots were greater, & contained a great deale of wine in them', and finally wonders if 'they were also ignorant, that to drinke a little at a time & often, was good & convenient for the health of the bodie' (195^{r-v}).

This is a minor quibble, of course. The speaker is reasserting a practice commended as healthy by physicians, that drinking 'little and often' is best. Yet, the significance of the moment, of the speaker and the correction, is not lost. As one of the other diners offers: 'I greatlie commend your opinion [. . .] wherby you giue us to wit, that we ought perfectlie to conceiue & understand the sentences of our auncestors, & measure them with their customes: otherwise ther would arise many errors' (195^{v}). The principle is plain: let us work out for ourselves how much is enough, interpreting advice as suits our practice rather than following rules laid down by medical authority or past practice. The act of doing so as wine and conversation are shared ensures the good health of this mixed civil society.

The interlinked genres of regimens and table philosophies bring, then, a new dimension to the burgeoning debate about humanism, wit, and intoxication. This debate has tended to privilege 'hard [male] drinkers'. In contrast, these books encourage a drinking culture which prioritizes light drunkenness and in which intoxication helps conversation; it facilitates the turning over, testing and adaptation of advice. The forms underlying this different tradition derive from a particular masculine humanist culture. Regimens, table philosophies, even the very idea of 'civil conversation', develop out of the habits of collecting and debating *in utramque partem* of the grammar school and the university: hence the variation of views. But the resulting conversation need not be exclusively male, not least because its location is often the household. Indeed, it is the noblewomen of Guazzo's fictional *Ciuile Conuersation* who are the catalysts for both the drinking and talking.

Little attention has been paid to this other Renaissance drinking culture, but its ramifications for male and female identities are tantalizing. If we were to seek to recover it then we would need to look for different literary sources, shifting the emphasis from Ben Jonson and the 'pot poets' to writings which make the banquet the pinnacle of celebration and keep a place for women drinkers. This might include the foreign language phrase books that exemplify the 'familiar talkes' extended to women: 'So I meane maistres, but I would that we should drinke once first' ('Cosi s'intende Signora; ma io verrei

For this interpretation see Amedeo Quondam, 'per quanto riguarda i bicchieri di vino non è questione soltanto di numero, ma sopratutto di dimensioni', Stefano Guazzo, *La civil conversatione. II. Apparati: note e indici*, ed. Amedeo Quondam (Roma, 2010), 436, fn. 191.

che primo bevessimo una volta'); 'I will do you reason, but it is not the part of a woman to drinke to much' ('Io farò ben ragion, ma non s'appartiene à donne a bere troppo').[47] Or vernacular literary texts like *The Tragicall and True Historie which happened between two English louers* (1565), which represent a banquet in mixed company. The narrator of this poem recognizes and records that talk 'common is at euery feast, / where Bacchus wares do walke', and he will not conclude his feast until the bride has had the chance, after all the other speakers, to 'frankly speake her inward thought, / and so her mynd declare'.[48]

[47] This phrase book is appended to Guazzo, *La Civil Conversatione* (1581), 349^{v}–350^{r}. All of these phrases are underlined by Harvey.

[48] B[ernard] G[arter], *The Tragicall and True Historie which happened betwene two English louers, 1563* (London, 1565), D5^{v}, D8^{v}.

Psychedelic Drugs and the Problem of Experience*

Sarah Shortall

Over fifty years since the criminalization of LSD brought medical research on the drug to a halt, researchers in Europe have reopened investigations into the possible therapeutic benefits of the controversial substance.[1] This might come as something of a surprise to those who remember the public outcry against psychedelic drugs in the 1960s, when the American media echoed with sensational stories of LSD-induced violence and psychosis.[2] But before it became 'the nation's newest scourge', LSD was hailed as a 'wonder drug' by medical researchers and psychotherapists convinced of its therapeutic potential. This paper investigates how and why psychedelic drugs made the remarkable transition from medical tool to countercultural sacrament, and from panacea to medical, legal, and cultural pariah.

Jordan Goodman, Paul Lovejoy, and Andrew Sherratt have already done much to demonstrate the fluidity of the boundary between licit and illicit drug use. They argue for the need to deconstruct the dominant western discourse on drugs, which artificially distinguishes between nutritional, medicinal, and recreational drug consumption. Instead, they look to 'the social contexts in which particular substances are consumed' in order 'to understand the meanings which they have for their users'.[3] Deconstructing the prevailing drugs discourse, however, requires more than replacing hegemonic definitions of drugs use with the meaning it has for consumers, as this meaning is itself highly contested and far from ideologically neutral.

* The author would like to thank Peter E. Gordon, Stuart Henderson, Harold Mah, Joshua Specht, Judith Surkis, and the anonymous readers at *Past and Present* for their support and invaluable comments on earlier drafts of this article.

[1] 'LSD: Acid Tests', *Economist* (23 Jun. 2011).

[2] This paper will employ the term 'psychedelic' to refer to a category of psychoactive substances including, but not limited to, LSD (acid), mescaline, peyote, and psilocybin.

[3] Jordan Goodman, Paul E. Lovejoy, and Andrew Sherratt (eds), *Consuming Habits: Drugs in History and Anthropology: Global and Historical Perspectives on How Cultures Define Drugs*, 2nd edn (New York, 2007), 4.

 © The Past and Present Society

Rather than asking which definition comes closest to encapsulating the true drug experience, this paper instead focuses on how various stakeholders describe this experience, for the cultural power of drugs lies in the various and competing ways they are represented. It is here, at the level of discourse, that we can glimpse the crucial role these substances play in the articulation of cultural distinctions which ramify well beyond the world of drugs—distinctions between the natural and the artificial, truth and illusion, interiority and exteriority, or self and other. Discourse on drugs thus not only reflects the broader historical or cultural context it inhabits, as Sherratt et al. have shown, but also helps to shape it.

While recreational drug use has long been identified with illusion, artifice, and toxicity, leaders of the 1960s psychedelic counterculture sought to turn these epithets back against the 'non-drug' culture itself. It was mainstream American society, they argued, which was unnatural, inauthentic, and dangerous, while psychedelic drugs provided access to a more authentic and liberating realm of experience.[4] Rather than questioning the nature/artifice, reality/illusion binaries which underwrote mainstream approaches to drug use, countercultural leaders simply inverted them and appropriated their positive terms for the drug experience. To the extent that both the pro- and anti-drug discourse remained beholden to this same set of hierarchical distinctions, they thus shared a 'common metaphysics' and 'general logic', as Jacques Derrida put it in his essay on 'The Rhetoric of Drugs'.[5] I shall have recourse to Derrida's work throughout this paper, as it provides critical insight into the way psychedelics were used to both uphold and destabilize metaphysical hierarchies. In particular, Derrida's notion of 'supplementarity' aptly encapsulates the paradox that these drugs could be treated both as artificial and dangerous supplements to the natural body, and as 'apt for the liberation of this same 'ideal' or 'perfect body' from social oppression, suppression, and repression'.[6] The rhetoric of drugs thus functions to erect boundaries between nature and artifice, essence and accident, interiority and exteriority, but because psychedelics invariably inhabit both sides of these boundaries at once, they can also be used to undermine them. This helps to explain why the drugs have been so polarizing, but also so flexible in their capacity to acquire a wide range of cultural meanings.

[4] The use of drugs as vehicles for a critique of modern society dates at least to the early nineteenth century and runs through much modern literature, including the work of Baudelaire, Rimbaud, Benjamin, Artaud, and Michaux.

[5] Jacques Derrida, 'The Rhetoric of Drugs', *Points. . .: Interviews, 1974–1994*, ed. Elisabeth Weber, trans. Peggy Kamuf et al. (Stanford, 1995), 247–8.

[6] Ibid., 244.

Whereas scholars have tended to focus on the legal or anti-drugs discourse, this paper will concern itself with the countercultural discourse on psychedelic drugs and the way it negotiated the aporias, or paradoxes, outlined above. While countercultural leaders claimed the psychedelic experience as a vehicle for spiritual transcendence, communal harmony, and psychosocial liberation, their accounts nevertheless reveal that the experience defied any categorical separation between liberation and control, self and other, or nature and artifice. Indeed, this was a tension inherited from the medical engagement with psychedelic drugs and it helps to explain the continuities between the two contexts. Already in the 1950s, North American researchers had begun to realize the extent to which reactions to psychedelic drugs varied enormously with the individual subject's disposition and the environment in which they were administered—what Leary would later term 'set' and 'setting'. As a result, medical researchers acknowledged a space for the drug 'experience' which mediated between its chemical make-up and subjective effects.

I shall argue that it was precisely this ambiguous experiential space which enabled psychedelics to be mobilized for such disparate ends—as both a cause and a cure for mental illness; both a medical tool and a countercultural agent. Faced with these aporias, proponents of the drugs sought to distance their benefits from their limitations, rooting the authenticity of the experience in its ability to transcend the specificities of race, class, and gender. Even as the counterculture vaunted the emancipatory power of psychedelic drugs, it thus occluded the way certain power relations shaped its own engagement with the drugs. This aspect of the discourse on psychedelics, I argue, is particularly significant for the theory and practice of history more broadly. The paper accordingly concludes with an argument for the suggestive parallels between the psychedelic counterculture's appeals to the rhetoric of 'experience' and those of historians who have made this a paradigmatic term since the 1960s.

I

Before they became the focus of a cultural conflict that split the nation, psychedelics were promising new compounds being tested for their medical value in North American labs. The post-war period saw a dramatic expansion of the mental health profession and a veritable revolution in psychopharmacology, fuelled largely by the development of 'major' and 'minor' tranquilizers such as Thorazine and Miltown.[7] The result was not only a massive rise

[7] On the psychopharmacological revolution, see David Healy, *The Creation of Psychopharmacology* (Cambridge, MA, 2002); Andrea Tone, *The Age of Anxiety: A History of America's Turbulent Affair with Tranquilizers* (New York, 2009).

in drug prescriptions for the treatment of psychological ailments, but also that such drug consumption became increasingly normalized and mainstream. In 1965 alone, for instance, American doctors prescribed twenty-four million doses of amphetamines and 123 million doses of tranquillizers.[8] In this context, the scientific profession played a key role in arbitrating between 'legitimate medicines' and 'dangerous narcotics'. Yet, because psychedelic drugs elicited 'widely disparate subjective effects', medical opinion was deeply divided over their value.[9]

After accidentally discovering d-lysergic acid diethylamide (LSD) in 1942, the Swiss company Sandoz Pharmaceuticals began shipping the substance to American scientists in 1949, advertising that its peculiar properties would deepen scientific understanding of the biochemistry of mental illness. Such claims were based on a view, current at the time, that hallucinogenic substances like LSD and mescaline gave rise to a temporary 'model psychosis' akin to schizophrenia. This approach, known as the 'psychotomimetic model', would dominate the psychedelic research agenda through the 1950s.[10] A characteristic medical manual from 1959, for instance, recorded that subjects under the influence of LSD experienced ' "illusions, hallucinations, paranoid delusions of reference, influence, persecution and grandeur" '.[11] It was findings such as these which inspired the CIA's research into the drug's potential military value as an interrogation tool and agent of chemical warfare.[12] Launched in 1953, 'Operation MK-ULTRA' presupposed that LSD induced terror and psychosis.

The medical association between psychedelics and madness would likewise underwrite public policy after the drugs attracted controversy in the mid-1960s. As early as 1962, Sidney Cohen and Keith Ditman—two of the leading medical authorities on LSD—issued a report warning of newly discovered dangers associated with the drug, including long-term psychosis and suicide, and of the risks posed by an emerging black market that allowed for

[8] Jay Stevens, *Storming Heaven: LSD and the American Dream* (New York, 1987), 306.

[9] Rick Strassman, 'Hallucinogens', in Mitch Earleywine (ed.), *Mind-Altering Drugs: The Science of Subjective Experience* (Oxford, 2005), 54.

[10] Healy, *Creation of Psychopharmacology*, 178–91. See also, Robert M. Yoder, 'Help for the Living Dead', *Saturday Evening Post* (22 Oct. 1955).

[11] Quoted in Erika Dyck, *Psychedelic Psychiatry: LSD from Clinic to Campus* (Baltimore, 2008), 69–70.

[12] See Martin A. Lee and Bruce Schlain, *Acid Dreams: The Complete Social History of LSD: The CIA, the Sixties, and Beyond* (New York, 1992).

psychedelic experimentation without medical supervision.[13] By 1966, a widespread moral panic had taken hold under the influence of sensational media reports of LSD-induced mental breakdowns, culminating in the criminalization of LSD and effective termination of scientific research in 1968.[14] It is nevertheless crucial to differentiate the earlier psychotomimetic research model, which understood psychedelic psychosis as a temporary and artificial simulation of true mental illness, from the reports that such substances could actually trigger real and lasting mental breakdowns, which gained currency in the media during the later backlash against LSD. According to the former, psychedelics offered an artificial simulation of the ' "experiential world of the schizophrenic" ', while the latter claimed that psychedelics rendered their consumers permanently insane.[15]

Although the 'model psychosis' paradigm initially dominated the psychedelic research agenda, by 1957 psychiatrists began to argue that it fell short of accounting for the substances' therapeutic potential. Arthur Chandler and Mortimer Hartman, for instance, had begun to employ LSD as a ' "facilitating agent" ' in psychotherapy, claiming that it provided access to the repressed material stored in a patient's unconscious.[16] Meanwhile in Canada, Abram Hoffer and Humphry Osmond were using high doses of LSD to cure chronic alcoholics who had failed AA treatment, attributing their success to the drug's ability to elicit 'a single intense experience' of personal insight capable of altering entrenched behaviours.[17] By 1959, LSD was at the height of its medical legitimacy, hailed as a 'wonder drug' with therapeutic potential for conditions as diverse as alcoholism, autism, obsessive-compulsive disorder, and terminal illness.[18]

What is particularly significant about these cases is that researchers did not ascribe the drug's therapeutic potential to its pharmacological effects, but rather to the experience it elicited. As Hoffer put it, ' "we considered not the chemical, but the experience as a key factor in therapy—in fact, we used a sort

[13] Donald Janson, 'Doctors Report a Black Market in Drug That Causes Delusions', *New York Times* (14 July 1962).

[14] See, e.g., 'The Dangers of LSD', *Time* (22 Apr. 1966); Bill Davidson, 'The Hidden Evils of LSD', *Saturday Evening Post* (12 Aug. 1967); Tom Buckley, 'The LSD Trigger: Crystal Palaces and Absolute Horror', *New Republic* (14 May 1966).

[15] Humphry Osmond, quoted in Dyck, *Psychedelic Psychiatry*, 60.

[16] 'The Psyche in 3-D', *Time* (28 Mar. 1960).

[17] Dyck, *Psychedelic Psychiatry*, 8.

[18] See Steven J. Novak, 'LSD before Leary: Sidney Cohen's Critique of 1950s Psychedelic Drug Research', in Sarah W. Tracy and Caroline Jean Acker (eds), *Altering American Consciousness: The History of Alcohol and Drug Use in the United States, 1800–2000* (Amherst, MA, 2004), 359–62; Lee and Schlain, *Acid Dreams*, 89–90, 57.

of psychotherapy made possible by the nature of the experience" '.[19] Similarly, when Sidney Cohen and Betty Eisner began administering LSD to psychotherapy patients and recorded an unprecedented 73 per cent improvement rate, they attributed it to an LSD-induced ' "integrative experience. . .wherein the patient accepts himself as he is" '.[20] Then a psychologist teaching at Harvard, Timothy Leary likewise framed his project to treat criminal recidivism with psilocybin in terms of a drug-induced ' "visionary experience" ' of personal insight inspiring behavioural change.[21] Experiential approaches such as these drew upon both the anti-psychiatry movement associated with R. D. Laing and the emerging 'humanistic' psychology of Carl Rogers and Abraham Maslow. In opposition to the dominant behaviourist and psychoanalytic paradigms, Maslow and Rogers sought to 'return conscious human experience to the center of psychology'.[22] Indeed, Maslow explicitly singled out psychedelic drugs as promising agents of therapeutic 'peak-experiences'.[23] By 1965, 30,000 to 40,000 patients had received LSD in a therapeutic context.[24]

Despite their apparently contradictory agendas, the therapeutic and psychotomimetic approaches to psychedelic drugs were in fact bound together by the same logic. Yet, how could the psychedelic experience be capable of at once simulating and curing mental illness? The answer, for many researchers, was that the therapeutic value of psychedelics lay in their very ability to replicate the symptoms of psychosis. For instance, R. D. Laing held that 'freaking out' during an LSD trip often heralded a positive breakthrough in working through repression.[25] Hoffer and Osmond accounted for their success in curing alcoholism by theorizing that 'the traumatic drug experience resembled the delirium tremens (DTs) of hitting bottom', a harrowing experience that shocked alcoholics into changing their lives.[26]

Such accounts reveal the aporia at the heart of the medical debate over psychedelic drugs, as researchers did not simply claim that psychedelics were

[19] Quoted in Dyck, *Psychedelic Psychiatry*, 59.

[20] Quoted in Novak, 'LSD before Leary', 359.

[21] Quoted in Robin M. Wasserman, 'Tuning In: Timothy Leary, Harvard, and the Boundaries of Experimental Psychology' (Harvard Univ. A.B. thesis, 2000), 59.

[22] Ibid., 16. See also, R. D. Laing, *The Politics of Experience and the Bird of Paradise* (New York, 1967).

[23] Abraham Maslow, *Religions, Values, and Peak-Experiences* (New York, 1964), 27.

[24] Jill Jonnes, *Hep-Cats, Narcs, and Pipe Dreams: A History of America's Romance with Illegal Drugs* (Baltimore, 1996), 228.

[25] Lee and Schlain, *Acid Dreams*, 64.

[26] Novak, 'LSD Before Leary', 360.

either therapeutic or toxic and psychotomimetic. Rather, many considered them to be therapeutic precisely because they elicited feelings of terror and psychosis. Even the initial psychotomimetic paradigm was premised upon the notion that the 'model psychosis' induced by psychedelic drugs would help scientists to understand and treat mental illness. Yet in order for psychedelic psychosis to yield such insights, it necessarily had to be both temporary and artificial. In other words, it was precisely because these drugs were artificial supplements that they could offer fundamental therapeutic insight into the functioning of the natural body. Psychedelic drugs, as the 1950s medical discourse understood them, thus typify the Derridean notion of the *pharmakon*—that which is conceived as 'both antidote and poison'.[27] This interdependence between toxicity and therapy was effectively silenced by the late 1960s, when the public outcry over psychedelic drugs blamed them for triggering real and permanent psychological damage.

By then, psychedelics had moved far beyond the purview of medical science. Because of the enormous publicity it garnered, Timothy Leary's dismissal from Harvard in 1963 has come to represent the decisive moment in this symbolic shift, when psychedelics became identified with the values of 1960s cultural rebellion rather than investigative science. It is nevertheless important to recognize that these substances had long inhabited a murky borderland between science, religion, and art. Although largely unpublicized in the media, a small coterie of artists and intellectuals had already begun to congregate around psychedelics in the 1950s, led by figures like Aldous Huxley and Gerald Heard. Huxley became fascinated with the drugs after reading one of Humphry Osmond's articles on mescaline in 1953, and famously recounted his own quasi-mystical psychedelic experience (under Osmond's supervision) in *The Doors of Perception*. Although Huxley's approach remained relatively peripheral during the 1950s, the line between science and religion was never very clear when it came to these drugs. Huxley in fact lectured the New York Academy of Sciences on the prospect of a psychedelic revolution uniting the forces of religion and pharmacology, while some researchers even devised scientific experiments to demonstrate the drugs' capacity to induce mystical experiences.[28]

Perhaps no one embodied this ambiguity better than Leary. While the Harvard psychologist initially framed his research on psilocybin in scientific-experimental terms, he quickly realized that 'the nature of the [drug]

[27] Derrida, 'The Rhetoric of Drugs', 235.

[28] See, e.g., Walter N. Pahnke and William A. Richards, 'Implications of LSD and Experimental Mysticism', *Journal of Religion and Health*, v (July 1966).

experience depends almost entirely on set and setting'.[29] It was therefore ill-suited to the growing emphasis on experimental controls in pharmacological research, which were designed to isolate a drug's intrinsic effects from any external variables. For Leary, it was 'meaningless' to talk about psychedelics in terms of 'the "effect of the drug" ', as they simply did not produce replicable results that could be isolated from the context in which they were taken.[30] He thus became increasingly disenchanted with what he called the ' "science game" ', perceiving it as an obstacle rather than an aid to getting the 'deepest experience out of the drugs'.[31] Meanwhile, Leary's colleagues grew uneasy with the ' "anti-intellectual atmosphere" ' and ' "outright attacks on science" ' emanating from an academic who seemed less concerned with scientific research than with spreading a cultural revolution.[32]

The dismissal of Leary and his colleague Richard Alpert, along with the advent of a black market in LSD, effectively broke the scientific community's monopoly over the supply and cultural meaning of psychedelic drugs. In the months before he was fired, Leary had already begun to cast himself more explicitly as a prophet and revolutionary, by advancing the cause of psychedelics as a religious, political, and civil-liberties issue. To this end, he established the International Foundation for Internal Freedom (IFIF) as an advocacy group promoting the freedom of all ' "to undertake research into the expansion of their own consciousness" ', and eventually headquartered himself with his followers at Millbrook Farm.[33] Leary's dismissal and subsequent activities helped shift media attention decisively to the non-medical applications of psychedelic drugs.[34] Despite a growing legal crackdown, recreational use of the drugs skyrocketed through 1966 and 1967, as young people flocked to hippie enclaves like San Francisco's Haight-Ashbury district. Ken Kesey—author of *One Flew over the Cuckoo's Nest*—and his quirky band of 'Merry Pranksters' played a key role in this popularization, staging mass LSD sessions known as 'Acid Tests' and shuttling across the country in a Day-Glo

[29] Timothy Leary, Ralph Metzner, and Richard Alpert, *The Psychedelic Experience: A Manual Based on the Tibetan Book of the Dead* (Secaucus, NJ, 1964), 11.

[30] Timothy Leary, 'Foreword', in Alan Watts, *The Joyous Cosmology: Adventures in the Chemistry of Consciousness* (New York, 1962), xii.

[31] Jonnes, *Hep-Cats, Narcs, and Pipe Dreams*, 229; Untitled article, *Boston Globe* (28 May 1963), Harvard University Archives, Cambridge, MA, HUG 300.

[32] Herbert Kelman, quoted in Robert E. Smith, 'Psychologists Disagree on Psilocybin Research', *Harvard Crimson* (15 Mar. 1962); David McLelland, quoted in Wasserman, 'Tuning In', 71.

[33] Quoted in John Kobler, 'The Dangerous Magic of LSD', *Saturday Evening Post* (11 Feb. 1963), 35.

[34] See, e.g., 'Psychic Drug Testers Living in Retreat', *New York Times* (15 Dec. 1963).

bus to spread the word about acid. By 1967, the notion of a 'psychedelic movement' or 'psychedelic revolution' had gained widespread currency.[35]

II

Both Leary and the medical researchers who preceded him had observed the way psychedelics subverted the boundary between interiority and exteriority—between internal drug effect and external environment, or between the natural body and the artificial chemical supplement. It was paradoxes such as these—much like the way medical researchers derived therapeutic benefit from the drugs' toxic properties—which likewise underwrote the countercultural engagement with psychedelic drugs and help to account for the continuity between the two contexts.

These aporias are evident, for instance, in the way countercultural leaders styled the drugs as religious sacraments offering an experience of transcendence. In doing so, they drew upon the precedent set by Huxley as well as a growing fascination with Native American traditions that had long employed peyote and psilocybin for religious purposes. The heightened feeling of significance so frequently invoked by psychedelic users seemed to lend itself quite naturally to a spiritual interpretation. Studies such as Walter Pahnke's 'Good Friday' experiment, for instance, claimed that psilocybin elicited 'intense mystico-religious responses' in 75 per cent of subjects when taken in a 'supportive setting'.[36] Books exploring psychedelic spirituality also proliferated, including one by the theologian and Zen popularizer Alan Watts, who claimed that there was 'no essential difference' between the LSD experience and 'the illuminated consciousness of the mystic'.[37] Leary was thus by no means alone in describing the psychedelic trip as 'the deepest religious experience of my life'.[38] He was so impressed with the drug's spiritual powers that he founded his own church, the League for Spiritual Discovery (LSD), based around the sacramental use of psychedelics. Yet, none conveyed the spiritual transfiguration associated with these drugs as eloquently as Aldous Huxley, for whom mescaline fulfilled the Blakean

[35] Gladwin Hill, 'Turn On, Tune In and Drop Out: LSD Users Describe their Experiences during a Psychedelic Trip', *New York Times* (23 Feb. 1967), 43; Malcom W. Brown, '9 Experts on LSD Urge More Study', *New York Times* (19 Oct. 1967).

[36] Timothy Leary, 'The Religious Experience: Its Production and Interpretation', in Gunther M. Weil, Ralph Metzner, and Timothy Leary (eds), *The Psychedelic Reader: Selected from the Psychedelic Review* (New York, 1971), 192.

[37] Watts, *Joyous Cosmology*, 17. See also William Barrett, 'Accept Life and Live', *New York Times* (18 Dec. 1960).

[38] Timothy Leary, *The Politics of Ecstasy* (Berkeley, 1998), 13.

promise that '"if the doors of perception were cleansed every thing would appear to man as it is, infinite"'.[39] Much more than a mere medical tool for the treatment of mental illness, these figures credited the psychedelic experience with offering hidden insights of fundamental value to healthy individuals.

Any transcendent experience achieved through recourse to psychedelic drugs, however, could not divorce itself from the materiality of the sacrament itself—a problem which tended to frustrate the claims of its apostles. If psychedelics enabled people to transcend the material world, this was nevertheless achieved through recourse to a material substance—one artificially produced in a laboratory. Critics of psychedelic spirituality were quick to point out this apparent contradiction. They disparaged Leary and his cohort for relying upon a 'Drugstore for the Soul' that afforded little more than '"false . . . Instant mysticism"'.[40] Given that mystical experience is traditionally defined as a gift of grace bestowed by a higher power or as the result of great spiritual labour, many felt it 'illegitimate to take a short-cut to enlightenment by popping a pill'.[41] Clearly sensitive to charges like these, Watts explicitly denied that the mystical psychedelic experience was 'spurious or artificial in contrast to those that come through religious discipline', on the grounds that 'mystical insight is no more in the chemical itself than biological knowledge is in the microscope'.[42] Leary adopted a similar line of reasoning, arguing that the drug 'merely acts as a chemical key. . . [that] frees the nervous system of its ordinary patterns and structures'.[43] According to this logic, the drug was at once merely an instrument—and therefore ancillary to the spiritual truth of the psychedelic experience—as well as a necessary instrument—one required in order to free the brain from the perceptual structures preventing humans from experiencing the world 'as it is, infinite'. The experience of reality in its truest form was thus parasitic upon something artificial—an external technical supplement added on to the natural body only to reveal and substitute a lack at its very heart. The countercultural mobilization of psychedelic drugs thus represents a classic case of the

[39] Aldous Huxley, *The Doors of Perception and Heaven and Hell* (New York, 2004), epigraph.
[40] Stuart Hampshire, quoted in Charles M. Holmes, *Aldous Huxley and the Way to Reality* (Bloomington, IN, 1970), 171; Arthur Koestler, quoted in Ken Goffman and Dan Joy, *Counterculture Through the Ages: From Abraham to Acid House* (New York, 2004), 252.
[41] Nicholas Murray, *Aldous Huxley: An English Intellectual* (London, 2002), 401.
[42] Watts, *Joyous Cosmology*, 19, 26.
[43] Leary et al., *The Psychedelic Experience*, 11.

Derridean supplement—of that which is 'at once accidental and essential. Like any good parasite, it is at once inside and outside'.[44]

This inseparable relationship between interiority and exteriority likewise disrupted countercultural claims that the psychedelic experience brought individuals into greater communion with one another. For those who came of age in a post-war climate of racial tension and Cold War conflict, promises such as these resonated deeply. While mainstream America seemed to be a society of estranged individuals, these barriers appeared to melt away under the influence of psychedelic drugs, leading many to hail them as a panacea for the social ills bedevilling American society. Allen Ginsberg claimed that LSD allowed individuals to merge with ' "the vastness beyond our conditioned selves" '.[45] For Tom Wolfe, it gave rise to 'the *experience* of the barrier between the subjective and objective, the personal and the impersonal, the *I* and the *not-I* disappearing'.[46] Many strove to translate this experience of radical self-transcendence into new forms of communal living and interpersonal engagement. Such was the vision informing Leary's project of forming a 'transpersonative community' in which members ingested psychedelics with the goal of jettisoning their egos and merging into a 'group mind'.[47] It was likewise central to the Merry Pranksters' project to 're-negotiate social space' with 'Acid Tests'.[48] Watts was particularly optimistic about the social possibilities suggested by these drugs, predicting that they would replace the 'imaginary, socially fabricated' ego with a 'strong sensation of oneness with others. . . a far better basis for social love and order than the fiction of the separate will'.[49] The psychedelic vision thus held out the promise of a cure for the diseases of alienation and individualism rampant in mainstream America—a vision intimately allied with the hippie values of peace, love, and social harmony.

Although this quest for self-transcendence was central to the countercultural discourse on psychedelics, it paradoxically emerged from an emphatically internal and incommunicable experience occurring at the level of individual consciousness. Again and again, psychedelic users spoke of

[44] Derrida, 'Rhetoric of Drugs', 234.

[45] Quoted in Ann Charters (ed.), *The Portable Sixties Reader* (New York, 2003), 329.

[46] Tom Wolfe, *The Electric Kool-Aid Acid Test* (New York, 1999 [1968]), 45. Italics in original.

[47] Stevens, *Storming Heaven*, 185, 198.

[48] David Farber, 'The Intoxicated State/Illegal Nation: Drugs in the Sixties Counterculture', in Peter Braunstein and Michael William Doyle (eds), *Imagine Nation: The American Counterculture of the 1960s and '70s* (New York, 2002), 24.

[49] Watts, *Joyous Cosmology*, 96.

'experiences for which our language has no vocabulary', which utterly transcended 'the narrow limitations of words and concepts' and therefore could not be communicated to those without first-hand experience.[50] By figuring the psychedelic experience in these terms, countercultural leaders could claim a special expertise and authority to speak about the drug experience that could be wielded against the drugs' critics (most of whom had never themselves 'experienced' the drugs). For leaders of the New Left, however, the ineffability of the LSD experience made it an escapist distraction that 'drew persons inward, removing them "from the arena of social consciousness" '.[51]

Yet such critiques failed to grasp the extent to which the psychedelic vision of outward social harmony depended upon the very interiority and ineffability of the drug experience. Only by using drugs to jettison the 'tyrannical verbal brain', could people realize the ' "original identity" ' of all beings 'which ordinary language . . . so completely conceal[s]'.[52] The experience of an internal reality prior to the artificial imposition of ego or language thus became the (paradoxical) precondition for outward communion. Not surprisingly, the very incommunicability of the drug experience inspired a particularly strong sense of kinship between fellow psychedelic initiates. But it did so precisely by alienating them from the uninitiated masses of 'straight' America, spawning exclusive cliques like the Pranksters or Leary's Millbrook coterie. The criminalization of LSD only widened this gulf by creating a vast 'illegal nation' of marginalized drug users defined as fundamentally alien to mainstream society.[53] The countercultural discourse on psychedelic drugs thus reveals the way in which an internal, pre-discursive experience can paradoxically serve to ground a communal identity, although it necessarily does so by defining this community against another. In other words, psychedelics were mobilized to both erect and to subvert boundaries between interiority and exteriority, identity and difference.

While proponents of psychedelic drugs often eschewed traditional political activism, this was not because they were apolitical. Instead, many considered psychedelics to be more revolutionary than any organized political movement, for they served to liberate individuals from the inside. Such an approach sought the roots of the nation's social and political problems within human consciousness and was by no means exclusive to the psychedelic drug culture, or indeed, to the 1960s. Leary thus drew upon a common countercultural trope when he argued that America's institutions of authority had

[50] Leary, 'Foreword', in ibid., ix, xii.

[51] Timothy Miller, *The Hippies and American Values* (Knoxville, TN, 1991), 49.

[52] Watts, *Joyous Cosmology*, 68.

[53] See Farber, 'Intoxicated State/ Illegal Nation'.

corrupted the natural state of the human mind, conditioning consciousness into 'artificial, repetitive sequences' that promoted intolerant, competitive, and consumerist behaviours.[54] Many—including, most notably, Herbert Marcuse—shared Leary's faith that psychedelics could act as a ' "cultural detoxicant' ".[55] By suspending pernicious conditioning and 're-imprinting... new belief systems and attitudes about others and society', these substances would engender 'a profound revolution in consciousness' with vital sociopolitical ramifications.[56] Countercultural leaders thus appealed to the physical brain as a site of counter-hegemonic re-inscription, mobilizing it to resist an oppressive subjectivity artificially imposed from without. From the liberated individual brain, they argued, a healthier social body would emerge.

Despite the emancipatory role the counterculture attributed to these substances, however, it soon became clear that they possessed an equally great oppressive potential. At a very basic level, the liberating and controlling elements of the psychedelic experience were inextricable because the very liberation it was meant to bestow required 'handing over [one's] cortex to a drug company'.[57] Yet such a criticism presupposes the natural self-sufficiency and enclosure of the individual body, to which the drug would necessarily be external and supplementary, as well as attributing undue agency to the drug's chemical properties. No such rigid distinction between interiority and exteriority was possible in the case of the psychedelic experience, as it both amplified the consumer's own disposition and rendered him or her more vulnerable to external suggestion. This problem became painfully evident when hippie enclaves like the Haight-Ashbury were inundated with teenagers, for they also attracted a slew of predators seeking to take advantage of the suggestibility of the psychedelic state.[58]

Neither were psychedelic propagandists innocent of employing the drugs for the purposes of social control. The countercultural project to deploy psychedelics as revolutionary political tools was at times eerily reminiscent of the CIA's plan to mobilize the drugs as weapons of chemical warfare capable of manipulating consciousness on a mass scale. While the CIA sought to programme trips in such a way as to consistently incapacitate their consumer,

[54] Leary, *Politics of Ecstasy*, 222.

[55] Miller, *Hippies and American Values*, 35.

[56] Ibid.; Timothy Leary, 'Tim Leary's Magic Bullet', *Psychology Today* (July 1983), Harvard University Archives, Cambridge, MA, HUG 300.

[57] Martin Mayer, quoted in Leary, *Politics of Ecstasy*, 73.

[58] See Goffman and Joy, *Counterculture Through the Ages*, 270–1; Farber, 'Intoxicated State/Illegal Nation', 35.

Leary instead designed a guidebook for the psychedelic trip that would elicit a reproducible spiritual experience. This he justified with the logic that an already 'free consciousness' liberated by psychedelics nevertheless remained dependent on the guidebook's teachings 'in order to be liberated'.[59] Kesey would likewise 'order and shape' the Pranksters' trips and manipulate the audio-visual equipment at the Acid Tests so as to control the group experience, even as he encouraged his followers to 'freak freely'.[60] All this points to the remarkably coercive tendencies at work within the communities around Leary and Kesey, focused as they were upon a charismatic leader with virtually unchecked authority over the supply, method, and meaning of drug use. It also suggests that both Kesey and Leary were themselves aware that the psychedelic experience had to be controlled in order to liberate—another of its aporias. It was not enough to de-condition inherited norms through recourse to psychedelic drugs; new ones had to be supplied to take their place.

In many ways, the medical discourse had set the conditions for these paradoxes precisely by figuring the psychedelic experience as an experience, rather than as a determined and replicable drug-effect. Rooted in the amorphous category of experience, psychedelics could accrue a wide range of contradictory discursive associations whose aporias frustrated any exclusive appropriation. While critics denigrated the drugs as dangerous, artificial supplements that invaded the natural self-sufficiency of the body and drew users into an unreal world of hallucination, countercultural leaders appealed to the rhetoric of experience to reverse this argument. They did so, moreover, by appealing to the very same naturalist metaphysics as their opponents, remaining bound to the same hierarchical distinctions between nature and artifice, inside and outside, medicine and poison. Countercultural discourse simply re-appropriated the psychedelic experience as in fact more natural and authentic than mainstream social life, branding the latter as itself the unnatural pathology in need of a cure. The rhetoric of experience was central to this authorizing project, as it allowed the drugs' proponents to divert attention away from the artificial nature of the drug and onto the experience of truth to which it purportedly gave rise. In doing so, they did not dispute the metaphysical binaries at the heart of the mainstream culture they criticized, but instead reinforced the privilege it placed on nature over artifice, truth over illusion, essence over accident, and identity over difference.

[59] Leary et al., *The Psychedelic Experience*, 12.

[60] Elliot M. Zashin, 'Political Theorist and Demiurge: The Rise and Fall of Ken Kesey', *The Centennial Review*, 17: 2 (1973), 211.

In order for the psychedelic experience to be identified with these privileged qualities, its aporias had to be effectively silenced. Either psychedelic drugs provided access to a more fundamental and beneficial set of truths, or they were merely artificial hallucinogens. Psychedelic activists therefore consistently downplayed both the ambivalence of the drug experience and any other internal differences which threatened to disrupt its claims to universality. In order for the psychedelic experience to be truly authentic and universal, in other words, it necessarily had to occur at a level more fundamental than differences based on race, gender, and class. Allen Ginsberg, for instance, claimed that LSD transcended all human boundaries, 'particularly black and white, particularly square and hippie . . . particularly Birchite and faggot individualist'.[61] Because spiritual transcendence, communal harmony, and personal liberation affected 'man at the very center of his nature', the psychedelic crusaders assumed these substances to be universally valuable, and that their goal '"was Every Man's"'.[62] Such sweeping claims to universality concealed, however, the distinctly white, male, middle-class bias within the countercultural discourse on psychedelics, obscuring how certain power relations and forms of difference affected it.

This experiential rhetoric of universality masked, for instance, the psychedelic counterculture's appropriation of non-white cultural markers. Even though psychedelic drug use attracted a predominantly white demographic, proponents tended to associate the drugs with non-white cultures in order to trumpet the authenticity of the psychedelic experience, over and against the artificiality of western norms. Drawing upon a long orientalist tradition, these propagandists identified their cause with the exotic Other, presenting it as the source of truths undiscovered by western culture. Nowhere was this clearer than in the relationship between the counterculture and Native American traditions. Most psychedelic drugs aside from LSD—such as peyote, mescaline, and psilocybin—were imported from an indigenous cultural setting, which allowed psychedelic activists to present their movement as the heir to an age-old Native tradition of sacramental drug use. Leary compared his own campaign to legalize LSD, for instance, with the plight of Southwestern tribes who had struggled against colonial priests seeking to deprive them of their sacred plants.[63] Yet, few Native Americans themselves identified with the psychedelic counterculture and the accounts of Native psychedelic rituals

[61] Allen Ginsberg, *Spontaneous Mind: Selected Interviews, 1958–1996*, ed. David Carter (New York, 2001), 91.

[62] Leary, in Charters, *Portable Sixties Reader*, 343; Michael Hollingshead, quoted in Lee and Schlain, *Acid Dreams*, 99.

[63] See especially his entry in Charters, *Portable Sixties Reader*.

upon which it drew were usually penned by outside observers. The Native American Church's ritual use of peyote was also an entirely distinct phenomenon from the hippie 'dope churches' organized primarily for the purpose of drug use.[64]

In articulating the spiritual aspect of the psychedelic experience, countercultural leaders also relied heavily upon the language of eastern mysticism, tending to conflate a variety of disparate religious traditions. For instance, Huxley's description of the mescaline state fused the vocabulary of the Christian 'Beatific Vision', the Hindu '*Sat Chit Ananda*', and the Buddhist 'Dharma-Body' into a single essentialized mystical vision.[65] Similarly, the atmosphere at Millbrook mingled drug use with Hindu chants, Buddhist meditation, and readings from the ancient Chinese *I Ching*.[66] Leary's manual for the psychedelic experience, based as it was on the *Tibetan Book of the Dead*, appropriated an esoteric religious tradition designed to be passed down from master to initiate, in the service of a public and entirely foreign cultural project. The psychedelic discourse thus relied upon both an affirmation and an overcoming of the cultural specificity and otherness of 'eastern' and Native American traditions.

Likewise absent from the countercultural discourse was an account of the way gender mediated and differentiated the drug experience. While psychedelic activists painted the psychedelic experience as a great emancipator from mainstream social norms, this did not appear to extend to the questioning of traditional gender roles. The poet Diane di Prima published an account of her stay at Millbrook that is instructive in this regard. Despite the unorthodox lifestyle at the mansion, di Prima reveals that female guests were nevertheless expected to cook and care for any children, while the men were freer to engage in drug experimentation.[67] Moreover, the literature on drug exploration that proliferated in the 1950s and 1960s rarely presented women in an active role. Instead, their stories appeared in the 'passive context' of patient case histories and sensationalized media reports of drug-induced sexual impropriety, or were published pseudonymously. Many of the wives of prominent psychedelic advocates, such as Laura Huxley and Rosemary Leary, actively participated in the psychedelic movement but did so in the shadow of their

[64] See the discussion in Miller, *Hippies and American Values*, 31–4.

[65] Huxley, Doors of Perception, 18.

[66] See the account in Charters, *Portable Sixties Reader*, 336–49; Marcus Boon, *The Road of Excess: A History of Writers on Drugs* (Cambridge, MA, 2002), 263.

[67] Diane di Prima, 'The Holidays at Millbrook—1966', in Charters, *Portable Sixties Reader*.

husbands' fame.[68] The counterculture's rhetoric of universality thus consistently veiled the particularity of women's engagement with psychedelic drugs.

This rhetoric likewise obscured the mediating role of class. While the drugs' promoters presented their cause as a battle against the Establishment, the psychedelic culture in fact originated within elite social circles and institutions. That psychedelic experimentation began among cultural elites is perhaps not surprising given the substances' initial confinement to the sphere of academic research. Leary and Alpert gained access to the drugs through these official channels, and after realizing their wider potential, Huxley advised the two to target 'the talented, the well-born, the intelligent rich, and others in positions of influence' as the best means of spreading a 'psychedelic revolution'.[69] Implementing this advice, Leary attracted a following of scientists, artists, intellectuals, and businessmen, just as a circle of cultural luminaries interested in psychedelics had formed around Huxley and Heard a decade earlier. Yet, as the black market in LSD flourished and made it accessible to the masses, tensions between elitism and populism began to emerge within the psychedelic leadership. While Kesey and Ginsberg advocated the popularization of psychedelics on a mass scale, Huxley, Hoffer, and Leary sought to restrict their use to adults with 'special needs and skills', who would undertake 'the experience in a responsible way' under the supervision of trained experts.[70] Leary thus conceived of his Millbrook coterie as the 'vanguard of a psychic revolution', while Kesey cultivated a more grassroots, working-class sensibility that was openly hostile to Leary's approach.[71] In contrast to Leary's 'high church psychedelic', with its staid piety, scholarly methods, and aristocratic sensibility, Kesey's 'low church psychedelic' prized spontaneity, fun, and shock-value.[72] Class dynamics thus affected and differentiated the psychedelic culture in critical ways.

III

In demonstrating the various ways the countercultural discourse on psychedelic drugs elided the mediating role of ethnic, gender, and class identities, I do not wish to suggest that the experiences defined by these identities were necessarily more authentic or real than those articulated by countercultural

[68] See Boon, *Road of Excess*, 253.

[69] Leary, in Charters, *Portable Sixties Reader*, 340.

[70] Abram Hoffer, 'The Confrontation between the Psychedelic Experience and Society', *Canadian Dimension* 4 (1967), 7.

[71] Lee and Schlain, *Acid Dreams*, 99; See the account of the meeting between the two groups in Wolfe, *Electric Kool-Aid Acid Test*, 104–7.

[72] Leary, *Politics of Ecstasy*, 105.

leaders. Instead, I simply aim to illustrate how each appeal to the rhetoric of experience involves a choice as to what is authentic and central to that experience and what is ancillary to it—a choice which can always be challenged by competing claims to experiential authenticity. It is this aspect of the psychedelic discourse which is significant for the practice of history more broadly. I shall therefore conclude by highlighting some of the striking parallels between appeals to the rhetoric of experience on behalf of psychedelic drugs and those of historians who have made 'experience' a foundational term in the discipline since the 1960s. In this way, I hope to underscore the wider methodological implications of the history of psychedelic drugs.

Countercultural leaders were neither the first nor the last to appeal to the authority of experience to legitimize their project. Around the same time that psychedelic researchers began invoking the language of experience to open up a space between the drugs' pharmacology and their subjective effects, a group of Marxist historians in Britain turned to the very same category to provide a mediating space between economic structures and class-consciousness. In 1963, the same year Timothy Leary was fired from Harvard, E. P. Thompson published *The Making of the English Working Class*. In it, he sought to recover 'the agency of working people' located in 'the raw material of [their] experience'—something he claimed was irreducible to the ideology of the dominant class.[73] 'Through the missing term, "experience"', he argued, 'structure is transmuted into process, and the subject re-enters history'.[74] In appealing to 'experience' as a site of working-class agency and authenticity, Thompson was deeply indebted to Raymond Williams' holistic understanding of this concept, which he once defined as 'the fullest, most open, most active kind of consciousness', in contrast to 'more specialized or limited states or faculties'.[75] This powerful experiential rhetoric of authenticity is remarkably close to the language employed by the counterculture to legitimize the psychedelic experience. Both groups invoked 'experience' as the source of a communal identity capable of resisting the oppressive norms and structures of the dominant culture. In doing so, moreover, both denuded other identity-based claims upon the authority of experience.

[73] E. P. Thompson, *The Making of the English Working Class* (New York, 1964), 12, 9.

[74] E. P. Thompson, 'The Poverty of Theory or an Orrery of Errors', *The Poverty of Theory and Other Essays* (London, 1978), 362.

[75] Raymond Williams, *Keywords: A Vocabulary of Culture and Society*, rev. edn (New York, 1985), 127.

In the decades that followed, Williams and Thompson began to attract criticism for the way their holistic account of working-class experience tended to occlude—just as the psychedelic drug discourse had—differences based on gender, race, or sexuality.[76] And yet, these critiques frequently appealed to the very same rhetoric of experiential authenticity and agency to ground their claims on behalf of competing identities. In calling for historians to attend to 'the material conditions of the collective black experience', for instance, Thomas Holt defended its status as 'an experience semi-autonomous from and/or contradictory to . . . the dominant discourse of a slave society'.[77] The notion of experience as an authentic space that resists the ideology of the powerful was here redeployed to ground a racial rather than a class identity, re-inscribing what was previously considered supplementary as in fact the most fundamental aspect of experience. Much like the psychedelic counterculture, historians thus mobilized the rhetoric of experience to underwrite distinctions between insiders and outsiders and ground a shared group identity. Each such appeal necessarily involved both an authorization and a de-legitimation—a choice distinguishing what is real or essential from that which is supplementary or super-structural.

In her 1991 essay on 'The Evidence of Experience', Joan Scott took issue with the way these historians have appealed to the experiences of women, the working class, or other marginalized groups as historically 'uncontestable evidence'. Doing so only naturalizes these differences, she argued, with the result that 'the evidence of experience then becomes evidence for the fact of difference, rather than a way of exploring how difference is established'.[78] Treating identity-based experiences as objective historical data thus serves to authorize a politics based on the primacy of these identities. But it also shores up the historian's own authority as an objective observer, by obscuring his or her interpretive role in deciding what counts as experience. By presenting 'women's experience' or 'working-class experience' as a historical given, Scott argued, such appeals elide the historian's 'own role in determining the salience of certain things and not others'—the way he or she 'excludes whole realms of human activity by simply not counting them as experience'.[79]

[76] See, e.g., Carolyn Steedman, 'The Price of Experience: Women and the Making of the English Working Class', *Radical History Review*, lix (Spring 1994).

[77] Thomas C. Holt, 'Experience and the Politics of Intellectual Inquiry', in James Chandler, Arnold Davidson, and Harry Harootunian (eds), *Questions of Evidence: Proof, Practice, and Persuasion Across the Disciplines* (Chicago, 1994), 395, 391.

[78] Joan W. Scott, 'The Evidence of Experience', *Critical Inquiry*, xvii, 4 (Summer 1991), 777.

[79] Ibid., 785; On this problem, see Martin Jay, *Songs of Experience: Modern American and European Variations on a Universal Theme* (Berkeley, 2005), ch. 6. Jay's work is a

In other words, experience is never simply given as a historical object; nor does it operate a priori as a site of agency and authenticity. Precisely by mobilizing the category of experience in these terms, however, both psychedelic propagandists and historians have obscured the historicity and the strategic nature of their own appeals to experience. By treating experience as an unmediated source of truth, they have masked the work performed by the appeal to experience itself—the way such appeals underwrite the authority of the speaker and his or her political project. Beyond asking whether historians can recover the evidence of experience, in other words, it might also prove worthwhile to consider how appeals to such evidence underwrite the epistemic authority of the historian, as well as the role they play in policing the boundary between the 'real' stuff of history and what is considered epiphenomenal or even irrelevant to it.

It is therefore fitting that the story of psychedelic drugs, which has been (understandably) eclipsed in the historiography of the 1960s by the Civil Rights Movement, second-wave feminism, and the New Left, should serve as a vehicle for these insights into the functioning of a major historical category. If the psychedelic drug culture has been deemed relatively insignificant, this suggests that historians have tended to accept dominant cultural narratives defining non-medical drug use as escapist or artificial, and therefore as historically and politically irrelevant. In accordance with the logic of supplementarity, however, these substances tell us much about the operation of fundamental cultural distinctions—between truth and illusion, inside and outside—which organize discourses far beyond those specifically concerned with drugs. What initially appears to be just a story about hallucinogens thus sheds light on key categories structuring the contemporary writing of history and the inevitable decisions it involves about what counts as historically significant. It also reveals the extraordinary purchase and wide-ranging applicability that the category of experience acquired during the 1950s and 1960s, enabling it to be deployed across registers as diverse as scientific research, countercultural advocacy, and historical writing.

---

testimony to the wider history of such appeals to the authority of experience, demonstrating how they have been deployed to serve a wide range of political, religious, aesthetic, philosophical, and historiographical ends from antiquity to the present.

Target America: Visual Culture, Neuroimaging, and the 'Hijacked Brain' Theory of Addiction

Timothy A. Hickman[1]

The historical study of drugs and addiction has always been a broadly interdisciplinary venture. Conferences and edited volumes on intoxicants and intoxication frequently include contributions from medical researchers and addiction treatment professionals alongside the usual give and take between historians, literary critics, and social scientists. The exchange is rewarding but the interface can be difficult, particularly since the mid-1990s as new theories of addiction and their rhetorical means of dissemination have become all but paradigmatic in the neurosciences. This new 'brain science' argues that neurological function, in this case addiction, can be pictured, mapped, and studied in real time, inside the skull of a living subject. The case has been argued in fascinating presentations based upon vividly detailed brain scans—visual images produced by the latest and most advanced digital imaging technologies. Seeing seems to be believing, and humanists and social scientists, most of whom understand addiction to be at least partly a socially constructed rather than an empirical or strictly physiological condition, have found themselves on the defensive.[2] After all, if we now know what addiction *really is*, then studies of its past construction lose much of their critical edge. Relegated to the status of antiquarian amusement, historical studies threaten to become mere illustrations along a teleological pathway

[1] In addition to the volume's editors and readers, I would like to thank Andrew Brennand, Nicola Caldwell, David T. Courtwright, Derek Heim, and Derek Sayer for their contributions to this article. Comments are welcome at T.A.Hickman@Lancaster.ac.uk

[2] On the interface between the clinical and social sciences of addiction, see David T. Courtwright, 'Addiction and the Science of History', *Addiction*, 107 (2012), 489. See also Howard Kushner, 'Toward a Cultural Biology of Addiction', *Biosocieties*, 5 (2010), 8–24. Courtwright's article, which calls for cooperation between scientists and historians was debated at length at *Points: The Blog of the Alcohol and Drugs History Society*: http://pointsadhsblog.wordpress.com/ On the persuasiveness of visual images in scholarly debates, see Phaedra Daipha, 'Visual Perception at Work: Lessons from the World of Meteorology', *Poetics*, 38 (2010), 150–64.

Past and Present (2014), Supplement 9
Advance Access published on 17 September 2013
© The Past and Present Society

that winds toward the final triumph of science over superstition. Just as remarkable is that this reaction to *a set of pictures* comes from people who are sensitive to and often have expertise in reading visual images.

This article therefore asks two questions that are standard in any cultural historian's repertoire: why have these images been so convincing and how might we understand them to be embedded in their broader cultural context? To answer those questions, I will look more closely at brain scan images themselves, concentrating particularly on the ways that they create visual meaning. The essay then shifts its focus to written language, examining what is perhaps the most influential use of these images, Alan I. Leshner's 1997 'hijacked brain' theory of addiction, which is the description promoted by the US National Institute on Drug Abuse (NIDA). Finally, we will return to the visual by looking at the US Drug Enforcement Association's 2002 'Target America' exhibition, which offered a striking juxtaposition of hijacking and addiction in a broader cultural context. By examining these recent visual descriptions of addiction, I hope to show that the historian's tools for cultural and social analysis can complement even the latest and most technologically advanced addiction research.

The invisibility of addiction has always been a challenge for those who have sought to define the condition. As early as 1897, the United States' best-known addiction cure doctor, Leslie E. Keeley, identified the visual ambiguity of narcotic addiction as among its most frustrating features, claiming that only those with specialized professional knowledge could hope to recognize the condition by its appearance.[3] Since then, physical side-effects like abscesses caused by injection, extreme thinness as an effect of amphetamine use, darkened eyes, hollowed cheeks, chaotic and impoverished living conditions, and even fashion choices have all been mobilized as visible markers of addiction, but none of these show anything like a tissue response that might reliably locate habitual drug use as a physiological or psychological condition.[4]

[3] Leslie E. Keeley, *Opium: Its Use, Abuse and Cure; or, From Bondage to Freedom* (Chicago, 1897), 23.

[4] For a fuller history of the visualization of addiction, see Timothy A. Hickman, 'Heroin Chic: The Visual Culture of Narcotic Addiction', *Third Text: Critical Perspectives on Contemporary Art and Culture*, 16:2 (June 2002), 119–36. See also Richard Huggins, 'The Addict's Body: Embodiment, Drug Use and Representation', in Dennis Waskul and Philip Vannine (eds), *Body/Embodiment: Symbolic Interaction and the Sociology of the Body* (Farnham, UK, 2006), 165–79; Richard Huggins, 'Images of Addiction', in Lisa Moore and Mary E. Kosut (eds), *The Body Reader: Essential Social and Cultural Readings* (New York, 2010), 384–98.

All of that appears to have changed, however, with the arrival of PET (Positron Emission Tomography) and fMRI (functional Magnetic Resonance Imaging). These are technologies that produce brain-scan images, analytical representations of living brains, which proponents claim offer very strong suggestions, or even concrete evidence, of addiction's physiological status as a 'brain disease'. The images and the theories of addiction attendant upon them have been very influential in scientific and policy circles and indeed in public culture more broadly. This is the case because PET and fMRI both offer means of recording and picturing the functionality of a living brain—especially glucose and oxygen metabolism—in real time.

PET records brain activity by tagging selected molecules with radioactive isotopes that emit positrons as they decay. The positron travels a short way before it collides with an electron, which causes the two particles to annihilate one another. As they do so, they produce two gamma rays that travel in opposite directions at a nearly 180-degree angle. A monitoring device picks up the rays, and the location of the original molecule, or concentrations of the original molecule, can be inferred and mapped via some extremely complex statistical computing. The metabolism of water, glucose, or any number of chemical products can be mapped in this way.[5] fMRI on the other hand, is a process that charts blood flow and oxygen levels that are associated with the brain's neural activity. It does so by producing a powerful magnetic field, which causes the nuclei of selected hydrogen atoms—single protons which, when combined with an oxygen atom, make up water—to become aligned within the field. A strong radio signal further energizes the selected nuclei. When the magnetic field and radio signal are cut back, the nuclei re-approach their normal state and release their acquired energy as photons, which are detectable by a scanner. Active brain areas demand more densely oxygenated blood than do inactive areas, and by the above means can be detected and mapped by an fMRI machine.[6] Among fMRI's advantages is that it maps brain activity without exposing patients to even the very small doses of radiation encountered in PET.

[5] Joseph Dumit, *Picturing Personality: Brain Scans and Biomedical Identity* (Princeton, 2004), 24–31.

[6] Kelly A. Joyce, 'From Numbers to Pictures: The Development of Magnetic Resonance Imaging and the Visual Turn in Medicine', *Science as Culture*, 15:1 (March 2006), 1–22. For a detailed description of the operation of MRI, see William R. Hendee and Christopher J. Morgan, 'Magnetic Resonance Imaging Part 1—Physical Principles', *Western Journal of Medicine*, 141:4 (October 1984), 491–500.

Both of these technologies were developed in the second half of the twentieth century. George de Hevesey, a Hungarian-born chemist working in Copenhagen and Stockholm, laid the groundwork for what would later become PET. In 1943 he won the Nobel Prize for chemistry when he showed that the radioactive isotope of a molecule is chemically indistinguishable from its original, but that its radioactivity made it traceable. Other chemists worked to develop and use more effective tracers, particularly positron emitters, whose rapid yet steady decay adds precision and detail to their traceability. The brief half-life of the positron emitters also adds to the cost of using them—a lab or medical facility needs an on-site cyclotron to produce the isotopes. The groundwork for fMRI, on the other hand, emerged at least as early as the 1890s, when University of Cambridge medical researchers C. S. Roy and C. S. Sherington showed that blood and oxygen flow to the brain increased with stimulation.[7] The relationship between neural activity and blood oxygen, or, the theory of haemodynamics, is at the centre of fMRI, which measures cerebral blood and oxygen levels. The hardware that made these theories applicable took a great deal of development, much of which occurred within the broadly supportive context of the US Atomic Energy Commission's efforts to find peace-time uses for nuclear technology after the Second World War.[8]

The development of PET and fMRI—which includes the development of computers and software to make sense of the collected data—encompasses a great deal of the histories of science, medicine, and technology in the twentieth century and is too long a story to tell here. The first widespread application of these technologies, however, began in the 1970s with a set of improvements to the detection devices used in PET. The most recent of the scanning technologies, fMRI, has only emerged since 1990 and it has rapidly become the most widely used brain scanning technology. Especially striking is the sheer scope of the enterprise that lay behind the brain scan images that had become so familiar in both the scientific and popular media by the end of the twentieth century. Those pictures are at least partly underwritten by the vast amount of scientific and medical research, not to mention the funding and institutional commitment, which went into their development.

Most importantly, both PET and fMRI produce data that scientists attempt to correlate with external or internal stimuli. Here, however, we must be cautious because correlation is not the same as causation. Put another way,

[7] C. S. Roy and C. S. Sherington, 'The Regulation of the Blood Supply of the Brain', *Journal of Physiology*, 11 (1890), 85–108.

[8] Dumit, *Picturing Personality*, 24–31. See Joyce, *From Numbers to Pictures*, 3, on the influence of the 'twentieth-century fascination with the atom' on the development of MRI.

while these imaging technologies are suggestive in mapping brain activity, positing a causal link to human behaviour based on that mapping is more controversial. Brains are extremely complex organs—a single square millimetre of brain tissue contains about 100,000 neurons, all of which are operating at the same time. Brain plasticity adds to the complexity. The brain is often able to adapt to injury or other stimuli and relocate its activities to other areas. For these and other reasons, the meaning of a brain scan remains controversial, particularly within its own field. UC San Diego researcher Ed Vul attacked what he called 'voodoo correlations' in a 2009 paper published in *Perspectives on Psychological Science.* Vul showed that the correlations between brain activity, as measured in fMRI scans, and human behaviour were frequently overstated because the researchers cherry-picked the most reactive parts of the scan, assumed that those reactions were 'average', and then based predictions of future brain activity on those misleading selections.[9] In terms of the claims made specifically about drug addiction, Stanton Peele has argued in the pages of *Radiology Today* that, while scans do correlate brain activity with drug use, they cannot differentiate between recreational use and addiction, which for Peele means that the scans are of limited use to addiction researchers.[10] Most frequently those who are critical of neuroimaging research call it 'high-tech phrenology'. This tag is not resented by most brain scientists, who point out that nineteenth-century phrenologists, though empirically wrong, were indeed path-breaking in their attempts to locate human behaviour in specific regions of the brain. What phrenology lacked was the technology to pursue its hunches—technology that is today supplied by PET, fMRI, and other neuroimaging systems.[11]

[9] Edward Vul, Christine Harris, Piotr Winkielman, and Harold Pashler, 'Puzzlingly High Correlations in fMRI Studies of Emotion, Personality, and Social Cognition', in *Perspectives on Psychological Science*, 4:3 (2009), 274–90. The journal published a full set of responses to Vul's findings alongside his original article. These are available online at http://www.psychologicalscience.org/journals/pps/4_3.cfm

[10] Stanton Peele, quoted by Dan Harvey, 'Imaging Addiction—PET and fMRI are Tools for Better Understanding Drugs' Effect on the Brain', in *Radiology Today*, 10:10 (2009), 16. The strongest arguments in favour of the use of brain scans in the study of addiction are those made below by researchers at NIDA.

[11] Harvey, *Imaging Addiction*, 16; Dumit, *Picturing Personality*, 23–4. Phrenology was the nineteenth-century 'science' that tried to explain human behaviour via the external configuration of the skull. On the history of phrenology, see Roger Cooter, *The Cultural Meaning of Popular Science: Phrenology and the Organization of Consent in Nineteenth-Century Britain* (Cambridge, 1984). For the connection of phrenology to

This article does not take sides on the medical aspects of this debate. It simply points out that the meaning of the data produced by neuroimaging is controversial within its own field. Medical researchers can now, in a sense, 'see' a living human brain in action, but interpreting that activity and linking it to behaviour remains problematic. The scientists involved in the enterprise know this, and they spend much of their time debating precisely these issues. They are generally circumspect, reflective, and cautious in their claims.[12] This is not always the case, however, for the ways that their findings are reported and used.

In the first instance, the machinery itself is often an important feature in the visual representation of the findings of brain science. As I suggested above, neuroimaging is a massive techno-historical enterprise. In 2003, a PET scanner—and the cyclotron required to produce the isotopes that it needs for molecular tagging—cost about $4 million to purchase and as much as $700,000 per annum to operate.[13] Additionally, a PET project requires the expertise of physicians, nuclear chemists, mathematicians, computer scientists, pharmacologists, and neurologists. fMRI is somewhat less institutionally demanding than PET (it does not require a cyclotron), but it is nonetheless a huge commitment. Neuroimaging projects thus require massive institutional and financial backing from the outset. The machinery itself can be seen as the materialization of this commitment—its simple presence evokes the vast medical, economic, scientific, and historical discourse that underwrites and indeed endorses it. As such, we should not be surprised when images like Figure 1 include some of that machinery within the view.

In Figure 1, the machinery quite literally backs the scientist, who looks directly into the camera, suggesting competence, integrity, honesty, and reliability—qualities that are enhanced and confirmed by the institutional support which the computers represent. Just as when scholars in the humanities and social sciences insist on having their photographs taken in front of their office bookcases, images like this suggest that the scientist personifies knowledge, prestige, and technological sophistication. She returns the viewer's gaze and demands respect, yet her friendly smile warms the image and invites onlookers into the lab to share in its findings. Such images humanize what might otherwise be a frightening or even threatening high-tech project.

---

recent neuroscience, see William R. Uttal, *The New Phrenology: The Limits of Localizing Cognitive Processes in the Brain* (Cambridge, MA , 2001).

12 See Dumit's ethnographic analysis and particularly his interviews with the scientists. The debate published alongside Vul's piece (see n. 9 above) offers further evidence of the self-reflexivity of many of the researchers involved.

13 Dumit, *Picturing Personality*, 31.

Figure 1. Dr. Nora Volkow and her work are backed by the institutional support that is embodied in the neuroimaging machinery behind her. (Courtesy of NIH/NIDA).

Besides establishing institutional commitment to a particular lab or scientist's research project, images like this one work the other way as well. Their emphasis on the competence and compassion of the scientist serves to justify the institutional commitment embodied by the machine. This linkage of the scientist to her tools is an important element in the visual rhetoric of the messages that brain scan images are meant to convey.

The message is clear in Figure 2, which offers an example of the main visual product of brain imaging technology—the brain scan itself. The image and its caption are drawn from the NIDA website, where it is used to show the difference between a brain under the influence of cocaine, and one that is not. It does so, first and foremost, by the striking use of bold colour to make its point. Strong tones of red, blue, yellow, and green leap out at the viewer, and, no less so than in the paintings of Henri Matisse or Vincent Van Gogh, the colour carries the message.[14] In this case, the varied colours suggest that these brains are different from one another. This is confirmed by the caption that accompanies the image. Red, yellow, and blue are, of course, primary colours. They are near opposites on any colour wheel. By their very natures as wavelengths and by our learned habits of viewing, they offer the strongest of contrasts to one another.[15] Red often signifies warmth or heat. It can appear as

[14] On the use of colour in Van Gogh and Matisse, see Richard T. Brettell, *Modern Art 1851–1929: Capitalism and Representation* (Oxford, 1999), 22; 29.

[15] Isaac Newton's 1672 spectral colour disc is perhaps the best-known placement of these colours in opposition to one another. For an overview of the field of colour theory in

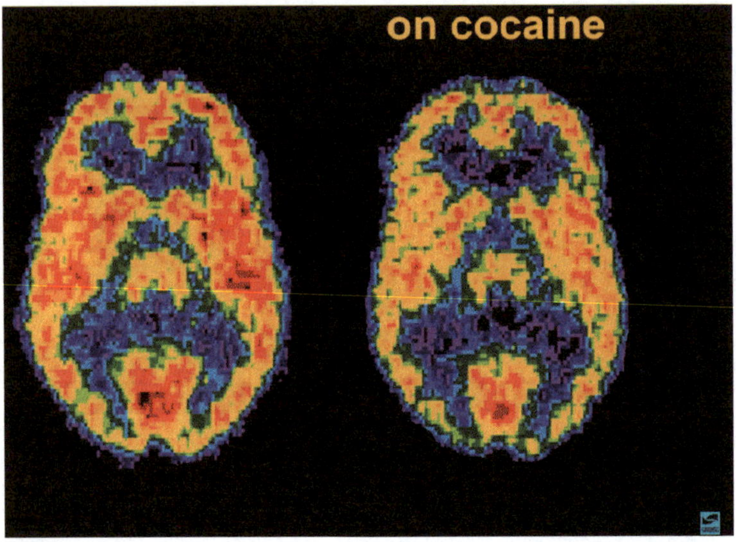

Figure 2. 'The left scan is taken from a normal, awake person. The red colour shows the highest level of glucose utilization (yellow represents less utilization and blue shows the least). The right scan is taken from a cocaine abuser on cocaine. It shows that the brain cannot use glucose nearly as effectively - show the loss of red compared to the left scan'*. (Courtesy of NIH/NIDA).
*'Understanding Drug Abuse and Addiction: What Science Says', section 2, slide 2, NIDA website, http://www.drugabuse.gov/publications/teaching-packets/understanding-drug-abuse-addiction, [accessed 11 July 2013].

vital, passionate, and active. Blue, on the other hand, can look cool, if not cold. It is the colour of a drowning man or of a freezing child, the colour of ice. Yellow enhances and helps to emphasize the difference between red and blue. The contrast of red, yellow, and blue draws strong emotions from viewers—there is little room for subtlety or ambiguity in such a colour scheme. It suggests a bold, stark, and above all unmistakable differentiation between

psychology and a set of preliminary findings on the meaning of the colour red, see Andrew J. Elliot and Markus Maier, 'Color and Psychological Functioning', *Current Directions in Psychological Science*, 16:5 (2007), 250–4. Marketing and business studies offer a rich archive of work on the meaning of colour. For a historical overview of the cultural meaning of colour, see Maureen M. Aslam, 'Are You Selling the Right Colour? A Cross-Cultural Review of Colour as a Marketing Cue', *Journal of Marketing Communications*, 12:1 (2006), 15–30. For the broader cultural resonance of the most popular colour schemes in neuroimaging, see Joyce, *From Numbers to Pictures*, 11.

the two scans and unambiguous knowledge about what that difference means. In NIDA's words, scan images like Figure 2 are 'literally the brain on drugs'.[16]

Perhaps it is too obvious to mention, but a brain scan is not 'literally the brain on drugs'. It is a visual representation of a hypothesis about brain response that is produced by a complicated process of statistical computing. Such heavy manipulation is necessary because the data produced by neuroimaging machines is, in the first instance, quantitative. It appears as a set of numbers that register the reactions of tiny units of brain analysis called 'voxels'. Brain researchers must determine in advance the numerical threshold that will mark a *significant* reaction. In doing so, they programme their computers to decide when a voxel will 'light up' on the scan, and when it will remain dark. The consequent image, therefore, is a conversion into visual form of quantitative data whose significance has already been decided by neuroimaging researchers.[17] This by no means suggests that neuroscientists merely find what they are looking for. I simply wish to point out that brain scans are not transparent representations of reality. As philosopher of science Colin Klein has put it, the images are 'auxiliaries to evidence rather than evidence proper'.[18] Scan images are better thought of as visual metaphors or as *figures of sight.* They are illustrations of hypotheses about neurological process, not simple snapshots of biomedical function.

In his pioneering work on neuroimaging, anthropologist Joseph Dumit argues that the primary difficulty for neuroimaging researchers is how to convert their quantitative data into a form that is comprehensible to others. One way to do so is to assign each of the numerical values a grey scale, which makes it possible to produce a picture, a virtual map of the brain, whose varying shades might show where, when, and for how long, brain activity is present. For this to work, however, one must determine how to group the shades of grey into larger clusters because simply assigning each of the numbers its own scale value would produce too many shades with too slight a variation between them. During the 1970s, Louis Sokoloff, working at the National Institutes of Health, argued that the grey shades were too subtle for researchers' eyes to see, so he pioneered another solution to the problem.

[16] 'Bringing the Power of Science to Bear on Drug Abuse and Addiction', section 2, slide 3, NIDA website, http://www.nida.nih.gov/pubs/teaching/Teaching5/Teaching3.html [accessed 11 July 2013].

[17] Joyce, *From Numbers to Pictures*, 5; Colin Klein, 'Images are not the Evidence in Neuroimaging', *British Journal of the Philosophy of Science*, 61 (2010), 266–7.

[18] Klein, 'Images', 266.

He assigned different colours to the varying numerical values. This produced images that were much more visually engaging and which also conveyed their information more effectively than grey scale images. As Dumit points out, however, the distinct resolution of the colour images also suggests that the brain is divided into regions far more sharply bounded and functionally differentiated than they really are. Further, because the colours do not exist in nature, and lacking a standardized colour scale, their selection is arbitrary.[19] We must bear in mind, therefore, that adding colour to an image is a meaningful choice made by scientists. In itself, this is not a problem if we remember that the images are meant to support and explain various theories about brain activity—that the scans play an expository role. But the potential for a significant slippage of meaning is obvious. Instead of an illustrative aid for scientific explanation or even an analytical tool, the images can appear to be simple photographs of the phenomenon itself. This is what happens when NIDA declares that a scan image is 'literally' a brain on drugs.

The careful and cautionary tone adopted by most neuroscientists makes neither headlines nor policy, but the demands of both media and politics for quick, unambiguous, and easily grasped information, and perhaps of both public and private funding bodies who are keen to establish the 'impact' of their support, offer great incentive to ignore those cautions. Figure 1 above is a photo of Nora Volkow, and no brain scientist has been more visible in media and policy circles than she. Volkow is an inherently interesting person. She is the great-granddaughter of Leon Trotsky and grew up in the house where he was murdered. Her work has won several major awards and she has headed a variety of laboratories and research institutes. Primarily, however, she is an influential neuroscientist with particular expertise in the application of neuroimaging to the study of drug addiction.[20] By 2010, she had published over 440 peer-reviewed articles, 75 book chapters and 3 books on the use of neuroimaging in mental and addictive disorders.[21] Most importantly, however, since 2003 she has been the director of NIDA, which claims to fund over 85 per cent of the world's research on illicit drug use. This means that what NIDA says, matters, and NIDA is a chief proponent of the 'brain disease'

[19] Dumit, *Picturing Personality*, 91–3.

[20] For an overview of Volkow's life and career, including her use of brain scan images to support her ideas, see her interview for the American television show *60 Minutes* (29 April 2012), online at http://www.cbsnews.com/video/watch/?id=7406968n&tag=contentBody;storyMediaBox [accessed 19 June 2012].

[21] Director's Page, NIDA website, http://drugabuse.gov/about/welcome/volkowpage.html [accessed 5 September 2011].

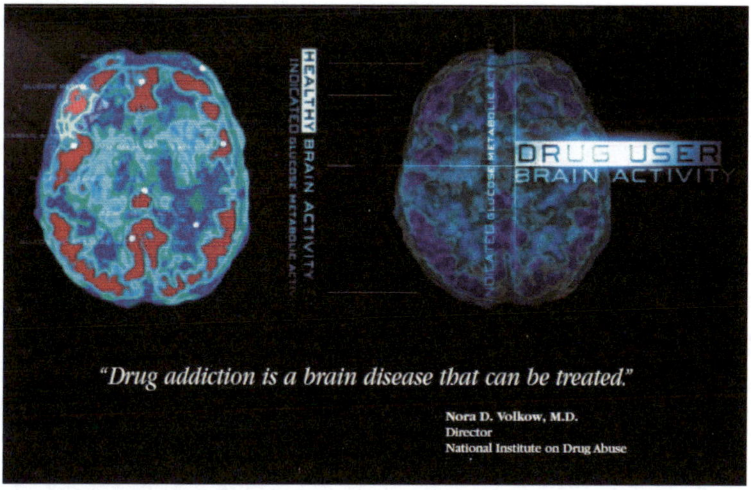

Figure 3. The frontispiece of NIDA's booklet, *Drugs, Brains and Behavior: The Science of Addiction*, NIH Pub. No. 07-5605 (April 2007). (Courtesy of NIH/NIDA).

model of addiction, supported by evidence drawn from neuroimaging.[22] The NIDA website offers a vast archive of information to the general public and to schools, all free of charge. There are many downloadable PowerPoint presentations on the site, with hundreds of brain scan images—all accompanied by text that is intended to be read out in order to explain them. NIDA is very generous with its information. Its publications are in the public domain and researchers need not gain permission to reproduce its materials.

Figure 3 is the frontispiece of what is perhaps NIDA's flagship publication for the general public. Clearly, the evidence provided by brain scans is at the foundation of NIDA's argument. This image makes its point very directly, and supports it textually, that is, by invoking the words, name and credentials of Nora Volkow. But more spectacularly, it does so through a comparison of brain images, one labelled 'healthy,' the other identified as that of a

[22] On the political history of 'the NIDA paradigm', see David T. Courtwright, 'The NIDA Brain Disease Paradigm: History, Resistance and Spinoffs', *Biosocieties*, 5:1 (2010), 137–47. For the history of science behind NIDA's theory, see Scott Vrecko, 'Birth of a Brain Disease: Science, the State and Addiction Neuropolitics', *History of the Human Sciences*, 23:4, 52–67. To understand the theory in terms of changing conceptions of the brain, see Nancy D. Campbell, 'The Metapharmacology of the "Addicted Brain"', *History of the Present*, 1:2 (Fall 2011), 194–218; and also Fernando Vidal, 'Brainhood, Anthropological Figure of Modernity', *History of the Human Sciences*, 22:5 (2009), 5–36.

'drug user'. These images do indeed look very different, but that is largely because they employ two different colour schemes—one emphasizing red, the other purple. NIDA is, of course, very aware of the way that colour carries meaning and they want everyone else to be aware of that as well. Their interpretation is made clear, for instance, in the text provided to accompany another set of brain scan images that are intended for use in secondary schools. Near the end of the presentation, teachers are directed to ask a question: 'As we look at side-by-side PET scans of a person who has never used cocaine compared with a cocaine addict, can you tell which brain is more active and healthy? Take a guess. Yes, the brain on the left with an abundance of *red* is the healthy, active brain' [emphasis original]. NIDA thus guides readers by combining a common sense attitude to the 'obviousness' of visual evidence (i.e. 'seeing is believing' or 'a picture is worth a thousand words') with friendly medical advice. The website suggests that teachers conclude by stating: 'With a little bit of knowledge about what drug addiction actually is, *anyone*—not just neuroscientists and neurobiologists—can see the changes in brain activity caused by drug abuse and addiction. The PET scans we've looked at today prove that.'[23] If anything is clear about neuroimaging, it is that 'seeing' a change in brain activity is a complicated project that requires caution and care. None of the subtleties of interpretation, none of the care taken by brain scientists when debating the meaning of neuroimaging and none of their cautious, circumspect negotiation of the tricky relationship of correlation to causation make it into this presentation.[24] For NIDA, the meaning of the scans and the nature of addiction are clear for anyone to see. Addicts have brains that are different from 'normal, healthy' brains, and they have been made so because their hosts were able to obtain and take drugs.

On the other hand, NIDA is aware that this can be a difficult notion for much of the lay public to understand. In the June 2008 edition of *NIDA Notes*, Volkow explained that 'thanks to science, our views and our responses to drug abuse have changed dramatically, but many people today still do not understand why people become addicted to drugs or how drugs change the brain to foster compulsive drug abuse'. She therefore supplemented the visual argument provided by the scans with a very powerful rhetorical figure, explaining that: 'Drugs change the brain, disrupting and *hijacking* its normal functions.'[25] NIDA in effect simplified the subtleties and ambiguities of neuroscience by turning to the metaphor of hijacking.

[23] 'Bringing the Power of Science', slide 14, NIDA website, http://www.nida.nih.gov/pubs/teaching/teaching5/teaching5.html [accessed 12 July 2010].

[24] See, for instance, the debate around Ed Vul's work (n. 9 above).

[25] Dr. Nora D. Volkow, *NIDA Notes*, 21:6 (June 2008), 17.

Dr Alan I. Leshner coined the hijacking metaphor during his time as director of NIDA between 1994 and 2001, when he became the CEO of the American Association for the Advancement of Science. The so-called hijacked brain hypothesis was launched in a special volume of the journal *Science* in October 1997, which Leshner edited.[26] Leshner used his own essay to summarize the implications of what he described as the 'dramatic advances' in the neuroscientific and behavioural views of addiction that had emerged over the preceding twenty years. He lamented the 'dramatic lag between these advances in science and their appreciation by the general public or their application in either practice or public policy settings'. Most importantly, Leshner defined addiction as 'a chronic, relapsing brain disorder characterized by compulsive drug seeking and use'. This was a significant intervention because, as Leshner pointed out, 'the more common view is that drug addicts are weak or bad people, unwilling to lead moral lives and to control their behavior and gratifications'. Leshner was critical of such views, which underwrite the strictest drug-warrior penal approaches to drug addiction. Instead, he hoped to convince his audience that addiction was a curable disease. This is why he declared that 'it is time to replace ideology with science'.[27] For Leshner, neuroscience showed that 'prolonged drug use causes pervasive changes in brain function that persist long after the individual stops taking the drug'. These effects are felt at 'all levels: molecular, cellular, structural and functional'. The result is that 'the addicted brain is distinctly different from the non-addicted brain, as manifested by changes in brain metabolic activity, receptor availability, gene expression, and responsiveness to environmental cues'.[28]

Leshner did not use 'hijacking' as a metaphor for what happens to the brain of a habitual drug user in his 1997 essay. The abstract of another article in the same volume of the journal claimed that a positive emotion produced by drug use 'hijacks incentive mechanisms of "liking" and "wanting" ', but the term does not appear in Leshner's own writing.[29] Nor does it appear in the *JAMA*, where Leshner reiterated his argument two years later in 1999.[30] Though these two articles are generally credited with launching or at least formalizing

[26] Alan I. Leshner, 'Addiction is a Brain Disease, and It Matters', *Science*, 278 (3 October 1997), 45–70.

[27] Ibid., 45.

[28] Ibid., 46.

[29] Randolph M. Nesse and Kent C. Berridge, 'Psychoactive Drug Use in Evolutionary Perspective', *Science*, 278 (3 October 1997), 63.

[30] Alan I. Leshner, 'Science-Based Views of Drug Addiction and Its Treatment', *JAMA*, (13 October 1999), 1314–16.

the hijacked brain theory, Leshner's clearest association with the phrase came in Bill Moyers' Emmy-winning PBS television series *Moyers on Addiction* in 1998. In the second episode of the five-part series, which was entitled 'The Hijacked Brain', viewers saw Leshner explain the theory to middle-school students. Three years later the popular American magazine *Newsweek* ran a cover story that celebrated the findings of fMRI and PET researchers looking into addiction. Journalist Sharon Begley quoted Leshner who stated that drugs change the brain, that they 'hijack its motivational systems, and even change how its genes function'.[31] We can thus be certain that by February 2001 the fully enunciated 'hijacked brain theory', based primarily on evidence drawn from neuroimaging, was in wide medical, scientific, and popular use. The theory was meant not only to be more accurate, but also to be a more compassionate view of addicts and addiction. In his 1997 *Science* article, Leshner had explained that 'a metaphorical switch in the brain seems to be thrown as a result of prolonged drug use . . . when that switch is thrown, the individual moves into the state of addiction'.[32] Leshner advanced this physiological, if not mechanistic view in order to take discussions of addiction treatment outside the dominion of drug-war morals and into the presumably value-free territory of science and medicine.

The hijacked brain advocates had thus made their intentions clear, but not one of them, neither Alan Leshner nor Nora Volkow, nor anyone at NIDA nor indeed anyone who watched *Moyers on Addiction* or read the *Newsweek* article could have foreseen the magnitude of the 'metaphorical switch' that history had in store for the hijacked brain theory. Only seven months after the *Newsweek* article appeared, on 11 September 2001, the figure of 'hijacking' lost its metaphorical status and became all too literal for the families and friends of the 2996 victims of the terrorist attacks on New York City and Washington DC. This spectacular transformation of the social and historical context that surrounded the brain science of addiction inevitably augmented the meaning of its language by enhancing the urgency and the sense of menace that were always associated with the word 'hijacking'.

As we saw above, Leshner, Volkow, and others who used the hijacking metaphor did so as a way to challenge a popular view of drug addiction as moral failure. They hoped that addicts might be seen as patients rather than as criminals and that such a shift in perception might lead to better quality treatment. In the wake of the September 11 attacks, however, the resonance

[31] Sharon Begley, 'How it all Starts Inside Your Brain', *Newsweek*, 137:7 (12 Feb. 2001), 40–2. http://search.proquest.com/docview/214299470?accountid=11979 [accessed 11 July 2013].

[32] Leshner, 'Addiction is a Brain Disease', 46.

of the hijacking metaphor took on a darker tone. Hijacking became the very epitome of cunning and evil. It was the chief tool of terrorism, and worse, it also appeared as a viable means to wage war. President George W. Bush's response was unequivocal: 'Our war on terror begins with al-Qaida, but it does not end there. It will not end until every terrorist group of global reach has been found, stopped and defeated.'[33] This mobilization against an abstract 'terror' drew upon a widely felt desire to take revenge upon a nebulous band of criminals whose modus operandi was hijacking. As such, the word hijacking was confirmed and enhanced in its association with both terrorism and the US government's response to it. It became inseparably associated with al-Qaida. The choice of hijacking as a metaphor for addiction now seemed much less objective and, regardless of the aims of its proponents, easily harmonized with the language of a 'war on terror'. Those whose concern had always been to pursue a 'war on drugs' were quick to see the connection, and the stated intentions of the hijacked brain theorists were quickly overwhelmed by the fickle wind of historical serendipity.

On 4 December 2001, less than three months after the September 11 attacks, the US Drug Enforcement Administration (DEA) convened 'Target America: Traffickers, Terrorists and Your Kids: A National Symposium on Narco-Terrorism'. The meeting was held at the DEA's Museum and Visitors Centre and was not concerned with brain science, nor with health, but rather with law enforcement. Its focus was on stopping the supply of illegal drugs, which it connected to the funding of world terrorism. The meeting was substantial and is worthy of closer investigation in its own right, but for my purposes what matters is its declaration to be only the 'first major proactive DEA event of its kind on narco-terrorism'.[34] The next event was to be a museum exhibition, which the transcript of the symposium confirms was in planning within three months of the attacks.

33 George W. Bush, Joint Speech to Congress, 20 Sept. 2001, at *The History Place*, http://www.historyplace.com/speeches/gw-bush-9-11.htm [accessed 11 September 2011].

34 Peter Bensinger, quoted in US Department of Justice, Drug Enforcement Administration, *Target America: Traffickers, Terrorists, and Your Kids, A National Symposium on Narco-Terrorism* (Washington, DC, 2001), 121. The association of political violence with the Latin-American drug trade had been in wide circulation throughout the 1990s. See Paul Gootenberg, 'Cocaine's Blowback North: A Pre-History of Mexican Drug Violence', in *Latin American Studies Association Forum*, 43:2 (Spring 2011), 7–10. The Latin-American connection is still stronger when we note the presence of General Jose Rosso Serrano—retired Head Chief General of the Columbian National Police—among the six invited panellists at the DEA symposium.

'Target America: Traffickers, Terrorists and You' opened its doors to the public on 3 September 2002, eight days before the first anniversary of the attacks. The date of the opening was by no means coincidental, nor were the guests of honour. New York Mayor Rudy Giuliani joined Attorney General John Ashcroft in cutting the ribbon to an exhibition which, at its entrance, offered a mixed media reproduction of the skeletal ruins of the World Trade Centre's South Tower augmented by real pieces of the tower (Figure 4). On the reverse of the cylindrical sculpture, which is titled 'September 11 2001', there is a similar image of the Pentagon, likewise authorized by chunks of the building. The piece was the symbol of the exhibition and its source images—the famous photos of the ruins of the South Tower—are among the most powerful visual symbols of September 11 itself. Target America's chief aim was to inform the American public of alleged funding links between international terrorism and the drug trade, and the piece seemed to imply that the September 11 hijackings had been funded by drug money.[35] That linkage allowed the exhibition to argue directly, emphatically, and repeatedly that every individual drug user was a supporter of international terrorism. In the DEA's news release, which accompanied the exhibition's opening, President Bush stated that 'it's so important for Americans to know that the traffic in drugs finances the works of terror, sustaining terrorists . . . [who] use drug profits to fund their cells to commit acts of murder'.[36] Target America linked drug use to international terrorism and murder, all of which could be seen as episodes of hijacking. This intensified demonization of the drug user was not what promoters of the hijacked brain theory intended, but metaphors are slippery and events are hard to predict. Language that was intended to escape drug war moralism was drawn back into the vocabulary of demonization that it was meant to escape.

In 2005 the exhibition expanded its scope and changed its name to 'Target America: Opening Eyes to the Damage that Drugs Cause', perhaps reflecting the 9/11 Commission's July 2004 conclusion that 'there is no reliable evidence

[35] Kari Lydersen, 'Drug-Terror Connection Disputed: DEA Defends Traveling Exhibit as Critics Draw Parallels to Prohibition Era', *Washington Post* (Saturday 12 August 2006). Online at http://www.washingtonpost.com/wp-dyn/content/article/2006/08/11/AR2006081101524.html [accessed 19 June 2012]. See also Michele Garcia, 'New DEA Exhibit Ties Drug Use to Financing Terrorist Groups', *Washington Post* (Sunday 19 September 2004), A02. Online at http://www.washingtonpost.com/wp-dyn/articles/A32168-2004Sep18.html [accessed 19 June 2012].

[36] DEA and Giuliani open National Museum Exhibit on Drugs and Terrorism, News Release, 3 Sept. 2002. DEA website, http://www.justice.gov/dea/pubs/pressrel/pr090302.html [accessed 11 September 2011].

Figure 4. 'September 11, 2001'. Mixed media sculpture that is part of the Target America exhibition. (Photo courtesy of the DEA museum, Dennis Young.)

that Bin Laden was involved in or made his money through drug trafficking'.[37] As the focus widened to a more general investigation of 'damage', the sculpture in Figure 4 moved away from the exhibition entrance and became the central object in its own narco-terrorism section. By June 2011 Target America had visited ten venues in nine cities as part of its permanent tour. Most important for the current discussion, however, is an image that appears in the sensational banner that tops the exhibition brochure and also the

[37] National Commission on Terrorist Attacks upon the United States, *The 911 Commission Report: Final Report of the National Commission on Terrorist Attacks upon the United States*, 171. Full text at http://www.911commission.gov/report/911Report.pdf [accessed 19 September 2011].

Figure 5. A representation of a PET lab in the science section of Target America. (Photo courtesy of the DEA museum, Dennis Young.)

homepage of the exhibition website. It is the left-hand brain scan from Figure 3 above, which appears alongside pictures of an abandoned child, a burning landscape, an automobile accident, and the DEA's insignia. As we saw above, NIDA explained that this is the scan of a healthy brain. One assumes that its brightness and predominance of red, which brings out the red in the rest of the composition, suited the layout designer's needs more closely than that of the addicted brain, which would have been more in keeping with the tone of the other pictures. The image's placement alongside pictures of 'damage', however, begs the question of NIDA's insistence on the self-evidence of brain scan imagery. It also shows how scan imagery can be re-packaged and incorporated into visual narratives whose purposes are very different from those stated by the neuroscientists who made the images in the first place. At the very least, the scan's presence makes clear that addiction science, in the form of the hijacked brain theory, has been used to support and is very much a part of the Target America exhibition. NIDA is listed among the exhibition's developmental partners and its website is linked from the Target America homepage. This helps us to understand the role of Figure 5 within the exhibition. As the wall plaque explains, it is a reproduction of a PET scanner and lab, and it anchors the addiction science section of the exhibition. As we saw above, the visual reproduction of scanning machinery often serves to underwrite the conclusions of the neuroscientists who study addiction, but in this case it does more. Its presence underwrites the much broader argument and goals of the Target America exhibition.

The presence of addiction science in the Target America exhibition asks us to consider an important question: was the hijacked brain theory itself hijacked by post-September 11 political imperatives, or does its inclusion in the DEA exhibition expose the theory's complicity with long-standing penal approaches to drug addiction?[38] The answer, which lies beyond the scope of this essay, requires further research into the history of NIDA's relationship to the DEA, but by posing it I hope to clarify the broader issue, which is that the hijacked brain theory, based as it is on the findings of neuroimaging research, was indelibly and inevitably inflected by its historical context as it became entangled with the problem of hijacking more generally after 11 September 2001.

Those who are familiar with the history of intoxicants and intoxication will not be surprised to see older social threats like drug use re-cast into the newest and most resonant language of social menace. That, however, is my point. Despite scientific claims to the contrary, we have no more arrived at the 'truth' of addiction now than we have at any other time in the past. This is not the case because science is not yet good enough, but rather because scientists, just like everyone else, use words and pictures to communicate. As long as they do so, which is to say as long as they participate in language, they will be entangled hopelessly in history because language is an inherently historical animal. Its meaning, expressed in written and visual metaphors, in linguistic tropes and figures, is generated within the context in which it is expressed. All who use language have intentions, but their aims can never account for the play of meaning and interpretation, nor can they anticipate shifts, big or small, within the broader context that their words and pictures must negotiate if they are to make any sense at all. As Michel Foucault put it, 'people know what they do; frequently they know why they do what they do; but what they don't know is what what they do does'.[39] As I am putting it, an actor's control of meaning is at best only partial.

This essay has therefore demonstrated at least three ways to think historically and critically about recent claims by neuroscientists to have found, or very nearly found, what addiction *really is*. First, we have seen how standard cultural/historical questions about aesthetic form—about how composition and colour create meaning—can help us to think critically about the visual

[38] On the resonance of the hijacked brain theory with the logic of 'strict supply reduction', see Courtwright, 'NIDA Paradigm', 142.

[39] Hubert L. Dreyfus and Paul Rabinow, *Michel Foucault. Beyond Structuralism and Hermeneutics*, (Chicago, 1982), 187.

images that are central to the dissemination of neuroimaging research. Secondly, we have examined the way that the figurative language of the hijacking metaphor operated within its broader historical context to generate at least some of its power. Finally, I have argued that by engaging one of the fundamental theoretical principles of cultural history—that the intentions of those who use language do not exhaust its meaning—we might generate a broader historical understanding of hijacked brain science. As such I hope to have shown that the methods of interdisciplinary cultural history, drawn from the arts, humanities, and social sciences, still have a great deal to offer, that they are, in fact, indispensable if we wish to make broader sense of even the most recent and technologically advanced research in the science of addiction.

The Taste of Opium: Science, Monopoly, and the Japanese Colonization in Taiwan, 1895–1945

Hung Bin Hsu

Many people in Taiwan today do not know that the island was once home to a large number of opium smokers. People smoked opium in Taiwan from the early Chinese Qing Period (1683–1895) onward and the practice continued well into the Japanese colonial period (1895–1945), but memories of the practice quickly faded and it was seldom mentioned in post-war Taiwanese society. In 2005 the television drama 'Beautiful Life' was broadcast island-wide in Taiwan. The show dramatized the glorious victory of modern medicine over a seemingly incurable addiction and its helpless victims, and also told the story of the conscience of local intellectuals, their resistance against the greedy and inactive colonial regime. Opium is the addictive substance, opium smokers the incorrigible addicts, and both are reduced to simplistic, villainous roles.

The image of opium and its users presented in this popular television drama is shared by many historians, and has significantly shaped the contours of the modern historiography of opium in Taiwan.[1] Scholars often fail to see that opium and opium smokers have their own history. If opium is merely an addictive, poisonous substance, and smokers only hopeless addicts, it seems natural to conclude that they do not merit serious study.

[1] For an example of research on policy-making and anti-opium intellectual activities, see especially Ryū Meishu [Itō Kiyoshi], *Taiwan tōchi to ahen mondai* (Taiwan Governance and the Opium Problem) (Tokyo, 1983). For a discussion of spirit-possession writing—a popular religious practice that helped smokers stop smoking opium in the late nineteenth and early twentieth centuries—see Wang Shiqing, 'Riju chuqi taiwan zhi jiangbi hui yu jieyan yundong' (The Spirit-Possession Writing and Opium-Abandonment Movement in Taiwan during the Early Japanese Occupation Period), *Taiwan wenxian*, xxxvii, iv (1986), 111–51. On modern medicine and opium-addiction treatment, see, e.g., Fan Yanqiu, 'Riben diguo fazhan xia zhimindi Taiwan de renzhong weisheng, 1895–1945' (Racial Hygiene in Taiwan within the context of the Development of the Japanese Empire) (National Chengchi Univ. Ph.D. thesis, 2001), 124–65.

 © The Past and Present Society

Recent years have witnessed growing awareness of the importance of the social, economic, and experiential aspects of the consumption of psychoactive substances, including opium.[2] Moreover, the material itself tells its own history. The very composition of the substance we call 'opium' is not fixed. Its ingredients and taste were changed according to the demands of its users. Opium can be dissolved in alcohol, becoming laudanum, one of the many opiate-based medical preparations popular in nineteenth-century England.[3] It can be mixed with a large quantity of dross and adulterants, forming cheap opium paste, favoured by labourers in late nineteenth-century China.[4] If we accept that opium played an important role in the everyday lives of many users, then its production, sale, price, and taste, as well as its 'material nature', certainly deserve more attention.

I want in this article to recapture the subtle relationship between opium and science in a specific colonial setting. That is, I would like to describe how the political rationality of Japanese colonialism became manifest in a technoscientific discourse on bodily taste, hands-on practice and the management of related materials and personnel. I am suggesting, in particular, that in researching and developing new opium pastes, colonial officers were endeavouring to reassemble a flexible, and sometimes unstable and fragile, framework for constituting superior authorities and colonial bodies. Experiencing the new taste of opium thus could be a means of experiencing colonial modernity.

Regarding science and its significance in the context of colonial India, David Arnold has argued, 'Science was intimately bound up with both colonial and Indian concepts of what constituted the modern world; it gave shape and authority to the understanding of modernity.'[5] After taking Taiwan as its first colony in 1895, the Japanese colonial officials constantly stressed that a 'scientific' approach should be adopted to solve the wide range of problems—social, economic, political, and sanitary—encountered by the newly arrived

[2] See especially Virginia Berridge, *Opium and the People: Opiate Use and Drug Control Policy in Nineteenth and Early Twentieth Century England* (London, 1999), 38–48. See also Carl A. Trocki, *Opium, Empire, and the Global Political Economy: A Study of the Asian Opium Trade, 1750–1950* (London, 1999), 7–10. On the complicated experience of opium smoking in modern China, see, e.g., Frank Dikötter, Lars Laaman, and Zhou Xun, *Narcotic Culture: A History of Drugs in China* (London, 2004), 57–62, 79–83. See also Zheng Yangwen, *The Social Life of Opium in China* (Cambridge, 2005), 10–24.

[3] Berridge, *Opium and the People*, 22–8.

[4] Dikötter, *Narcotic Culture*, 63–4.

[5] David Arnold, *Science, Technology and Medicine in Colonial India*, (Cambridge, 2000), 15.

colonizers.[6] Focusing on the techniques applied by the colonial authorities to understand the island, Yao Jen-to argues that 'the Japanese governmentality [in Taiwan] was a number-, knowledge-, and truth-producing machine' and that 'what was created by number in colonial Taiwan was not an illusion but a sufficient authority'.[7] Here the concept of laboratory was important. For colonial officers, the laboratory allowed a manipulation of the scale of things, so that macro may become micro and then be magnified again.[8] As Warwick Anderson, in the context of Americn colonialism in the Philippines, once put it, 'This scalar technology proved especially alluring in a colonial setting, where so much seemed macroscopically complex or otherwise uncontrollable until translated into docile specimens.'[9] The Japanese authorities were keen producers of knowledge on opium, and set up the very early modern laboratory and factory in Taiwan, the Opium Production Office. But the conditions here were never thoroughly laboratory-like. Rather than a site of absolute control, the Office was also a site of contestation and negotiation.

By the end of the Qing period, opium preparation and retail in Taiwan had become a well-developed business. Opium shops usually started with imported raw materials and made their own pastes with their own recipes. Different opium mixtures with different proportions of Indian opium, Persian opium, Qing opium and other adulterants were prepared for different customers with different economic means and tastes. Chinese pharmacies, barber's shops, and brothels also made their own paste. In the late 1890s, most opium shops in Taiwan provided at least three kinds of paste. Some had as many as six preparations.[10]

Things changed dramatically in Taiwan after the island was ceded by Qing China (1644–1912) to Meiji Japan (1868–1912) in 1895, following

[6] Mark R. Peattie, 'Japanese Attitudes toward Colonialism, 1895–1945', in Ramon H. Myers and Mark R. Peattie (eds), *The Japanese Colonial Empire, 1895–1945* (Princeton, 1984), 84–5.

[7] Yao Jen-to, 'The Japanese Colonial State and its Form of Knowledge in Taiwan', in Liao Ping-hui and Wang Der-wei David (eds), *Taiwan under Japanese Colonial Rule, 1895–1945: History, Culture, Memory* (New York, 2006), 43–5.

[8] On the political implications of making and consolidating scientific facts within a laboratory, see Bruno Latour, *Science in Action: How to Follow Scientists and Engineers through Society* (Cambridge, Mass., 1987).

[9] Warwick Anderson, *Colonial Pathologies: American Tropical Medicine, Race, and Hygiene in the Philippines* (Durham, 2006), 6.

[10] Cheng Daxue and Xu Xizhuan (eds and trans.), *Riju chuqi zhi yapian zhengce* (Collection of the Official Documents regarding Opium Policy during the Early Japanese Occupation Period), 2 vols (Taizhong, 1978), i, 119–29.

the Sino-Japanese War. Although opium smoking was rarely seen in Japan, the Japanese fear of opium began in the mid-nineteenth century and the practice was heavily criminalized and strictly prohibited.[11] In order to secure this important source of revenue while preventing its spread to Japan and stirring up anti-Japanese feeling among the Taiwanese, the Meiji government decided to adopt Gotō Shinpei's proposals to implement a government monopoly on opium and a gradually suppressive approach to opium smoking. Gotō was a physician trained in Germany and later became an influential politician in colonial Taiwan, Manchuria, and Japan. He viewed opium smoking from the perspective of disease, classifying opium as a poison and smokers in Taiwan as poisoned patients. According to his proposal, the practice of opium smoking would be confined to those who were medically diagnosed as dependent on the drug, and a licence issued by the authorities would be needed for purchasing and smoking opium.[12]

In subsequent decades, the number of smokers on the island decreased steadily and by the end of the colonial rule of the island in 1945 the practice of opium smoking had almost completely vanished.[13] The opium monopoly also became the most important source of revenue in the early stages of the colonial period. Until Taiwan was deprived of financial aid from Tokyo in 1904, opium contributed from 23 per cent to 46 per cent of all revenue collected from the island every year.[14] This drew the attention of other colonial powers. In a report published in 1905 by the Opium Investigation Committee, appointed by the Philippine Commission of the United States of America to investigate the use of opium in East and Southeast Asia, the committee reached an admiring conclusion: '[the opium system in Taiwan] is more effective in decreasing the use of opium than any other system the Committee has cognizance of among a people where morphomania is a common vice'.[15]

[11] Bob Tadashi Wakabayashi, 'From Peril to Profit: Opium in Late-Edo to Meiji Eyes', in Timothy Brook and Bob Tadashi Wakabayashi (eds), *Opium Regimes: China, Britain, and Japan, 1839–1952* (London, 2000), 64–73.

[12] Ryū, *Taiwan tōchi to ahen mondai*, 44–60.

[13] Du Congming, 'Taiwan apian yinzhe zhi tongji de diaocha diba baogao' (The Eighth Report of the Statistical Research on Opium Addicts in Taiwan), in Du Congming (ed.), *Yanlunji* (Collection of Du Congming's Writings and Speeches), 3 vols (Gaoxiong, 1964), ii, 563–601.

[14] Ryū , *Taiwan tōchi to ahen mondai*, 106–7.

[15] Opium Investigation Committee appointed by the Philippine Commission, *Report of the Committee Appointed by the Philippine Commission to Investigate the Use of Opium and the Traffic therein and the Rules, Ordinances, and Laws regulating such Use and Traffic in Japan, Formosa, Shanghai, Hongkong, Saigon, Singapore, Burmah, Java, and the Philippine Islands* (Washington, 1905), 20.

The monopoly system in Taiwan was distinguished by the Government-General's plan to control every aspect of opium: import, production, transport, and retail. Although the Japanese authorities held very negative images of opium smoking from the mid-nineteenth century onwards, they knew little about what opium smoking was or how to make opium paste. In order to start its monopoly enterprise in Taiwan, the Government-General first had to learn everything from the locals. In April 1896, *Taiwan sōtokufu seiyaku sho* (The Opium Production Office of the Taiwan Government-General) was established in Taipei, and made responsible for the examination, production, and transport of opium. In order to produce paste that would be quantitatively and qualitatively sufficient for all smokers in Taiwan, three stages were followed: 1) learning from locals the methods for making opium; 2) analysing and comparing the methods; and 3) improving the methods for mass production.[16]

Soon after the establishment of the Opium Production Office, two officials were sent on missions to investigate opium-related issues, including consumption, import, sales, and production. Their report, *Ahen jikō chōsa hōkokusho* (Report on Opium-Related Matters) was presented in August 1896. This was the first wide-scale study devoted to opium in Taiwan.[17] Places targeted for investigation outside of Taiwan included Amoy, Hong Kong, India, the Dutch East Indies, Burma, Persia, and Singapore. Simultaneously, non-Japanese materials, including the reports of the Chinese Imperial Maritime Customs and those of the Royal Commission on Opium, were translated into Japanese.[18]

In addition to acquiring knowledge about opium, the Office began to conduct experiments on manufacturing paste. Local makers and retailers were consulted, sometimes with payments, about methods of making paste, and all the details were recorded and translated into Japanese. Every step of making paste was investigated: the appearance and packaging of different varieties of raw opium; methods for making adulterants; methods for making different types of paste; preservation and fermentation; the amount of ash produced in different pipes; types of local wines used for making paste;

[16] Taiwan sōtokufu seiyaku sho, *Taiwan sōtokufu seiyaku sho jigyō dai-ichi nenpō* (The First Annual Report of the Opium Production Office of the Taiwan Government-General) (Tokyo, 1898), 8.

[17] Ibid., 7–8.

[18] Ibid., 47–50. Taiwan sōtokufu seiyaku sho, *Taiwan sōtokufu seiyaku sho jigyō dai-ni nenpō* (The Second Annual Report of the Opium Production Office of the Taiwan Government-General) (Tokyo, 1899), 4. See also Cheng and Xu, *Riju chuqi zhi yapian zhengce*, ii, 87–8.

the tastes of different pastes; types of containers; tools for making paste; local weighing scales; and the processes of packing paste.[19] The investigations illustrated that producing paste was far more complex than simply importing raw opium and reselling it to consumers. It involved knowledge about proper techniques and tastes, as well as the organization and management of materials and personnel.

However, despite precise and detailed investigations, opium remained mysterious to the Japanese officials. What did opium taste like? What kind of taste was favoured? More importantly, how could they produce such a taste? The non-smoking Japanese officials, even after widely collecting and studying materials on opium, still found it difficult to apprehend the way in which smokers described the paste of a superior grade. Descriptions of pure and fragrant taste, thick smoke, and tender, dense, evenly spread bubbles meant little to them.[20] Therefore, the Office relied on the opinions and judgements of local expert examiners. Following instructions they had received from the local makers, Japanese officials and technicians would make samples, and then let the expert examiners judge the taste and quality. However, to achieve the goal of mass production, the officials had to find a way to understand and manage taste themselves.

Soon after the Office was founded, a laboratory was set up. The laboratory was the first department established in the Office, before the construction of a factory or other facilities. It was through a series of technoscientific practices that the officials learned to manage the taste of opium. At first, the officials collected sampled pastes from different shops in the market and conducted chemical examinations with a local expert examiner. Their results are shown in Table 1, which compares the grade, chemical composition, and the expert examiner's opinion of each paste.

The terms used by the expert examiner, as recorded in Table 1, were abstract and subjective, including, for example, 'pure', 'strong', 'tender', 'wild' and 'foul'. To the officials, the importance of the table lay not with the remarks themselves, but in the comparison between local grades, analytical figures, and the expert examiner's descriptions. This comparison was one that could be actualized only in a laboratory. Here, Japanese officials paid special attention to the percentage of morphine in each paste, and concluded that better pastes contained higher percentages of morphine. For them, a lower percentage of morphine implied a higher proportion of adulterants and, therefore, indicated an inferior grade.[21] In other words, the Japanese

[19] Taiwan sōtokufu seiyaku sho, *Taiwan sōtokufu seiyaku sho jigyō dai-ichi nenpō*, 9–36.

[20] Ibid., 20–3.

[21] Ibid., 21.

Table 1. Comparative Table of the Laboratory Analysis of Opium Pastes from the Market

	Water (%)	Soluble proportion (%)	Morphine (%)	Insoluble proportion (%)	Expert examiner's remarks
Fuyan (1st-grade)[22]	22.39	73.55	11.73	4.23	This is made of Persian and Sichuan opium; the colour is black and purple, and the taste is strong.
Luyan (2nd-grade)	23.24	73.35	9.74	3.50	This is made of Sichuan opium and Wanchengtu (an adulterant); the bubble is restrained by the fire and the taste is wild and weak.
Jingui (1st-grade)	22.35	74.20	7.42	5.75	This is made with Benares and good Sichuan opium; the taste is strong and without any fragrance.
Yugui (2nd-grade)	23.30	75.70	8.56	4.26	This is made of Persian and Sichuan opium; the character is plain, with good bubble, and a strong and fragrant taste.
Mangui (3rd-grade)	22.80	73.60	5.19	4.98	This is made of Persian and Wenzhou opium; the taste is wild and the character is soft, with a strange bubble.
Tanggui (4th-grade)	22.73	72.72	4.65	5.51	This is made of Wenzhou opium; the taste is wild, the bubble is weak and black, and the character is plain.
Shanggui (1st-grade)	23.21	73.70	7.40	3.50	This is made of Persian opium and the skin of Benares opium; the taste is fragrant and strong, the bubble is red, and the character is plain.
Zhonggui (2nd-grade)	24.00	72.42	6.42	2.53	This is made of Persian and Wenzhou opium; the taste is strong and the bubble is good.
Xiagui (3rd-grade)	21.36	72.10		1.35	This is made of Persian, Wenzhou opium and a bit of Wanchengtu; the taste is wild and the bubble is weak, big and red.

Source: Taiwan sōtokufu seiyaku sho, *Taiwan sōtokufu seiyaku sho jigyō dai-ichi nenpō*, 20–1.

[22] The grades inside the parentheses have been added by the author according to the original name of the paste. It should be noted that the pastes were collected from different shops, and the quality grades assigned to each paste by different shops did not usually have the same meaning.

officials did not try to understand the taste of opium in the local context, but defined and translated opium based upon analyses, calculations, and deductive observations within the new context of a laboratory.

Figure 1 demonstrates that the local expert examiner was deprived of his usual smoking environment. Instead, he was relocated to a well-equipped laboratory, surrounded by scientific instruments, and observed by a group of Japanese officials. In contrast to the confident officials, the anxious countenance of the expert examiner reveals the disadvantages of his position as a symbol of local knowledge waiting to be studied and translated into modern, scientific language. Through the laboratory practices, the Japanese officials—without ever inhaling a single puff of opium—could gain access to the secrets of its taste.

After that, the officials moved on and tried to make their own paste. They did this according to the method they learned from local makers. The amount of adulterants used was significantly decreased and, as a result, the percentage of morphine in the pastes increased more than 20 per cent. The Office believed that the pastes made with these modified methods would be of a

Figure 1. The examination of paste in the laboratory of the Opium Production Office. On the right hand side was a local opium expert examiner. *Source:* Taiwan sōtokufu seiyaku sho, *Taiwan sōtokufu seiyaku sho jigyō dai-ni nenpō*. Courtesy of National Taiwan Library.

better quality than alternative pastes on the market.[23] The pastes were divided into three grades. The 1st-grade was aimed at higher classes of consumers; the 2nd-grade was marketed to the middle classes; and the 3rd-grade was for the lower classes.[24] The composition standards for government-made pastes were regulated and expressed in the form of analytical figures, as shown in Table 2. The remarks and opinions of the local expert examiner had no role in this enterprise of standardized mass production.

In 1897 the Office began to supply smokers in Taiwan with its pastes. Before long, negative opinions caught its attention. It was reported that the quality of the pastes was so poor as to make them unsmokable, and the 3rd-grade paste was especially bad. Reports documented complaints about the paste causing sore throats and headaches. It was also said that some poisons must have been added to the paste by the colonial authorities, and that the paste was made to kill islanders: smoking 1st-grade paste would cause death in ten years; smoking the 2nd caused death within five years, while using the awful 3rd-grade paste could kill you in just one to three years.[25] Another report stated that the 3rd-grade paste was regarded as not only inferior in flavour, but also as having a strong taste of medicine and alcohol that caused headaches and hurt the smoker's throat.[26]

The Office considered these opinions to be malicious rumours, and remained confident about its paste. The officials rationalized that the development of these pastes through a series of laboratory and factory practices was scientifically sound, and argued that a local expert had examined all the pastes before sale, so the quality could not be inferior.[27] The Office considered other factors that may have contributed to the inferior quality of opium, including the deterioration of the paste after long-term storage or long-distance transportation, the quality of the adulterants, and further adulteration with harmful substances by the local retailers.[28] The Office then devoted resources to studying the fermentation of pastes and tried to

[23] Taiwan sōtokufu seiyaku sho, *Taiwan sōtokufu seiyaku sho jigyō dai-san nenpō* (The Third Annual Report of the Opium Production Office of the Taiwan Government-General) (Taipei, 1900), 24–5.

[24] Taiwan sōtokufu seiyaku sho, *Taiwan sōtokufu seiyaku sho jigyō dai-ichi nenpō*, 24, 50–1.

[25] Taiwan sōtokufu seiyaku sho, *Taiwan sōtokufu seiyaku sho jigyō dai-ni nenpō*, 9.

[26] 'Ahen enkō no hinshitsu oyobi hihyō shinchiku ken hōkoku (The Report on the Quality and Criticism of Opium Paste from Shinchiku County)', in *Taiwan sōtokufu kōbun ruisan* (Official Documents Archive of the Taiwan Government-General), vol. 4524, division 6, no. 8.

[27] Taiwan sōtokufu seiyaku sho, *Taiwan sōtokufu seiyaku sho jigyō dai-ni nenpō*, 9. See also Taiwan sōtokufu seiyaku sho, *Taiwan sōtokufu seiyaku sho jigyō dai-ichi nenpō*, 38–9.

[28] Taiwan sōtokufu seiyaku sho, *Taiwan sōtokufu seiyaku sho jigyō dai-ni nenpō*, 9–10.

Table 2. Standards of Morphine Composition for Government-Made Opium Pastes in the Early Colonial Period

	Morphia (%)	Insoluble remainders (%)	Water (%)
1st-class	9.5–10.5	4.5–5.5	22–23
2nd-class	11.5–13.0	2.5–3.5	22–23
3rd-class	10.0–11.0	3.0–3.5	22–23

Source: Taiwan sōtokufu seiyaku sho, *Taiwan sōtokufu seiyaku sho jigyō dai-ni nenpō*, 29–30, 62.

find the best environment for preserving pastes. Studies to come up with better packaging were also conducted. And a new adulterant was invented to replace the old one. Furthermore, in 1898 a regulation was introduced to prohibit licensed opium retailers from changing the composition of government-made pastes by adding other adulterants or mixing together pastes of different grades.[29]

The Office also thought that rumours about its poisonous pastes had been spread by dealers who lost their businesses after the introduction of the monopoly. Thanks to enforcement by the police and the above remedial methods, the Office happily reported that these rumours had gradually disappeared.[30] However, the attachment of smokers to their old preferences was stronger than expected by the Office. When the Opium Investigation Committee of the Philippine Mission visited Taiwan in 1903, the Director of the Bureau of Monopolies acknowledged that the local smokers' distaste for government pastes had led to increased smuggling:

> At first smuggling was due to the peculiar taste of government opium, which the people did not like. It was also due to the difference in price, but the chief cause was that the taste of government opium did not suit them. Some smokers like it strong and others weak, and the taste of the opium differed according to the method of preparation.[31]

Gradually, the Japanese government realized that taste had important implications for its opium monopoly, and that smokers of different regions had their own peculiar tastes. For example, when a Japanese official was

[29] Taiwan sōtokufu minsei bu eisei ka, *Jitsumu shuchi: Taiwan ahen seido yōshi* (Necessary Notices for Opium Practice: The Points of Opium System in Taiwan) (Taipei, 1899), 32.

[30] Taiwan sōtokufu seiyaku sho, *Taiwan sōtokufu seiyaku sho jigyō dai-san nenpō*, 3.

[31] Opium Investigation Committee appointed by the Philippine Commission, *Report of the Committee Appointed by the Philippine Commission*, 62.

commissioned to investigate opium issues along the Chinese coastal areas in 1899, he noticed that smokers in South Fujian were 'strangely' fond of pastes with a higher proportion of dross, and the paste made by the Office was not welcomed there.[32] When the Japanese government began to set up an opium monopoly in Kwantung Leased Territory in 1928, the government controlled only the sale and delivery of raw opium but left the manufacture of paste to licensed retailers in order to satisfy the peculiar tastes of smokers in Kwantung.[33]

Through the processes of collecting, learning, and translating local knowledge, Japanese officials not only acquired knowledge of how to make paste, but also how to manage the taste. The Office linked the taste of pastes and the percentage of morphine they contained, and transformed the abstract and subjective descriptions of taste given by local expert examiners into empirical data and figures that could be revealed and reproduced through laboratory practices. The Office came to be an authority on opium-related affairs and, as a gradually suppressive policy was carried into effect in Taiwan, was very often entrusted with the task of inspecting pastes seized by police officers or courts.[34] In other words, it was no longer the smokers or local expert examiners, but the Office, who possessed the real knowledge about opium.

However, the method developed in the laboratory was not naturally applicable for mass production. The process of production developed by the Office was distinguished by its united method and the uniform quality of its product, as compared with the great variations of the pastes available in late Qing Taiwan. In order to provide sufficient pastes for all smokers on the island efficiently and economically, the whole process of paste production needed to be re-networked, and every element made manageable.

The local method of paste production had several uncontrollable elements that made mass production a challenge. The first was the quality of the raw opium, which was imported from different places in the world through different channels. Persian opium, Indian opium, and Chinese opium were the main types used on the island before 1895. Of these types only Benares opium, under the management of the East India Company, showed a stable quality. Raw opium from other areas, in particular the popular Persian opium, was

32 *Taiwan kyōkai kaihō* (Bulletin of Taiwan Association), xxviii (Taipei, 20 Jan. 1901), 43–4.

33 League of Nations Commission of Enquiry into the Control of Opium Smoking in the Far East, *Report to the Council, Volume II: Detailed Memoranda on Each Territory Visited by the Commission* (Geneva, 1931), 442–3.

34 Taiwan sōtokufu seiyaku sho, *Seiyaku sho shiken ihō dai-ichi gō* (The First Collection of Test Reports of the Opium Production Office), (Taipei, 1900), 94–6.

made by local factories and had varying quality.[35] From October 1896, following the implementation of the opium monopoly in Taiwan, the two companies allowed to import the drug under governmental contract began to purchase raw opium in Hong Kong.[36] Initially they relied on the opinions of local expert examiners in Hong Kong, usually those who were knowledgeable and old-hands in the business, to judge the quality of the drug based on their long-term experience. However, the Japanese authorities felt that the way these experts conducted their examinations was not particularly reliable. In 1899, a Japanese official commissioned to investigate the state of raw opium in Hong Kong commented on these methods:

> In short, the local method of examining raw opium was to choose the one that contains a higher percentage of soluble components, cook it and then examine the quality according to the smell and taste of the paste made of it. But, what is the standard of smell and taste? Every day there are so many chests to be examined, how could it be possible to make correct judgements? Particularly, is it not rude to judge the quality of raw opium by smoking the ready-made paste? It is hard to understand that the highly civilised Europeans would pay the expensive fee for these unscientific tests.[37]

Japanese officials strongly believed that the quality of raw opium depended on the percentage of morphine in it, and, therefore, a large amount of samples were dispatched from Hong Kong to the laboratory of the Opium Production Office to be tested. Just as the Office expressed the taste of opium in terms of its chemical composition, the judgements of Hong Kong experts were replaced by analytical chemical results, and further translated into physical results. By converting the chemical method into a physical method, the efficiency of examining raw opium improved, and, therefore, the quality of the imported opium could be guaranteed. It became possible for a single Japanese technician to examine more than five hundred chests of opium per day.[38]

In addition to raw opium, the management of other ingredients and adulterants was also crucial for the successful mass production of opium paste. In order to maintain composition and quality, all ingredients and adulterants used for making government opium had to be supplied in a steady and stable

[35] Robert L. Jarman (ed.), *Taiwan Political and Economic Reports, 1861–1960,* 10 vols. (Slough, 1997), iii, 123.

[36] Taiwan sōtokufu seiyaku sho, *Taiwan sōtokufu seiyaku sho jigyō dai-ichi nenpō*, 82.

[37] *Taiwan kyōkai kaihō*, xxvii (Taipei, 20 Dec. 1900), 26–9. See also Cheng and Xu, *Riju chuqi zhi yapian zhengce*, ii, 124–9.

[38] Taiwan sōtokufu seiyaku sho, *Taiwan sōtokufu seiyaku sho jigyō dai-san nenpō*, 55–6.

manner. Opium ash and Chinese wine, two important ingredients widely used in the local production method, were soon found problematic. Opium ash is the remainder of the paste left inside the opium pipe after smoking, and was a popular ingredient in making paste. Because of the difficulty of collecting opium ash, controlling its quality and maintaining a stable supply, the Office excluded opium ash from their list of ingredients for making paste.[39]

The Office also replaced Chinese wine with its own imitative wine. According to its analytical studies, the function of Chinese wine was to dissolve otherwise insoluble elements in the raw opium, and was relevant to the smell and bubble of opium paste. Initially, the Office bought Chinese wine from several different local makers. Naturally, the quality of the wine was not consistent, and the wine was hard to preserve. The Office replaced the unmanageable Chinese wine with its own alcohol product in November 1897. These substitutions and changes in the composition of the paste were not implemented abruptly. Rather, they resulted from a process of learning, translating, and modifying, and samples made with the new ingredients and adulterants had to be judged by the expert examiners.[40]

Although the Office was established in April 1896, it was not until March 1898 that installation of steam engines and other machines was finished. Before the installation of the new factory and machines, production was carried out manually, resembling local techniques. The Office had to learn from local makers about the various tools used for making paste.[41] The capacity of this manual production averaged 127.5 kg of paste per day. This was just a fraction of daily consumption in Taiwan at that time, estimated at 544.32 kg.[42] After moving into the new factory with its new machines in March 1898, productivity rose to 575.34 kg per day.[43]

Steam engines and machines were introduced to replace local tools. By doing so, the Opium Production Office tried to make every step of the process more manageable, efficient, and precise. For example, a crushing machine

[39] Taiwan sōtokufu seiyaku sho, *Taiwan sōtokufu seiyaku sho jigyō dai-ichi nenpō*, 17–18; Taiwan sōtokufu seiyaku sho, *Taiwan sōtokufu seiyaku sho jigyō dai-san nenpō*, 57–9. See also Cheng and Xu, *Riju chuqi zhi yapian zhengce*, i, 104–11.

[40] See the following annual reports, Taiwan sōtokufu seiyaku sho, *Taiwan sōtokufu seiyaku sho jigyō dai-ichi nenpō*, 18–20; Taiwan sōtokufu seiyaku sho, *Taiwan sōtokufu seiyaku sho jigyō dai-ni nenpō*, 20–1; Taiwan sōtokufu seiyaku sho, *Taiwan sōtokufu seiyaku sho jigyō dai-san nenpō*, 23–4.

[41] Taiwan sōtokufu seiyaku sho, *Taiwan sōtokufu seiyaku sho jigyō dai-ichi nenpō*, 26–7.

[42] Taiwan sōtokufu seiyaku sho, *Taiwan sōtokufu seiyaku sho jigyō dai-ni nenpō*, 8–10.

[43] Taiwan sōtokufu seiyaku sho, *Taiwan sōtokufu seiyaku sho jigyō dai-san nenpō*, 2.

replaced the manual chopping of opium flesh into small pieces. A newly designed two-layer copper pan was substituted for the local copper pan. A pressing filter machine replaced the flat bamboo basket customarily used to filter the opium solution.[44] As always, taste was a consideration, and before the installation of the machines, expert examiners tested samples of pastes made by steam heat.[45]

As the scale of production expanded, the number of workers recruited by the Office also increased. However, the recruitment of workers was not indiscriminate. The Office had strict regulations specifying who would be qualified to work for the Office and how they should behave in the factory. Workers had to be born in Taiwan, be able to speak Taiwanese, be married, strong, and competent, with no disabilities, between 25 and 40 years old, with more than seven years experience making pastes, free from the habit of smoking opium, and of an upright and obedient disposition. Every day before work, workers needed to report to security guards before changing into factory uniforms. The uniforms were made in two colours, grey and light yellow, for islander and Japanese inlander workers respectively. After work, before workers signed the registry book, their bodies were examined for stolen opium.[46] The environment also needed regular cleaning and a hygiene committee was set up to supervise matters of cleanliness.[47] Through these regulations, the Office not only made use of the existing experienced makers, but also turned them into workers capable of operating a modern, mass production factory.

The Opium Production Office created what was apparently the first modern, fully functional factory in Taiwan. It was characterized not only by the installation of steam engines and machinery, but also by its modern management of material, working processes, and personnel. In the last few years of the nineteenth century, the Office was also one of the few providers of electric power. The electric power provided by the steam engines of the Office

[44] Taiwan sōtokufu seiyaku sho, *Taiwan sōtokufu seiyaku sho jigyō dai-ni nenpō*, 17–19. See also Taiwan sōtokufu seiyaku sho, *Taiwan sōtokufu seiyaku sho jigyō dai-san nenpō*, 14–15.

[45] Taiwan sōtokufu seiyaku sho, *Taiwan sōtokufu seiyaku sho jigyō dai-ni nenpō*, 11.

[46] Taiwan sōtokufu seiyaku sho, *Taiwan sōtokufu seiyaku sho jigyō dai-ichi nenpō*, 42–3. See also Taiwan sōtokufu seiyaku sho, *Taiwan sōtokufu seiyaku sho jigyō dai-go nenpō* (The Fifth Annual Report of the Opium Production Office of the Taiwan Government-General) (Taipei, 1902), 65–6.

[47] Taiwan sōtokufu seiyaku sho, *Taiwan sōtokufu seiyaku sho jigyō dai-yon nenpō* (The Fourth Annual Report of the Opium Production Office of the Taiwan Government-General) (Taipei, 1902), 33–5. See also Taiwan sōtokufu seiyaku sho, *Taiwan sōtokufu seiyaku sho jigyō dai-go nenpō*, 67–8.

was mainly used for the production of paste and the security of the Office during the night. However, for a period, the electric light bulbs of the Government-General and the official residences of the Governor-General and the Chief of the Civil Administration were also powered by the Office.[48] The lighting facilities of the Office were presented by the colonial government as one of its modernization achievements and many islanders gathered in front of the Office to see the unusual phenomena of electric lamps during the early colonial years.[49]

The Office was frequently visited by people of different backgrounds, including the Governor-General, the Chief of the Civil Administration, foreign consuls, soldiers, officials, police, teachers, students, doctors, and local entrepreneurs.[50] Furthermore, in 1900 the Government-General sponsored the founding of the *Yōbun kai* (Society for Uplifting Culture), aimed at winning the understanding and cooperation of the island's literati, and invited all gentry holding the grade of *lingsheng* or higher to attend the society's inauguration ceremonies in Taipei. Around half of the island's top gentry accepted the invitation and were shown around the colonial government's modern, advanced institutions and facilities, including the Office.[51] One attendee described in his diary the scenes of opium manufacture, the steam engines and the paste examinations. He was impressed by the efficiency of the machinery and by the wondrous chemistry used to distinguish the government-made pastes from poisonous and unhealthy local pastes. The Government-General also prepared tea, sweets, fruits, and opium pastes for visitors.[52] Scenes of the opium production and examination were also recorded in the first documentary film made about Taiwan, *Taiwan jikkyō shōkai* ('An Introduction to the Real Conditions in Taiwan'), which was commissioned by the Government-General for the Tokyo Exhibition of

[48] Taiwan sōtokufu seiyaku sho, *Taiwan sōtokufu seiyaku sho jigyō dai-san nenpō*, 33–4.

[49] Wu Jen-shen, *Fanxing diandian: Jindai taiwan diandeng fazhan (1895–1945)* (A Starry Sky: The Development of Electric Light in Modern Taiwan, (1895–1945)) (Taipei, 1999), 32, 263–9.

[50] Taiwan sōtokufu seiyaku sho, *Taiwan sōtokufu seiyaku sho jigyō dai-san nenpō*, 104–5; Taiwan sōtokufu seiyaku sho, *Taiwan sōtokufu seiyaku sho jigyō dai-yon nenpō*, 39; Taiwan sōtokufu seiyaku sho, *Taiwan sōtokufu seiyaku sho jigyō dai-go nenpō*, 71–2.

[51] Patricia Tsurumi, *Japanese Colonial Education in Taiwan, 1895–1945* (Cambridge, Mass., 1977), 38–9.

[52] Wu Degong, 'Guanguang riji' (Sightseeing Diaries), in Taiwan yinhang jingji yanjiushi (ed.), *Taiwan youji* (Accounts of Journeys in Taiwan), *Taiwan wenxian congkan*, lxxxix, (Taipei, 1960), 27–8, 34.

1907 in order to show the advancements made on the island after the arrival of the Japanese colonial government.[53]

After the establishment of the monopoly, the Government-General became the only producer and provider of opium paste in Taiwan. In the following decades of its rule over the island, the colonial regime continued manipulating the production of opium and, eventually, left smokers in Taiwan with only one choice of paste.

In the early years of colonial rule, the 3rd-grade paste—made of Persian opium and other adulterants—was the most popular kind on the island, followed by the 2nd-grade, whilst few smokers used the 1st-grade paste made of Indian Benares opium. This pattern of consumption, of primarily Persian opium, was consistent with consumption in late Qing Taiwan, and indicated a more economical and practical way of smoking. As the new century unfolded, this pattern changed. An increasing amount of 1st-grade paste was sold and gradually overtook the 2nd- and 3rd-grades. By 1906, 1st-grade paste had surpassed the 3rd-grade and become the most popular kind of paste in Taiwan. The consumption of 2nd-grade paste decreased and in 1908 the Government-General stopped producing this kind of paste altogether. In subsequent years, the market continued favouring the 1st-grade paste and production of the 3rd-grade paste ceased in 1928. [54] The shift from 3rd- to 1st-grade paste demonstrates a significant change in Taiwanese opium taste towards the Indian description. During the 1900s the import of Indian opium increased dramatically, from 27,000 kg in 1900 to 102,000 kg in 1907.[55] This change seems to represent a shift from practical and economical uses to recreational and medical ones.

In 1897 the average price of paste in Taiwan was 17.78 *yen* per kilogram. This increased to 31.30 *yen* in 1905, 58.83 *yen* in 1915, 117.21 *yen* in 1925 and

[53] Ye Longyan, 'Rizhi shidai Taiwan jilupian zhi lishixing fenxi' (A Historical Analysis of the Documentaries in Taiwan during the Japanese Colonial Period), in Li Daoming and Zhang Changyan (eds), *Jilu Taiwan: Taiwan jilupian yanjiu shumu yu wenxian xuanji* (Collection of Bibliographies and Literature on Taiwan Documentary Studies) (Taipei, 2000), 39.

[54] Taiwan sōtokufu keimu kyoku eisei ka, 'Taiwan no ahen seido' (Opium System in Taiwan, orig. 1939), in Ōtomo Masako and Shen Jie (eds), *Iryō to eisei–kyūryō to ahen mondai* (Medical Treatments and Hygiene–Treatments and the Opium Problem), *Shokuminchi shakai jigyō kankei shiryō shū, Taiwan hen* (Collection of Materials Related to Social Enterprise in Japanese Colonies, Taiwan Volume), 30 vols (Tokyo, 2001), xxii, 312–14. See also International Opium Commission, *Report of the International Opium Commission, Shanghai, China, February 1 to February 26, 1909* (Shanghai, 1909), 280–1.

[55] Taiwan sōtokufu keimu kyoku eisei ka, 'Taiwan no ahen seido', 37–9.

120 *yen* in 1935.[56] Simultaneously, the number of opium houses, which provided coolies a cheap place to rest and socialize, slowly decreased, from 258 in 1897 to only 29 in 1929. In 1929 the operation of opium houses was officially banned.[57] Although it was reported in 1908 that a few smokers still used opium as a working drug during the night time, these were more often self-employed freelancers, rather than coolies.[58] The increasing price of paste and the disappearance of the 3rd-grade paste and opium houses indicated that opium gradually ceased to function as a work aid or source of relief to coolies as it had in late nineteenth-century Taiwan.

An increasing demand of a multilateral drug control regime, a decreasing number of smokers and a rising standard of living in Taiwan in the early twentieth century might account for the increasing price of government opium. As the twentieth century unfolded, opium smoking became a multinational concern, with a focus on opium issues in China and on the control of supply. The International Opium Commission was held in 1909 at Shanghai.[59] Due to the rising prices of imported raw opium after the Shanghai meeting and the decreasing number of smokers on the island, in order to control opium smoking and maintain profits from the monopoly enterprise, the colonial government gradually raised the price of its own paste.[60]

The colonial authorities also intentionally lowered the percentage of morphine in the paste. The 1st-grade paste contained between 11 and 11.5 per cent in 1897, and over the next few years, the percentage was kept between 10 to 12 per cent. However, from 1900 the percentage decreased steadily, from 9–9.5 per cent in the years 1900–01 to 8–8.5 per cent in 1912.[61] The percentage of morphine in 3rd-grade paste was also reduced from 10–11 per cent in 1897 to

56 Ibid., 312–14.

57 Ibid., 344–6.

58 Lin Qingyue, 'Ahen insha no kenkyū ni tsuite' (Research on Opium Addicts), *Taiwan igakukai zasshi*, lxv (Mar. 1908), 84.

59 William B. McAllister, *Drug Diplomacy in the Twentieth Century: An International History* (London and New York, 2000), 28–30.

60 Fujiwara Tetsutarō, 'Ahen seido chōsa hōkoku' (Report on Investigating Opium Systems, orig. 1923), in Okada Yoshimasa, Tatai Yoshio, and Takahashi Masae (eds), *Zoku gendaishi shiryō* (A Sequel of the Collection on Materials of Modern history), 12 vols (Tokyo, 1986), *zyū-ni, ahen mondai* (xii, Opium Problem), 176. See also Kurihara Jun, 'Taishoki ni okeru Taiwan sōtokufu senbaikyoku no ahen seisaku' (The Opium Policy of the Taiwan Government-General during the Taisho Period), *Shiron* (Historica), lxvi (Mar. 2013), 26–36.

61 Arakawa Asakichi, *Ahen no ninshiki* (The Understanding of Opium) (Taipei, 1943), 213.

7 per cent in 1908.[62] Furthermore, from the early 1910s, the Government-General was no longer able to purchase raw opium from the Hong Kong market because the Indian government had stopped the export of opium for the China market. This forced the Government-General to purchase its supply directly from London, New York, Calcutta, and Mumbai.[63] Interestingly, the Japanese technicians of the Opium Department (the former Opium Production Office) within the Monopoly Bureau soon realized that the morphine percentage of the new raw opium supply was higher than that from Hong Kong, and, consequently, found it harder to maintain the low proportion of morphine in government pastes.[64] Arakawa Asakichi, Chief of the Opium Department, recalled in 1943 that in order to maintain a low percentage of morphine in the paste with the new supply, they considered adding more adulterants. However, raising the proportion of adulterants beyond a certain point would damage the taste of the paste. The technicians from the Opium Department and a private pharmaceutical company—Hoshi Pharmaceuticals, which was granted the right to import raw opium into Taiwan from 1917 to 1926—began to study methods of extracting crude morphine from raw opium, attaining results in 1915. This allowed the Government-General to control the percentage of morphine in the paste and gradually lessen its proportion without adding more adulterants.[65] At the same time, the Government-General and Hoshi Pharmaceuticals could benefit from the sale of crude morphine, which could be made into much-needed medicinal morphine during World War I (1914–18) when German supplies were blocked.[66] In the early 1930s, the percentage of morphine in 1st-grade opium, then the only kind of paste available in Taiwan, was further reduced to 5 per cent.[67] The Japanese officials of the Monopoly Bureau were proud of their efforts to maintain a high quality of opium paste in Taiwan. In a pamphlet prepared for the International Opium Conference at Geneva in 1924, the chief of the Monopoly Bureau emphasized the importance of

[62] Lin, 'Ahen insha no kenkyū ni tsuite', 100.

[63] Gregory Blue, 'Opium for China: The British Connection', in Brook and Wakabayashi (eds), *Opium regimes*, 41–2.

[64] League of Nations Commission of Enquiry into the Control of Opium-Smoking in the Far East, *Report to the Council, Volume II*, 413.

[65] John M. Jennings, *The Opium Empire: Japanese Imperialism and Drug Trafficking in Asia, 1895–1945* (Westport, Conn. and London, 1997), 42–3.

[66] Arakawa, *Ahen no ninshiki*, 214–17.

[67] League of Nations Commission of Enquiry into the Control of Opium-Smoking in the Far East, *Report to the Council, Volume II*, 413. See also Du Congming, *Huiyi lu* (Du Congming's Reminiscences) (Taipei, 1973), 80; Du Congming, 'Taiwan apian yinzhe zhi tongji de diaocha diba baogao', 567.

providing smokers with a paste of united quality, good taste, smooth bubble, and beautiful colour for protecting their health and, at the same time, preventing them from conducting illegal opium businesses.[68]

From 1928 onwards only one kind of opium paste with one unified taste was available in Taiwan. In contrast to the environment of late nineteenth-century Taiwan, in which smokers of different socio-economic backgrounds chose different pastes for a diversity of functions, smokers in the early twentieth century were described by the Japanese colonial regime as poisoned patients; there was only one reason for them to smoke: to stop the craving for morphine. Equipped with a modern laboratory and factory, the Government-General not only turned the 'opium problem' into a manageable and profitable business, but also made opium production a showcase of science, modernity, and efficient colonial administration. As the twentieth century unfolded, aided by the establishment of strict surveillance systems and an authoritative knowledge of smokers, the Government-General cared less about smokers' needs and tastes than they did in the early stages of the colonial period. By increasing the price of opium and decreasing the percentage of morphine it contained, the administration manipulated the situation to move slowly towards the eradication of opium smoking. It is clear that during the colonial period, local preferences shifted from Persian to Indian opium, and the pattern of consumption shifted from economical and practical to medical and recreational. These shifts are not explained by the addictive nature of opium or by the laziness and fecklessness authorities saw in smokers. The reasons for these shifts in consumption are that the price of the drug was gradually lifted beyond the reach of working class smokers, and the practice of using opium was deprived of all its functions excepting recreation and medicine.

The Opium Production Office was one of the most important governmental institutions in the early stages of the colonial period. It consisted of the first modern laboratory and modern factory in Taiwan, and successfully transformed the Japanese authorities from neophytes to experts, allowing them to become the exclusive provider of opium in Taiwan. This was not attained by colonial forces or political ideas alone, but rather through a series of laboratory and factory practices that enabled the Office to manipulate the very substance, opium, not only to learn what opium was, but also, more importantly, to translate, modify, manage, and produce the drug. Before the colonial government could execute its power to modernize smokers in Taiwan, the

[68] Kaku Sagatarō, 'Nihon teikoku no ahen seisaku' (Japanese Empire's Opium Policy, orig. 1928), in Okada, Tatai, and Takahashi (eds), *Zoku gendaishi shiryō, zyū-ni, ahen mondai*, 39–40.

Office already scientifically modernized opium. Opium was purified (deprived of its variety and complexity), reduced into clear scientific figures, standardized, mass-produced, distributed, and smoked by every smoker on the island. At the same time, it was made transparent, manageable, and profitable. However, it should also be noted that the whole process of translation and mass-production was carried out within a specific colonial context. The history of opium reminds readers of the power structure that was behind and sustained the modern nature of opium and the political implications of colonial science. It was the isolated environment of the island, and vast investment that made the Office into the primary, authoritative representation of the truth about the substance and made opium smokers into manageable, obedient subjects. It was the imbalance of power between colonizer and colonized that enabled the Office to deprive local opium expert examiners of their smoking environments and relocate them to a laboratory, the stronghold of modern science. It was the presence of strong police forces that lessened resistance among smokers to the new taste of government paste; and this same imbalance that made local workers obedient to the new methods, processes, and rules of the opium factory. Therefore, on the one hand it was the science and laboratory practices that made it possible for the Government-General to understand, translate, manage, and produce opium, and, on the other hand, it was the presence of the colonial regime in Taiwan that made opium a ready experimental sample under the modern, scientific gaze. Through the taste of opium, the Taiwanese began to experience the flavour the Japanese colonization that operated under the rhetoric of scientific modernization.

Material Culture and 'Political Drinking' in Seventeenth-Century England

Angela McShane

I

A post-7/7 sketch from the satirical programme 'Bremner, Bird, and Fortune' joked that the best way to integrate disaffected young Islamists into British culture was to teach them how to binge drink.[1] This joke played upon two prevalent but contradictory attitudes in contemporary British society: medical, social, and moral concerns over the destructive relationship the British are thought to have with intoxicating drink; and a pervasive popular belief that there is something fundamentally suspicious about someone who doesn't drink alcohol in company, suggesting a refusal to join together in fellowship with the community.[2] Neither the joke itself nor the cultural mores and prejudices (however self-deprecating) it illuminates are modern. It was mirrored, for example, in numerous seventeenth-century jests, such as a popular 1683 ballad, inspired by the failed Ottoman siege of Vienna that claimed 'Mahomet was',

> A coffee-drinking drousie rogue,
> The use of grape so much in vogue,
> to deny to those adore him:
> Had he allowed the fruits of the vine,
> and gave them leave to Carrouse in wine
> They had freely passed the Rhine,
> and conquer'd all before them.[3]

Similarly, in William Congreve's *Way of the World*, Sir Wilful drunkenly rants against Turkish infidels who 'believe not in the Grape'. He explains (in song),

Place of Publication London unless otherwise stated.

[1] BBC 2005: exact date of transmission unknown.

[2] James Nicholls, *The Politics of Alcohol: A History of the Drink Question in England* (Manchester, 2009); Medical Research Council Report 'Middle-Age Drinkers Facing Peer Pressure', 12 December 2011.

[3] Ballad publication data from Angela McShane, *Political Broadside Ballads of Seventeenth Century England. A Critical Bibliography* (2011) [hereafter *PBB*]. Anon., *A Carrouse to the Emperor* (4 edns, 1683; 1684; 1700s), *PBB* 693X.

 © The Past and Present Society

To drink is a Christian Diversion
Unknown to the Turk and the Persian
Let Mahometan fools
Live by Heathenish Rules
And be damned over teacups and coffee
But let British Lads sing
Crown a health to the King
And a Fig for your Sultan and Sophy.[4]

Moreover, an anonymous ballad entitled *The Loyal Subject (as it is reason) Drinks good sack and is free from Treason,* printed in 1663 and 1681, pointed out that drinking alcohol both indicated and ensured loyalty to the monarchical state, while also furnishing Charles II's much depleted royal treasury with income from the excise on wine and beer.[5] This article traces just one thread in the Gordian knot of relations between alcohol, state, and subject that have lasted to the present day—disrupting any easy sense of a 'modernity' that is entirely separated from a longer past. It shows how, over the course of the late sixteenth and seventeenth centuries, the material and gestural elements of two socially and politically binding drinking rites—the sacred Protestant Holy Communion and the classically inspired 'loyal-health'—overlapped, creating a new kind of 'prophane sacrament' (as it was dubbed), with which any and all who professed loyalty to the monarchical state and Protestant religion were expected to comply.[6] Modern scholars have largely interpreted healthing and pledging rituals as ways of bonding or competing between equals.[7] In contrast, early-modern observers located the origins of health-drinking rituals in the unequal but necessarily symbiotic relations between God and man, king and subject, ruler and ruled.[8] Drinking

[4] William Congreve, *The Way of the World* (1700), Act 4, Sc. i (65).

[5] *PBB* 400.

[6] Charles Morton [attrib.], *The Great Evil of Health Drinking* (1684), 10. On social and religious importance of ritual see Edward Muir, *Ritual in Early Modern Europe*, 2nd edn, (Cambridge, 2005).

[7] See e.g., B. Ann Tlusty, *Bacchus and Civic Order: The Culture of Drink in Early Modern Germany* (Charlottesville, 2001); Alan Bray, *The Friend* (Chicago, 2003); Alexandra Shepard, *Meanings of Manhood in Early Modern England* (Oxford, 2003); and Alexandra Shepard, '"Swil-bolls and tos-pots": Drink Culture and Male Bonding in England, *c*.1560–1640', in L. Gowing, M. Hunter, and M. Rubin (eds), *Love, Friendship, and Faith in Europe, 1300–1800* (Basingstoke, 2005).

[8] See, e.g., Thomas Young, *Englands Bane* (1617), 75; Robert Bolton *Some Generall Directions . . . Walking with God* (1626), 204; William Prynne, *Healthes:Sicknesse* (1628), 52–3; Morton, *Great Evil*, 47, 61–2, 128.

a 'health' in this sense had been embedded in the English context for centuries as a mark of loyalty and fealty in both courtly and civic circles; events that were memorialized and symbolized through the gifting of drinking vessels from lords to vassals.[9] This chapter argues that, from the late sixteenth century onwards, the material and intellectual symbolism of these elite loyal-healthing rituals migrated into the population at large, becoming increasingly ubiquitous, both socially and geographically; a process that was catalysed by the dissemination and application of Christian humanism across English society and by deep social and political divisions created by the civil wars and their aftermath.[10] It focuses on three key moments in which the ritual and social significance of the loyal-health was profoundly altered. First, the Elizabethan religious settlement (*c.*1558–1603) brought about a permanent shift in the material experience of the Eucharist, creating a new cultural framework for ritual drinking not only in religious but also in civil contexts. Secondly, the disruptions of the civil wars and interregnum (1640–1659) saw an increasingly widespread practice of loyal-healthing—modelled on classical precedents—begin consciously to appropriate the exclusive tests that defined who could participate in ritual drinking and the sanctification of secular vessels by 'words, gestures and actions'.[11] This combination of Christian humanist authority and example created a powerful ideological tool with which to elicit and challenge political and religious allegiance at all levels of society. Finally, during the period from Restoration to 'Glorious Revolution' (1660s-1690s), loyal-healthing acquired sacral status and began

[9] Thomas Valpy French, *A History of Toasting* (1881); Thomas Valpy French, *Nineteen Centuries of Drink in England* (1890); Peter Brown and Marla Helane Schwartz, *Come Drink the Bowl Dry: Alcoholic Liquors and Their Place in 18th Century Society* (York Civic Trust, 1996); Judith Bennett, 'Conviviality and Charity in Mediaeval and Early Modern England', *Past and Present*, 134 (Feb. 1992) 19–41; Gervase Rosser, 'Going to the Fraternity Feast: Commensality and Social Relations in Late Mediaeval England', *Journal of British Studies*, 33:4 (Oct.1994), 409–46. For courtly healthing and gifting see, e.g., Letters from Antonio Foscarini, May 1608, *Calendar of State Papers Relating to English Affairs in the Archives of Venice, Vol.11: 1607–1610* (1904), 129–37; *August 1611, Vol.12: 1610–1613* (1905), 191–200; *Miscellaneous, 1616, Vol.14: 1615–1617* (1908), 592–600. Albert J. Loomie (ed.), *Ceremonies of Charles I: The Notebooks of John Finet, 1628–41* (New York, 1988), 60–1, 96. Pusey Horn: V&A:M.220&A-1938: http://collections.vam.ac.uk/item/O84673; Wassail Bowl: V&A:W.8A-1976: http://collections.vam.ac.uk/item/O70551.

[10] See Phil Withington, *The Politics of Commonwealth: Citizens and Freemen in Early Modern England* (Cambridge, 2005).

[11] Peter Browne, *A Second Part of Drinking in Remembrance of the Dead* (Dublin, 1715), 16–17.

to be given official support at all levels of governance. The public, ritual consumption of alcohol became so essential to any and all 'loyal subjects' (a category vulnerable to partisan interpretation) that it became increasingly dangerous—and by the 1680s not infrequently fatal—to refuse the secular sacrament of the loyal-health. By 1716, this remarkable shift led Peter Browne, Bishop of Cork and Ross to remark that loyal-healthing had elided with and overtaken Communion as the most significant bonding ritual in early modern England.[12]

The article concentrates on the radicalization phase of a much longer history of the loyal-health, which was officially incorporated into virtually every institution of state and society by the nineteenth century.[13] This later history, however, saw further important shifts in the material culture and practice of the ritual, especially the use of individual vessels (influenced by changes in dining and drinking manners) and its renaming as 'toasting', which effaced the sacral origins and meanings revealed by the earlier period.[14] Though contemporaries noted its ubiquity, the vast majority of loyal-healthing rituals taking place daily in public and private venues all over early modern England went unrecorded. Tracing the practice across a broad swathe of society in seventeenth-century court records and archives has necessitated using many descriptions of *disloyal* drinking to dethroned or exiled Stuart monarchs, successful or failed Pretenders. However, the loyal-health was not a ritual exclusive to Cavalier or Jacobite supporters of the Stuart monarchy. It was equally important to Whigs, Tories, and those for whom these terms had little meaning; and later to Hanoverians and Victorians, under whose auspices it continued to function as a tool, both official and unofficial, for demonstrating, determining, and even inculcating affection and allegiance to the legitimately established state.

II

The Holy Communion rite was a nexus of theological differences between Catholics and Protestants. While the Catholic Church restricted the drinking of Communion wine in the Mass only to ordained clergy, Protestant reformers insisted all Christians should partake in both bread and wine, as part of a purely commemorative service. Consequently, the English Reformation set in train a series of material and gestural changes in the celebration of Holy Communion, resulting in an enormous shift in ritual

[12] See discussion below.

[13] See French, *Nineteen Centuries.*

[14] OED gives the first use of 'toast' in the sense of a health from B. E. *A new dictionary of the terms ancient and modern of the canting crew* (1699).

experience.[15] In principle every person in the country aged sixteen or over, no matter how poor or lowly, could handle and drink wine from a fine cup as part of a communal ritual three or more times each year.[16] Moreover, by demystifying and domesticating the ritual elements of Communion, Protestant reformers inadvertently 'constructed, redefined and blurred' the boundaries between sacred and profane spaces.[17]

English Church authorities struggled to prescribe and proscribe the material, verbal, and gestural elements of the new Protestant Eucharist in accordance with shifting theological and political ideologies and disputes between moderate and radical reformers.[18] By 1571, the Archbishops of Canterbury and York had both ordered the remodelling of communion plate along domestic lines. Any sense that communion-ware was intrinsically sacred was to be eradicated, but in order to maintain 'decency', no 'profane cup or glass' was to be used. Cups were to be made of 'pure' metal of intrinsic worth—such as silver—and were to have the added honour of a cover that could double as a plate for bread.[19] Thousands of parish cups were reworked or renewed in the wake of these instructions. Exeter goldsmith John Jones literally re-formed a Catholic, goblet-shaped chalice into a Protestant, beaker-shaped communion-cup (see Figures 1 and 2).[20] He engraved the cup with 'secular' Moresque decoration and its cover with a Tudor rose: a resounding affirmation of crown authority. Communion wine was to be

[15] The literature is extensive. For a useful summary see Peter Marshall, '(Re)defining the English Reformation', *Journal of British Studies*, 48:3 (July 2009), 564–86; Peter Marshall, *Reformation England, 1480–1642* (2003); Judith Maltby, *Prayer Book and People in Elizabethan and Early Stuart England* (Cambridge, 1998). See also Debora Shuger, 'A Protesting Catholic Puritan in Elizabethan England', *Journal of British Studies*, 48:3 (July 2009).

[16] On post-reformation Communion practice see Christopher Marsh, *Popular Religion in Sixteenth-Century England* (1998), 38–40.

[17] Andrew Spicer and Sarah Hamilton, 'Introduction' in Andrew Spicer and Sarah Hamilton (eds), *Defining the Holy: Sacred Space in Medieval And Early Modern Europe* (2005), 1–26.

[18] See Robert Whiting, *The Reformation of the English Parish Church* (Cambridge, 2010); Kenneth Fincham and Nicholas Tyacke, *Altars Restored: The Changing Face of English Religious Worship, 1547–c.1700* (Oxford, 2007); Kenneth Fincham (ed.), *Visitation Articles and Injunctions of the Early Stuart Church*, Church of England Record Society (Woodbridge, 1994), vol. I, xiv-xvi; Gerald Bray (ed.), *The Anglican Canons 1529–1947* (Woodbridge, 1998), vol. 6.

[19] Whiting, *Parish Church*, 64–6.

[20] V&A:4636–1858 http://collections.vam.ac.uk/item/O10949/. For pre-Reformation goblet shape see V&A:M.488A-1911 http://collections.vam.ac.uk/item/O110440/.

Figure 1. Communion cup and paten cover, engraved silver, John Jones, Exeter, 1571–74, V&A: 4636–1858 [http://collections.vam.ac.uk/item/O10949/communion-cup-and-jones-john/] © Victoria and Albert Museum, London.

brought to the altar-table 'in a clean and sweet standing pot or stoop of pewter—if not of purer metal'.[21] Such 'stoups' (usually flagons or tankards) also followed secular shapes and forms (see Figures 3, 4, and 5). Only the prayer-book 'words of institution', a narrative of Christ's injunctions at the Last Supper, spoken over the cup and wine before distribution to communicants, clearly differentiated this from any secular cup and drink.[22]

The gestural practice of Communion was also changed radically. By 1600, most communicants in English parishes sat or stood around a centrally placed communion table, or stayed in their pews, many still wearing hats, while the communion cup was passed from person to person, much as might happen at home, or in an alehouse or tavern. In the 1630s, Archbishop Laud

[21] Bancroft, 1603/4: Art.20; Bray, *Anglican Canons*, 291; on cups see 290, fn.93.

[22] On this precise point see Browne, *Second Part*, 12–17.

Figure 2. Detail of paten cover, engraved silver, John Jones, Exeter, 1571–74, V&A: 4636–1858 [http://collections.vam.ac.uk/item/O10949/communion-cup-and-jones-john/] © Victoria and Albert Museum, London.

attempted to reform this 'indecent' lack of ceremonial with a more formal ritual. He instructed that communicants were to remove their hats and were to come to the altar table (preferably placed at the top end of the chancel) to receive Communion while kneeling (Figure 3). Laud's changes were much disputed, and might be said to have contributed to the outbreak of the civil wars. However, by 1678 it was common for ministers to place the cup into the hands of communicants who knelt, bare-headed at a 'Table placed Altar wise' (Figure 4). [23]

Some unexpected consequences arose from these new rituals. Despite canonical insistence, many parishes lost control over the clear distinction

[23] See Whiting, *Parish Churches*, 24–31; Nigel Yates, *Buildings, Faith, and Worship: The Liturgical Arrangement of Anglican Churches 1600–1900* (Oxford, 1991, rev. edn, 2001), 28–32. See also Fincham and Tyacke, *Altars Restored*; Maltby, *Prayer Book*; *The Diary of John Evelyn*, ed. E. D. de Beer (1 vol., 1959), 648; John Spurr, *The Restoration Church of England 1646–1689* (1991), 362–6. John Kettlewell believed this gestural practice kept people away from Communion, *An Help and Exhortation to Worthy Communicating* (1683), 392–410.

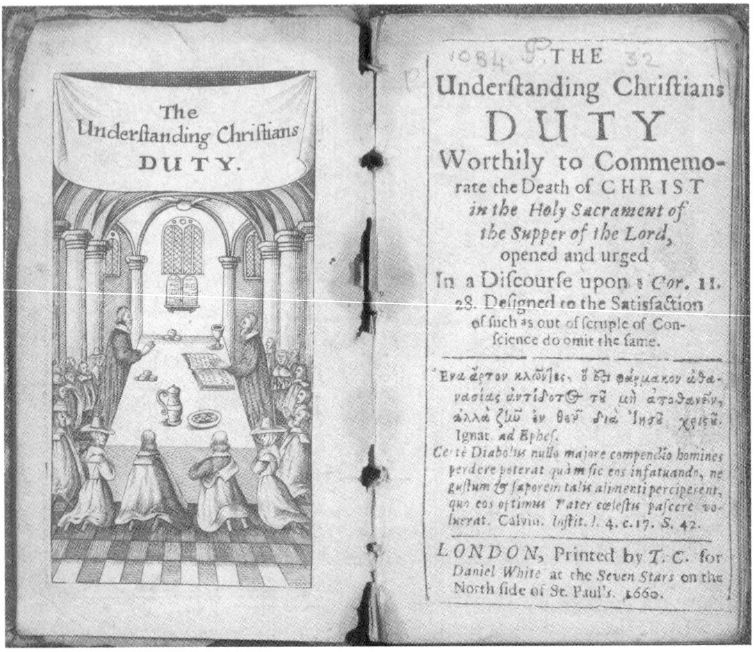

Figure 3. Frontispiece from: Lewis du Moulin, *The Understanding Christians Duty*, printed book, London, 1660 © Trustees of Dr Williams Library, London.

between a 'decent' communion cup and a 'profane' secular one.[24] The material demands of the new Protestant Communion service put considerable pressure on parish resources. Communion cups needed to be much larger—some holding a quart or more—and more robust for handing round to people unaccustomed to such luxurious drinking. Large flagons, alms-plates and, in densely populated parishes, chargers for bread were also needed on the altar (Figure 5).[25] In response, many domestic items were donated to churches, regardless of previously 'profane' use, or inappropriately secular decoration.

'Idolatrous' iconography was stripped from communion objects, but was replaced by political iconographies, such as the Tudor rose on John Jones's cup. Generous donations of costly 'fashioned' wares, decorated with personal inscriptions and images, also offered scope for local social positioning by

[24] See Browne, *Second Part*, 17–20.

[25] Whiting, *Parish Church*, 66–7.

Figure 4. Frontispiece from: Charles Drelincourt, *Directions with Prayers and Meditations*, printed book, London, 1680 © Lambeth Palace Library, London.

displaying wealth, power, and status to the whole community. Surviving examples include a silver flagon, expensively engraved with Christ as the Good Shepherd and the names of the donors;[26] a far less costly pewter flagon, gifted by churchwardens and roughly inscribed with their names;[27]

[26] V&A:Loan: http://collections.vam.ac.uk/item/O118535/.

[27] V&A:511–1901: http://collections.vam.ac.uk/item/O76220/.

Figure 5. Frontispiece from: Charles Wheatly, *The Church of England Man's Companion*, printed book, Oxford, 1714. Reproduced by kind permission of the Syndics of Cambridge University Library.

a fine silver-gilt cup professionally engraved with a long religious essay, donated by a printer's widow.[28] In 1633, William Laud himself gifted a simple, silver communion cup to St Michaels in Manningtree, Essex,

[28] V&A:Loan: http://collections.vam.ac.uk/item/O108924/.

inscribed with his name and arms as Bishop of London.[29] Much less appropriate examples include a fine domestic cup, sporting a classical head, acquired by St Margaret Pattens, London;[30] a gilt beer jug donated to a Kent parish;[31] huge wooden goblets, carved with royal heraldic devices and religious texts, that apparently doubled as salts;[32] or a monumental 'flint' baluster glass—a form usually associated with healthing—whose domed lid was topped with a cross.[33] Parishes often used materials other than silver or pewter, perhaps from principle (as Puritan John Trapp pointed out, sacramental cups had been 'Anciently of Glasse, afterwards of wood and lastly of silver or gold') or compromise, as in West Malling in Kent where, from 1581, a ceramic vessel topped with a silver lid was used.[34]

Reformed Communion had inadvertently opened the way for domestic vessels to acquire new meanings, as they were translated between church, home, alehouse, or tavern. The inability to maintain control over the shape, size, materials, and decoration of communion-ware allowed secular and sacred vessels to become visually indistinguishable. In some cases, altar tables too were literally transformed from religious to secular drinking spaces. In Sandwich, Kent, for example, the mayoral election was regularly held in St Clement's church: aldermen 'brought in half a dozen bottles of wine, clapped them on the communion table and there sat as at an alehouse bench, smoked tobacco and drank and committed some other filthy things'.[35] Other confusions also arose: on one hand divines were anxious to rebuff Catholic accusations that reformers had turned the Eucharist into little more than a health; on the other hand, it was not uncommon for divines to use healthing as a religious metaphor, as in 1616, when Thomas Adams described Christ's sacrifice as 'drinking to us in his own bloud, a saving Health to all Nations'.[36]

[29] V&A:Loan: http://collections.vam.ac.uk/item/O109393/.

[30] V&A:Loan: http://collections.vam.ac.uk/item/O118331/.

[31] Kent beer-jug held in Canterbury Cathedral Treasury (seen 2003; uncatalogued; photographs not permitted).

[32] V&A:W.34–1947 and V&A:W.50–1913.

[33] Glass communion vessel, *c.*1670s-90s; Burrell Collection, Glasgow, uncatalogued.

[34] John Trapp, *A Commentary Upon the Gospel according to St Matthew* (1642), 579; http://www.britishmuseum.org/explore/highlights/highlight_objects/pe_mla/m/malling_jug.aspx.

[35] 14 November 1683, *Calendar of State Papers Domestic* [hereafter *CSPD*]*: Charles II, 1683–4* (1938), 70–127.

[36] Thomas Adams, *A Divine Herball* (1616), 24, 29. Prynne complained at the confusion caused by such language: *Healthes:Sicknesse*, 42–3. On Catholic accusations see Browne, *Of Drinking to the Memory of the Dead* (Dublin, 1713), 18; and Browne, *Second Part*, 26–7, 65–6.

That some misunderstanding was created among the laity may be suggested by the case of Immanuel Bradley, who, in 1639, was fined forty pounds for drinking a health at the altar.[37]

Further unwanted consequences of Reformation changes also had a profound impact on political drinking rituals. The communal divisions that emerged in the wake of the changes and compromises of the Reformation familiarized the wider population with a religious drinking ritual that was as much about testing and excluding members of the community as it was about including them in communal worship.[38] Church and state authorities were concerned to encourage as many people as possible to communicate, but also to expel non-conforming members from the Communion service. Communicants needed to show that they lived in the parish, were catechised according to officially sanctioned Protestant precepts, and were in 'good charity' with their neighbours, friends, and kin.[39] During the civil war and interregnum, Puritan-inspired changes in parish worship saw thousands of people, especially royalists, excluded from parish Communion, either from personal choice or compulsion.[40] After the Restoration of crown and episcopacy in 1660, decorative schemes, objects, words, prayers, music, and rituals in parish churches re-emphasized links between monarchy and state religion.[41] Taking Communion now became a test of both religious and political loyalties. It was even described as a 'tool for conversion', a ritual

[37] 7 November 1639, 'Acts of the Court of High Commission', *CSPD*: *Charles I, 1640* (1880), 378–434.

[38] Spurr, *Restoration Church*, 200–2; 286–9; Amy Nelson Burnett, 'The Social History of Communion and the Reformation of the Eucharist', *Past and Present* 211:1 (2011), 77–119; Maltby, *Prayer Book*, 51–2,108.

[39] This was the implication of Anglican canons and visiting injunctions throughout the period—see Articles 1603(4): 2–12, 22, 26, 27, 28, 41; Articles 1640: 1, 3, 4, 5: Bray, *Canons*, 265–81, 293, 297, 299–301, 413, 445, 561–2, 565–7.

[40] Bernard Capp, *England's Culture Wars: Puritan Reformation and its Enemies in the Interregnum, 1649–1660* (Oxford, 2012), ch. 6; W. W. Biggs, 'The Controversy Concerning Free Admission to The Lord's Supper, 1652–60', *Transactions of the Congregational Historical Society*, 16:4 (1951), 178–89; Christopher Haigh, '"A matter of much contention in the realm": Parish Controversies over Communion Bread in Post-Reformation England, *History*, 88:291 (2003), 393–404; Spurr, *Restoration Church*, 17–18.

[41] Capp, *Culture Wars*, 14–16. See also Gerald Randall, *Church Furnishing and Decoration in England and Wales* (1980); Yates, *Buildings*, 42; Edward Fawcett, *Royal Arms and Achievements in Somerset Churches* (Taunton, 1937), 2–3; and Rosemary A. Pardoe's various regional *Royal Arms* pamphlets.

that could effect change from within.[42] Church injunctions not only required the examination and public repentance of anyone recently 'reformed' (whether from Catholicism, Presbyterianism, or sectarianism), before they could be admitted to Communion, but also anyone suspected of disloyal behaviour.[43] Contemporaries were concerned that using Communion for political ends had brought it into disrepute, causing the numbers of willing communicants to decrease markedly.[44] In contrast, the increasingly popular loyal-healthing ritual seemed to offer an alternative vehicle for social and political union; combining customary practices of hospitality and communal 'caritas'.[45]

III

Early-modern commentators were certain that healthing practices, along with drunkenness, had been increasing in frequency and spreading across the social orders of England from the late sixteenth century onwards.[46] Quantifying that increase is problematic, but one clear sign was the growing number of sermons and treatises on the subject published by leading divines and moralists. Among the most cited and numerous were Thomas Young's *Englands Bane* (editions in 1617 and 1634); Robert Bolton's *Walking with God* (six editions between 1625 and 1641); Robert Harris's *The Drvnkards Cvp* (eight editions between 1619 and 1630) and John Hart's, *The Dreadful Character of a Drunkard* (printed in 1663, 1679, and 1686). Richard Younge (aka Junius Florilegus), issued three separate publications on drunkenness in at least ten different editions between 1655 and 1664.[47] While railing against drunkenness in general, each writer dedicated a section of his discourse to attacks on healthing rituals. In 1628, the Puritan pamphleteer, William Prynne, decided healthing had become so ubiquitous that it

[42] See Kettlewell, *Help and Exhortation*, Sig.A4, Part III; Spurr, *Restoration Church*, 200–2, 286–7, 344, 345–51.

[43] See visitation questions for Ely, 1665, ch. 2, arts. 7 and 10; 1671, 5; Llandaff, 1671, 4; Chichester, 1679, 1–2, 6: art. xv; Bristol, 1683.

[44] Arnold Hunt,'The Lord's Supper in Early Modern England', *Past and Present*, 161(1998), 39–83; Spurr, *Restoration Church*, 200–2, 286–7, 351–3.

[45] See Felicity Heal, *Hospitality in Early Modern England* (Oxford, 1991); Victoria Kahn '"The Duty to Love": Passion and Obligation in Early Modern Political Theory', *Representations*, 68:1 (October 1999), 84–107.

[46] See Prynne, *Healthes:Sickness*, 1–2; Robert Harris, *The Drunkards Cup* (1622), Sig.A2–3, 22; Anon., *Tom Tell Troth* (*c.*1622), 3; Bolton, *Some Generall Directions*, 196; Morton, *Great Evil*, xiii, 9.

[47] See I. Green, 'Younge, Richard (fl. 1636–1673)' *Oxford Dictionary of National Biography* [hereafter *ODNB*] for full bibliography.

warranted treatment as a topic in itself; his highly influential pamphlet *Healthes:Sicknesse* (*sic*) was reprinted and cited in moralist texts for the next two hundred years.[48] Further treatments followed, including John Geree, *Θειοφαρμακον. A Divine Potion to preserve spirituall health, by the cure of unnaturall health-drinking* (1648); Charles Morton [attrib.], *The Great Evil of Health Drinking* (1684) and Bishop Peter Browne's several tracts, especially his *Discourse of Drinking Healths* (1716).[49]

Barnabe Rich described the healthing ritual in 1617:

> The institution of drinking an Health, is full of ceremony, and observed by Tradition, as the Papists doe their praying to Saints. He that begins the health . . . first uncovering his head, hee takes a full cup in his hand, and settling his countenance with a grave aspect, he craves for audience . . . [he names] some Honourable personage . . . worthy of a better regard than to have his name polluted . . . among a company of drunkards . . . [and] turnes the bottome of the cup upward. The cup being newly replenished to the breadth of an haire . . . thus it goes round through the whole company.[50]

Outraged by the religious, material, and gestural connotations of the practice Rich parodied gospel and prayer book accounts of the Last Supper: a cup is chosen and filled with wine, words are spoken in prayer, the cup is passed around the company, who must all drink. Finally (though Rich does not mention this) the Last Supper ends with the apostles singing.[51] Rich intended to shock, but from the 1640s changes in loyal-healthing made the mirroring of the Last Supper increasingly more real than Rich's caricature. The ceremony was not only freighted as a sign of trustworthy neighbourliness, credit, and reputation, but, by naming the king, whose 'two bodies' continued to be imbued with religious meaning, and by deliberately appropriating material and ritual aspects of the Protestant Eucharist, it began to take on an equally sacral and communal significance. It also became, like Communion, an exclusive ritual that could be used to challenge the political or religious loyalties of strangers or neighbours gathered in a public place.

The most striking feature of the innumerable healthing incidents to be found in court records (a tiny fraction of all loyal-healthing) is that, despite

48 E.g., French, *Nineteen Centuries*, 190–3.

49 See Toby Barnard, 'Browne, Peter (d. 1735)', *ODNB* and discussion below.

50 Barnabe Rich, *The Irish Hubbub* (1617), 24.

51 In both Mark 14:23 and Matthew 26:27 the disciples sing a hymn after supper. On ballads replacing hymns in health drinking see Morton, *Great Evil*, 108. See also Luke 22:17, 20.

the threat of prosecution, violence or even death, ordinary men and women, drunk or sober, would refuse to comply with loyal (or disloyal)-healths they found unpalatable. Why not, as some contemporaries advised, simply 'drink the Cup, which they that require it call a Health, tho not in the same Notion and Formality in which it was urged and imposed'?[52] Because oaths and public declarations carried civic and religious weight, a far worse fate than temporal punishment threatened for those who drank 'unworthily'. As Paul's letter to the Corinthians warned, 'he that eateth and drinketh unworthily, eateth and drinketh his own damnation'.[53] This doctrine was everywhere: reiterated in sermons and inscribed on communion cups and altar-tables.[54] Biblical exemplars were compelling. At the Last Supper Judas was already 'out of charity' with Christ and his followers: Christ gave him a piece of wine-dipped bread and 'Satan entered his soul'.[55] The popular Old Testament story of Belshazzar's feast emphasized that the misuse of sacred objects could also bring destruction on the heads of drinkers.[56] Pamphlets and ballads also told dire stories of people suffering a terrible end after drinking Communion wine unworthily or healths to God or the Devil.[57] A growing similarity between Communion and loyal-healthing rituals transferred this religious fear into the secular arena.

Significantly, the divisions of the 1640s saw a change in the 'words of institution' used for a loyal-health; combining a prayer and a curse in which the 'health' of the king and the 'confusion' [or worse] of his enemies were drunk.[58] For instance, Hugh Sheldon was indicted in 1651 for drinking the king's health and for disparaging Cromwell.[59] In Hereford in 1685, Stephen Arundell drank to the health of the Duke of Monmouth and the death of James II.[60] Either prayer or curse could lead to indictment, as in 1641 when one Readman 'drank a health to the confusion of the protestants in Ireland', or in 1650 when William Norman drank 'to the confusion of

[52] Morton, *Great Evil*, 36–7; See Browne, *Of Drinking* (1713), 22–3, 40–1 on healthers seeking to amend their words to avoid profanation.

[53] I Corinthians 11:29; on sacrament as oath see Browne, *Second Part*, 72.

[54] See, e.g., John Downame, *A Treatise Tending to Direct the Weak Christian* (1645), Sig.A3–4; Whiting, *Parish Church*, 31, 68.

[55] John 13:26–7.

[56] Daniel 5:25.

[57] See, e.g., Young, *England's Bane* (1617 edn), Sig.C2; (1634 edn), 12–13; *Perfect Passages of Each Days Proceeding*, No. 20, 5–10 March 1645, 160; Richard Baxter, *A Dreadful Warning to Lewd Livers* (*c.*1670s).

[58] Morton, *Great Evil*, 42, 47, 56, 68–71, 99–104; Browne, *Discourse* (1716), 10–11, 17–18.

[59] 20 September 1651, Derbyshire RO Q/SB/2/650.

[60] Herefordshire RO: BG11/17/5/69.

parliament'.[61] At the same time, the seventeenth-century practice of administering politico-religious oaths to the general public had sensitized large swathes of the population to their religious and legal significance.[62]

The shared cup over which the words of a loyal-health were spoken also had an important role to play. Protestant Communion practice implied that ritual use and spoken words could together 'inscribe a cup' with religious authority, regardless of its material or decorative qualities.[63] Though supposedly stripped of intrinsic sacred attributes, providential occurrences could render the most ordinary cup as an object of extraordinary, even spiritual significance.[64] John Aubrey recounted how, in 1648, a royalist clergyman,

> standing up, with his head uncover'd to Drink his Majesties Health, saying *God bless our Gracious Sovereign*, as he was going to put the Cup to his lips, a swallow flew in at the Window, and pitched on the brim of the little earthen-cup (not half a pint), and sipt, and so flew out again . . . the Cup is preserved there still, as a Rarity.

Breakages during communion or healthing rituals could also be subject to sinister interpretation. For example, as Aubrey also relates,

> Mr Ployden [a Catholic] to avoid the penalty [of the Test Acts], went to his parish church [for Communion] [but] when . . . the chalice [was put] into [his] hand, the Cup of it . . . fell off. 'Tis true it was out of order before, and he had a tremor in his hand [but the] Communion was stopt by this accident.[65]

It was also seen as inauspicious when during a loyal-health to Cromwell the shared glass broke.[66] Such providential tales made explicit a belief that objects involved in secular or sacred drinking rituals were capable themselves of

[61] Cheshire RO: DCC/47/5; LMA: MJ/SR/1046/233.

[62] The literature is extensive, see, e.g., Edward Vallance, *Revolutionary England and the National Covenant: State Oaths, Protestantism and the Political Nation, 1553–1682* (Woodbridge, 2005); John Spurr, '"The Strongest Bond of Conscience": Oaths and the Limits of Tolerance in Early Modern England', in Harold E. Braun and Edward Vallance (eds), *Contexts of Conscience in Early Modern Europe 1500–1700* (Basingstoke, 2004), 151–65.

[63] Morton, *Great Evil*, 2, 18, 36, 75. On potential slippage between consecrated plate in church and secular spaces see Browne, *Of Drinking* (1713), 26–8.

[64] On this important concept see Alexandra Walsham, *Providence in Early Modern England* (Oxford, 1999).

[65] John Aubrey, *Miscellanies* (1696), 99–100.

[66] A. G. H. Bachrach and R. G. Colmer (eds), *Lodewijk Huygens The English Journal 1651–1652* (Leiden, 1982), 146–7.

making revelations about the integrity of drinkers. The wealthy routinely possessed precious vessels decorated with royal arms, but taverns and alehouses could provide even ordinary health-drinkers with fine silver vessels, or pewter tankards, perhaps decorated with loyal iconography, or mere earthenware mugs, decorated with slip mottos, such as 'Obey the King'.[67] Court records show tavern and alehouse drinkers could change the vessels they drank from over an evening; as in 1684, when James Fulham and two friends 'called for Drink [and] after having had a Pot and a Glass, desired a Silver Cup', perhaps to drink a health.[68] The size of vessel chosen was also of importance, as the quantity to be drunk by each healther had to be exactly the same.[69] Christ's instructions 'Drink ye all of this' (sometimes inscribed on communion cups), could be interpreted to mean everyone should drink and that they should each drink all of the contents.[70]

That intoxicating drink was drunk during a health was just as important as the vessel it was drunk from, the quantity consumed, the gestures used, and the 'words of institution' spoken. Wine was preferred, although anything would do in extremity. In 1686, George Wright of Bolton drank healths to the 'rightful King' (the Duke of Monmouth) in puddle water.[71] In 1648, field reports mentioned the royalist healthing that went on behind the walls of Colchester during its infamous siege. One pamphlet claimed that here too the king's health was defiantly drunk in water, though a royalist play insisted sherry had been specially reserved for the purpose. In 1650, a group of inebriated royalists in Milton, Bedfordshire, were discovered drinking healths to the exiled Charles II in a mixture of their own blood and wine.[72] In 1654, Irish cavaliers proudly declared they drank loyal-healths in 'good Usquaba [whiskey] and brave brown ale'.[73]

[67] V&A:Loan: BM.1030–2001: http://collections.vam.ac.uk/item/O78303; William Lowndes, *A Further Essay for the Amendment of the Gold and Silver Coins* (1695), 9–10: 'every alehouse-keeper . . . [has] 100 or 200[lbs] in plate . . . scarce a session happens, but some one . . . is Arraigned for stealing a Tankard or the like'. Sessions papers support this claim.

[68] *Old Bailey Proceedings Online* [hereafter *OBPO*] 16 January 1685, t16850116–27.

[69] Young, *Englands Bane* (1634), 22.

[70] Prynne, *Healthes:Sicknesse*, 42–3.

[71] Berwick RO DDKE/acc. 7840 HMC/599.

[72] See Angela McShane, 'The Extraordinary Case of the Flesh-Eating and Blood-Drinking Cavaliers' in A. J. McShane and G. Walker (eds), *The Extraordinary and the Everyday in Early Modern England: A Celebration of the Work of Bernard Capp* (2010), 198–9, 201, 210.

[73] Thomas Birch (ed.), *A Collection of the State Papers of John Thurloe* (1742), vol.2, Lord Dudop to lieutenant general Dalzyell, 14 November 1654, 718–733.

Echoing the gestural changes in Communion practice, loyal-healthers frequently demanded the ceremonious removal of hats and the performance of obeisance to the sacral authority of the crown while drinking; transforming a social and convivial space into a religiously and politically charged one. Describing just such an incident, John Cannon remarked on how a convivial scene 'altered suddenly'.[74] In 1649, Daniel Holt of Loughborough pinned a victualler's hat to the ceiling with his sword and threatened to run him through for refusing to drink or take his hat off for a loyal-health to Charles II.[75] The appropriation of sacral gestures was particularly explicit in one Chester tavern in 1682: 'some Lords and gentlemen . . . fell to drinking, sticking all their swords on the top of the room [creating an altar-like appearance] and made their servants doe the like, then fell down on their knees and drunk an health to the prosperity of the D of York and the damnation of the D. of Monmouth.'[76] Like communion cups, the special vessels chosen for healthing also did 'hat honour': lids being ceremoniously removed or lifted from tankards or baluster glasses before a health was begun.

The liturgical form of words used in loyal-healthing rituals made it almost impossible for men or women of conscience to comply when challenged to drink and swear. If the outcome of falsely drinking a loyal-health was to drink damnation on oneself, then the only possible answer, no matter what the consequences, was a refusal, or even a rebuttal; as in 1645, when Francis Church was stung into retorting that Charles I was 'a rascal and rebel and no King'.[77] Drinkers could be trapped into a disloyal and sacrilegious act with words, as in 1694, when Francis Paleing accompanied an unsuspecting watchman into an alehouse and 'demanding a mugg of ale', drank to 'King William and Mary, George and Ann'. As the watchman drank in return, Paleing suddenly added the words: 'four such children the devil never had'.[78] The political and religious anxieties that loyal-healthing created led, as one sermon put it, to some cases where drinkers 'loved their friends to death'.[79] In May 1689, Clement Pomfret proposed a health to James II and died in the fight that ensued when his friend Thomas Alcroft (acquitted) tried to persuade him not

[74] See, J. Money (ed.), *The Chronicles of John Cannon, Excise Officer and Writing Master*, 2 vols (Oxford, 2009), vol. I, 138. See also Morton, *Great Evil*, 34; Browne, *Of Drinking* (1713), 19.

[75] LMA MJ/SR 1030/95; Capp, *Cultural Wars*, 164.

[76] J. Horsefall Turner (ed.), *The Rev. Oliver Heywood, B.A. 1630–1702* (4 vols: Brighouse, 1882–85), vol. ii, 288.

[77] Affidavits of David Cassey, 10–19 February 1645, House of Lords, HL/PO/JO/10/1/180.

[78] *OBPO*, February 1694, t16940221–34.

[79] Morton, *Great Evil*, 6.

to drink it.[80] William Blundell noted in his diary that men who refused a duel on their own account were prepared to engage in violence if the royal honour was maligned.[81]

IV

Moral critics were at pains to historicize, demonize, and dismiss 'all those ordinary Objections, Excuses, [or] Pretences which are made to justifie, extenuate, or excuse the drinking or pledging of healths'.[82] They pointed out the foreign and pagan origins of healthing, blaming ancient Greeks and Romans (including Jupiter himself), Jews, Saxons, and the Dutch in turn.[83] Yet the dialogic form of their expositions meant they also spelt out how the use of alcohol in communal bonding rituals could be legitimated through Judaic, Christian, and especially classical traditions. Treatises admitted that Christians (unlike Turks or Jews) were released from prohibitive consumption laws by New Testament teaching; hence Sir Wilful's claim that only 'unchristian' souls would attempt to restrict alcohol consumption.[84] Thomas Heywood's *Philocothonista, or, The drunkard, opened, dissected, and anatomized* (1635), though appearing to decry them, in fact revelled in details about the fabulous cups used in Greek and Roman drinking rituals and the language and arts of drinking they inspired, as well as amusing stories of drunkenness taken from a range of classical and other authors.

Moralizers complained that those with classical education, or pretensions to civil sophistication, were encouraged to 'drink like Greeks', or to be 'merry' or even 'mad' like Greeks'; to enjoy symposiatic excess.[85] As Congreve's drunken healther Sir Wilful put it in his discussion of theological practices: 'Orthodox is a hard word ... [hiccough] Greek for Claret'.[86] Drinking, even to excess, could have form, style, and meaning.[87] Young's *England's Bane* bewailed 'There are in London drinking schools: so that drunkennesse is professed with us as a liberall

[80] *OBPO*, May 1689, t16890516–9; see also *OBPO*, May 1689, trial of John Stanninot Thomas Newton t16890516–30.

[81] T. Ellison Gibson (ed.), *A Cavaliers Notebook* (1880), 154–5.

[82] Prynne, *Healthes:Sicknesse*, Frontispiece.

[83] See, e.g., Young, *Englands Bane* (1634); 35 (1617), Sig.D1 + 3: Adams, *Divine Herball*, 24; *Great Evil*, 28–9, 40–65; Browne, *Discourse*, 15–16, 35–8, 82, ch IV.

[84] Acts 10: 14–15.

[85] Prynne, *Healthes:Sicknesse*, Sig. A3v; Morton, *Great Evil*, 49–56.

[86] Congreve, *The Way of the World* (1700), Act 4, Sc.i, 65.

[87] M. O'Callaghan, 'Tavern Societies, the Inns of Court, and the Culture of Conviviality in Early Seventeenth-Century London', in Smyth (ed.), *A Pleasing Sinne*, 37–54.

arte and science'.[88] Prynne complained bitterly at the dignified and heroic languages used to describe the styles, rules, and excesses of drinking, while sober moderation was always portrayed in derogatory terms.[89]

Despite its learned roots, knowledge about the form and cultural background of healthing practices was disseminated widely across the social spectrum, through observation and emulation of elite behaviour in taverns and alehouses and via a range of freely accessible visual, literary, and aural media that were full of allusion; such as the ubiquitous name signs of English drinking houses and shops and their interior decoration.[90] 'The Three Cups', a popular alehouse or tavern name, referred to the three healths offered at the end of Roman banquets: to Jupiter Olympus, the Heroes, and Jupiter the Saviour.[91] Historical, mythological, and biblical images were painted or pinned onto alehouse and tavern walls. Well-known drinking subjects were Balthazar's Feast, Bacchus, and Alexander (who killed his best friend, and was said to have died himself, in health-drinking bouts).

Easily obtainable cheap texts, such as political drinking ballads, described and encouraged the contrarieties of good fellowship and violence that characterized loyal-health drinking.[92] At least three hundred separate songs, published from the mid- to late-seventeenth century, mentioned healthing, many offering visual or textual evidence of healthing procedure.[93] Both woodcuts and words described the ritual uncovering of the head, standing or kneeling while sharing the cup as 'loyal healths' went round (Figure 6). They disseminated a classically constructed style of drinking that promoted excess for politically beneficial reasons, but verses also threatened violence—to 'cripple your shanks' or 'a full one on the face'—to anyone who 'baulked at a brimmer' (refused to drink a full glass in a loyal-health). [94]

[88] See also *A Solemne Ioviall disputation, theoreticke and practicke; briefely shadowing the Law of Drinking together, with the solemnities and controversies occurring* (1617).

[89] Prynne, *Healthes:Sicknesse*, Sigs.A3v-b1, b2, 2.

[90] See J. Fleming, *Graffiti and the Writing Arts of Early Modern England* (Pennsylvania, 2001); Andrew Gordon, '"If my sign could speak"; The Signboard and the Visual Culture of Early Modern London', *Early Theatre*, 8.1 (2005), 35–51.

[91] *Chronicles of John Cannon*, I, 127 and Castle Cary Tavern below. On interpretation see Morton, *Great Evil*, 51, 53; Browne, *Discourse*, 36.

[92] Browne, *Second Part*, 7–8, pointed out they were used as a vehicle to defend the practice.

[93] *PBB* Index 547–8.

[94] See A. McShane-Jones, 'Roaring Royalists and Ranting Brewers: The Politicisation of Drink and Drunkenness in Political Broadside Ballads from 1640–1689' in A. Smyth (ed.), *A Pleasing Sinne. Drink and Conviviality in 17th-Century England* (Woodbridge, 2004), 55–88.

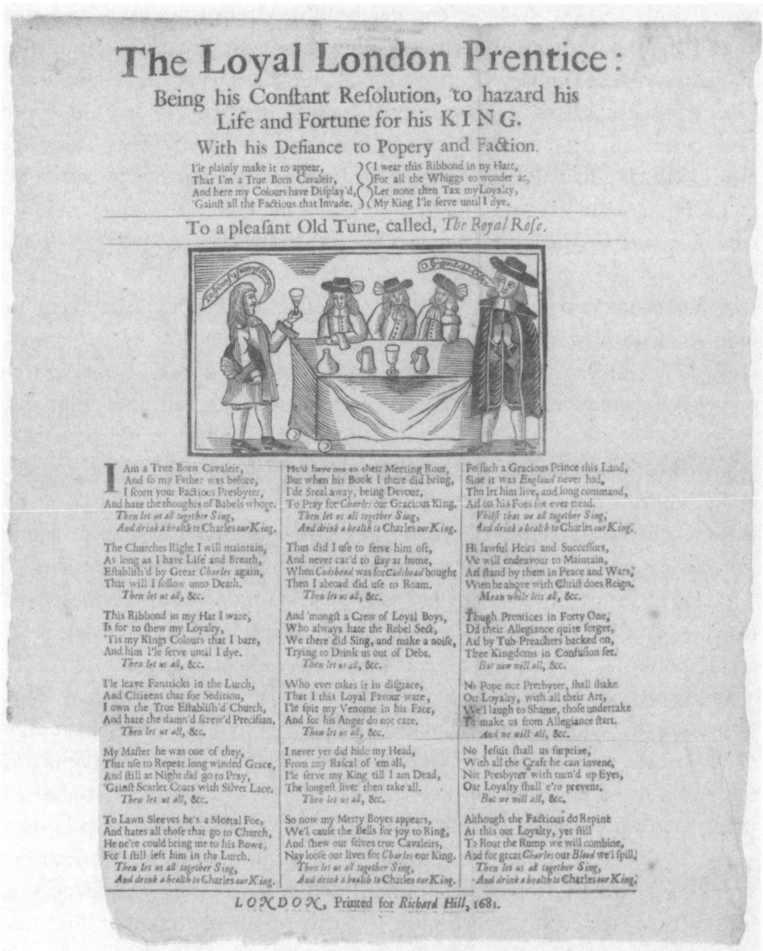

The Loyal London Prentice:

Being his Conſtant Reſolution, to hazard his Life and Fortune for his KING.

With his Defiance to Popery and Faction.

I'le plainly make it to appear,
That I'm a True Born Cavaleir,
And here my Colours have Diſplay'd,
'Gainſt all the Factious that Invade.

I wear this Ribbond in ny Hatt,
For all the Whiggs to wonder at,
Let none then Tax my Loyalty,
My King I'le ſerve until I dye.

To a pleaſant Old Tune, called, *The Royal Roſe.*

I Am a True Born Cavaleir,
And ſo my Father was before,
I ſcorn your Factious Presbyter,
And hate the thoughts of Babels whore.
Then let us all together Sing,
And drink a health to Charles *our King.*

The Churches Right I will maintain,
As long as I have Life and Breath,
Eſtabliſh'd by Great *Charles* again,
That will I follow unto Death.
Then let us all, &c.

This Ribbond in my Hat I ware,
Is for to ſhew my Loyalty,
'Tis my Kings Colours that I bare,
And him I'le ſerve until I dye.
Then let us all, &c.

I'le leave Fanaticks in the Lurch,
And Citizens that ſoe Sedition,
I own the True Eſtabliſh'd Church,
And hate the damn'd ſcrew'd Preciſian.
Then let us all, &c.

My Maſter he was one of they,
That uſe to Repeat long winded Grace,
And ſtill at Night did go to Pray,
'Gainſt Scarlet Coats with Silver Lace.
Then let us all, &c.

To Lawn Sleeves he's a Mortal Foe,
And hates all thoſe that go to Church,
He ne're could bring me to his Bowe,
For I ſtill left him in the Lurch.
Then let us all together Sing,
And drink a health to Charles *our King.*

He'd have me to their Meeting Rout,
But when his Book I there did bring,
I'de Steal away, being Devout,
To Pray for *Charles* our Gracious King.
Then let us all together Sing,
And drink a health to Charles *our King.*

Thus did I uſe to ſerve him oft,
And never car'd to ſtay at home,
When *Codshead* was for *Codshead* bought
Then I abroad did uſe to Roam.
Then let us all, &c.

And 'mongſt a Crew of Loyal Boys,
Who always hate the Rebel Sect,
We there did Sing, and make a noiſe,
Trying to Drink us out of Debt.
Then let us all, &c.

Who ever takes it in diſgrace,
That I this Loyal Favour ware,
I'le ſpit my Venome in his Face,
And for his Anger do not care.
Then let us all, &c.

I never yet did hide my Head,
From any Raſcal of 'em all,
I'le ſerve my King till I am Dead,
The longeſt liver then take all.
Then let us all, &c.

So now my Merry Boyes appears,
We'l cauſe the Bells for joy to Ring,
And ſhew our ſelves true Cavaleirs,
Nay looſe our lives for *Charles* our King.
Then let us all together Sing,
And drink a health to Charles *our King.*

Fo ſuch a Gracious Prince this Land,
Sine it was *England* never had,
Thn let him live, and long command,
Ad on his Foes for ever tread.
Whilſt that we all together Sing,
And drink a health to Charles *our King.*

Hi lawful Heirs and Succeſſors,
We will endeavour to Maintain,
And ſtand by them in Peace and Wars,
When he above with Chriſt does Reign.
Mean while lets all, &c.

Though Prentices in Forty One,
Did their Allegiance quite forget,
And by Tub-Preachers backed on,
Three Kingdoms in Confuſion ſet.
But now will all, &c.

No Pope nor Presbyter, ſhall ſhake
Our Loyalty, with all their Art,
We'l laugh to Shame, thoſe undertake
To make us from Allegiance ſtart.
And we will all, &c.

No Jeſuit ſhall us ſurprize,
With all the Craft he can invent,
Nor Presbyter with turn'd up Eyes,
Our Loyalty ſhall e're prevent.
But we will all, &c.

Although the Factious do Repine
At this our Loyalty, yet ſtill
To Rout the Rump we will combine,
And for great *Charles* our *Blood* we'l ſpill,
Then let us all together Sing,
And drink a health to Charles *our King.*

LONDON, Printed for *Richard Hill*, 1681.

Figure 6. *The Loyal London Prentice*, printed ballad, London, 1681, p EBB65. Reproduced by kind permission of Houghton Library, Harvard University.

Loyal- and disloyal-healths recorded by the courts give a clear indication of how classical models, whether acquired directly through schooling or second-hand through observation, could influence ideas and impact directly on behaviour. One unusually detailed case from Hereford illustrates this. In 1694, at the 'Catherine Wheel', Pelham Corbett began a health to King William. Rowland Andrews refused it. The company demanded that he should leave, but instead, Andrews began a counter-health to 'him who lost fifteen shillings' (i.e. three 'crowns'). Incensed, Samuel Lestoken threw his glass of cider in Andrews' face. Timothy Geers attacked James Neda with a pair of tongs and a drawn sword. Andrews then struck Pelham Corbett and, taking him by the neck-cloth, almost choked him. At the same time, Andrews' widowed mother, the landlady, hit Corbett with a basting ladle and was joined in her attack by her daughter and the maid. On coming before the court, the men seem to have escaped punishment, but Widow Andrews had her licence revoked for harbouring Jacobites.[95]

A closer look at this event reveals how the behaviour of these drinkers was redolent with classical structures. In the 'Catherine Wheel' we see a well-known Ciceronian proverb in action, '*Aut bibat, aut abeat*' ('drink with us or begone'; some versions add, 'lest the wine drinkers fall upon him with violence'). Rowland Andrews' refusal to drink a health should have been followed by his departure. His refusal to leave provoked legitimate violence, including the dishonouring act of drink thrown in the face.[96] The company was socially mixed. Pelham Corbett came from a relatively well-to-do family (he may have been a soldier at this time) and Timothy Geers was the son of a sergeant at arms; both probably received a grammar school education.[97] Rowland Andrews was a skilled joiner, while James Neda's profession is uncertain, but his evidence made clear that they could all read.

Humanist commentaries on drinking were also brought into play in interpreting the seditious import of healthing rituals that came to the attention of the courts. Erasmus and Plato had both argued that the most dangerous thing at a drunken feast was a sober man, who could reveal what was said while men were unguarded and in their cups.[98] This was the antithesis of 'good company'.[99] It was the acknowledged dishonour of such behaviour that saved Lord Altham from prosecution in 1686, when a tavern vintner accused him of proposing a disloyal-health. Judge Wythens commented 'that men should be responsible indeed for words they spoak in drinke, but much more for Actions' and fined the vintner 'for the disorders of his house', warning that

95 Herefordshire RO BG11/17/5/86–7; 'The corporation of Hereford: Miscellaneous papers, 1601–1760', *The Manuscripts of Rye and Hereford Corporations*, Thirteenth report, Appendix Part IV (1892), 338–53.

96 Morton, *Great Evil*, 11, 44–5; Prynne, *Healthes:Sicknesse*, 58–9.

97 See House of Lords PO/JO/10/6/44/1921, 16 Nov 1703.

98 Robert Bland (ed.), *Proverbs: Chiefly Taken from the Adagia of Erasmus, with Explanations* (1814), vol. 1, 225–9.

99 Phil Withington, 'Company and Sociability in Early Modern England', *Social History*, 32:3 (2007), 291–307.

'people will be carefull how they go drinke at such a mans house as serves them so'.[100]

V

The changes in the social extent and sacral significance of loyal-healthing rituals mapped out above were matched by an about-face by political and religious authorities in their attitudes towards the practice, culminating by the end of the century in their official enforcement. In 1628, William Prynne hoped to engage Charles I in a campaign against loyal-healthing that was detrimental to the king's honour. He assured readers no official retribution could follow refusals to participate in immoral healthing rituals.[101] Yet from the 1640s authorities increasingly *did* threaten action if loyal-healths were refused (or disloyal-healths proposed). In 1645, the governor of royalist Berwick was asked to pardon James Grieve, as 'meaning no irreverence', when he soberly refused to drink the king's health.[102] The drinking practices of cavaliers have been much studied, especially by literary scholars, but in fact loyal-healthing was so socially entrenched that they continued to be drunk by both sides of the political and religious divide.[103] For example, on entering Newcastle in 1640 the Scots military leaders began their occupation by drinking a loyal-health with the surrendering mayor, while in 1647 a curfew was prompted in London because parliamentary soldiers were stopping people and forcing them to drink loyal-healths in the street.[104] In 1651, a parliamentary soldier in Cornwall was sentenced to run the gauntlet for beginning two healths to the king and queen and, despite laws to the contrary, loyal-healths were drunk to Cromwell as Protector (though a great many more to his confusion are recorded).[105]

Immediately after the Restoration, in May 1660, loyal-healthing was ostensibly restored to its pre-war status as a secular and immoral practice. William Prynne's pamphlet *Health Sickness* was twice reissued that year,

[100] *The Entring Book of Roger Morrice III. The Reign of James II 1685–87,* ed. Tim Harris, 7 vols (2007), 309.

[101] Prynne, *Healthes:Sicknesse*, Preface, 5–6.

[102] Berwick RO: BRO17/2/e) and g).

[103] See, e.g., L. Potter, *Secret Rites and Secret Writing: Royalist Literature, 1641–1660* (Cambridge, 1989), 134–8; and essays by S. Achilleos and M. Keblusek in Smyth (ed.), *A Pleasing Sinne,* 21–35, 69–88.

[104] Capp, *Cultural Wars,* 165; 2 and 8 December, 1647, *Journal of the House of Lords, Vol. 9 1646 (7)* (1767–1830), 553–5; 565–6.

[105] See, e.g., A letter of intelligence from Monsieur Augier's secretary, 27 November 1654, *Journal of the House of Commons, Vol. 7 1651–1660* (1802), 390–2; *Huygens English Journal,* 146–7. For further examples see Capp, *Cultural Wars,* 162–7.

alongside two royal proclamations, promulgated in June and August (and often reprinted), against 'vicious and debauched' persons whose loyal-healthing brought dishonour to the king and disruption to the state.[106] Apparently, in the new political world of the Restoration, Charles II, son of the king that had overseen the removal of Prynne's ears, was now directly following the old Presbyterian's advice. Yet in practice, the legal and moral status of loyal-healthing in Restoration England was far less clear, as exemplified by a case from Castle Cary in Somerset. In January 1661, the broad-weaver Philip Leigh sat drinking for three hours in the 'Three Cups', sharing one flagon of beer with a friend from Wincanton and then another with a local friend, Ralph Simes. They were accosted by a group of local men, led by the landlady, who challenged Leigh to drink a loyal-health. He complied, but also reminded them that the king's proclamation had expressly forbidden the practice. In response, they challenged him again, this time to drink 'to the confusion of all Anabaptists, Quakers and Presbyterians'. Leigh was unwilling to drink to the confusion of anyone, but the company warned that he was 'a rogue if he would not drink it' because 'these are all the Kings enemies'. Steadfastly pointing out 'we have broken the Kings law already', Leigh was attacked, imprisoned, and brought before the magistrate the next day on a trumped up charge of treasonable words.[107] The deposition by Leigh's friend, the illiterate (non-signing) Ralph Simes, indicates most tellingly how difficult it was for subjects to steer a safe course between ambivalent legalities. Simes declared in his evidence that he had not joined in the loyal-health; did this unlikely claim make him disloyal or law abiding?

The early modern state's attitude towards alcohol reflected the Christian humanist tradition of the *via media*.[108] On one hand, too much alcohol could lead to someone being 'disguised' in drink—transformed into a disloyal or disruptive subject. In 1661, a Glastonbury man excused himself from expressing the wish that 'Times will turne' claiming he was 'not himself being much overcome with beere'.[109] In 1676, a Scottish seaman, who had fought in the Dutch wars, pleaded his drunkenness with tears in his eyes when it was reported that he had disparaged the king and declared, with admirable

[106] *The Diary of Bulstrode Whitlocke 1605–1675*, ed. Ruth Spalding (Records of Social and Economic History, NS XIII, 1990), noted their promulgation on 13 June (p. 606) and 13 August (p. 612). Reprinted by Prynne, *Health Sickness* (1660) and Morton, *Great Evil*, 122–7.

[107] Somerset RO Q\SPET/1/20; Q/S9 99 No 23, 21 January 1661.

[108] J. Scodel, *Excess and the Mean in Early Modern Literature* (Princeton and Oxford, 2002), especially ch.7.

[109] Somerset RO Q/S9 99 No 13.

inclusivity, that he 'Did not care if the whole nation were damn'd and destroyed'.[110] On the other hand, consuming too little or no alcohol led to 'crazy-brained' and 'hot-headed sedition'. Cavaliers and subsequently Tories satirised 'Jewish' Dissenters and Whiggish 'Turks' because they did not drink like loyal subjects. On the contrary, they infected the body politic with seditious sobriety.[111]

Despite its official proclamations and its support for campaigns like the reformation of manners in the 1690s, the British monarchical state linked affection for the state with a willingness to drink alcohol in a public ritual. Test Acts enforced the sacrament on office holders, and anyone whose loyalty to Church or state was questioned, in a way that some argued was just like loyal-healthing.[112] Unlike bonfires and bells, loyal-healths were not expressly ordered for national public celebrations in the seventeenth century. They were nevertheless provided for and expected by governors at every level and in every branch of the state.[113] Conduits ran with wine at the Restoration for this purpose; mass healthing events, led by civil authorities, took place in towns in the 1680s, while money with which to drink loyal-healths was frequently provided to soldiers and sailors by military authorities throughout the period.[114] It was the express hope of these authorities that loyal-healthing rituals 'would not only increase but beget an affection to his Majesty', bringing about a loving bond between subjects and legitimate government.[115] Only

[110] *OBPO*, August 1676: t16760823.

[111] See McShane-Jones, 'Roaring Royalists'.

[112] Morton, *Great Evil*, 109–10; Anon., *The unreasonableness of compelling men to the Holy Sacrament of the Lords Supper* (1684).

[113] Stafford. Sampson Byrch, Mayor, to [Secretary Jenkins], 25 September 1682, *CSPD*: Charles II, 1682 (1932), 362–448.

[114] There are far too many examples to cite here: see, e.g., Civic events: The Earl of Bath to [the Earl of Sunderland], 28 September 1688, *CSPD: James II, 1687–9, vol. III* (1972), 286; 16 Feb. 1689, 'The corporation of Lincoln: Registers, vols VI and VII (1653–1710)', *The Manuscripts of Lincoln, Bury St. Edmunds etc.: Fourteenth report, Appendix; part VIII* (1895), 102–15; 18 February 1689, A. Hewitson (ed.), *Diary of Thomas Bellingham, an officer under William III* (Preston, 1908), 52. Loyal-health money for soldiers and sailors: May 1660, B. Lubbock (ed.), *Barlow's journal of his life at sea . . .* (2 vols, 1934): I, 42; 18 July 1689, *Narcissus Luttrell, A Brief Historical Relation of State Affairs*, 6 vols (Oxford, 1857), I, 549.

[115] 12 September 1683, John Gelson to —; and Under-Sheriff J. Hillier to Secretary Jenkins, 15 September 1683, *CSPD: Charles II, 1683: July-September* (1934), 390–1, 398. See also Lieutenant-Governor Stede to Lords of Trade and Plantations, 19 May 1686, *Calendar of State Papers Colonial [CSPC], America and West Indies, Volume 12: 1685–1688 and Addenda 1653–1687* (1899), 182–200.

very full and frequently refilled loyal cups could cement allegiances and establish social and national bonds, by balancing the humours of the body politic, promoting social virtue, and combating self-destructive melancholia.[116]

Loyal-healthing acted as an effective weapon for wheedling out groups or individuals in society that secretly harboured animosities detrimental to the harmonious state. In 1686, for example, a group of soldiers broke into a licensed Quaker meeting in Leicester and demanded they drink a loyal-health. Fundamentally opposed to any form of oath-taking or sacramental ritual, Quakers were easy prey. On the health being refused, the Captain-Lieutenant threatened 'if thou drinkest not my masters health I will cuckold thy wife before thy eyes'; the soldiers locked the doors 'and used and abused the women much . . . some of the young girls so affrighted their recovery is questioned'.[117] Post-Restoration, careful investigations were made into reports of refused loyal-healths, or proposed disloyal ones, especially those involving officials, clerics, or military officers. John Cannon, a government excise man, reported several accusations motivated by personal grievances.[118] Punishments included loss of position, large fines, imprisonment or even execution. Serious consequences were avoided only with difficulty, although ambivalent attitudes towards the effect of drink in 'disguising the subject' could sometimes work in the accused's favour.[119] In 1689, for example, Roger Morrice noted that three Members of Parliament were accused of drinking healths to the prosperity of the recently deposed King James II. The investigating judge Sir Thomas Littleton thought it best 'to let the accusations fall' because the accuser confessed he was drunk and the Commons 'were never like to punish any one for what he said in his drinke.'[120] It became a common defence for those indicted for sedition to claim that they had publicly drunk the king's health. In 1678, colonists exchanged accusations over support for loyal-healths dating back to the 1640s and 1660s.[121] Leonard Po-Jenner, indicted in 1693, was acquitted on these grounds, despite one deposition that

116 McShane, 'The Extraordinary Case'.

117 *Morrice III*, ed. Harris, 275.

118 *Chronicles of John Cannon*, I, 138, 145, 152–3.

119 See D. Rabin, 'Drunkenness and Responsibility for Crime in the Eighteenth Century', *Journal of British Studies*, 44 (Jul. 2005), 457–77.

120 *The Entring Book of Roger Morrice V, The Reign of William III 1689–91*, ed. Mark Knights (7 vols, 2007), 332.

121 Dispute between William Stoughton and Peter Bulkeley of Massachusetts and Randall Holden and John Greene of Rhode Island, July 1678, *CSPC, America and West Indies, Volume 10: 1677–1680* (1896), 268–81.

'lately he used to drink it by the name of the King's Health, without naming King William and Queen Mary'.[122]

Most remarkably, religious authorities too changed their stance on the legitimacy of loyal-health drinking over the course of the century. Moralists had all singled out the loyal-health from other forms of pledging because it presented a unique problem, which was not only moral and religious but also political. How could a subject refuse a health that might impugn his or her loyalty to the king or state?[123] Until the 1660s, the moralist consensus was that all should refuse to participate in a ritual that was of no benefit to the state, society, or the individual; Francis Bacon's quasi-proverbial reply 'I will pray for the king's health and drink for my own' was almost universally tripped out. Treatises like Prynne's had confidently assured readers that magistrates and governors would respect a sober response, while complying would do no more than put the drinker's immortal soul at risk. Meanwhile, the laxity of magistrates in prosecuting drinkers was criticized as setting a bad example.[124]

By the 1670s, however, none other than the nonconformist divine, Richard Baxter, expressly broke with this moral consensus. In his *Christian Directory* (1673 and 1678), after excoriating the custom of pledging in traditional manner with a long line of dire biblical warnings, Baxter's advice in the case of loyal-healthing was to participate: 'As possibly in some cases and Companies [where] the offence given by denying it may be such as will do more hurt far, than yielding would do. (As if a malignant company would lay ones Loyalty to the King upon it.)' In addition he advised: 'To be bare when others lay the honour of the King or Superiours upon it, is a Ceremony that on the aforesaid reason may be complyed with. . . . it is meet that we join such words (where we have liberty) as may prevent the scandal'.[125] The willingness of even the most severe detractors to advise compliance reflected not only the very real and ever-present threat of violence against those who refused to comply, whether from religious or political conviction, but also an acceptance of the need to demonstrate loyalty through the ritual imbibing of alcohol.

122 *OBPO*, May 1693, t16930531–46. See also Thomas Norton to Col. Worden, 9 November 1682, *CSPD: Charles II, 1682* (1932), 532.

123 Prynne, *Healthes:Sicknesse*, 52–4 and passim. Morton, *Great Evil*, 32–4, 68–71, 87–91, 96, 98, 114–15, 122.

124 Harris, *Drunkards Cup*, 28–9; Bolton, *Walking* (1638 edn), 204; Prynne, *Healthes: Sicknesse*, 5–6.

125 Baxter, *Christian Directory*, 388.

Following Baxter's capitulation, in 1684 *The Great Evil of Health Drinking* described loyal-healthing as 'a prophane sacrament' and expressed concern that 'loyal-healthing' was not only 'exacted from them that have no inclination to it' but was also expected as a 'stated and solemn service', 'approaching the Altar of Duties'.[126] After William III's death in 1702, a controversy broke out over the implications of Whigs drinking to his memory (termed the 'litany health'), which, as Bishop Peter Browne fulsomely argued, was a blasphemous appropriation of the sacrament.[127] Unlike any previous detractor from loyal-healthing, Browne faced fierce opposition from both lay and clerical writers, who accused him of partisan Tory motivations.[128] Undeterred, and at some professional cost, Browne continued to bemoan the fact that loyal-healthing had become common among churchmen and tipplers alike, for all ranks and degrees, 'becoming the only modern way of expressing all mens good wishes and desires' and such a daily practice in homes, that children had learned to drink a loyal-health long before they took Communion.[129] His inference was that the loyal-health was in danger of replacing Communion as the key ritual of communal and national bonding in early modern England.

VI Conclusion

The ostensible differences in context and behaviour between Communion drinking and health drinking—one a sober sipping of Communion wine in a church, the other a downing of whole cups of drink, in a secular context, that could provoke violence—has not unreasonably led historians to see them as essentially different things: sacred and profane. And yet in 1715 an Anglican bishop saw them as dangerously and inextricably linked. An apposite example of objects that moved explicitly from secular healthing to sacred Communion

126 Morton, *Great Evil*, v, 31–3.

127 Peter Browne, *Of Drinking to the Memory of the Dead* (Dublin, 1713; London, 1715), 6; Browne, *Second Part* (Dublin, 1714); Peter Browne, *An Answer to a Right Reverend Prelate's Defence of the Eating and Drinking in Remembrance of the Dead* (Dublin, 1715), 13, 15–16, 18–23, 32–5; Browne, *Discourse* (1716), 152; Peter Browne, *A Letter to a Reverend Gentleman in Oxford on the subject of drinking healths* (1722).

128 See, e.g., Anon., *Remarks upon the Lord Bishop of Cork's Second Part of Drinking in Remembrance of the Dead by a Country Curate* (Dublin, 1715), 23–7; Anon, *Alectruonophonia: Or, The controversy about drinking to the memory of the dead, impartially consider'd* (1716); see also Richard Steele's objections in *The Englishman* (28 January 1714), No. 50.

129 Browne, *Discourse*, 34, 51–2, 94–6, 211; Browne, *Of Drinking* (1713), 3, 18–19, 36; Browne, *Second Part*, 60–1. Morton, *Great Evil*, xiii-iv also aimed to deter clerics from 'conformity' with healthing.

Figure 7. 'Rolleston Tankard'. Image Courtesy of Dr Julian Ellis, O.B.E., Church Warden, Holy Trinity Church, Rolleston, Nottinghamshire.

is offered by a recently discovered seventeenth-century, pewter communion-tankard, highly decorated with youthful images of Charles II and his (Catholic) Queen Catherine of Braganza (Figure 7).[130] The maker's marks suggest it was commissioned as an unambiguous declaration of loyalty in the 1680s. Large enough to hold a wine quart, the date of its donation is unknown, but it was used for parish Communion in Rolleston, Nottinghamshire until the 1760s.[131] In church, the 'Rolleston Tankard' promoted communal 'caritas' and tested conformity to state and religion, through its unambiguously loyal decoration and its function in bringing the Communion wine to be verbally consecrated and shared at the altar. In taverns, and homes too, objects like the Rolleston tankard enabled the promotion of loving hospitality alongside the testing of loyalty to state and

130 Image Courtesy of Julian Ellis, Church Warden, Holy Trinity Church, Rolleston, Nottingham.

131 See parish website http://www.rollestonchurch.org.uk/pewter.html, which includes article from *Journal of the Pewter Society* (Spring, 2012).

Church, through loyal-healthing rituals. A ballad verse, taken from a theatre song by Thomas Shadwell and extended to ballad length by a Whig hack for use in loyal-health drinking rituals, summed up the symbiotic importance of intoxication and Christian 'caritas' in the ritual politics of early modern England:

> Love and Wine are the bonds that fasten us all
> The world but for this to confusion would fall
> Were it not for the pleasures of love and good wine
> Man-kind for each trifle their lives would resign
> they'd not value dull life, or would live without thinking
> Nor Kings rule the world but for love and good drinking.[132]

This article has argued that seventeenth-century England saw a slippage take place between sacred and secular drinking that came about through the interplay of ritual words, gestures, alcohol, and objects, with political and religious division. It proposes that the effect, over time, was to embed a notion that to qualify as a socialized subject, a willingness to drink alcohol was crucial. Although the social and moral acceptability of sobriety is probably at its greatest height today, and loyal-healthing, though still in use, has become a relic of older times and mores, the refusal to drink alcohol in company can still elicit a suspicious response. This suggests that these long-embedded traits have remained fundamental to the cultural baggage of British drinking practices through to the modern day; perhaps explaining how, in contemporary Britain, 'Bremner, Bird, and Fortune' can still get a laugh out of a seventeenth-century joke.

[132] *The Delights of the Bottle* (4 edns: 1675, 1678), *PBB* 489.

Wine, Corruption, and the Politics of Intoxication in Eighteenth-Century Stockholm

Karin Sennefelt

The first decree regulating the meetings of the Swedish diet, from 1582, had to do not with the order of sessions or regulation of membership but with intoxication. It stipulated that members of the diet were not to drink so much when at the diet that they then got into fights with the city guards.[1] This type of regulation is symptomatic of political culture in early modern Sweden. Alcohol and politics were intimately connected in debates, economy, and sociability.

Meetings of the four-estate diet occurred with increased regularity in the eighteenth century, bringing men from all over the realm to one place for months at a time. Often they had time, and sometimes money to spend. Certainly they needed to forge alliances and enforce loyalties. Political sociability in eighteenth-century Stockholm involved navigating an array of vices and corruption. The meetings of the diet drew around a thousand members to the city. The estates included representatives of the nobility, clergy, and burghers of the realm, but also representatives of the large portion of the peasantry who were freeholders. Following the fall of absolutism at the end of the Great Northern War (1721), the Swedish diet not only established power over war and peace, taxation and occasionally judicial power; it also fixed a permanent meeting place in Stockholm with a sociable world around it. Political sociability had been scarce and clandestine during the autocracy of Charles XII. His death in late 1718, and the establishment of parliamentary rule thereafter, saw political sociability move into coffeehouses, wineshops, and taverns as politicians from all over the realm gathered in the city. It was here that members of the diet, together with many others, drank, mobilized support for votes, and demonstrated their political aptitude as honest, Swedish men in toasts, songs, and verse.[2]

[1] Johan Holm, *Konstruktionen av en stormakt: Kungamakt, skattebönder och statsbildning 1595–1640* (Stockholm, 2007), 185.

[2] Lennart Thanner, *Revolutionen i Sverige efter Karl XII:s död. Den inrikespolitiska maktkampen under tidigare delen av Ulrika Eleonora d.y:s regering* (Uppsala, 1953);

 © The Past and Present Society

Political sociability, involving large sums of money from the purses of rival factions and foreign ambassadors, has been seen as a sign of the inherent corruption of Sweden's so-called Age of Liberty. Foreign influence on politics, the lack of political principle, an unprecedented cynicism, and the privileging of faction over fatherland have been taken to be emblematic of rule by the estates. Viewed in these somewhat moralistic terms, sociability has until recently been treated merely as the means of establishing the political sympathies of individual politicians. More recent research has emphasized how elites used social exchange and personal relations—not least sociability, entertaining, and drink—to uphold their political positions.[3] Drinking culture, on the other hand, has a historiography in Sweden largely separated from politics. Instead, festive traditions and rituals have been outlined but often without any discussion about their social significance in historical context.[4] The implications of intoxication and intoxicating substances, both political and bodily, therefore remain to be explored.

While this chapter recognizes that eighteenth-century political sociability was characterized by corruption, it argues that corruption must be understood in historical context rather than evaluated according to modern norms of political independence and individuality. In particular, corruption in eighteenth-century Sweden must be considered in relation to the human body, the social order, and tensions between old and new luxuries. What follows suggests that the corruptive aspects of politics converged in one transformative beverage: wine. The chapter accordingly examines the role of wine, and its intoxicating effects, in political sociability. It discusses the benefits and risks of drinking in a strictly hierarchical society and how wine could transform social relationships, create alternative equalities, alter the bodies and status of men, and endanger the welfare of the fatherland.

Karin Sennefelt, 'Social and Political Thresholds in Stockholm, *c.*1720–1770', *Urban History*, xxxv (2008), 187–8.

[3] Ingemar Carlsson, *Parti – partiväsen – partipolitiker. Kring uppkomsten av våra första politiska* partier (Stockholm, 1981); Patrik Winton, *Frihetstidens politiska praktik. Nätverk och offentlighet 1746–66* (Uppsala, 2006), 315–16. For a moralistic historiography on political sociability see, e.g., Michael Roberts, *The Age of Liberty: Sweden 1719–1772* (Cambridge, 1986); Michael F. Metcalf, 'The First 'Modern' Party System? Political Parties, Sweden's Age of Liberty, and the Historians', *Scandinavian Journal of History*, ii (1977).

[4] See, e.g., Christina Mattsson, *Från helan till lilla manasse. Den svenska snapsvisans historia* (Stockholm, 2002).

I

Swedish male politicians are often described as forming 'teams' or 'companies' (*lag*) in eighteenth-century Stockholm. Members of the diet had specific 'companies' that they dined with daily (*matlag*); suffering affronts in company was much worse than in private settings.[5] The term *lag* therefore connoted a very specific group of people which was simultaneously closed to outsiders and in which actions, though enclosed, were nevertheless public. Regardless of social standing, sociability was built on creating this type of company. These were more or less temporary groupings with shared views on appropriate behaviour in given situations. Forming these ties of loyalty was an essential facet of male sociability throughout the early modern period and its importance did not diminish because new ideals of sociability began to influence the higher orders.[6] Political sociability can therefore not easily be divided into either 'elite', 'popular', or indeed 'polite', because this was a meeting ground between the representatives of the four estates and others. In eighteenth-century political sociability the creation of loyalty was the utmost goal. Drinking was central to these 'companies' of comrades from the same estate, establishing allegiance to a patron or forming commitment to a particular issue among members of different estates.

Dining or drinking entailed accepting social allegiances that could be used for political purposes. These occasions enforced the social rule that every gift, while apparently free, carried obligations. A favour must be returned and a drink reciprocated for the giver and recipient to remain equals. If not, hierarchy and allegiance was established. For those without opportunity or funds, an alternative to buying drinks and proposing toasts was political favours. It is this which encouraged historians to view eighteenth-century Swedish politics as especially corrupt. However, political entertaining was not new to the parliamentary epoch; nor did it disappear when royal autocracy was restored in 1772. Attempts at 'bribery' were a regular feature of sociability; favours and bonds of loyalty were the point of political sociability for mature, responsible men. To stand aloof from such practices was to disassociate from that collective, and the few politicians who attempted it were derided accordingly.

[5] Äldre kommittéer, nr 57, Kommissorialrätten om riksdagsmannen Nils Persson för utlåtelser mot arvprinsen, 22 April 1747, Riksarkivet, Stockholm (hereafter ÄK 57), 4 Aug. 1747, fol. 214; *Prästeståndets riksdagsprotokoll*, 24 vols (Stockholm, 1921–2011), x, 1740–1741, 18 Aug. 1741, 393.

[6] B. Ann Tlusty, *Bacchus and the Civic Order: The Culture of Drink in Early Modern Germany* (Charlottesville and London, 2001); Alexandra Shepard, *Meanings of Manhood in Early Modern England* (Oxford, 2003), 4–5; Phil Withington 'Company and Sociability in Early Modern England', *Social History*, xxxii (2007), 295, 297, 304–7.

Independence was a sign of dishonour rather than honour. As one contemporary put it, a politician must both be free and bound: he was freed by the Instrument of Government and bound by social commitments. Contemporaries did not perceive the political system to be corrupted by gift-giving but by those who did not return favours, give promises, or submit to the host.[7]

When men drank together feelings of submission and patronage flowed with the wine. Sociability transformed men who took part in company. A peasant entering a wineshop with the help of a patron became a client, even though it might only be for one evening.[8] The role of client meant that he must fulfil a set of obligations that mirrored those that his patron had accepted by taking him under his wing. By taking on roles as clients and patrons, responsible masculinity was confirmed. It created a man who knew his place in society and performed his role correctly in relation to other men and in relation to patriarchal norms. The contract created political masters and subordinates out of previously unrelated people and these associations came with expectations of fulfilling a range of political duties.

This ideology was clearly reflected in drinking practices at the diet where a patron treated a company or prospective clients. A patron could either secure a private room at a wineshop or treat members of the diet in his own home or temporary lodgings in Stockholm. The host did not always take part in the actual drinking himself. Instead he could turn up during the party, make a little speech about how pleased he was to be treating everyone to drinks, perhaps pass some money around, leave and pay the bill later. This type of entertaining emulated the strict formality of a royal audience of the seventeenth century more than eighteenth-century civil society, which encouraged social heterogeneity, politeness, and conviviality. Accordingly, guests were usually socially homogeneous. At one occasion in 1734, the royal councillor Carl Gyllenborg treated representatives of the three non-noble estates

[7] V 7, Uppsala University Library (hereafter UUB), unpaginated; Johan Arckenholtz, *Sagu-Brott af 1734 Års Riksdag i Stockholm*, ed. Ingemar Carlsson (Stockhom, 2003), 102–3; Riksdagens kommissioner, kommissionen över Christopher Springer, R 5643, Riksarkivet, Stockholm (hereafter R 5643), 24 April 1747, fols 237, 240–1; Gustaf Fredrik Gyllenborg, *Mitt lefverne 1731–1775. Självbiografiska anteckningar af Gustaf Fredrik Gyllenborg* (Stockholm 1885), 60–1; Clas Julius Ekeblads journal, I:e 14:1–3, 36, Vf 68:3, 29–30, Kungliga biblioteket (hereafter KB), Stockholm. On the principles of gift giving and reciprocating, see Marcel Mauss, *The Gift*, trans. W. D. Wells (Abingdon, 2005).

[8] For patron–client relationships in Swedish science and politics, see Hjalmar Fors, *Mutual Favours: The Social and Scientific Practice of Eighteenth-Century Swedish Chemistry* (Uppsala, 2003) and Winton, *Frihetstidens politiska praktik.*

to parties. But whereas the clergy and burghers were invited to Gyllenborg's home, the peasants were invited to the outskirts of town where the councillor's brother made an appearance. All the way down to the peasant estate, internal hierarchy within the estate was also important to uphold. When the object was to create a specific allegiance in a particular political cause, separate rooms were used for separate estates, even within the same wineshop. As the century wore on, social hierarchy became easier to transgress in political sociability. By the 1750s, men from all four estates patronized both coffeehouses and wineshops. Then, certain public houses had obtained reputations for being gathering places for supporters of the two political parties, the Caps or the Hats, or for being the haunts of those with other political persuasions, such as royalists. Hierarchies nevertheless remained. It was still noteworthy to a young nobleman in 1769 that a group 'of all sorts and estates, like on Noah's ark' met at the home of the noble government official Skiöldebrand.[9]

Companies not only organized in formalistic courtly fashion in order to form patron-client relationships, however. Within companies ostensible equality was celebrated by drinkers and hosts. Loyalties among drinkers, not only to superiors or hosts, were equally important, and this was created through toasting and singing. Drinking in excess was in this case not necessarily a problem; camaraderie correlated with levels of inebriation. Even though intoxication was associated with uninformed political discourse, it did not follow that intoxication as a mode of political sociability was condemned. Intoxication was an accepted manner of behaviour, both in company and on the streets. The key issue was controlling the effects of the intoxicant. Swedish men were often inebriated. Well into the eighteenth century intoxication was an extenuating circumstance in criminal cases, and the first law against inebriation, in 1733, indicated that only observable intoxication equated with drunkenness. Violation risked a fine, doubled for the nobility and 'non-nobles of high standing'.[10] This was because the higher

[9] Arckenholtz, *Sagu-Brott*, 127; Johan Gabriel Oxenstierna, *Dagboks-anteckningar af Johan Gabriel Oxenstierna åren 1769–1771*, ed. Gustaf Stjernström (Uppsala, 1881), 7 March 1769, 11; Jacques Revel, 'The Uses of Civility', in Philippe Ariès, Georges Duby, and Roger Chartier (eds), *A History of Private Life*, 3 vols, iii, *Passions of the Renaissance* (Cambridge Mass. and London, 1989), 184, 190–205; Karin Sennefelt, *Politikens hjärta. Medborgarskap, manlighet och plats i frihetstidens Stockholm* (Stockholm, 2011), 180–97. Hanna Enefalk incorrectly assumes that homosocial drinking only emerged in Sweden around 1800, see 'En gustaviansk brygd: dryckesvanor och genus i högreståndskretsar ca 1772–1809', *Historisk tidskrift*, cxxx (2011), 741–2.

[10] 'Förordning emot Swalg och Dryckenskap', 17 Apr. 1733, *Utdrag utur alle ifrån [. . .] års slut utkomne Publique Handlingar, Placater, Förordningar, Resolutioner och Publicationer*, 15 vols *(Stockholm, 1746)*, ii, 998; Christer Ahlberger, *Konsumtionsrevolutionen. Om det*

social orders were expected to have greater self-control—a capacity for masculine self-discipline which also equated with maturity.[11]

Among the loyalties most celebrated among drinkers were brotherhood and love of fatherland. Toasts were introduced as 'brother's toasts' (*brorskål*) or 'cousin's toasts' (*kusinskål*) which dissolved any hierarchy among the drinkers and made them brothers or cousins who could dispense with titles. Noble drinkers from the provinces Skåne and Finland drank a 'cousin's toast' to underscore their common condition as living on the borders of the realm. When Axel Reuterholm, a young nobleman, entered the wineshop Kastenhof in November 1738, he was greeted by a group of eleven other noblemen. Eight of them offered him a 'brother's toast', which he accepted. The drinkers treated him to drink, kissed his cheeks and proposed a toast to his father, engaging him as an equal within that select company. Charged with treason a burgher from the city of Stockholm, Christoffer Springer, denied having drunk a 'brother's toast' in 1747 with Alexander Blackwell, the king's former physician currently on trial for attempting to overthrow the royal succession. He did concede, however, that 'you can have many brothers, and when someone calls you brother you must address them in the same manner'. Reciprocity was just as important a component of equality as it was in establishing social hierarchy.[12]

Drinking parties celebrated political virtues that underscored citizenship. Patriotism was not only propagated in political debates, but also in sociability, especially in songs and toasts to different political entities such as the king, the diet, and the four estates. Drinkers, by singing, became equals in their shared passion for the realm and its government. Loyalty to the royal family was enacted in kneeling down and recounting their names before emptying glasses. In the eighteenth-century songs to Bacchus and the camaraderie of drinking were superseded in political sociability by songs and verses that celebrated the political order under parliamentary rule. Songs and verses

---

moderna konsumtionssamhällets framväxt 1750–1900 (Göteborg, 1996), 26–7; Niklas Ericsson, *Den törstiges val. Dryckernas svenska historia* (Stockholm 2003), 21; Beat Kümin, 'Drinking and Public Space in Early Modern German Lands', *Contemporary Drug Problems*, xxxii (2005), 13.

[11] Lyndal Roper, *Oedipus and the Devil: Witchcraft, Sexuality and Religion in Early Modern Europe* (London, 1994), 108, 111, 119; Philip Carter, *Men and the Emergence of Polite Society, Britain 1660–1800* (Harlow, 2001), 83 and note; Shepard, *Meanings of Manhood*, 26, 28.

[12] Arckenholtz, *Sagu-Brott*, 106–7; Axel Reuterholm, *Axel Reuterholms dagboksanteckningar under riksdagen i Stockholm 1738–39*, ed. Göran Nilzén (Stockholm, 2006), 21 Nov. 1738, 182–3; R 5643, 11 April 1747, fol. 171.

dwelt on the ideological foundations of the constitution and its balance of freedom and sovereignty. Others described the traditional social roles of the estates: warfare and nobility, clergy and learning, burghers and trade, and the peasantry's labour. Songs also idealized personal attributes and claimed manly virtues like patriotism, bravery, reason, and incorruptibility. Equality as self-defined citizens was imagined, if not achieved.[13]

II

Within company drunkenness, as opposed to light intoxication, presented an array of complexities. Though losing control in many cases was degrading, hearty drunkenness was an important part of a man's social life and hard drinking a rite of passage into mature manhood. Swedish drinking songs of the early modern period were part of a European Bacchanalian tradition, celebrating drunkenness in its riotous, boisterous forms, but also recorded the repentant remorse that followed festivities. As far as we can tell, this also reflects how drunkenness was experienced by the social elites at the time. Great intoxication among male drinkers was a measure of the success of a social occasion expressed in metaphors of having willingly surrendered to Bacchus. Women also drank and took part in toasting and singing, but did not succumb to drunkenness to the same degree.[14] When hosts, toasts, and songs encouraged excessive consumption, striking the balance between degrading and polite behaviour was not an easy task.

Intoxication made men seem young and irresponsible, with consequences for those interested in cultivating political competency. The discourse of moderation that was propagated in conduct literature was not without its contradictions.[15] In early modern Europe in general, young men were at once expected to live in excess—drink too much, eat too much, feel too much, fight

[13] Vs 52 II, 4, 7–8, 140, 146, Vs 169 (unpaginated), KB; F 376, (unpaginated), N 1139, fols 154–5, 164–8, UUB; *Nya Små-Saker Til Nöje och Tidsfördrif*, 1 (Stockholm, 1768), 27; Per Hanselli, *Ur en samlares papper*, 2 (Uppsala, 1869), 3–5. For toasts and songs, see Karin Sennefelt, 'Masculinity, Sociability, and Citizenship in Stockholm in the Age of Liberty', in Michael Bregnsbo, Pasi Ihalainen, Karin Sennefelt, and Patrik Winton (eds), *Scandinavia in the Age of Revolutions: Nordic Political Cultures, 1740–1820* (Farnham, 2011).

[14] See, e.g., Torkel Stålmarck, *Bellman i verkligheten* (Stockholm, 2000), 31–4; Lucidor, *Samlade dikter. Texten*, 2 vols (Stockholm, 1914) i; Enefalk, 'En gustaviansk brygd', 737; Alexander Engström, 'Bacchus and the Social Order: Noble Drinking Culture and the Making of Identity in Early Modern Sweden' (Uppsala University Master's thesis, 2013).

[15] See Jennifer Richards, 'Health, Intoxication, and Civil Conversation in Renaissance England', this volume, 168–86.

too much, lust too much—and were scorned for doing so. Honour and respectability, both crucial components of political capability, diminished accordingly. In Sweden, intoxication was attractive to all men as a disassociation from patriarchal norms. Older, married men might very well take part in excessive drinking now and again and sought status in the same way as other men did in the camaraderie of excess.[16] When Carl Linnaeus, who was working as a physician in Stockholm in the 1730s, commented on the consequences of drinking he referred to the stages of manhood. In his description, an older man, a lover of Bacchus took one step backwards on the age-ladder for every glass. He became a man, a youth, a boy, and finally, a babbling baby. In the end, the company had all regressed into animals, their humanity gone.[17]

Tensions between the social significance of drink and its degrading effects were evident in diet debates, especially among the peasant estate. Drunkenness was unacceptable at political sessions or in public as it reflected particularly badly on the lowest estate. To gain respect among the higher estates members of the peasantry sought to break their stereotypical association with beastly rusticity, to defy the contempt of their superiors, and to pose as figures of modest respectability and restraint. Often regarded as the direct opposites of the ideal *l'hônnete homme*, peasants' social behaviour needed to stay within these strict boundaries in order for them to be regarded as political subjects.[18] Intoxication might damage the peasantry's political legitimacy; but it was also an age-old tactic to avoid political responsibility. By claiming to have been intoxicated, peasants could get away with criticisms of the constitution and government which otherwise could engender harsh

[16] Lars Magnusson, 'En bråkig kultur – Socialt drickande i Eskilstuna före industrialiseringen', in Anders Gustavsson (ed.), *Alkohol och nykterhet. Aktuell forskning i Norden presenterad vid ett symposium i Uppsala*, (Uppsala, 1989), 29–34; Roper, *Oedipus and the Devil*, 110–13, 119, 153; Shepard, *Meanings of Manhood*, 67, 84, 94, 101, 103, 105–6, 111, 211, 248; David Tjeder, *The Power of Character: Middle-Class Masculinities, 1800–1900* (Stockholm, 2003), 77, 82–3, 104–11; Andreas Marklund, *I hans hus. Svensk manlighet i historisk belysning* (Umeå, 2004), 283.

[17] Elis Malmeström, *Carl von Linné: Geniets kamp för klarhet* (Stockholm, 1964), 239; Carl Gyllenborg, *Swenska Sprätthöken. Comédie uti 5 Acter*, Stockholm 1740, Svenska litteratursällskapets klassikerutgåvor (Uppsala, 1959), 22, 74.

[18] Peter Englund, *Det hotade huset. Adliga föreställningar om samhället under stormaktstiden* (Stockholm, 1989), 92–101, 196–200; Anders Claréus, 'Primitiva bönder? Något om allmogens syn på statsmakt, politik och nation under 1700-talet', in Åsa Karlsson and Bo Lindberg (eds), *Nationalism och nationell identitet i 1700-talets Sverige* (Uppsala, 2002); Peter Henningsen, *I sansernes vold. Bondekultur og kultursammenstød i enevældens Danmark*, 2 vols (København, 2006) ii, 557–68, 580–4.

punishment. This was the case in 1723, when a peasant member of a diet commission investigating crimes against the Instrument of Government refused to swear an oath on the very document he was meant to uphold. The peasant, Olof Larsson, claimed the Instrument of Government needed improvement and the powers of the king increased. On being investigated for treason he revoked his words, claiming drunkenness—an argument acceptable to the commission. Hereby he escaped execution or life imprisonment and was merely sent home.[19] More normally, however, staying not drunk (if not sober) was crucial for preserving the honour of the estate and the peasantry's bargaining power at the diet. Yet the pressures of political sociability made it difficult to refuse a drink. One former speaker of the peasant estate defended his drunkenness at an estate meeting in 1723 by saying that he had been visited by comrades from his home parish and they had treated him to so much sociability that he could not remember what he said during the meeting or anything else that happened that day.[20]

The accentuated caution of the peasant estate was not misplaced. At the diet of 1727 the queen invited all four estates to a dinner at her summer palace outside Stockholm. Because logistically it was impossible for all 1000 or so members to attend, the estates were required to send small delegations. The peasant estate was allotted thirteen seats. However, some of the excluded peasant members went anyway. The extra guests were accommodated and seated at dinner. Eskil Kilium, a Finnish member and one of the gate-crashers, had only ever drunk wine at Communion and now became excessively intoxicated, falling over in the dining room and requiring servants to help him. The other members of the peasantry were deeply embarrassed. On the boat carrying him back to Stockholm Kilium died, either of alcohol poisoning or suffocation. His behaviour at a formal dinner, in front of the queen and the higher estates, precipitated debate within the peasant estate which led to a request to the speaker of the nobility for advice on regulating behaviour.[21]

A similar affair was discussed by the clergy, but was treated rather differently. Only days after arriving at the diet superintendent Johannes Esberg was seen staggering along the streets and, at one point, losing consciousness. Initially, the estate planned to silence the matter, perhaps only warning

[19] See, e.g., Riksdagens kommissioner, kommissionen över stämplingar mot regeringsformen, R 5615, Riksarkivet, Stockholm (hereafter R 5615), 10, 13 May 1723, fols 8–9, 12–13, 49–50.

[20] *Bondeståndets riksdagsprotokoll*, 13 vols, (Stockholm, 1939–86), i, 1720–1727, 16 Feb. 1723, 24 Sept. 1726, 115, 357, ii, 1731–1734, 28 May 1731, 7 Jun., 10 Aug. 1734, 293, 305, 392–3.

[21] *Bondeståndets riksdagsprotokoll*, i, 8 Jun. 1727, 617–20.

him for his behaviour. But soon there were rumours against the whole estate in town and it was decided Esberg should suffer the full force of the Church Law. He was suspended from his post and ejected from the estate meetings. Esberg did not seem to take full responsibility for his actions, stating early on that he had been drinking '*aqvam vitae* (it should be called *mortis*)' in order to cure a tooth ache but had been overcome by fainting, although reports from his diocese indicated problems with drink over a long time. He promised never to touch aquavit again. After a lengthy apology in Latin to the estate, he was reinstated as superintendent and member of the clergy. The estate explicitly discussed the issue as a question of their corporate honour. Esberg was completely shunned so that his disgrace would not rub off on the estate; his full repentance meant he could be shown mercy. The clergy did not defer to a higher authority as the peasantry had done.[22]

That the peasantry and clergy investigated and discussed the drunkenness of their members did not mean they had a greater propensity toward heavy drinking. Rather the peasant estate in particular had much to lose from the failure of its members to maintain a trustworthy and mature façade in front of the other estates and the wider Stockholm public. Strong behavioural controls therefore became a necessity, especially because many peasant members were unaccustomed to the urban, polite, and manly sociability that confronted them in town.

The nobility, the highest estate, did not seem to have the same concerns.[23] The higher orders lost in social status among their peers as they drank excessively. Young noblemen, influenced by ideals of *l'hônnete homme* criticized their peers for immoderate drinking. Claes Julius Ekeblad commented that noble officers who were members of the diet became 'lackeys and rabble' when they were treated to drink at the palace at Karlberg. At political clubs and wineshops, noblemen were reduced to a 'blind mob', according to noble observer Johan Gabriel Oxenstierna. Noblemen too, according to their peers, could be reduced to fools comparable to the masses.[24] The estate had greater expectations of self-control, but their control and status was something only their peers should judge. Whereas the peasant estate was quick to apologize

[22] *Prästeståndets riksdagsprotokoll*, 24 vols (Stockholm, 1921–2011), vi, 26, 29 March, 24, 27 April, 6, 11, 15 May, 18, 19, 21 June, 9 July 1723, 81, 84, 104–5, 116, 122–3, 130, 141, 191–2, 196–7, 200, 227, appendices 4, 5, 7, 10, 13, 464–5, 467–8, 471–2, 477–8. The clergy did refer the matter to the royal council, but this was to confirm Esberg's suspension from his post which according to the Church Law of 1686 must be done by the King in Council.

[23] See also Elizabeth A. Foyster, *Manhood in Early Modern England: Honour, Sex, and Marriage* (London, 1999), 121.

[24] Ekeblads journal, 21 Feb. 1761, 21; Oxenstierna, *Dagboks-anteckningar*, 3 Nov. 1769, 58.

for Kilium and the inebriated transgressions of others, and the clergy sought to distance itself from Esberg, the nobility defended a member who was found lying in a snowdrift in a stupor in 1741. City guards brought the nobleman to their quarters, where he proceeded to offend both them and the county governor. This nobleman was shielded by the noble estate on the grounds of his noble status, which made him immune from all criticism by those below him on the social scale. According to the nobility, any 'honest member of the diet' could happen to find himself in the same circumstances. His insults at the noble county governor, on the other hand, led to censure from his own estate. Casting judgement on intoxication was a prerogative based on social hierarchy.[25]

Older, married, high-status men took part in drinking regularly, and were transformed by the same means as younger men, in the camaraderie of excess. Sociability and company served as a site for transformation when men were intoxicated. Drunkenness temporarily altered a man's status, not only from a mature man into a young man, or indeed a child, but also his social status: he could move from nobleman to rabble in the matter of an evening (and back again in the course of the following day). For members of the peasantry, in contrast, the imperative was to avoid public drunkenness in order to uphold their social and political status.

III

The social importance and concurrent dangers of intoxication made for a complex political sociability in eighteenth-century Sweden. In the meantime, intoxicating beverages and the corruptive aspects of their consumption also figured as political questions. That certain drinks had specific connotations was not new. In Sweden in the eighteenth century, these connotations were reinforced by economic doctrine and political alliances.

As part of sumptuary legislation, coffee imports were stopped and consumption forbidden in Sweden in 1756–61 and 1766–69, although, as in many countries, sumptuary laws were ignored and smuggling increased. The fact that legislators banned coffee was at once a sign that this 'new luxury' was a morally and medicinally problematic product and that imports impaired Sweden's foreign trade. This view was related to the steep increase in coffee consumption in the eighteenth century, especially from the 1760s onwards.[26]

[25] Stockholms slottsrätt, protokoll, Stockholm City Archives, 16 Jan.–3 Feb., 11 Jul. 1741; see also, *Sveriges ridderskaps och adels riksdags-protokoll från och med år 1719*, 32 vols (Stockholm 1875–1982) xii, 1741–1742, 7, 12, 26 Jan. 1741, 62–7, 70, 75, 90–8.

[26] Leos Müller, 'Kolonialprodukter i Sveriges handel och konsumtionskultur', *Historisk tidskrift*, cxxiii (2004), 236–7, 241.

When a new product became popular it accrued transformative properties. The goods must be placed within a system of social codes in order to become understandable. Old luxuries, according to Jan de Vries, functioned as markers of discrimination, as distinguishers of social difference, and were reserved for the privileged few who did not have to answer to social strictures. Colonial goods formed the newer luxuries that communicated other types of meaning. They invited reciprocal relations in consumption and through commercialization and homogenization. New luxuries fostered good taste and behaviour, which anyone could display. Consuming these wares was a way, almost, of personally promoting virtue in a society.[27] This dichotomy of old and new luxuries is complicated when we consider that imports all arrived to markets conditioned by corporate order. In a society where equality in sociability largely was illusory, luxuries, whether we term them old or new, could take on and change meanings. What followed were debates on the minutiae of consumption and its social implications.

In addition to coffee, products that were discussed as unnecessary foreign wares were tea, chocolate, snuff, hair powder, and various types of wine. While some products, like coffee, were banned for short periods of time, legislators also took pains to set tax rates on particular products. These taxes were determined according to whether or not the product was domestic or imported and the presumed social status of the consumer. Assumptions about taste and behaviour also played an important part in defining who might consume new luxuries. Luxury consumption might be defined as excessive consumption, as in the case of aquavit. Or commodities were equated with types of behaviour which could not be expected among the majority of people. A member of the burgher estate acknowledged the importance of acquiring both taste and correct behaviour when he noted that most ordinary people had never seen coffee, tea, or chocolate and were even less likely to 'have the ability to use these kinds of beverages'. However diligent legislators in the diet were in setting tax rates and determining who might consume what according to social status, they could never expect sumptuary laws to be adhered to in practice. As one member of the clergy stated before the ban on coffee, 'human's taste and habits will not be tamed by law'.[28] Sumptuary legislation reflected an idealized social hierarchy in reaction to changing consumption patterns. It was not a social reality.

[27] Jan de Vries, *The Industrious Revolution: Consumer Behaviour and Household Economy, 1650 to the Present* (Cambridge, 2008), 44–6.

[28] See, e.g., 'Extract af Collegie Cleri Conitialis protocoll d. 20 Maji 1720', 'Ödmiukt Memorial från bondeståndet', Riksdagen 1720, utskottshandlingar, '1720 års akter', R 2393, Riksarkivet, fols 996–9, Stockholm; *Borgarståndets riksdagsprotokoll*, 10 vols (Stockholm 1945–2008), ii, 1723, 17 Sept. 1723, 402, v, 25 Oct. 1734, 202–4, x, 15

The distinction between old and new luxuries reads as irrelevant in this case. What was important was what transformative properties a specific ware had on a specific social group, and these connections were not simply determined by how long a commodity had been imported. Crucially, it was not peasant participation in the consumption of new luxuries that became a political issue. Instead, peasants were brought to trial for consuming one of the long-standing old luxuries—wine—and for doing so in a manner that promoted patron–client relationships. Coffee and tea drinking were part of a distinctly urban consumption pattern in eighteenth-century Sweden in which members of the peasantry nevertheless participated. If members of the peasant estate did overstep the corporate boundaries of appropriate consumption when it came to tea and coffee, this was not subject to any particular disapproval. They could consume these new luxuries in drink and sociability without challenging the social hierarchy. The middling orders, on the other hand, the many young bureaucrats and non-noble officers also present in the city during diet meetings, were censured in a manner reminiscent of other European coffee drinkers. Their presence at coffeehouses was criticized for creating effeminate, politically uninformed busybodies and this behaviour was put in stark contrast to the honourable masculinity displayed by officers taking part in Sweden's wars.[29] The transformative properties of these different luxuries, then, were not the same for all commoners and it seems as though censure of consumption was based in two different world views—one corporate and hierarchical, and one based in civil society and a culture of politeness. Both paradigms defined appropriate consumption along social lines.

Wine had increased greatly in popularity in Sweden in the seventeenth century, due in part to the post-Reformation demand for Communion wine. Initially this was not a drink exclusively for the elites. In the seventeenth century, local court records from Stockholm show that crimes committed by intoxicated burghers, guards, and soldiers were equally reported to have happened after drinking wine or beer. By the eighteenth century aquavit had established its prominence among the lower orders: new techniques for distilling aquavit from domestic grain, and later potatoes, led to a great increase in consumption at the expense of beer. A low alcoholic malt beverage called *svagdricka* (literally weak drink) complemented aquavit at mealtimes.

Feb., 20 May, 9 June 1752, 132–3, 220, 296; *Prästeståndets riksdagsprotokoll*, 24 vols (Stockholm, 1921–2011), viii, 29 Nov. 1734, 320, xiii, 1751–1752, 18 Feb., 7 April, 7, 18, 25 May 1752, 164, 212–13, 247, 259, 287.

[29] Sennefelt, *Politikens hjärta*, 140–1, 167–76.

Simultaneously, in the early eighteenth century sumptuary laws reserved the drinking of wine to the social elites.[30] Alcoholic beverages took on new meanings as social markers in the eighteenth century. And there were many arguments to support this division.

Both aquavit and wine became highly politicized drinks, but for different reasons. Throughout the eighteenth century the peasant estate fought to keep the right to distil aquavit for household consumption. Aquavit was important for a range of reasons, besides its intoxicating properties. Members of the peasantry argued for its importance for both agriculture and in raising cattle (cattle was fed the by-products from distilling during winter). Also, peasants argued as employers that aquavit was essential in order to attract skilled help to their farms. The diet prohibited home distilling in 1740–41, 1756–60 and in 1772. This was during periods of domestic grain shortage and did not result in any protests from the peasantry. The household heads who acted as representatives of the peasant estate were just as eager not to let grain go to waste in times of scarcity, and could very well sell their own grain at higher prices without refining it into aquavit. Simultaneously, however, the Crown was interested in taking over distilling and the revenues connected to its sales, and prohibited home distilling late in the century, a measure that was later revoked.[31] The peasant estate's high political profile in the issue of distilling branded the consumption of aquavit as distinctly provincial and low-class.

Wine functioned as a social contrast to aquavit. It was considered refined and held significant status. Social norms, codified in an active and constantly varying sumptuary legislation and in diet and pamphlet debates, deemed wine a commodity—like silk shawls and marzipan—that was inappropriate for the peasantry. This does not mean, however, that members of the peasantry did not consume these wares. Rather, the need for sumptuary laws and luxury debates can be seen as attempts enforce what was invented as old and established social values: attempts to counteract the slow dissolution of corporate society and its gendered norms.[32] Another reason to oppose wine consumption among the lower orders was patriotic. Some wines, according to both the estates and pamphleteers, were more necessary to a society than others and it would be best to restrict the imports of some of these wines. In a report on 'foreign beverages' in 1727, a diet commission concluded that wines

[30] Ericsson, *Den töstiges val*, 25, 71, 97–100, 129, 143, 146–9.

[31] Kalle Bäck, *Bondeopposition och bondeinflytande under frihetstiden: Centralmakten och östgötaböndernas reaktioner i näringspolitiska frågor* (Stockholm, 1984), 174–83.

[32] Karin Hassan Jansson, 'When Sweden Harboured Idlers: Gender and Luxury in Public Debates, *c.*1760–1830', in Göran Rydén (ed.), *Sweden in the Eighteenth-Century World: Provincial Cosmopolitans* (Farnham, 2013).

were the drinks that were most detrimental to domestic economy. The committee defined some wines 'necessary' and others 'dispensable'. Necessary wines were those that had been imported for a long time: Rhineland wines, moselle, 'ordinary' French white and Spanish and Portugese red wines. Dispensable wines were Hungarian, Italian, or champagne and burgundy or other types of wine and liqueurs imported in bottles.[33] As in discussions on coffee and tea, medicinal, moral, and mercantile arguments against consumption converged. Carl Linnaeus and a member of the peasant estate both shared the opinion that the consumption of wine brought disease to Swedish men, such as gout and digestive disorders.[34] And in line with mercantilist policies promoting the production of luxury goods within the realm, the diet supported experiments in making Swedish wine out of berries and fruit, although this venture never was successful.[35]

Sumptuary laws made incursions into people's everyday lives in ways that were not motivated by trade balance. Rather, the most important reason for laws against what was called 'luxuriance and superfluity', to be reinforced time after time in the eighteenth century, was to alter consumption and lifestyle. Luxury products created pride, wantonness, and un-Swedishness according to debaters and politicians. Perhaps most detrimental of all, they disrupted social order. Political commentators discussed how two members of the burgher estate were treated to a glass wine and a pipe of tobacco in the home of a noble councillor in 1734. The goods connoted the breakdown of traditional boundaries: the burghers risking illusions of grandeur, the councillor sinking to their level.[36] As the philosopher and theologian Daniel Annerstedt commented in 1766, something was superfluous when 'I without any regard for estate, circumstances or wealth, stretch my custom much further than Nature loves: this is Luxuriance, when the lower person wants to ape the dignified, and the poor person the rich.'[37]

Pamphlet debates over luxuriousness are a reminder that until the late eighteenth century Sweden was a society of estates. The nobility, clergy,

[33] *Borgarståndets riksdagsprotokoll*, 10 vols (Stockholm 1945–2008), iii, 1726–27, appendix 64, 750. See also Bo Peterson, '"Yppighets Nytta och Torftighets Fägnad": Pamflettdebatten om 1766 års Överflödsförordning', *Historisk tidskrift*, ciii (1984), 16.

[34] *Bondeståndets riksdagsprotokoll*, 13 vols (Stockholm 1939–86), xi, 1769–1770, appendix 13, 591; Malmeström, *Carl von Linné*, 235.

[35] Ericsson, *Den törstiges val*, 146.

[36] Arckenholtz, *Sagu-Brott*, 48.

[37] Peterson, '"Yppighets Nytta"', 3, 16, 25, 30–1; Leif Runefelt, 'Från yppighets nytta till dygdens försvar – den frihetstida debatten om lyx', *Historisk tidskrift*, cxxiii (2004), 215–16.

burghers, and peasantry were considered social realities that should be recognisable through dress, consumption, and habits. The emergence of groups which did not fit into this corporate order, such as the aforementioned 'non-nobles of high standing', was socially disruptive. At a time when the peasantry's political power was increasing, burghers contested noble privileges, and the middling sorts competed with the nobility in lifestyle and consumption, setting social boundaries became acutely important and increasingly difficult. Although wine drinking among the lower orders had not seemed socially threatening in the seventeenth century, social change made wine a luxury product which now had the ability to break and confuse social and gender order.

The stigmatizing effects of drink could work both ways. Just as the lower orders could emulate high status through consumption, so a nobleman's choice of comestible could take away the honour and virtue that drinking in company otherwise might lend him. The noble members of the Order of Awazu and Wallassis (two types of wine), found drinking aquavit 'highly ignominious'. One member, Claes Ekeblad was accused by a brother of having drunk twenty shots of cinnamon aquavit. What he had drunk was so important to him that he provided witnesses to the fact that he had in fact drunk burgundy and cinnamon water for his stomach pains. Similarly, a member of the burgher estate, mayor Sebaldt, was ridiculed at the diet for coming into a wineshop and ordering malt drink rather than the French wine that was more appropriate for his station.[38]

IV

Political drinking was largely a means of creating and maintaining loyalties and establishing patronage. As discussed above, it encouraged camaraderie among men and signified hierarchies. Treating others to alcohol created bonds and obligations between patrons and clients. Although the diet brought together men from all estates they had very different means of sustaining urban consumption patterns. Less wealthy people had difficulties avoiding the obligations created by drink: while it was impolite to decline a drink, it was also impossible for many men to treat their social superiors in return. Instead they must be repaid politically. When intoxication's many corruptive effects converged—weakening manly reason, creating political allegiances and identities, transforming status—a commodity like wine became truly dangerous.

[38] Claes Lundin and August Strindberg, *Gamla Stockholm. Anteckningar ur tryckta och otryckta källor* (Stockholm, 1882), 430; Vs 56, KB, Stockholm; Enefalk, 'En gustaviansk brygd', 734.

In such complicated circumstances the act of treating a social subordinate to wine inevitably carried the whiff of bribery and corruption. When members of the peasantry treated each other, it was often with simpler wares, such as beer, aquavit or a malt drink: natural, harmless sociability was to drink beer with one's comrades from the provinces. At the diet in 1755, the prospective member Jonas Carlsson Öhrman tried to gain a seat by treating his fellow peasants to aquavit and biscuits. Members of the peasantry were at the wineshops, but it appears that when they were in the company of their equals their consumption was not luxurious, or above their station. At most they might smoke a pipe of tobacco while they were at the wineshops.[39] As Eskil Kilium's death attests, many were simply not accustomed to the manner in which to drink wine. At Anton Springer's wineshop in 1755, two members of the peasantry were drinking malt drink and aquavit and smoking when the proprietor suggested they try some wine. They ordered the same amount as they would aquavit (*circa* 300 ml), which would amount to a large glass of wine. The proprietor suggested they order a tankard (*circa* 1300 ml) instead.[40]

When peasants were entertained by a superior however, it was with wine. One court steward came in to a wineshop in 1755 and changed the habits of a group of peasants sitting there. Previously they had been smoking tobacco and drinking malt drink and aquavit. The steward offered the peasants the same wares initially, but then moved on to offering them three or four glasses of wine each. The same pattern emerges when the person taking on the position as host did so due to his superior experience as a member of the peasantry. Influential members of the peasant estate with money to spend came to entertain in the same ways that otherwise characterized the higher orders.[41] Wine came to mark a relation as hierarchical, as a patron–client relationship between host and guest because it was not always possible for peasants to entertain in return and thereby release themselves from obligations of loyalty.

The many social and cultural dynamics at play here came together in a court case brought by the diet against some of its own members. Despite there being no legal grounds to prosecute anyone for political sociability, a group of

[39] Riksdagens kommissioner, kommissionen vid riksdagen 1755–56, R 5651, 23, 30 Dec. 1755, fols 325, 356, 358, R 5661, 21 Nov., 11, 12, 15 Dec. 1755, fols 33, 86, 94–5, 100, Riksarkivet, Stockholm (hereafter R 5651, R 5661); See also R 5615, 16 May 1723, fol. 111.

[40] R 5661, 13, 14 1755, fols 22, 24, 25.

[41] Svea hovrätts arkiv, Huvudarkivet, protokoll i särskilda mål, Målet mellan Börje Filip Skekta och Abraham Hedman 1748–50, AId vol. 7, Riksarkivet, Stockholm (hereafter SHP Hedman), 16 April 1748, unpaginated; ÄK 57, 4, 5 Aug. 1747, fols 208–9, 214–15, 220–1, appendix 6; R 5651, 24 Dec. 1755, fol. 334; R 5661, 12, 13, 14, 21, 22 Nov., 11, 15 Dec.1755, fols 17, 19, 21, 23, 33, 36, 46, 83–4, 99–100.

peasants were charged by the diet with having taken part in and organizing what was deemed 'illegal entertaining' in 1747. This was later defined as any type of sociability that served the purpose of 'persuading others to take part in any plans or aims that might lead to [political] parties or plotting'. Sociability as the means to political alliances and plotting was, of course, ubiquitous at the diet, but it was only members of the peasantry and the lower ranks of the burgher estate who risked prosecution. The real perceived danger was not so much plotting as the effects of treating and drinking wine on the lower orders.[42]

At the centre of the case was a member of the peasant estate, Jonas Nilsson, who was accused of having hosted 'suspicious and harmful parties'. In November and December of 1746 he had regularly treated other members of the peasant estate at a wineshop called the Golden Dove. They drank beer and aquavit, but also French, Spanish, and Rhineland wine and ate meals and biscuits. The remaining receipts also show that they broke a couple of glasses in the process. They had usually been a company of four to nine, sometimes up to eighteen men, seated in different rooms. Nilsson could not afford to pay for these parties himself. He had received money from an agent of the Russian ambassador. All Nilsson had to do was to show a receipt to the agent and the money was refunded (encouraging Nilsson to ask the proprietor to double the sums on the receipts so that he could pocket the remainder).[43] The prosecutor in 1747 found it 'reprehensible and worthy of punishment that a member of the diet should live in daily pleasure and enjoy himself in sociability'. The 'immodest level of pleasure', his colleague added, was determined by the fact that the entertaining had been hosted by peasants.[44] Another accused, the burgher Christopher Springer, testified that his entertainment of different members of the estates and foreign ambassadors had not been superfluous. He had only treated his friends and without any ceremony. Among equals, he inferred, consumption did not have to involve luxury, either old or new. On the other hand, demarcating hierarchy and establishing loyalty required certain drinks.[45]

If a man wanted to profess his innocence of political crimes he needed to underscore that his consumption had not been transformative: no clients were created, no confusions in status had arisen. With code words like *friends* and *malt drink* Jan Persson, a member of the peasantry, pointed to the fact

[42] 'Kongl. Maj:ts Kundgiörelse, angående några omständigheter, som wid Riksdagarne komma at tagas', 6 Sept. 1751, *Publique Handlingar*, v, 3095.

[43] Sennefelt, *Politikens hjärta*, 210.

[44] SHP Hedman, 13, 14 May 1748, unpaginated.

[45] R 5643, 22 April 1747, fol. 215.

that the entertaining of which he was accused had promoted equality and reciprocity and had not involved drinks which were socially inappropriate. He made a point of regretting not being able to entertain with finer drinks. But what he was really saying was that he had not corrupted anyone in any of the many ways that wine could.[46] These trials against 'illegal entertaining' died down in the 1760s, partly because the hypocrisy of putting the lower orders on trial for something that was legion among the other estates gradually became apparent and partly because the diet, which initiated the prosecutions, became dominated by non-noble estates reluctant to prosecute their own. Political sociability and its transformative properties became accepted, at least in practice.

V

Intoxication not only destabilized men's walk, it in fact destabilized a range of social roles. Men's status oscillated back and forth, depending on their level of inebriation, their manner of drinking, and the company they kept. In eighteenth-century Sweden, many facets of the transformative effects of alcohol converged into a common conception of wine as the most corruptive drink of all. Drink would corrupt not only the body, but affected patriotism; it transformed social standing and political alliances, and in turn the limits of political subjectivity. A certain alcoholic beverage, then, was the corruptive agent of both men's bodies and the social order. Tracing practices and discourse surrounding what at the time was deemed corruptive, we find that this had to do with the multi-layered symbolic value of wine-drinking in relation to economic doctrine and social standing. Sociability stood at the centre of creating political articulacy, and it was in a negotiation over competency and wine that these issues were most clearly formulated. Political companions had to balance their levels of intoxication with the proprieties of social status, masculine camaraderie, patronage, and citizenship. Depending on the circumstances, wine drinking could create desirable or reprehensible allegiances; it intoxicated men, thereby levelling them socially; it brought a man's faithfulness to the fatherland into question. By doing all this, wine both upheld a stagnating social system and upset the social order.

[46] R 5661, 20 Nov. 1755, fol. 29–30; *Bondeståndets riksdagsprotokoll*, 13 vols (Stockholm, 1939–86), vii, 1751–1756, 10 Dec. 1756, 148.

List of Contributors

Rebecca Earle is a Professor in the Department of History, University of Warwick.

Timothy A. Hickman is Senior Lecturer in the Department of History, Lancaster University.

Hung Bin Hsu is Assistant Professor in the Department of History, National Chung Hsing University.

Geoffrey Hunt is a Professor at the Centre for Alcohol and Drug Research, University of Aarhus, and Senior Scientist at the Institute for Scientific Analysis, Alameda, CA.

Karen Joe Laidler is Professor, Sociology Director, Centre for Criminology, University of Hong Kong.

Rudi Matthee is John and Dorothy Munroe Professor of History, University of Delaware, Newark, DE.

Angela McShane is Senior Tutor and Head of Renaissance and Early Modern Postgraduate Studies in History of Design, V&A/Royal College of Art, London.

Molly Moloney is Senior Research Associate at the Institute for Scientific Analysis, Alameda, CA.

Tom Nichols is Head of Subject and Reader in History of Art, University of Glasgow.

Paul Nugent is Professor of Comparative African History and Director of Centre of African Studies, University of Edinburgh.

Robin Osborne is Professor of Ancient History, University of Cambridge, Faculty of Classics, Cambridge.

 © The Past and Present Society

Jennifer Richards is Professor of Early Modern Literature and Culture, School of English Literature, Language and Linguistics, Newcastle University.

Karin Sennefelt is Professor at the Department of History at Stockholm University.

Sarah Shortall is a Ph.D. Candidate in the History Department at Harvard University.

Phil Withington is Professor of History at the University of Sheffield.

Index to *Cultures of Intoxication*

(Page numbers in *italics* refer to illustrations.)

 © The Past and Present Society

PAST & PRESENT
Supplement Series

Transnationalism and Contemporary Global History
Edited by Matthew Hilton and Rana Mitter

Ritual and Violence:
Natalie Zemon Davis and Early Modern France
Edited by Graeme Murdock, Penny Roberts, and Andrew Spicer

Postwar Reconstruction in Europe:
International Perspectives 1945-1949
Edited by Mark Mazower, Jessica Reinisch, and David Feldman

Relics and Remains
Edited by Alexandra Walsham

The Politics of Gesture: Historical Perspectives
Edited by Michael J. Braddick

The Religion of Fools? Superstition Past and Present
Edited by S.A. Smith and Alan Knight

Rodney Hilton's Middle Ages:
An Exploration of Historical Themes
Edited by Christopher Dyer, Peter Coss, and Chris Wickham

The Art of Survival:
Essays in Honour of Olwen Hufton
Edited by Ruth Harris and Lyndal Roper

Visit us online for each supplement's full
table of contents, or to order:

www.oxfordjournals.org/past/supplement.html

OXFORD
UNIVERSITY PRESS